W9-CNS-657

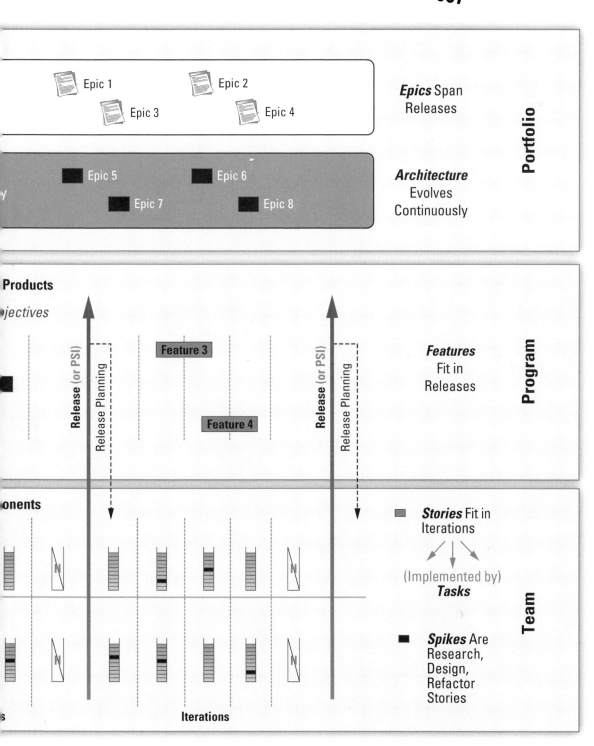

Epic 1
Epic 2
Epic 3
Epic 4

Epics Span
Releases

Epic 5
Epic 6
Epic 7
Epic 8

Architecture
Evolves
Continuously

Portfolio

Products

jectives

Release (or PSI)

Release Planning

Feature 3

Feature 4

Release (or PSI)

Release Planning

Features
Fit in
Releases

Program

onents

Stories Fit in
Iterations

(Implemented by)
Tasks

Spikes Are
Research,
Design,
Refactor
Stories

Team

Iterations

PRAISE FOR AGILE SOFTWARE REQUIREMENTS

"In my opinion, there is no book out there that more artfully addresses the specific needs of agile teams, programs, and portfolios all in one. I believe this book is an organizational necessity for any enterprise."

—Sarah Edrie, Director of Quality Engineering, Harvard Business School

"*Agile Software Requirements* and Mr. Leffingwell's teachings have been very influential and inspiring to our organization. They have allowed us to make critical cultural changes to the way we approach software development by following the framework he's outlined here. It has been an extraordinary experience."

—Chris Chapman, Software Development Manager, Discount Tire

"This book supplies empirical wisdom connected with strong and very well-structured theory of succeeding with software projects of different scales. People new to agile, practitioners, or accomplished agilists—we all were waiting for such a book."

—Oleksandr (Alex) Yakyma, Agile Consultant, www.enter-Agile.com

"This book presents practical and proven agile approaches for managing software requirements for a team, collaborating teams of teams, and all across the enterprise. However, this is not *only* a great book on agile requirements engineering; rather, Leffingwell describes the bigger picture of how the enterprise can achieve the benefits of business agility by implementing lean product development flow. His 'Big Picture' of agile requirements is an excellent reference for any organization pursuing an intrinsically lean software development operational mode. Best of all, we've applied many of these principles and practices at Nokia (and even helped create some of them), and therefore we know they *work*."

—Juha-Markus Aalto, Agile Change Program Manager, Nokia Corporation

"This pragmatic, easy-to-understand, yet thought-provoking book provides a hands-on guide to addressing a key problem that enterprises face: How to make requirements practices work effectively in large-scale agile environments. Dean Leffingwell's focus on lean principles is refreshing and much needed!"

—Per Kroll, author, and Chief Architect for Measured Improvements, IBM

"Agile programming is a fluid development environment. This book serves as a good starting point for learning."

—*Brad Jackson, SAS Institute Inc.*

"Dean Leffingwell captures the essence of agile in its entirety, all the way from the discrete user story in the 'trenches' to complex software portfolios at the enterprise level. The narrative balances software engineering theory with pragmatic implementation aspects in an easy-to-understand manner. It is a book that demands to be read in a single sitting."

—*Israel Gat, http://theAgileexecutive.com, @Agile_exec on Twitter*

"An incredibly complete, clear, concise, and pragmatic reference for agile software development. Much more than mere guidelines for creating requirements, building teams, and managing projects, this reference work belongs on the bookshelf of anyone and everyone involved with not only agile processes but software development in general."

—*R.L. Bogetti, Lead System Designer, Baxter Healthcare*

"This book covers software requirements from the team level to program and portfolio levels, including the architecture management and a consistent framework for the whole enterprise. We have practiced the multi-team release planning and the enterprise-level architecture work with kanban and achieved instant success in our organization. Combining the principles of the product development flow with the current large-scale agile and lean software development is a really novel concept. Well worth reading and trying out the ideas here."

—*Santeri Kangas, Chief Software Architect, and*
Gabor Gunyho, Lean Change Agent, F-Secure Corp

"Dean Leffingwell and his Agile Release Train (ART) concept guides us from team-level agile to enterprise-level agile. The ART concept is a very powerful tool in planning and managing large software programs and helps to identify and solve potential organizational roadblocks—early."

—*Markku Lukkarinen, Head of Programs, Nokia Siemens Networks*

AGILE SOFTWARE REQUIREMENTS

The Agile Software Development Series

Alistair Cockburn and Jim Highsmith, Series Editors

★Addison-Wesley

Visit **informit.com/agileseries** for a complete list of available publications.

Agile software development centers on four values, which are identified in the Agile Alliance's Manifesto:

1. Individuals and interactions over processes and tools
2. Working software over comprehensive documentation
3. Customer collaboration over contract negotiation
4. Responding to change over following a plan

The development of Agile software requires innovation and responsiveness, based on generating and sharing knowledge within a development team and with the customer. Agile software developers draw on the strengths of customers, users, and developers to find just enough process to balance quality and agility.

The books in The Agile Software Development Series focus on sharing the experiences of such Agile developers. Individual books address individual techniques (such as Use Cases), group techniques (such as collaborative decision making), and proven solutions to different problems from a variety of organizational cultures. The result is a core of Agile best practices that will enrich your experiences and improve your work.

★Addison-Wesley   **Cisco Press**   **EXAM/CRAM**   **IBM Press.**   **QUE**   **PRENTICE HALL**   **SAMS**   **Safari Books Online**

Agile Software Requirements

Lean Requirements Practices for Teams, Programs, and the Enterprise

Dean Leffingwell

✦✦Addison-Wesley

Upper Saddle River, NJ • Boston • Indianapolis • San Francisco
New York • Toronto • Montreal • London • Munich • Paris • Madrid
Capetown • Sydney • Tokyo • Singapore • Mexico City

Many of the designations used by manufacturers and sellers to distinguish their products are claimed as trademarks. Where those designations appear in this book, and the publisher was aware of a trademark claim, the designations have been printed with initial capital letters or in all capitals.

The author and publisher have taken care in the preparation of this book, but make no expressed or implied warranty of any kind and assume no responsibility for errors or omissions. No liability is assumed for incidental or consequential damages in connection with or arising out of the use of the information or programs contained herein.

The publisher offers excellent discounts on this book when ordered in quantity for bulk purchases or special sales, which may include electronic versions and/or custom covers and content particular to your business, training goals, marketing focus, and branding interests. For more information, please contact:

U.S. Corporate and Government Sales
(800) 382-3419
corpsales@pearsontechgroup.com

For sales outside the United States, please contact:

International Sales
international@pearson.com

Visit us on the Web: informit.com/aw

Library of Congress Cataloging-in-Publication Data

Leffingwell, Dean.
  Agile software requirements : lean requirements practices for teams,
programs, and the enterprise / Dean Leffingwell.
    p.   cm.
  Includes bibliographical references and index.
  ISBN-13: 978-0-321-63584-6 (hardcover : alk. paper)
  ISBN-10: 0-321-63584-1 (hardcover : alk. paper)
  1. Agile software development. I. Title.
  QA76.76.D47L4386 2011
  005.1—dc22

                          2010041221

Copyright © 2011 Pearson Education, Inc.

All rights reserved. Printed in the United States of America. This publication is protected by copyright, and permission must be obtained from the publisher prior to any prohibited reproduction, storage in a retrieval system, or transmission in any form or by any means, electronic, mechanical, photocopying, recording, or likewise. For information regarding permissions, write to:

Pearson Education, Inc.
Rights and Contracts Department
501 Boylston Street, Suite 900
Boston, MA 02116
Fax: (617) 671-3447

ISBN-13: 978-0-321-63584-6
ISBN-10:   0-321-63584-1
Text printed in the United States on recycled paper at Courier in Westford, Massachusetts.
First printing, December 2010

To Jenny and Marcy

Contents

FOREWORD

Why do product development projects miss their economic objectives? Studies show that 80 to 85 percent of project failures are due to incorrect requirements. Experienced developers know that managing requirements is a greater challenge than technical execution. And, although we have known this for decades, we really haven't gotten much better at it. Why? At first, we were functionally organized, so we simply displaced the problem outside the boundary of engineering—we blamed marketing and product management. Later, as we adopted cross-functional teams, we told these teams to listen to the voice of the customer and assumed that this would solve the problem.

It didn't. We never challenged the idea that it was feasible to develop valid requirements up front—we just told people to try harder. We just told them to pay more attention to what the customer was asking for. We ignored the fact that many customers don't know what they want. We ignored that fact that even when they know what they want, they can't describe it. We ignored the fact that even when they can describe it, they often describe a proposed solution rather than the real need. For example, customers told us that they wanted suitcases that were easy to carry, and asked us to make them lightweight. We did this, but they rejected our elegant designs and bought the heavier designs of our competitors—the ones with wheels on them!

The sad truth is that there is no one "voice of the customer." It is a cacophony of voices asking for different things. Even at a single customer, we need to balance the needs of technical decision makers, end users, system operators, and financial decision makers. All of these actors weigh different attributes differently, and they change their weighting as they acquire more experience using the product. We also need to understand the needs of distributors, regulators, manufacturing, and field service. If we focus only on the user, we could miss what Dean calls the "nonfunctional requirements."

And this problem is dynamic, not static. In the course of our development effort, the context constantly changes—competitors introduce new products and customer needs evolve. If it is not feasible to develop valid requirements before we begin design, what is our alternative? In my opinion, we should start with the belief that even the best requirements will contain major errors, and that these errors grow exponentially with time. This shifts our focus. Instead of believing that we are hearing a high-fidelity signal coming from the customer, we need to recognize that it is a noisy, low-fidelity signal—a signal that must be continually checked for errors. Rather than using heavy front-end investment to create perfect requirements, we invest in creating processes and infrastructure that can rapidly detect and correct poor fits between our solution and the customer's evolving needs.

What better test for this alternative approach than the development of large systems? Many of the methods that work superbly on small projects break down on large ones. For example, in small systems, costs and benefits are typically local. System performance does not suffer when a team makes locally optimal decisions. This is not true for large systems where we must deal with economic effects that are dispersed physically, temporally, and organizationally.

We need better approaches to understanding and managing software requirements, and Dean provides them in this book. He draws ideas from three very useful intellectual pools: classical management practices, agile methods, and lean product development. By combining the strengths of these three approaches, he has produced something that works better than any one approach in isolation.

First, although it might be unfashionable to say this, classic management practices still offer us some very useful methods. Not all of our predecessors were stupid dolts, incapable of recognizing a working solution. For decades I have seen relatively simple concepts like technology and product roadmaps producing great results. They ensure that work on technology begins early enough to keep it off the critical path. They create strong logical links between technology efforts and the programs that they serve. We don't need to blindly accept all traditional practices, but we'd be foolish to discard everything our predecessors already learned. Dean shows you how to apply some of these great ideas at the program and portfolio level.

Second, the agile community has developed a very powerful set of ideas that has already produced impressive results. These methods have grown rapidly for a very good reason—they work. Agile decomposes the large batches of the waterfall model into a series of time-boxed iterations. These smaller batches dramatically accelerate feedback, producing enormous benefits.

Since much of agile's success has occurred in smaller projects, it is natural to ask whether it is equally useful in large systems. While I deeply respect the value of agile methods, I think Dean is correct in recognizing that these methods must be extended to meet the needs of large system development. It is quite risky to assume that large system architectures will naturally emerge and that any shortcomings can be refactored away. For example, a naval warship is designed for a 30-year operating life. Good naval architects anticipate evolving threats, emerging technologies, and changing missions. We do not create such systems by letting architecture "emerge." Once we recognize the unique challenge of managing at the system level, we can start investing in the organizational infrastructure needed to meet this challenge. Dean shows you how to do this with agile method extensions such as architectural runways.

Dean also draws upon the ideas of what I call "second-generation lean product development." Many of the initial attempts to use lean in product development focused on ideas such as standardization of work and variability reduction. They lacked agile's intrinsic appreciation that developing great new solutions requires learning to thrive in the presence of uncertainty. These lean product development methods have now evolved, and the results are impressive. For example, today's "kanban" approaches are limiting WIP, accelerating feedback, and making flow visible to all participants. You can see the influence of these ideas on Dean's approaches at the program and portfolio levels. Dean has also recognized the importance of the new emphasis on economics. This emphasis helps us make better decisions and it enables us to explain our choices to management in terms they readily understand.

As you read this book, I suggest paying attention to several things. First, try to understand the reasons *why* certain of these approaches work, not just *what* they are. If you understand why things work, then you can more easily adapt them to your own unique context. Second, treat these ideas as a portfolio of useful patterns rather than a rigid set of practices that must be adopted as a group. This will reduce the batch size of your adoption process, produce less resistance, and provide faster results. Finally, as you use these ideas, strive for balance. You will have a natural tendency to prefer certain ideas—they address issues you feel are important, and they feel comfortable. You may have given other areas little attention for a long time. Often the areas that have received little attention hold great untapped opportunity.

—Don Reinertsen
Author of The Principles of Product Development Flow:
Second Generation Lean Product Development

Preface

Introduction to the Book

In the past decade, the movement to lighter-weight and increasingly agile methods has been the most significant change to affect the software enterprise since the advent of the waterfall model in the 1970s. Originated by a variety of thought and practice leaders and proven in real-world, successful experiments, the methods have proven themselves to deliver outstanding benefits on the "big four" measures: productivity, quality, morale, and time to market.

In the past five years, the methods spread virally. Within the larger enterprise, the initiatives usually started out with individual teams adopting some or all of the practices espoused by the various methods, primarily XP, Scrum, Lean, Kanban (later), and various combinations and variants.

However, as the methods spread to the enterprise level, a number of extensions to the basic agile methods were necessary to address the larger process, organizational, application scope, and governance challenges of the larger enterprise.

Not the least of these is the challenge of agile requirements, which is the necessity to scale the basic, lightweight practices of team agile—product backlogs, user stories, and the like—to the needs of the enterprise's *Program* and *Portfolio* levels. For example, agile development practices introduced, adopted, and extended the XP-originated "user story" as the primary currency for expressing application requirements. The just-in-time application of the user story provided a much leaner approach and helped eliminate many waterfall-like practices, such as imposing overly detailed and constraining requirements specifications on development teams.

However, as powerful as this innovative concept is, the user story by itself does not provide an adequate, nor sufficiently lean, construct for reasoning about investment, system-level requirements, and acceptance testing across the larger software enterprise's project Team, Program, and Portfolio organizational levels. That is the purpose of this book.

This book describes an agile requirements artifact model, corresponding practices, suggested roles, and an organizational model that provides a quintessentially lean and agile requirements subset for the agile project teams that write and test the code. Yet this model also scales to the full needs of the largest software enterprise.

WHY WRITE THIS BOOK?

In 2000, after about 25 years of managing software development as an entrepreneur and executive, along with my coauthor Don Widrig, I published my first book: *Managing Software Requirements: A Unified Approach*. In 2003, we updated the book with a second edition: *Managing Software Requirements: A Use Case Approach*. These are considered to be definitive texts on managing application requirements—a lot of copies were sold, and the books have been translated into five languages. More importantly, many individuals, teams, and companies told me that these works helped them achieve better software outcomes. That was always the goal.

In the following years, I turned my attention to agile development methods. I continue to be more and more impressed with the power of these innovative methods, the quality and productivity results they delivered, and the way in which they reenergized and empowered software teams. Though the methods were developed and proven in small team environments, the challenges of building software at scale is a more fascinating puzzle—part science, part art, part engineering, part organizational psychology. As a result, I became engaged in helping a number of larger enterprises in adopting and adapting these methods in projects affecting hundreds—and then thousands—of software practitioners. Fortunately, with some extensions, the methods did scale to the challenge. Based on these experiences, in 2007 I published *Scaling Software Agility: Best Practices for Large Enterprises*, a book designed to help larger enterprises achieve the benefits of agile development.

Scaling Software Agility took a broad view of software methods and didn't focus much on software requirements. Even though the management of requirements continued to be a struggle for many agile teams, there were bigger organizational and cultural challenges, as well as a number of emerging agile technical practices, that needed to be addressed.

In the past couple of years, the movement to lean thinking in software development captured my interest, in part because I have some background in lean manufacturing from earlier days. Generally, lean provides a comprehensive, deeply principled, rigorous, and mathematical framework for reasoning about product development economics and the increasingly important subset, software development.

So, my thinking, along with that of many others, evolved further. Many of us started to see agile development, especially agile at scale, as a "software instance of lean." In addition, lean scales beyond the software development labs and provides tools to address changes in other departments such as deployment, IT, distribution, and program and portfolio management. Simply put, lean provides a broader framework for organizational change, and it helps us address these larger challenges. I'm a big fan of lean thinking.

At its core, lean focuses on the value stream and provides philosophies, principles, and tools to continually decrease time to market, enhance value delivery, and eliminate waste and delays. As enterprises head down the lean path, it is again beneficial to focus on optimizing the understanding and implementation of software requirements, because they are the unique carriers—or at least the best proxy—for that value stream.

Lean thinking brings us full circle. Once again, it is useful to focus on requirements management practices in our agile—and increasingly lean—software development paradigm. That's why I wrote this book.

My hope is that the book will help the individual software practitioner, project team, program, and enterprise adopt and adapt agile and lean practices, deliver better solutions to their users and stakeholders, and thereby achieve the personal and business benefits that success engenders. After all, you can never be to too rich or too lean.

HOW TO READ THIS BOOK

With this book, I'm hoping to tell a somewhat complex story—how to address the challenge of managing software requirements in an agile enterprise that may employ just a few developers building a single product to those employing hundreds or even thousands of software practitioners building systems of previously unseen complexity—in a practical, straightforward, and understandable manner.

To do so, the book is written in four parts, the last three of which are dedicated to describing specific agile requirement practices at increasing levels of sophistication and scale.

Part I, Overview: The Big Picture of Agile Requirements in the Enterprise

In Part I, we describe an overall process model intended to communicate the "Big Picture" of how to apply agile requirements practices at the project Team, Program, and Portfolio levels.

We provide a brief history of software methods, describing the evolution from waterfall through iterative and incremental development, to agile and lean. We describe the big picture of agile requirements—an organization, requirements, and process model that works for the team and yet scales to the full needs of the enterprise.

We then provide an overview of the model and illustrate how it can be applied in agile requirements for the team, agile requirements for the program, and agile requirements for the portfolio.

If you need an introduction and orientation to the concepts, terms, and general practices of managing agile requirements, this part is intended to stand alone.

Part II, Agile Requirements for the Team

In Part II, we describe a simple yet comprehensive model for managing requirements for agile project teams. This portion of the model is designed to be as lightweight as possible, quintessentially agile, and to not encumber the agile teams with any unnecessary complexity and overhead. We introduce the agile team, user stories, stakeholders, users and user personas, iterating, agile estimating and velocity, acceptance testing, the role of the product owner, and, finally, methods for discovering requirements.

If your teams are using agile, this comprehensive, explanatory guide to applying agile requirements is intended for you.

Part III, Agile Requirements for the Program

Part III is intended for those involved in building more complex systems that often require the cooperation of a number of agile teams. We expand the picture and introduce additional requirements artifacts, roles, organizational constructs, and effective practices designed for this purpose. We describe Vision, product and system features, the product Roadmap, the role of the product manager, the Agile Release Train, release planning, nonfunctional requirements, techniques for requirements analysis, and use cases.

If you are a developer, tester, manager, team lead, QA, architect, project or program manager, or development director/executive involved in building systems of this scope, this part is intended for you.

Part IV, Agile Requirements for the Portfolio

In Part IV, we describe the final, *Portfolio* level, of requirements practices. This level is intended to guide enterprises building ever-larger systems of systems, application suites, and product portfolios. These often require the coordination and cooperation of large numbers (20 or 50 or 100 or more) of agile project teams. We introduce additional requirements artifacts, roles, organizational constructs, and practices designed for this purpose. We describe the role that larger-scale, intentional, system-level architectures play in agile development. We introduce a kanban system for reasoning about how to evolve and, when necessary, rearchitect, such systems in an agile manner. We also describe some of the legacy thinking in portfolio and project management and give some suggestions as to what to do about it. We conclude with a chapter describing investment themes, epics, and, finally, one of the ultimate objectives—agile portfolio planning.

If you are a program manager, development director, system architect, executive, or portfolio manager or planner who is involved in managing investments for a portfolio of products, systems, software services, or IT applications, this part is intended for you.

ACKNOWLEDGMENTS

It's a humbling process to acknowledge all the contributions of others who have collaborated on this book.

I'd like to thank Don Reinertsen, who provided permission to use elements of his breakthrough text, *Principles of Product Development Flow: Second Generation Lean Product Development*. The principles from his book helped me truly understand things I thought I understood before (even if it did cause me to rework some chapters). Thanks to Alistair Cockburn, who contributed directly to the use-case chapter, and other agile thought leaders whose work I have, I hope, acknowledged appropriately.

I am particularly appreciative of those individuals who contributed so much to the intellectual content in the book. They—and their employers—allowed me to develop and publish what were, at that time, experiments-in-process. These include my Finnish collaborators. Juha-Markus Aalto of Nokia Corporation was instrumental in the development of the lean and scalable requirements model and had the courage to put the Agile Release Train to work at theretofore unprecedented scale. The agilists and architects at F-Secure Corporation—Santeri Kangas, Gabor Gunyho, Kuan Eeik Tan, and others—contributed to the architecture chapters. Their enthusiasm and commitment to rethinking the roles of system architecture in large-scale systems development was lean, agile, and practical.

Don Widrig, coauthor of our earlier *Managing Software Requirements* texts, contributed heavily and drafted the requirements discovery and analysis chapters. Mauricio Zamora of CSG Systems was always ready to test an idea, read an early chapter, or "try this at work." Pete Behrens helped me see user stories, stakeholders, and personas more clearly and was instrumental in drafting those chapters. Jennifer Fawcett extended my understanding of the agile product owner and product manager roles and contributed extensive case study examples from her work at Tendril Inc. Stephen Baker and Joseph Thomas of DTE Energy provided the mental model for legacy mind-sets of portfolio management. Israel Gat contributed to the portfolio chapters. Oleksandr (Alex) Yakyma reviewed various works in process and translated pieces to his Russian and Ukrainian audience.

Even that list is not exhaustive. So many others—Mike Cottmeyer, Ryan Shriver, Keith Black, John Bartholomew, Chris Chapman, Craig Larman, Mike Cohn, Maarit Laanti, Ryan Martens, Matthew Balchin, and Richard Lawrence—directly contributed words, thoughts, critiques, or encouragement.

My Addison-Wesley editor Chris Guzikowski kept faith when the manuscript was lagging. Editorial assistant Raina Chrobak, along with full-service production manager Julie Nahil, helped turn the manuscript into a suitable production. Thanks to copyeditor Kim Wimpsett and production editor Molly Sharp for the great production support. And thanks to my Addison-Wesley reviewers, Robert Bogetti, Sarah Edrie, Alexander Yakima, Brad Jackson, and Gabor Gunyho. A special thanks is due Gabor Gunyho, who contributed directly to the intellectual content of the architecture chapters and who also provided an incredibly thorough concept, text, and methodology review.

If there is any quality to be found in this resulting product, much of the credit goes to these collaborators. I hope the book meets your requirements.

About the Author

Dean Leffingwell, a 30-year veteran of the software industry, is an entrepreneur, software executive, consultant, and author.

Mr. Leffingwell was cofounder and CEO of a number of software companies including publicly traded RELA/Colorado Medtech; Requisite, Inc., makers of RequisitePro and now part of IBM's Rational Division; and consumer Internet identity company ProQuo, Inc. Mr. Leffingwell formerly served as chief methodologist to Rally Software. Prior to that, he served as Vice President of Rational Software, now IBM's Rational Division, where his responsibilities included the Rational Unified Process and promulgation of the UML.

Mr. Leffingwell has been a student, coach, and author of contemporary software engineering and management practices throughout his career. He is the author of *Scaling Software Agility: Best Practices for Large Enterprises* (Addison-Wesley, 2007). He is also the lead author of the first and second editions of *Managing Software Requirements*, both from Addison-Wesley, which have been translated into five languages.

Mr. Leffingwell has a bachelor's degree in engineering from the University of Illinois and a master's degree in engineering from the University of Colorado. He has served as advisor and board member to a number of private and publicly held companies throughout his career.

PART I

OVERVIEW: THE BIG PICTURE

If you can't describe what you are doing as a process, you don't know what you're doing.

—W. Edwards Deming

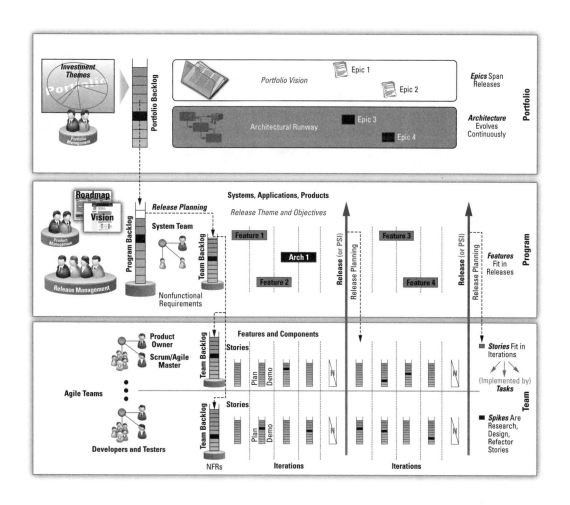

Chapter 1

A BRIEF HISTORY OF SOFTWARE REQUIREMENTS METHODS

Inertia is the residue of past innovation efforts. Left unmanaged, it consumes the resources required to fund next generation innovation.

—Geoffrey Moore, *Dealing with Darwin*

SOFTWARE REQUIREMENTS IN CONTEXT: DECADES OF ADVANCING SOFTWARE PROCESS MODELS

Software development has become one of the world's most important technologies. The software we produce today is rapidly becoming the embodiment of much of the world's intellectual property. Simply put, our modern world depends on software.

In support of our efforts over the past 40 to 50 years, we have implemented various software development methodologies—process frameworks we use to structure, manage, and control our work. Early on, it was a "cut-and-try" approach—ad hoc—as and where necessary. In large part, that worked.

Over time, the scope and reach of our endeavors, along with the power of the computers we programmed, increased by 10,000 fold. It seems like very quickly we went from simple simulations to flying commercial airliners internationally. So, the consequences of success or failure—whether measured in potential economic or human cost—increased exponentially as well. To mitigate all this new risk and help us produce only intended, rather than unintended, outcomes, we developed more structured and controlled methodologies.

Because what we produce is not physical goods but intangible ideas reflected in binary code, our methods all had a primary focus on "managing software requirements." *Software requirements* was the label we applied to the abstractions we use to carry the value stream into development and on to delivery to our customers. In large part, these newer practices worked too, and we owe much of our successes to these methods. Indeed, we shipped a *lot* of software.

But over time, the applications we developed became larger and larger still, and the methods we used to control our work became heavier and heavier. As an unintended consequence, we started slowing down the very thing we were trying to speed up—our ability to deliver higher-value, higher-quality software at faster and faster rates.

So, in the past two decades, the movement to more "agile" and "leaner" software development methodologies, including lighter weight but still safe and effective treatment of application requirements, has been one of the most significant factors affecting the industry. Simply, we need processes that provide even better safety and governance than we have experienced but without the burden. We want the best of both worlds.

So, this migration to more rapidly exploratory and lighter-weight processes has been a consistent theme over time, as Figure 1–1 shows.

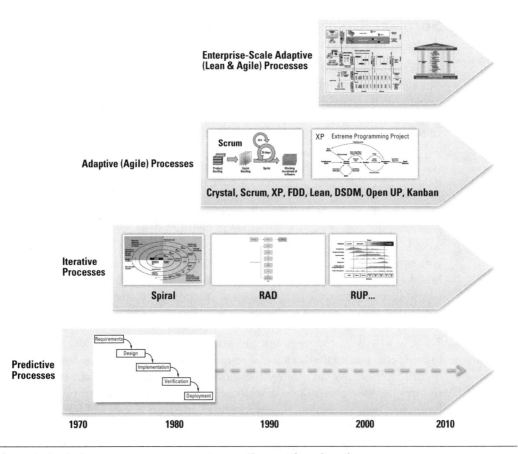

Figure 1–1   Software process movements over the past few decades
Adapted from Trail Ridge Consulting, LLC

A brief look at each of these mega-software process trends will tell us where we've been, where we are today, and perhaps a bit about where we are likely headed in the future.

PREDICTIVE, WATERFALL-LIKE PROCESSES

The software industry advanced quickly after its inception in the 1950s and 1960s. As it did so, the need to be able to better predict and control ever larger-scale software project outcomes somehow led us to what has become known as the sequential, stage-gated "waterfall" software process model, usually typified by a graphic such as Figure 1–2.

In this model, software development occurred in an orderly series of sequential stages. Requirements were agreed to, a design was created, and code followed thereafter. Lastly, the software was tested to verify its conformance to its requirements and design.

Winston Royce, who was at TRW at the time, is often credited with the creation of this model. Ironically, however, Royce actually described it as a model that could *not* be recommended for large-scale software development. In his seminal paper [Royce 1970], he wrote this:

> In my experience, the simpler model . . . [such as the one pictured in Figure 1–2] has never worked on large software development efforts.

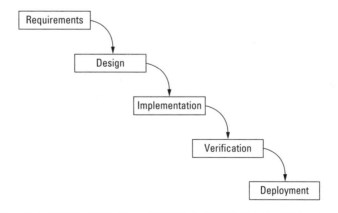

Figure 1–2   Simplified "waterfall" model. Progress flows top to bottom, like a waterfall.

He then went on to describe an enhanced model, which included building a prototype first and then using the prototype plus feedback between phases to build a final deployment. Unfortunately, his actual guidance is lost to history, or perhaps to the beguiling, construction-like thinking and oversimplification of the simple graphic in Figure 1–2. So, what came into common usage was not what Royce intended.

Problems with the Model

As Royce would have likely predicted, the model hasn't worked all that well for large software projects, and we have all struggled under the burden. Within just a decade or two, the resulting statistics were not very pretty. For example, the oft-cited Standish Group's Chaos report survey [Standish 1994[1]] noted the following.

- 31% of projects will be canceled before they are completed.
- 53% of the projects will cost more than 189% of their estimates.
- Only 16% of projects were completed on time and on budget.
- For the largest companies, completed projects delivered only 42% of the original features and functions.

In addition, it appears that an ineffective treatment of requirements was a primary root cause, because these were the three most common factors that caused projects to be "challenged":

- *Lack of user input:* 13% of all projects
- *Incomplete requirements and specifications:* 12% of all projects
- *Changing requirements and specifications:* 12% percent of all projects

Requirements in the Waterfall Model: The Iron Triangle

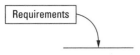

Of course, we can't say for certain that applying a rigid waterfall-based requirements process was the root cause, but in any case it's clear that misunderstood and changing requirements had a huge impact on project success, and the waterfall model was the dominant process model in effect at the time. Moreover, as generally applied, the deceptively simply "requirements box" pictured in the waterfall model implies that there is a set of requirements that can be reasonably determined "up front" and that these can then be used as a basis to estimate the schedule and budget of the project, as Figure 1–3 shows.

---

1. This often-cited report does have its critics. See *www.few.vu.nl/~x/chaos/chaos.pdf*. However, the general conclusions correlate pretty well to the author's experiences.

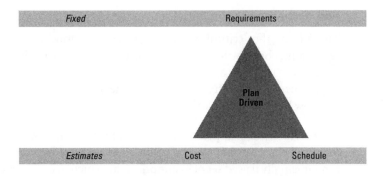

Figure 1–3   Once requirements are "known," you can estimate the cost and schedule.

Of course, from that point forward, the schedule and budget were likely also fixed (after all, what business could possibly plan for highly variable resources and project costing?). So, from a more realistic perspective, that led us to a simple "iron triangle" trap, as Figure 1–4 illustrates.

This "fixed requirements scope" assumption has indeed been found to be a root cause of project failure. For example, one key study of 1,027 IT projects in the United Kingdom [Thomas 2001] reported this: "Scope management related to attempting waterfall practices was the single largest contributing factor for failure." Here's the study's conclusion:

> This suggests that … the approach of full requirements definition, followed by a long gap before those requirements are delivered, is no longer appropriate. The high ranking of changing business requirements suggests that any assumption that there will be little significant change to requirements once they have been documented is fundamentally flawed.

Figure 1–4   The iron triangle trap of the waterfall model

And What About Quality?

There is another critical, implicit deficit of the model as well. Software veterans reading this book will likely note that there is another critical dimension, *quality*, which does not even appear in the iron triangle diagram. Since cost, schedule, and requirements were *all* fixed, quality was the only *variable* the teams could access. We all know how well that worked out.

So, it certainly does appear from the data that attempting to *fix the requirements up front* and then *carefully control change* and *use quality as the team's variable* was a fundamentally flawed set of assumptions on which to base a software process model. This kind of hard data, plus our aggregate personal experiences, led us to a "tipping point" that warranted serious consideration of substantially different process models for the industry, and indeed they did evolve in due course.

And Yet, the Waterfall Model Is Still Amongst Us

Even in light of this evidence, however, the waterfall model is *still* in widespread use today, as Figure 1–5 implies.

Given its deficiencies, one wonders why that may be the case in 2010 and beyond. Perhaps there are a number of understandable reasons.

- The model was itself born as a fix to an earlier problem, which was the "code it, fix-it, code-it-some-more-until-it's-quickly-not-maintainable" tendency of prior practices.
- It appears to be extremely logical and prescriptive. Understand requirements. Design a system that conforms. Code it. Test it. What could be more sensible and logical than that?
- It worked to a point (we did and still do ship a *lot* of software using the model). As a result, companies built their project and program governance models, including business case and investment approvals, project review and quality assurance milestones, and the like, around its flawed software life cycle.
- It reflects a continuing market reality—customers still do impose fixed-date/fixed-requirements agreements on suppliers, and they will likely continue to do so for years to come. (And, yes, sometimes we impose them on ourselves.)

So, we belabor it here, not to further "beat a dead horse" but to recognize that this particular horse is likely to be still alive and kicking in many business contexts. No matter how agile we want to be, we will have to avoid its flailing hooves well into the future. In turn, this can severely impact our operating freedom in implementing agile requirements practices. The bigger the opportunity for gain in the larger setting, the more likely the old model still exists—and the bigger the obstacles we are likely to encounter!

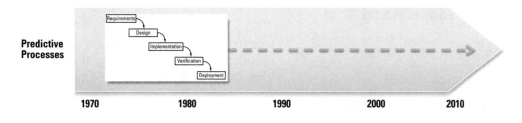

Figure 1–5   The model may have originated in the 1970s, but it is still in use today.

As agilists, our job is to help the business migrate to the new agile paradigm as efficiently as possible. Therefore, although we can agree that we don't want to support the waterfall model any longer than we absolutely have to, *we do have to understand it* and recognize that it still exists.

ITERATIVE AND INCREMENTAL PROCESSES

In the decades that followed, failures of the waterfall model, along with increasing time-to-market pressures and advances in software development tools and technologies, drove the need for more innovative, *discovery-based* models, which led us to the iterative processes of the 1980s and 1990s, as illustrated in Figure 1–6.

Generally, these can be seen as a continuum of increasingly iterative methods that used the following:

- Rapid development of understanding via experimental discovery (spiral)
- Rapid build of models, prototypes, and initial systems using more advanced tools (RAD)
- Iterative and incremental development of ever larger and more complex systems (RUP)

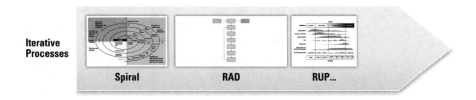

Figure 1–6   Iterative processes: spiral, RAD, and RUP

Spiral Model

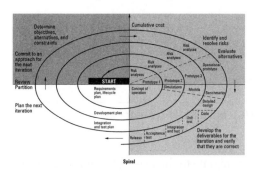

Spiral

Source: B.W. Boehm, "A Spiral Model of Software Development and Enhancement," IEEE Computer, Vol. 21, No. 5, 1988, pp. 61–72

One trendsetter in this continuum [Boehm 1988] is widely credited for initiating this trend with what has been described as the "spiral model of development."

In the spiral model, requirements still have a strong early placeholder. An initial pass around the spiral is intended primarily to understand requirements and perform some validation of the requirements before more serious development begins. Thereafter, the model assumed another, larger "spiral" intended to develop the solution in largely sequential steps of design, coding, integration, and testing. As such, this was the first published model based on a more discovery-based requirements process (albeit followed by a fairly traditional sequential, waterfall-like process, but one that incorporated constant feedback). Most give credit to this thinking as the starting point to the iterative and incremental (and now, increasingly agile) software development methods movement.

Rapid Application Development

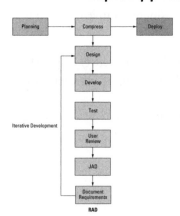

RAD

Rapid Application Development (RAD) is now considered to be a more generic term for a type of development process introduced by James Martin in the early 1990s. Although it was originally a fairly well-defined software process model focusing on the iterative development and construction of an increasingly capable series of prototypes, today it generally stands for any number of lighter-weight approaches, using fourth-generation languages and frameworks (such as web application frameworks), which accelerate the availability of working software. These frameworks and higher-level approaches often emphasize speed of deployment and feedback over performance and scalability. From a requirements perspective, the assumption was that if you could build it fast enough before the requirements changed, you would be more successful. And if you did get it wrong, the tools are sufficiently facile and lightweight that you could build it again faster than you could use traditional, paper-based requirements discovery methods. This thinking was indeed a harbinger of methods to come.

Rational Unified Process

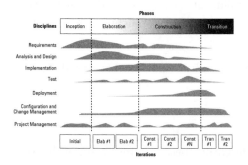

Source: Leffingwell, *Scaling Software Agility: Best Practices for Large Enterprises*, Figure "RUP," © 2007 Pearson Education, Inc. Reproduced by permission of Pearson Education, Inc.

Based more on the spiral model than RAD and intended for large-scale applications where robustness, scalability, and extensibility were mandatory, the Rational Unified Process (RUP) was launched in the late 1990s. RUP is a widely adopted iterative and incremental software process model, actively marketed and supported by the Rational Software Division of IBM. RUP has proven to be an effective framework for the practice guidance and management of large-scale application development. It has seen widespread industry use (more than a million practitioners) and has been applied with success on thousands of projects of all types, including projects at the very largest scale.

RUP was the first widely adopted software process that recognized the necessary overlap of the various *activities* that occurred during the life cycle *phases* of *inception*, *elaboration*, *construction*, and *transition*. For example, activities such as "requirements" were no longer relegated to a single phase. Although requirements activities were particularly intensive during the early inception and elaboration phases (as illustrated by the size of the "humps" in the diagram), requirements elaboration and requirements change are considered to be a continuous process that occurs throughout the life cycle.

More recently, a number of lighter-weight and more agile instantiations of RUP, including Agile RUP and OpenUP (an open source process under the auspices of the Eclipse foundation[2]), have become available.

Requirements in Iterative Processes

In iterative processes, we see a purposeful move away from the traditional *big, up-front design* (BUFD) requirements and design artifacts, such as software requirements specifications, design specifications, and the like, which served to define and govern implementations in waterfall implementations. In its place, we see a "discovery-based" approach. In the iterative model, we applied lighter-weight documents and models such as vision documents, use-case models, and so on, which are used to initially define what is to be built. Based on these initial understandings, the iterative process itself is then applied to more quickly discover the "real user requirements" in early iterations, thus substantially reducing the overall risk profile of the project.

---

2. *www.eclipse.org/epf/*

Once better defined in early iterations, these requirements were then implemented in a fairly robust but mostly traditional build-out of code, tests, and so on, to implement the requirements and provide assurances that the system conformed to the agreed-to behaviors.

Clearly, this was a giant step forward for the industry and one that started to soften the boundaries of the iron triangle.

ADAPTIVE (AGILE) PROCESSES

Starting in the late 1990s and through the current decade, software process has seen an explosion of lighter-weight and ever-more-adaptive models. Based on some fundamental changing software implementation paradigms such as object orientation, 3G languages, and test-driven development, these models were based on a different economic foundation. These models assumed that—with the right development tools and practices—it was simply more cost effective to write the code quickly, have it evaluated by customers in actual use, be "wrong" (if necessary), and quickly refactor it than it was to try to anticipate and document all the requirements up front.

Indeed, the number of methods—including Dynamic Systems Development Method (DSDM), Feature-Driven Development (FDD), Adaptive Software Development, Scrum, Extreme Programming (XP), Open Unified Process (Open UP), Agile RUP, Kanban, Lean, Crystal Methods, and so on—speaks to the industry's thirst and constant drive for more effective and lighter-weight processes.

The Agile Manifesto

In 2001, the creators of many of the agile software development methodologies came together with others who were also implementing various agile methods in the field and created an Agile Manifesto[3] summarizing their belief that there is a better way to produce software. Even today it does an excellent job of synthesizing and defining the core beliefs underlying the movement:

> *We are uncovering better ways of developing software by doing it and helping others do it. Through this work we have come to value:*

Individuals and interactions	over	processes and tools
Customer collaboration	over	contract negotiation

---

3. *www.agilemanifesto.org*

| Working software | over | comprehensive documentation |
| Responding to change | over | following a plan |

That is, while there is value in the items on the right, we value the items on the left more.

Behind the manifesto itself are a set of core principles that serve as a common framework for all agile methods.

- *Our highest priority is to satisfy the customer through early and continuous delivery of valuable software.*
- *Welcome changing requirements, even late in development. Agile processes harness change for the customer's competitive advantage.*
- *Working software is the primary measure of progress.*
- *Deliver working software frequently, from a couple of weeks to a couple of months, with a preference to the shorter timescale.*
- *Business people and developers must work together daily throughout the project.*
- *Build projects around motivated individuals. Give them the environment and support they need, and trust them to get the job done.*
- *The most efficient and effective method of conveying information to and within a development team is face-to-face conversation.*
- *Agile processes promote sustainable development. The sponsors, developers, and users should be able to maintain a constant pace indefinitely.*
- *Continuous attention to technical excellence and good design enhances agility.*
- *Simplicity—the art of maximizing the amount of work not done—is essential.*
- *The best architectures, requirements, and designs emerge from self-organizing teams.*
- *At regular intervals, the team reflects on how to become more effective, then tunes and adjusts its behavior accordingly.*

Given the number of agile methods, a reasonable treatment of each is outside our scope. However, according to a recent survey, it looks like these "method wars" have settled a bit, at least with respect to market share (for now), as Figure 1–7 shows.[4]

---

4. *www.versionone.com*

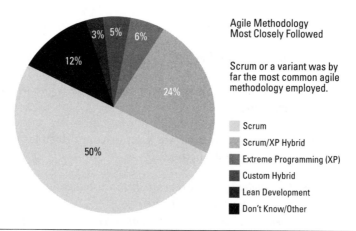

Figure 1–7   Survey of most widely adopted agile methods. Fourth Annual State of Agile Development Survey 2009. Courtesy of VersionOne, Inc.

Source: VersionOne's 2009 Agile Methodology Survey

The survey reflects that, currently, the most widely adopted agile methods are Scrum and XP. According to this survey, Scrum (with or without combination with XP) is now applied in 74% of agile implementations, and this has been our experience as well.

Based on their predominance, we'll be using these two methods as base practices for much of what we discuss in our agile requirements practices in this book, so a brief description of these is in order.

Extreme Programming (XP)

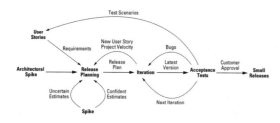

Source: Leffingwell, *Scaling Software Agility: Best Practices for Large Enterprises*, Figure "Extreme Programming Project" © 2007 Pearson Education, Inc. Reproduced by permission of Pearson Education, Inc.

XP is a widely used agile software development method that is described in a number of books by Beck and others [Beck 2000; Beck and Andres 2005]. Key practices of XP include the following.

- A team of five to ten programmers work at one location with customer representation on-site.
- Development occurs in frequent builds or iterations, which may or may not be releasable, and delivers incremental functionality.
- Requirements are specified as user stories, each a chunk of new functionality the user requires.

- Programmers work in pairs, follow strict coding standards, and do their own unit testing. Customers participate in acceptance testing.
- Requirements, architecture, and design emerge over the course of the project.

XP is prescriptive in scope and is typically applied in small teams of less than ten developers, where the customer is integral to the team or readily accessible. In addition, the *P* in XP stands for *programming*, and as opposed to other methods, XP describes some strict practices for coding that have been shown to produce extremely high-quality output.

Scrum

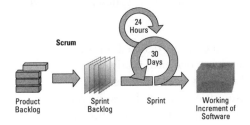

Scrum is an agile project management method [Schwaber 2004] that is enjoying increasing widespread use. Key Scrum practices include the following.

- Work is done in "sprints," which are timeboxed iterations of a fixed 30 days or fewer duration.
- Work within a sprint is fixed. Once the scope of a sprint is committed, no additional functionality can be added, except by the development team.
- All work to be done is characterized as product backlog, which includes new requirements to be delivered, the defect workload, and infrastructure and design activities.
- A *Scrum Master* mentors the empowered, self-organizing, and self-accountable teams that are responsible for delivery of successful outcomes at each sprint.
- A *product owner* plays the role of the customer proxy.
- A daily stand-up meeting is a primary communication method.
- A heavy focus is placed on timeboxing. Sprints, stand-up meetings, release review meetings, and the like are all completed in prescribed times.
- Typical Scrum guidance calls for fixed 30-day sprints, with approximately 3 sprints per release, thus supporting incremental market releases on a 90-day time frame.

Scrum is achieving widespread use because it is a lightweight framework, and—more importantly—it works. It also has the added benefit of a training certification process, administered by the Scrum Alliance,[5] which is also a good source for ongoing discussions about the Scrum method, its application, and adoption.

---

5. *www.scrumalliance.org*

REQUIREMENTS MANAGEMENT IN AGILE IS FUNDAMENTALLY DIFFERENT

No matter the specific method, agile's treatment of requirements is fundamentally different. We see it immediately in the core principles:

Manifesto principle #1—Our highest priority is to satisfy the customer through early and continuous delivery of valuable software.

Manifesto principle #2—Welcome changing requirements, even late in development. Agile processes harness change for the customer's competitive advantage.

Overall, the impact on the industry is dramatic and material. As described in *Scaling Software Agility* [Leffingwell 2007]:

> (with agile) instead of investing months in building detailed software requirements specifications…teams focus on delivering early, value-added stories into an integrated baseline. Early delivery serves to test the requirements and architectural assumptions, and it drives risk out by proving or disproving assumptions about integration of features and components.
>
> No longer do management and the user community wait breathlessly for months, hoping the team is building the right thing. At worst, the next checkpoint is only a week or so away, and…users may be able to deploy even the earliest iterations in their own working environment.

So, with agile, we take a far more flexible approach to requirements management: one that is far more temporal, interactive, and just-in-time. Gone are the traditional software requirements specifications, design specifications, and the like, and, along with them, the implied commitment to deliver "all that stuff" on a fixed schedule and fixed resource basis.

Goodbye Iron Triangle

The net effect of this change is to eliminate the iron triangle that has kept us from achieving our quality and dependability objectives. In the agile battle of date versus scope, the date wins. In other words, with agile methods, we'll fix two things, schedule and resources, and we'll float the remainder, scope (requirements), as the DSDM-inspired Figure 1–8 illustrates.[6]

---

6. Dynamic System Development Method: An agile method with roots in RAD

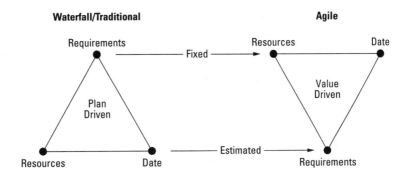

Figure 1–8   Agile fixes the date and resources and varies the scope.

Also, as we apply the appropriate agile technical practices, quality is also fixed. So, now we have a truly virtuous software cycle:

Fix quality—deliver a small increment in a timebox—repeat.

Agile Optimizes ROI Through Incremental Value Delivery

Agile is also based on a simplistically sound economic principle—the sooner we deliver a feature, the sooner our customers will pay us for it. This improves the return on investment for the cost of development, as Figure 1–9 illustrates.

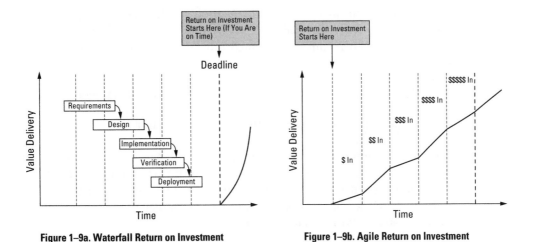

Figure 1–9   Value delivery and ROI in waterfall versus agile

In waterfall (Figure 1–9a), investment (cost) starts immediately and continues until delivery is reached. *No* return on investment is possible until such time as all committed requirements have been delivered to the customer, or the deadline is reached.

In agile (Figure 1–9b), value delivery starts with the first shippable increment. Therefore, whether business value is measured in customer retention or incremental pricing, return on investment starts then too.

If we assume the investment is constant (though, as we'll see later, the actual investment will actually be much lower in agile), then this is true:

ROI $$ (agile) > ROI $ (waterfall)

Wait, It Gets Even Better

However, even this simple example understates the case for increased ROI because it doesn't take into account the differential value of early market features. For example, when I bought my first iPhone, the initial price was an eye-popping $600. As an early adopter, I purchased mine within just a few months of launch and paid the full price. I did so because it was the only product on the market at that time that offered the feature set of a full-touch UI, integration with iTunes, and the promise of the future applications store. And I wanted it! Twenty-four months later, you could buy a much more powerful version, with 3G data network, integral GPS, video, and a host of other features, for about $199, which is *one-third the price* I paid just two years earlier for about *half* the capability.

Anyone entering the market later with a "me too" product had to compete at a much lower price. Moreover, they had to invest heavily to disrupt an incumbent market of early adopters who are unlikely to switch as the iPhone makes its way into its users' daily lives.

What this story describes is a well-known causal market ROI behavior:

The value of any marketable feature decreases over time.

Therefore, to capture the maximum gross profit, you have to be in the market first, or at least early enough to where the value/pricing differential is still in effect. When you superimpose that phenomenon on the curves of Figure 1–9, you get a truly startling effect. ROI actually increases at a rate even faster than the linear rate implied by Figure 1–9a, as is illustrated in Figure 1–10.

Taking this into account, the following becomes clear:

ROI $$$ (agile) >> ROI $ (waterfall)

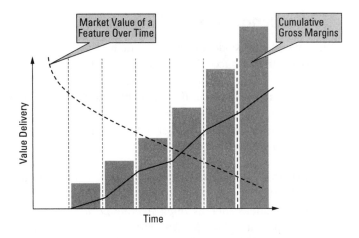

Figure 1–10 Agile ROI, taking into account differential feature value over time

Now we see why an already successful enterprise may be willing to transform itself to more agile practices, even in the face of serious political, operational, governance, and organizational impediments:

Because it makes economic sense to do so.

ENTERPRISE-SCALE ADAPTIVE PROCESSES

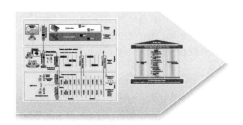

**Enterprise-Scale Adaptive
(Lean & Agile) Processes**

The compelling nature of this ROI data, coupled with the increases in productivity, quality, and morale achieved by agile teams, is incenting larger software enterprises to adopt agile methods. Although the methods we've described so far were developed in smaller team contexts, they are now being actively applied and extended in larger enterprises worldwide. Books such as *Scaling Software Agility: Best Practices for Large Enterprises* [Leffingwell 2007] and *Scaling Lean and Agile Development* [Larman and Vodde 2009] are adding momentum to this movement by providing additional practice guidance around the broader enterprise topic areas including organization, product line and systems architectures, governance, and portfolio management.

INTRODUCTION TO LEAN SOFTWARE

In a parallel universe, the roots of the lean software movement were evolving primarily from the successes of Toyota and the Toyota Production System (TPS), an alternative to the mass production systems in use at the time. TPS is a set of lean, economically-based manufacturing philosophies, principles, and practices used to vault Toyota to become the world's leading car manufacturer by 2007. This method has been described in a number of books, including classics such as *The Toyota Way* [Liker 2004].

In turn, this has spawned a growing *lean software* movement, (note: "lean" appears with about 3% market share in Figure 1–7) which is being promulgated by thought leaders in books such as *Implementing Lean Software Development* [Poppendieck and Poppendieck 2007], *Lean Software Strategies* [Middleton and Sutton 2005], and *Lean-Agile Software Development* [Shalloway 2010]. In addition, lean thinking has been applied successfully in product development in books such as *Managing the Design Factory* [Reinertsen 1997] and *Principles of Product Development Flow* [Reinertsen 2009]. The move to lean thinking in software and systems development is now also being actively supported by a body of knowledge and certification body, the Lean Software and Systems Consortium.[7]

With respect to product development, lean thinking is based on an extensive set of proven economic and mathematical principles that describe the flow of product information within the enterprise but that apply equally well to the supplier and customer elements of the larger business value chain. As such, it is broader and deeper than the specific agile software methods we have described so far.

Indeed, it is easy to view XP, Scrum, and others as "software instances of lean," and as such, lean provides an even broader framework for improving the economics of new product development in those enterprises dependent on software.

The impact of lean thinking is only beginning to be felt in the industry today, but it seems likely that the impact of lean over time will be as great or greater than the effect of the agile software development methods we have described so far. Therefore, we'll take some time to establish the framework for lean software thinking in the following sections, because this set of principles also underlies the premise for our approach to *lean requirements practices for teams, programs, and the enterprise.*

The House of Lean Software

As we mentioned, the principles and practices as applied to lean manufacturing, lean product development, lean services, and lean thinking in general are deep and extensive.

---

7. *www.leanssc.com*

Although the general body of work is enormous, Larman and Vodde[8] have described a framework for lean software thinking that translates many of the core principles and practices into a manageable software context. In so doing, they also reintroduced a "house of lean thinking" graphic, inspired by earlier houses of lean from Toyota and others. Perhaps because I'm a visual learner, I've always liked that graphic, so I've created a variant for our "house of lean software," which is illustrated in Figure 1–11.

Our house of lean software has five elements:

- *Roof, the Goal:* Sustainably delivering value fast
- *Pillar 1:* Respect for people
- *Pillar 2:* Continuous improvement
- *Foundation:* Management support
- *Contents:* Product development flow

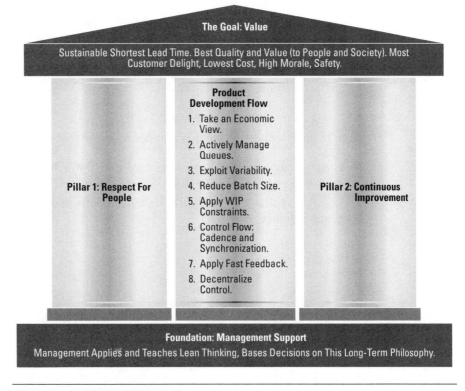

Figure 1–11 House of lean software

Adapted from Toyota Production System [Liker 2004], *www.leanprimer.org* [Larman and Vodde], Reinertsen 2009

---

8. *www.leanprimer.com/downloads/lean_primer.pdf*

The first four elements—the roof, pillars 1 and 2, and the foundation—provide the philosophical framework for lean software thinking. The fifth element, the product development flow, describes the specific lean principles we'll apply throughout this book.

We'll describe each of the elements of the house of lean in the following sections.

Roof, the Goal: Sustainably Delivering Value Fast

The goal of lean is unarguable: to deliver the maximum amount of value to the customer in the shortest possible time frame. Here's how others put it:

> *All we are doing is looking at the timeline, from the moment the customer gives us an order to the point where we collect the cash. And we are reducing the timeline by reducing the non-value-added wastes."*
>
> —Taiichi Ohno

> *"We need to figure out a way to deliver software so fast that our customers don't have time to change their minds."*
>
> —Poppendieck

> *"Focus on the baton, not the runners."*
>
> —Larman and Vodde[9]

So in our requirements work, we are reminded to do the following.

- Focus on customer requirements as they move through the system, rather than the people and organizations who manage them.
- Search for, and actively minimize, delays, handoffs, and other non-value-added activities.

---

9. Craig Larman commented: "In the Scrum-origins paper [The New, New Product Development Game, Harvard Business Review, 1986] the authors emphasize the importance of no handoff, and refer to the best approach as *not* handing off a ball or baton to other (specialist) teams, but rather, a cross-functional team that 'moves the ball down the field together' (rugby metaphor). [however] realistically today, there are still going to be handoffs—between sales, product mgmt, R&D, manufacturing, and operational support. Given this large-scale challenge, the 'watch the baton' (focus on the value flow and value/waste ratio, not the busy-ness of people or local optimization) viewpoint is still relevant to 'get' the lean-thinking viewpoint."

In addition, we must remember that requirements are not an end unto themselves. We don't really care if we've done a good job of discovering, organizing, prioritizing, and managing them. We only care how they ultimately serve us as the carriers of value delivery through the enterprise, from "concept to cash" [Poppendieck and Poppendieck 2007]—a proxy if you will—for what the customer needs and wants. In turn, all the associated process mechanisms we use to deliver value in our product, system, or service must serve that ultimate purpose.

From a software requirements perspective, we can visualize our enterprise's software delivery *value chain* as in Figure 1–12.

To optimize delivery time and increase ROI, we'll need to optimize the value chain of requirements-to-code-test-delivery by optimizing each of these functions. And to really accelerate value delivery, we will also need to minimize all the delays implied by the whitespace between.

Pillar 1: Respect for People

Although it is fair to "focus on the baton" (requirements), we must constantly be aware that it is our people who actually *do* all the value-added work, and respect for people is a comforting and fundamental principle of lean and agile.[10]

In addition, people are empowered in lean to evolve their own practices and improvements. Management challenges people to change and may even ask what to improve, but workers learn problem-solving and reflection skills and decide for themselves how to make the appropriate improvements.

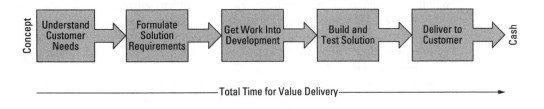

Figure 1–12 A software delivery value chain

---

10. Agile Manifesto synonym: *Build projects around motivated individuals. Give them the environment and support they need, and trust them to get the job done.*

Pillar 2: Continuous Improvement

This leads to the second pillar of lean, continuous improvement, or *kaizen*. With kaizen, we are guided to "become a learning organization through relentless reflection and continuous improvement." [Liker 2004][11]

- Solve problems and improve processes by going to the source and personally observing and verifying data.
- Make decisions slowly by consensus, thoroughly considering all options; implement decisions rapidly.
- Use continuous improvement to determine the root cause of inefficiencies and apply effective countermeasures.
- Protect the organizational knowledge base by developing stable personnel, slow promotion, and careful succession systems.
- Reflect at key milestones and after you finish a project to openly identify all the shortcomings of the project.

Foundation: Management Support

The foundation of lean thinking is management support. In fact, *support* is an inadequate word to describe the key and active role that management takes in implementing and driving lean. *Leadership* would be a better word. In lean, management is trained in the practices and tools of lean thinking and continuous improvement, applies them routinely, and teaches employees how to use them as well.

In this case, lean deviates from much of our experience with agile development. In our experience, agile has often been promoted as a team-based process that, in the worst case, tends to exclude management from key process and practices.[12] Of course, excluding management from participation and problem solving does not scale very well, and here is a key differentiator between agile and lean that we can leverage.

- In agile, it has been our expectation that management supports us and helps eliminates impediments.
- In lean, the expectation is that management leads us, is competent in the basic practices, and takes an active role in driving continuous improvement.

---

11. Agile Manifesto synonym: *At regular intervals, the team reflects on how to become more effective, then tunes and adjusts its behavior accordingly.*
12. In the Scrum story, there are "chickens" and "pigs." Those who actively write and test the software are pigs (fully "committed" to the "ham and eggs restaurant partnership"). Others, including management, are "chickens" and are only "involved." This otherwise cute story has led to a tendency in agile to assume that management is somehow not as committed as the team and is therefore not as necessary; perhaps they are not needed at all This is not helpful because it exacerbates organizational silos and inhibits successful adoption.

This key principle is one of the major drivers for lean in the software enterprise. Managers and executives lead, rather than follow, and are accountable for continuously advancing practices.

Contents: Principles of Product Development Flow

In the center of the house of lean software are the various principles and practices teams use to actually develop and deliver software to their end users. Of course, there is no one right way to do this, and the reference books mentioned earlier provide varying perspectives.

In his latest book, *Principles of Product Development Flow*, Reinertsen [2009] calls out eight key themes, each supported by a number of supporting principles. Together, the themes and principles provide comprehensive guidance for lean, flow-based product development. In my view, this is the best and most general description of lean principles as applied to product development, and by extension, they provide excellent, though nontrivial, guidance to the software development team. Reinertsen's book is a rigorous treatment, which contains more than 175 supporting lean and flow principles, so we can't possibly describe them here.

What we can do, however, is introduce the eight high-level themes and then apply various supporting principles throughout this book. The eight themes are as follows.

- Take an economic view.
- Actively manage queues.
- Understand and exploit variability.
- Reduce batch sizes.
- Apply work-in-process (WIP) constraints.
- Control flow under uncertainty—cadence and synchronization.
- Get feedback as fast as possible.
- Decentralize control.

Because these provide much of the underlying lean philosophy in this book, we'll describe each here.

- *Take an economic view:* Take an economic view to establish the decision framework for your specific context, whether it is at the team, program, or enterprise level. Understand the full value chain. Do not consider money already spent. Sequence high-risk, low-cost activities first. If you quantify only one thing, *quantify the cost of delay.*
- *Actively manage queues:* Long queues are universally bad because they create longer cycle times, increase risk, lower quality, and decrease motivation.

Actively manage queue lengths and provide predictable wait times by applying Little's law.[13] Operate at below-peak levels of utilization to increase responsiveness to change. Use cumulative flow diagrams to manage throughput.

- *Understand and exploit variability:* In manufacturing, variability must be minimized to create predictable results, efficiency, and quality. In software development, variability is inherent. Instead of eliminating variability, we must design systems that expect and address variability and even exploit it when appropriate.

- *Reduce batch sizes:* Large batch sizes create unnecessary variability and cause severe delays in delivery and quality. The most important batch is the transport (handoff) batch between teams and between roles within a team. Optimize proximity (co-location) to enable small batch sizes. Good infrastructure (test automation, continuous integration, and so on) and loose architectural coupling enable delivery of software in small increments (batches).

- *Apply WIP constraints:* The easiest way to control queue length is to apply constraints to work in process. Limiting work in process helps force the input rate to match available capacity. Timebox deliveries to help prevent uncontrolled expansion of work. Constrain global WIP pools by constraining local WIP pools. When WIP is too high, purge lower-value projects. Make WIP continuously visible (whiteboards and sticky notes).

- *Control flow under uncertainty—cadence and synchronization:* Even in the presence of variability and uncertainty, we can keep our software process in control with cadence and synchronization. *Cadence* is a predictable rhythm that helps us transform unpredictable events into predictable events. This makes waiting times predictable, lowers transaction costs, and increases dependability and reliability of the product development process. Periodic *resynchronization* allows us to limit variance and misalignment to a single time interval. Regular, system-wide integration (component synchronization) provides high-fidelity system tests and objective assessment of project status. Regular synchronization also facilitates cross-functional trade-offs and high-bandwidth information transfer.

- *Get feedback as fast as possible:* Software development cannot innovate without taking risks, and we need fast feedback to take fast corrective action. Fast feedback (short iterations, short release time frames, fast continuous integration, minimal delays between code and test, and so on) has many

---

13. Little's law tells us that the average waiting time in a queue is equal to the average length of the queue divided by the average processing rate. Long queues and slow cycle times beget long waits.

benefits: truncates unsuccessful paths quickly, reduces the inherent cost of failure in risk taking, and improves the efficiency of learning by reducing the time between cause and effect. Fast feedback is facilitated by small batch sizes but often requires increased investment in the development environment to understand smaller changes.

- *Decentralize control*: The faster we go, the less practical it is to have decisions move up and then back down the chain of command. Delays in decision making slow feedback and simultaneously decrease the fidelity of the decision, because of the decay in fact patterns that occur in the waiting time. Teams must be empowered to make decisions and act quickly and efficiently. There is little danger because the faster the feedback, the faster even a poor decision can be corrected.

These eight themes provide an economic, quantitative, and mathematically proven substrate for lean and agile software lean requirements management. However, there is one final theme that must be explored before we get on the work at hand.

A Systems View of Software Requirements

What we need to do is learn to work in the system, by which I mean that everybody, every team, every platform, every division, every component is there not for individual competitive profit or recognition, but for contribution to the system as a whole on a win-win basis.

—W. Edwards Deming

Lean thinking requires a *systemic* approach to managing operations throughout and across all the components (departments, artifacts, practices and processes, individuals, and so on) of the enterprise. Optimizing the behavior of any one function, such as requirements management or of a role such as the product owner or product manager or even an entire agile team or business unit—will not produce an optimum, system-level result. Rather, we must look beyond the project team and recognize and optimize all the facets of our requirements process in a comprehensive and systematic way.

For example, we must understand how our new agile requirements model impacts the definition and development of the enterprise-class systems architectures that are necessary to host the new value proposition. In addition, we'll need to understand the impact of requirements practices on departmental and organizational activities—not just at the individual project or team level but all the way to the enterprise portfolio—because that is where the new projects are formed.

We'll cover these perspectives in Part IV of this book.

Kanban: Another Software Method Emerges

Not surprisingly, the movement to lean has already inspired at least one software process that is based exclusively on lean principles. Kanban (the word means "signal" in Japanese) is the label for a way of scheduling and managing software work that is seeing increasing use in the agile community. As defined by the Limited WIP Society,[14] a software kanban system has the following characteristics.

- Visualizes some unit of value. This unit of value could be a user story, minimal marketable feature, requirement, or something else. This is different from a taskboard, which generally focuses on visualizing the current tasks.
- Manages the flow of these units of value, through the use of WIP limits.
- Deals with these units of value through the whole system, from when they enter a team's control until they leave it.
- By putting these three properties of a kanban system together, kanban allows value to flow through the whole system using WIP limits to create a sustainable pipeline of work.
- Further, the WIP limits provide a mechanism for the kanban system to demonstrate when there is capacity for new work to be added, thereby creating a pull system.
- Finally, the WIP Limits can be adjusted and their effect measured as the kanban system is continuously improved.

The pull system of kanban tends to quickly expose impediments, blocking issues, and bottlenecks in the flow (which may result from either a capacity constraint or noninstant availability of a resource). The team can then change their process for the better. As compared to a more traditional, prescriptive approach to change, this visible, adaptive approach can lower resistance and accelerate capability improvement. Therefore, it seems likely that this relatively lighter-weight method will be seeing increasing use in the software development community over time. The kanban method will be discussed further in Chapter 9. In addition, we'll be seeing many of these same kanban-based practices at work throughout this book.

SUMMARY

In this introductory chapter, we provided a brief history of requirements methods as they have evolved over the past 20 to 30 years. We did so for two reasons: to provide context for advancing methods based on lessons learned in the past, and since all these methods are still at work in the industry today, to help us understand the existing practices before we attempt to improve them.

---

14. *www.limitedwipsociety.org*

We introduced agile development methods that are being successfully applied at the team and enterprise levels. We noted how these methods are being further advanced, and further scaled, through the application of lean and flow principles. In understanding lean, we concluded that requirements management is not solely a local, team-based problem. Rather, we must also understand the impact of applying these methods to the development of enterprise-class architectures and enterprise project and portfolio management.

To address these challenges, we'll need to provide a systematic approach to applying lean and agile requirements practices that work efficiently for small teams and can also be scaled to the full needs of the enterprise. Our objective must be to help the enterprise achieve the *full* benefits of lean and agile development. In doing so, we must be careful to not encumber the agile teams that write and test all the new code, lest we risk killing the "goose that laid this golden egg."

Chapter 2

THE BIG PICTURE OF AGILE REQUIREMENTS

This would all be a lot easier to understand if you could just draw me a picture.

—Anonymous senior executive

Effectively implementing a new set of lean and agile requirements principles and practices in a project team, program, or enterprise is no small feat. Even the language is different and seemingly odd (user stories, sprints, velocity, story points, epics, backlog?). In addition, further "leaning" the organization often requires eliminating or reducing requirements specifications, design specifications, stage-gated governance models (with incumbent requirements reviews), sign-offs (with incumbent delays…), implementing work-in-process limits (which may seem counterproductive to those who measure "utilization"), and so on. So, there will likely be many challenges.

Even for the fully committed, it can take six months to a year to introduce and implement the basic practices and even more time to achieve the multiples of productivity and quality results that pay the ultimate dividends in customer satisfaction, revenue, or market share. To achieve these benefits, we must change many things, including virtually all of our former requirements management practices. However, many of the existing required artifacts, milestones, and so on, serve as safeguards to "help" avoid the types of project problems that software has often experienced. So, we have a dilemma—how do we practice this new high-wire act without a safety net, when the safety net itself is a big part of the problem?

Fortunately, we are now at the point in time where a number of organizations have made the transition before us and some common patterns for lean and agile software process success have started to emerge. In our discussions with teams, managers, and executives during this transition, we often struggled to find a language for discussion, a set of abstractions, and an appropriate graphic that we could use to quickly describe "what your enterprise would look like and how it would work after such an agile transformation."

To do so, we need to be able to describe the new software development and delivery process mechanisms, the new teams and organizational units, and some of the roles key individuals play in the new agile paradigm. In addition, any such *Big Picture* should highlight the requirements practices of the model, because those artifacts are the proxy for the value stream.

Eventually, and with help from others, we arrived at something that worked reasonably well for its purpose.[1] We call it the *Agile Enterprise Big Picture*, and it appears in Figure 2–1.

THE BIG PICTURE EXPLAINED

In this chapter, we'll explain the Big Picture in a summary format intended to provide the reader with a quick gestalt of this new, agile, leaner, and yet fully scalable software requirements model.

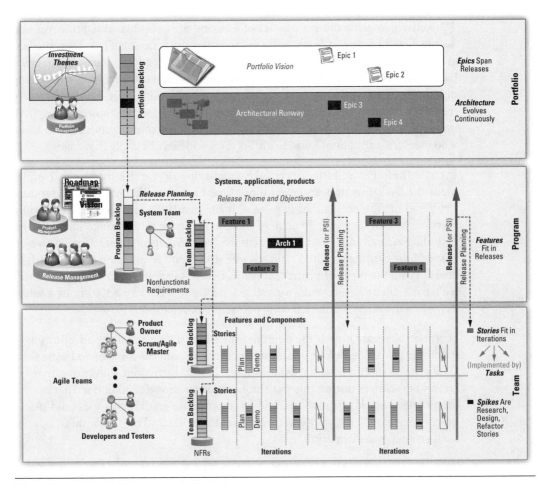

Figure 2–1   The Agile Enterprise Big Picture

---

1. Special thanks to Matthew Balchin and others at Symbian Software, Ltd., and Juha-Markus Aalto of Nokia Corporation.

In the remaining chapters of Part I of this book, we'll describe the basic big-picture requirements management practices for the individual *Team, Program,* and *Portfolio* levels. In Parts II, III, and IV, we'll further elaborate on the requirements management artifacts, roles, and activities at a level of detail suitable for implementation and action.

Big-Picture Highlights

Because this picture serves as both the organizational and process model for our agile requirements practices, we'll have time throughout this book to explore its many nuances. However, from an overview perspective, the following highlights emerge.

The Team Level

At the *Team level,* agile teams of 7±2 team members define, build, and test *user stories* in a series of *iterations* and *releases.* In the smallest enterprise, there may be only a few such teams. In larger enterprises, groups, or *pods,* of agile teams work together to support building up larger functionality into complete products, features, architectural components, subsystems, and so on. The responsibility for managing the *backlog* of user stories and other things the team needs to do belongs to the team's *product owner.*

The Program Level

At the *Program level,* the development of larger-scale systems functionality is accomplished via multiple teams in a synchronized *Agile Release Train* (ART). The ART is a standard cadence of timeboxed iterations and milestones that are date- and quality-fixed, but scope is variable (no iron triangle). The ART produces *releases* or *potentially shippable increments* (PSIs) at frequent, typically fixed, 60- to 120-day time boundaries. These evaluable increments can be released to the customer, or not, depending on the customer's capacity to absorb new product as well as external events that can drive timing.

We'll use the generic *product manager* label as the title for those who are responsible for defining the features of the system at this level, though we'll also see that many other titles can be applied to this role.

The Portfolio Level

At the *Portfolio level,* we'll talk about a mix of *investment themes* that are used to drive the investment priorities for the enterprise. We'll use that construct to assure that the work being performed is the work necessary for the enterprise to deliver on its chosen business strategy. Investment themes drive the portfolio vision, which will be expressed in as a series of larger, *epic*-scale initiatives, which will be allocated to various release trains over time.

In the rest of this chapter, we'll walk through the various elements of the Big Picture to describe how it works. While we'll highlight the requirements value delivery stream, we'll also expose the rest of the picture including the roles, teams, and processes that are necessary to deliver value. In this way, we'll provide a systemic view of our *lean and agile requirements process that works for teams and yet scales to the full needs of the enterprise.*

BIG PICTURE: TEAM LEVEL

Figure 2–2 summarizes the Team level of the Big Picture.

The Agile Team

The "front line" of software development consists of some number of *agile teams* that implement and test code and collaborate on building the larger system. It's appropriate to start with the team, because in agile, the *team is the thing,* because they write and test all the code that delivers value to the end user. Since it's an agile team, each has a maximum of seven to nine members and includes all the roles necessary to define/build/test[2] the software for their *feature or component.* The roles include a Scrum/Agile Master, product owner, and a small team of dedicated developers, testers and (ideally) test automation experts, and maybe a tech lead.

In its daily work, the team is supported by architects, external QA resources, documentation specialists, database specialists, source code management (SCM)/build/infrastructure support personnel, internal IT, and whoever else it takes such that the core team is fully capable of *defining, developing, testing, and delivering working and tested* software into the system baseline.

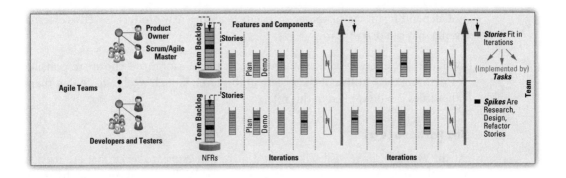

Figure 2–2   Team level of the Big Picture

---

2. See Chapter 6 of *Scaling Software Agility: Best Practices for Large Enterprises* [Leffingwell 2007].

Since testing software is integral to value delivery (teams get *no* credit for untested code), testers are integral to the team. Often the testers are logically part of the QA organization but are physically assigned and dedicated to an agile team. In this matrix fashion, their primary allegiance is to the team, but as members of the QA organization, they can leverage other QA teammates and managers for skills development, automation expertise, and any specialty testing capabilities that may be necessary at the system level. In any case, it must be clear that the agile team itself is responsible for the quality of their work product and that responsibility cannot be delegated (or abrogated!) to any other organization, in or out of house.

Teams are typically organized to deliver software *features or components*. Most enterprises will have a mix of both types—some *component teams* focused on shared infrastructure, subsystems, and persistent, service-oriented architectural components and some *feature teams* focused on vertical, user-facing, value-delivery initiatives. Agile teams are self-organizing and reorganize when necessary based on the work in the program backlog. Over time, the makeup of the teams themselves is more dynamic than static—static enough to "norm, storm, and perform"[3] for reasonable periods of time and dynamic enough to flex to the organization's changing priorities.

Pods of Agile Teams

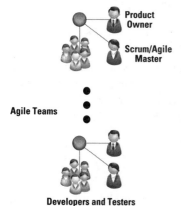

Product Owner

Scrum/Agile Master

Agile Teams

Developers and Testers

In addition, within the larger enterprise, there are typically some number (three to ten) or so of such teams that cooperate to build a larger feature, system, or subsystem (the *program* domain in the Big Picture). Although this isn't a hard or fast rule, experience has shown that even for *very* large systems, the logical partitions defined by system or product family architecture tend to cause "pods" of developers to be organized around the various implementation domains. This implies that perhaps 50 to 100 people must intensely collaborate on building their "next bigger thing" in the hierarchy, which we'll call a *program*. As we'll discover later, this is also about the maximum size for face-to-face, collaborative *release planning*.

Of course, even that's an oversimplification for a really large system, because there are likely to be a number of such *programs*, each contributing to the *portfolio* (product portfolio, application suite, systems of system).

---

3. See the Forming–Storming–Norming–Performing model of group development proposed by Bruce Tuckman at *http://en.wikipedia.org/wiki/Forming-storming-norming-performing*.

Roles in the Agile Team

Product Owner

As we have described, Scrum is the dominant agile method in use, and the product owner role is uniquely, if arbitrarily, defined therein. In Scrum, the product owner is responsible for determining and prioritizing user requirements and maintaining the product backlog. Moreover, even if a team is not using Scrum, it has been our experience that implementing the product owner role—as largely defined by Scrum—can deliver a real breakthrough in simplifying the team's work and organizing the entire team around a single, prioritized backlog.

But the product owner's responsibilities don't end there. In support of Agile Manifesto principle #4—*Business people and developers must work together daily throughout the project*—the product owner is ideally co-located with the team and participates *daily* with the team and its activities.

Scrum/Agile Master

For teams implementing Scrum, the Scrum Master is an important (though sometimes transitional[4]) role. The Scrum Master is the team-based management/leadership proxy whose role is to assist the team in its transition to the new method and continuously facilitate a team dynamic intended to maximize performance of the team.

In teams that do not adopt Scrum, a comparable leadership role typically falls to a team lead, an internal or external coach, or the team's line manager. As their skills develop, many of these *Agile Masters* become future leaders by illustrating their ability to deliver user value and by driving continuously improving agile practices.

Developers and Testers

**Developers and Testers
(Four to Six)**

The rest of the core team includes the developers and testers who write and test the code. Since this is an agile team, the team size is typically limited to about three to four developers plus one to two testers, who are (ideally) co-located and work together to *define, build, test, and deliver* stories into the code baseline.

Iterations

In agile development, new functionality is built in short timeboxed events called *iterations* (*sprints* in Scrum). In larger enterprises, agile teams typically adopt a

---

4. As the teams master the agile process, the role becomes less critical. Some very agile teams, even those who have adopted Scrum, no longer have a Scrum Master per se. Everybody knows the rules, and they are self-enforced.

standard iteration length and share start and stop boundaries so that code maturity is comparable at each iteration-boundary system integration point.

Each iteration represents a valuable increment of new functionality, accomplished via a constantly repeating standard pattern: *plan the iteration, build and test stories, demonstrate the new functionality to stakeholders, inspect and adapt, repeat.*

The iteration is the "heartbeat of agility" for the team, and teams are almost entirely focused on developing new functionality in these short timeboxes. In the Big Picture, the iteration lengths for all teams are the same since that is the simplest organizational and management model. Although there is no mandated length, most have converged on a recommended length of *two weeks*.

Number of Iterations per "Release"

A series of iterations is used to aggregate larger, system-wide, functionality for release (or potential release) to the external users. In the Big Picture, we've illustrated four *development* iterations (indicated by a full iteration backlog) followed by one *hardening* (or stabilization) iteration (indicated by an empty backlog) prior to each release increment.

This pattern is arbitrary, and there is no fixed rule for how many times a team iterates prior to a *potentially shippable increment* (PSI). Many teams apply this model with four to five development iterations and one hardening iteration per release, creating a cadence of a potentially shippable increment about every 90 days. This is a fairly natural production rhythm that corresponds to a reasonable external release frequency for customers, and it also provides a nice quarterly planning cadence for the enterprise itself.

In any case, the length and number of iterations per release increment, and the decision as to when to actually release an increment, are left to the judgment of the enterprise.

User Stories and the Team Backlog

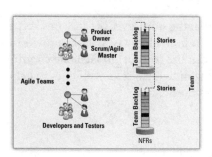

User stories (*stories* for short) are the general-purpose agile substitute for what traditionally has been referred to as *software requirements* (the stuff in the middle of the iron triangle of Chapter 1).

Originally developed within the constructs of XP, user stories are now endemic to agile development in general and are typically taught in Scrum, XP, and most other agile implementations. In agile, *user stories are the primary objects that carry the customer's requirements through the value stream—from needs analysis though code and implementation.*

As opposed to requirements (which by common definition represent something the system *must* do to fulfill a business need or contractual obligation), user stories are *brief statements of intent* that describe something the system *needs* to do for some *user*. As commonly taught, the user story often takes a standard user-voice form of the following:

> As a <user role>, I can <activity> so that <business value>.

With this form, the team learns to focus on both the user's role and the business benefit that the new functionality provides. This construct is integral to agile's intense focus on value delivery.

Team Backlog

The team's backlog (typically called a *project* or *product* backlog) consists of all the user stories the team has identified for implementation. Each team has its own backlog, which is maintained and prioritized by the team's product owner. Although there may be other things in the team's backlog as well—defects, refactors, infrastructure work, and so on—the yet-to-be-implemented user stories are the primary focus of the team.

> Identifying, maintaining, prioritizing, scheduling, elaborating, implementing, testing, and accepting user stories is the primary requirements management process at work in the agile enterprise.

Therefore, we will spend much of the rest of this book further describing processes and practices around user stories.

Tasks

For more detailed tracking of the activities involved in delivering stories, teams typically decompose stories into *tasks* that must be accomplished by individual team members in order to complete the story. Indeed, some agile training uses the task object as the basic estimating and tracking metaphor.

However, the iteration tracking focus should be at the story level, because this keeps the team focused on business value, rather than individual tasks. Tasks provide a micro–work breakdown structure that teams can use (or not) to facilitate coordinating, estimating, tracking status, and assigning individual responsibilities to help assure completion of the stories—and thereby—the iteration.

Big Picture: Program Level

Figure 2–3 summarizes the Program level of the Big Picture.

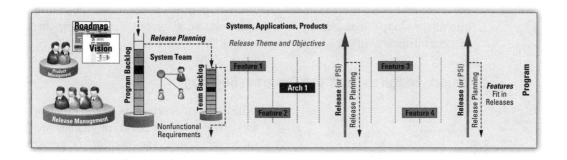

Figure 2–3   The Program level of the Big Picture

Here, we find additional organizational constructs, roles, processes, and requirements artifacts suited for building larger-scale systems, applications, products, and suites of products.

Releases and Potentially Shippable Increments

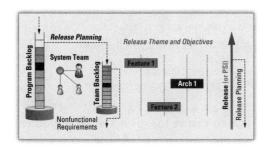

Although the goal of every iteration is to produce a shippable increment of software, teams (especially larger-scale enterprise teams) find that it may simply not be practical or appropriate to ship an increment at each iteration boundary. For example, during the course of a series of iterations, the team may accumulate some *technical debt* that needs to be addressed before shipment. Technical debt may include things such as defects to be resolved, minor code refactoring, deferred system-wide testing for performance, reliability, or standards compliance, or finalization of user documentation. *Hardening iterations* (indicated by an iteration with an empty backlog) are included in the Big Picture to provide the time necessary for these additional activities.

Moreover, there are legitimate business reasons why not every increment should be shipped to the customer. These include the following:

- Potential interference with a customer's licensing and service agreements
- Potential for customer overhead and business disruption for installation, user training, and so on
- Potential for disrupting customer's existing operations with minor regressions or defects

For these and other reasons, most programs aggregate a series of iterations into a potentially shippable increment, which can be released, or not, based on the then-current business context.

Vision, Features, and the Program Backlog

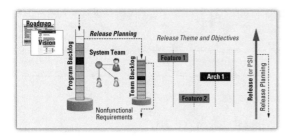

Within the enterprise, the product management (or possibly program management or business analyst) function is primarily responsible for maintaining the Vision of the products, systems, or application in their domain of influence.

The Vision answers the big questions for the system, application, or product, including the following.

- What problem does this particular solution solve?
- What features and benefits does it provide?
- For whom does it provide it?
- What performance, reliability, and so on, does it deliver?
- What platforms, standards, applications, and so on, will it support?

The Primary Content of the Vision Is a Set of Features

A Vision may be maintained in a document, in a backlog repository, or even in a simple briefing or presentation form. But no matter the form, the prime content of the Vision document is a prioritized set of *features* intended to deliver *benefits* to the users.

Nonfunctional Requirements

In addition, the Vision must also contain the various nonfunctional requirements, such as reliability, accuracy, performance, quality, compatibility standards, and so on, that are necessary for the system to meet its objectives.

Undelivered Features Fill the Program Backlog

In a manner similar to the team's backlog, which contains primarily *stories*, the program (or *release*) backlog contains the set of desired and prioritized *features* that have not yet been implemented. The program backlog may or may not also contain estimates for the features. However, any estimates at this scale are coarse-grained and imprecise, which prevents any temptation to over-invest in inventory of too-early feature elaboration and estimation.

Release Planning

In accordance with emerging agile enterprise practices, each release increment time-box has a kickoff release planning session that the enterprise uses to set the company context and to align the teams to common business objectives for the release. The input to the release planning session is the current Vision, along with a set of objectives and a desired, prioritized feature set for the upcoming release.

By breaking the features into stories and applying the agreed-to iteration cadence and knowledge of their velocity, the teams plan the release, typically in a group setting. During this process, the teams work out their interdependencies and design the release by laying stories into the iterations available within the PSI timebox. They also negotiate scope trade-offs with product management, using the physics of their known velocity and estimates for the new stories to determine what can and can't be done. In addition to the plan itself, another primary result of this process is a commitment to a set of release objectives, along with a prioritized feature set.

Thereafter, the teams endeavor to meet their commitment by satisfying the primary objectives of the release, even if it turns out that not every feature makes the deadline.

The Roadmap

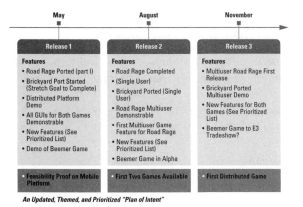

An Updated, Themed, and Prioritized "Plan of Intent"

The results of release planning are used to update the (product or solution) *Roadmap*, which provides a sense of how the enterprise hopes to deliver increasing value over time.

The Roadmap consists of a series of planned release dates, each of which has a theme, a set of objectives, and a prioritized feature set. The "next" release on the Roadmap is *committed to the enterprise*, based on the work done in the most recent release planning session. Releases beyond the next one are not committed, and their scope is fuzzy at best.

The Roadmap, then, represents the enterprise's current "plan of intent" for the next and future releases. However, it is subject to change—as development facts, business priorities, and customers need change—and therefore release plans beyond the next release should not generally be used to create any external commitments.

Product Management

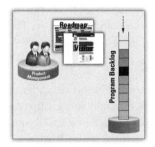

In agile, there can be a challenge with the apparently overlapping responsibilities of the *product manager* and the product owner. For example, in Scrum, the product owner is responsible for the following:

> representing the interests of everyone with a stake in the resulting project . . . achieves initial and ongoing funding by creating the initial requirements, return on investment objectives, and release plans.[5]

In some smaller organizational contexts, that definition works adequately, and one or two product owners are all that are needed to define and prioritize software requirements. However, in the larger software enterprise, the set of responsibilities imbued in the Scrum product owner is more typically a much broader set of responsibilities shared between team and technology-based product owners and market or program-based *product managers*, who carry out their traditional responsibilities of both defining the product *and* presenting the solution to the marketplace.

However, we also note that the title of the person who plays this role may vary by industry segment, as shown in Table 2–1.

Responsibilities of the Agile Product Manager in the Enterprise

No matter the title (we'll continue to use *product manager* generically), when an agile transition is afoot, the person playing that role must fulfill the following primary responsibilities:

- Own the Vision and program (release) backlog
- Manage release content
- Maintain the product Roadmap
- Build an effective product manager/product owner team

---

5. [Schwaber 2007]

Table 2–1   Product Manager Role May Have Different Titles

Industry Segment	Common Title for the Role
Information systems/information technology (IS/IT)	Business owner, business analyst, project or program manager
Embedded systems	Product, project, or program manager
Independent software vendor	Product manager

BIG-PICTURE ELEMENTS: PORTFOLIO LEVEL

Figure 2–4 summarizes the Portfolio level of the Big Picture.

At the top of the Big Picture, we find the portfolio management function, which includes those individuals, teams, and organizations dedicated to managing the investments of the enterprise in accordance with the enterprise business strategy. We also find two new artifact types, *investment themes* and *epics*, which together create the *portfolio vision*.

Investment Themes

A set of *investment themes* establishes the relative investment objectives for the enterprise or business unit. These themes drive the vision for all programs, and new epics are derived from these themes. The derivation of these decisions is the responsibility of the portfolio managers, either line-of-business owners, product councils, or others who have fiduciary responsibilities to their stakeholders.

The result of the decision process is a set of themes—*key product value propositions that provide marketplace differentiation and competitive advantage.* Themes have a much longer life span than epics, and a set of themes may be largely unchanged for up to a year or more.

Epics and the Portfolio Backlog

Epics represent the highest-level expression of a customer need. Epics are development initiatives that are intended to deliver the value of an investment theme and are identified, prioritized, estimated, and maintained in the *portfolio backlog*. Prior to release planning, epics are decomposed into specific features, which in turn are converted into more detailed stories for implementation.

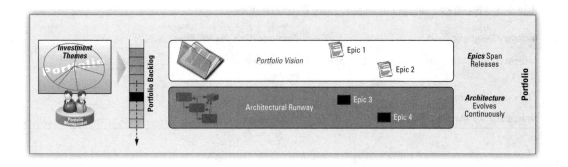

Figure 2–4   Portfolio level of the Big Picture

Epics may be expressed in bullet form, in user-voice story form, as a sentence or two, in video, in a prototype, or indeed in *any form* of expression suitable to express the intent of the product initiative. With epics, clearly, the objective is *strategic intent, not specificity*. In other words, the epic need only be described in detail sufficient to *initiate a further discussion* about what types of features an epic implies.

Architectural Runway

In Chapter 1, we described how design (architecture) and requirements are simply two sides of the same coin—the "what" and the "how." In this book, we'll have time to explore this topic in more detail, and we'll provide some discriminators that help us think about the differences in architecture and requirements, as well as the commonalities. However, even though this book focuses on requirements, we can't ignore architecture, because experience tells us that teams that build some amount of *architectural runway*, which is the ability to implement new features without excessive refactoring, will eventually emerge as the winners in the marketplace. So, any effective treatment of agile requirements must address the topic of architecture as well.

Therefore, system architecture is a first-class citizen of the Big Picture and is a routine portfolio investment consideration for the agile enterprise.

SUMMARY

In this chapter, we introduced the Big Picture as the basic requirements artifact, process, and organizational model for managing software requirements in a lean and agile manner. For agile teams, the model uses the minimum number of artifacts, roles, and practices that are necessary for a team to be effective. However, the model expands as needed to the Program and Portfolio levels, in each case providing the leanest possible approach to managing software requirements, even as teams of teams build larger and larger systems of systems. In the next few chapters, we'll elaborate on each of these levels.

Chapter 3

AGILE REQUIREMENTS FOR THE TEAM

When you're part of a team, you stand up for your teammates. Your loyalty is to them. You protect them through good and bad, because they'd do the same for you.

—Yogi Berra

INTRODUCTION TO THE TEAM LEVEL

In the previous chapter, we provided an overview of the basic organization, process, and requirements artifacts model we'll use to implement software agility. Of course, we won't get very far without first understanding the basic nature of the agile team itself and how it organizes its work to deliver the value stream to its customer. In this chapter, we'll elaborate on the Team level of the Big Picture, as illustrated in Figure 3–1.

Why the Discussion on Teams?

One might wonder why a book on software requirements leads with a discussion of the organization, roles and responsibilities, and activities of the agile project *team*. As we described in the previous chapters, the nature of agile development is so fundamentally different from that of traditional models that, by necessity, we must rethink many of the basic practices of software development. For many, adopting

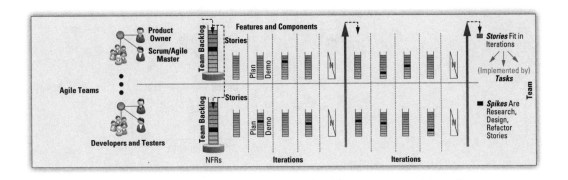

Figure 3–1 The Team level of the Big Picture

agile challenges the existing organizational structure, the assumptions about the relationships among team members, and even personnel reporting structures.

More importantly, in agile, the organization of the requirements and the organization of the team itself are not independent things. No longer do large batches of predetermined requirements defined by others get thrown "over the transom" to a set of developers for implementation—individuals that are organized, via matrix or other, for whatever purposes.

> Rather, the teams organize around the requirements so as to optimize the efficiency of defining, building, and testing code that delivers value to the end users.

The entire team is integrally involved in defining requirements, optimizing requirements and design trade-offs, implementing them, testing them, integrating them into a new baseline, and then seeing to it that they get delivered to the customers. That is the sole purpose of the team.

To understand the team organization challenge better, let's consider the challenge of "producing working code in a timebox" and see what type of organization might best accomplish this.

The basic unit of work for the team is the user story (the topic of Chapter 6). The team's objective is to define, build, and test some number of user stories in the scope of an iteration and thereby achieve some even larger value pile in the course of a release. Each story has a short, incredibly intense development life cycle, ideally followed by long-term residence in a software baseline that delivers user value for years to come. Pictorially, Figure 3–2 shows the life cycle of a story.

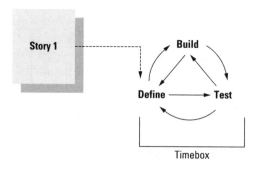

Figure 3–2 Defining/building/testing a user story

At the time of arrival, the story will likely have some amount of elaboration done during one or more prior iterations, or it may simply be a labeled placeholder for a "thing to do that we'll figure out later." At the iteration boundary, however, later is now. In essence, each story operates in the same pattern: Define the story, write the code and the test, and run the test against the code. These are all done in parallel so we call that sequence *define/build/test*. In so doing, we use the sequence as a verb to illustrate the fact that the process is concurrent, collaborative, and atomic. It is done completely, or it isn't *done*. However, even an atom has its constituent parts, and ours are as follows.

- *Define:* Even if the story is well-elaborated, the developer will likely still interact with the product owner to understand what is meant by the story. Also, some design will likely be present in the developer's mind, and if not, one will quickly be created and communicated to the product owner, peer developers, and testers. We use the word *define* to communicate that this function is a combination of both *requirements and design*. They are *inseparable*; neither has any meaning without the other. (If you don't know *how* to do IT, then you don't really know what IT is!)
- *Build:* The actual coding of the story provides an opportunity for new discovery as well. Conversations will again ensue between developer/product owner, developer/other developers, and developer/tester. Story understanding evolves during the coding process.
- *Test:* A "story" is not considered complete until it has passed an acceptance test (the topic of Chapter 10), which assures that the code meets the intent of the story. Building functional acceptance tests (plus unit tests) before, or in parallel with the code, again tests the team's understanding of the subject story.

Of course, this process happens every day; it happens in real time, and it happens multiple times a day for each story in the iteration!

How could such a process work in a traditional environment where a product owner or manager may not exist or has been be called away on another mission? How could it work if the developer is multiplexed across multiple projects or is working part-time "on assignment" from a resource pool? How could it work if the test resources are not dedicated and available at the same time that the code is written? The answer is, it doesn't.

Clearly, we are going to have refactor our organization to achieve this agile efficiency. We are going to have to *organize around the requirements* stream and build teams that have the full capability *to define, build, test, and accept* stories into the baseline—every day.

Eliminating the Functional Silos

Unfortunately, for many of us, we are not organized that way now. Instead, we are likely to be organized in functional silos, as illustrated in Figure 3–3.

Developers sit with, and communicate with, other developers. Product management, business analysts, and program managers are co-located with each other and often report to different departments entirely. For the larger organizations, architects may work together so as to help induce common architectures across business units, and so on, but may have little affinity or association with the development teams themselves. Product owners may not even exist, or if the function is filled by product managers, they are so multiplexed and/or unavailable that the team is constantly frozen, awaiting answers. Testers probably report to—and are co-located with—a separate QA organization, rather than development.

In agile, we must redefine what makes a team a team and eliminate the silos that separate the functions, as Figure 3–4 illustrates.

AGILE TEAM ROLES AND RESPONSIBILITIES

Fortunately, although it is no small matter to reorganize this way, the basic organizational structure of each agile team is largely the same, so at least we have a well-defined objective to achieve.

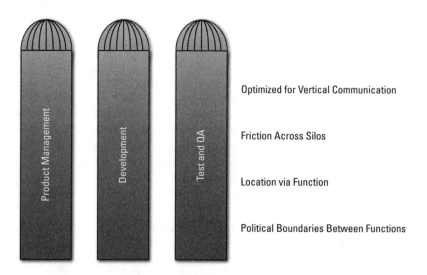

Figure 3–3   Typical functional silos

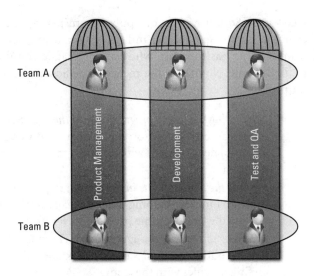

Figure 3–4 Reorganizing into agile teams

With Scrum, for example, there are three roles on an agile project team: the *product owner*, the *Scrum Master*, and the rest of the *team*, consisting primarily of the *developers* and *testers* who write and test the code.

Product Owner

Since the product owner is primarily responsible for defining and prioritizing requirements, it is clear why it is such a critical role in the agile project team. Chapter 11 is devoted to this topic.

In summary form, the product owner role is responsible for the following:

- Working with product managers, business analysts, customers, and other stakeholders to determine the requirements
- Maintaining the backlog and setting priorities based on relative user value
- Setting objectives for the iteration
- Elaborating stories, participating in progress reviews, and accepting new stories

Scrum Master/Agile Master

Scrum is quite specific about this role and provides specialized training and a specific title (Scrum Master) for those who assume this role. Although not every team will have a Scrum Master or apply Scrum per se, the method serves as a good example for all agile teams, and most agile teams have a Scrum Master or agile team lead, at least initially, who has some agile training and takes the initiative to fill this role. No matter the method, the Scrum/Agile Master is responsible for four things.

- *Facilitating the team's progress toward the goal:* Scrum/Agile Masters are trained as team facilitators and are constantly engaged in challenging the old norms of development while keeping the team focused on the goals of the iteration.
- *Leading the team's efforts in continuous improvement:* This includes helping the team improve, helping the team take responsibility for their actions, and helping the team become problem solvers for themselves.
- *Enforcing the rules of the agile process:* The rules of agile are lightweight and flexible, but they are rules nonetheless, and this role is responsible for reinforcing the rules with the team.
- *Eliminating impediments:* Many blocking issues will be beyond the team's authority or will require support from other teams. This role actively addresses these issues so that the team can remain focused on achieving the objectives of the iteration.

Developers

Developers write the code for the story. In so doing, they may work in a pair-programming model with another developer, they may be paired with a tester, or they may operate more independently and have interfaces to multiple testers and other developers. In any case, the responsibility is the same, and it includes the following:

- Collaborating with product owners and testers to make sure the right code is being developed
- Writing the code
- Writing and executing the unit test for the code
- Writing methods as necessary to support automated acceptance tests and other testing automation
- Checking new code into the shared repository every day

In addition, developers actively participate in improving the development environment.

Testers

Testers are an integral part of every agile team. They become part of the team just as soon as new code starts to be laid down, and they continue with the team throughout the release process. Their cycle is the same as the development cycle. Every new story that reaches an iteration boundary is subject to immediate review and analysis for acceptance testability. The tester's workflow in the course of the iteration parallels that of the developer:

- Writing the acceptance test case while the code is being written
- Interfacing with the developer and product owner to make sure the story is understood and that the acceptance tests track the desired functionality of the story
- Testing the code against the acceptance test
- Checking the test cases into the shared repository every day
- Developing ongoing test automation to integrate acceptance and component tests into the continuous testing environment

These are the primary roles on the agile team. At this level, that's all the understanding we will need to move forward with defining requirements practices for the team. In summary, Figure 3–5 illustrates an "ideal" agile team.

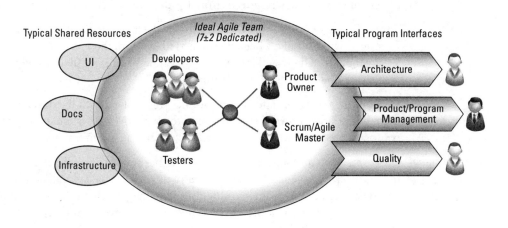

Figure 3–5   Ideal agile team with shared resources and typical interfaces

Other Team/Program Roles

You'll also note some shared resources and interfaces to other roles, including the following.

- *Architects:* Many agile teams do not contain people with titles containing the word *architect*,[1] and yet architecture does matter to agile teams. In these cases, the local architecture (that of the component, service, or feature that the team is accountable for) is most often determined by the local teams in a collaborative model. In this way, it can be said that "architecture emerges" from the activities of those teams.

  At the system level, however, architecture is often coordinated among system architects and business analysts who are responsible for determining the overall structure (components and services) of the system, as well as the system-level use cases and performance criteria that are to be imposed on the system as a whole. For this reason, it is likely that the agile team has a key interface to one or more architects who may live outside the team. (We'll discuss this in depth in Chapter 20.)

- *The role of quality assurance:* Quality assurance also plays a different role in agile. Since the primary responsibility for quality moves to the agile team (developers *and* testers), many QA personnel can typically reassume the role that was originally intended—that of overseeing overall, system-level quality by remaining "one step removed" from the daily team activities.

  Some of these QA personnel will live outside the team, while others (primarily testers) will have likely been dispatched to live with the product team. There, they work daily with developers to test new code and thereby help assure new code quality on a real-time basis.

  In addition, as we'll see later, QA personnel are involved with the development of the system-level testing required to assure overall system quality and conformance to nonfunctional, as well as functional, requirements.

- *Other specialists and supporting personnel:* Other supporting roles may include user-experience designers, documentation specialists, database designers and administrators, configuration management, build and deployment specialists, and whomever else is necessary to develop and deploy a whole product solution.

---

1. Agile Manifesto principle #11—*The best architectures, requirements, and designs emerge from self-organizing teams.*

USER STORIES AND THE TEAM BACKLOG

Since the efficiency of these agile teams is paramount to the overall organizational efficiency, we need to assure that the agile teams apply the simplest and leanest possible requirements model. To build a lean and scalable model, we need to make sure that the team's requirements artifacts are the simplest thing that could possibly support the needs of *all* stakeholders and particularly sensitive to the needs of the team members. Moreover, that subset must be quintessentially agile so that the artifacts described are consistent with most agile training as well as common practice. (In other words, it isn't mucked up with administrative overhead, manual traceability, reporting, detailed requirements cram down, or any of the other ways enterprises can unnecessarily burden the teams!)

Backlog

The term *backlog* was first introduced by Scrum, where it was described as a *product backlog*. However, in our enterprise model, *product* can be a pretty nebulous thing because various teams may be working at various levels, so there are multiple types of backlogs in the Big Picture. Therefore, our use of the term *backlog* is more generalized than in Scrum. In the Big Picture, we identified the particular backlog we are describing here as the team's local backlog, as shown in Figure 3–6.

This backlog is the one and only definitive source of work for the team. It holds all the work (primarily user stories) that needs to be done. It is local to them and is managed by them. It is their repository for all identified work items, and the contents are typically of little concern to others in the enterprise. They manage it, tool it, and put things in and out of it as it suits their needs in order to meet their iteration objectives. If "a thing to do" is in there, then it is likely to happen. If it isn't, then it won't.

Within the team, maintenance and prioritization of the backlog are the responsibility of the product owner, who is a resident of the team.

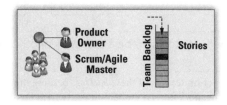

Figure 3–6 Stories and the team backlog

The team's backlog consists of all the work items the team has identified. In the meta-model, we generically call these work items *stories*[2] (some call them *backlogs* or *backlog items*) because that's what most agile teams and tools call them. For our purposes, we'll define a story simply as follows:

A story is a work item contained in the team's backlog.

From a model perspective, a *story is a kind of backlog item*, as Figure 3–7 illustrates.[3]

User Stories

Although that definition is simple, it belies the underlying strength of agile in that it is a special kind of story, the *user story*, that agile teams use to define the system behavior and value for the user. Indeed, the user story is inseparable from agile's focus on value delivery. To make the user story explicit, we need to extend the model a little, as shown in Figure 3–8.

Figure 3–7   A story is a kind of backlog item.

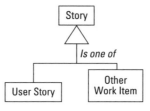

Figure 3–8   A story may be a user story or other work item.

---

2. Many Scrum teams call these *backlogs* because they are items in the product backlog. Strictly speaking, *work items* is probably a better term than story or backlogs, but we are trying to follow the most common usage as well as encouraging the use of the user story format.
3. The triangle indicator connecting the Story to Backlog item is the UML generalization relationship, indicating that the thing the arrow points to is a generalization of the special case of the pointing thing. In other words, in this case, story *is a special kind* of backlog item.

With this small addition, we now see that the backlog is composed of user stories and other work items. Other work items include things such as refactors, defects, support and maintenance, and tooling and infrastructure work. We'll discuss the rationale for specifically calling out these other work items later, but for now we just need to know that they help the team keep track of *all* the work they have to do to deliver value. They also help the team better estimate the time it will take to actually deliver the user stories.

User Story Basics

User stories are the agile replacement for most of what has been traditionally expressed as software requirements statements (or use cases in RUP and UML), and they are the workhorses of agile development. Developed initially within the constructs of XP, they are now endemic to agile development in general and are taught in most Scrum classes as well. We'll define a user story as follows:

> A user story is a brief statement of intent that describes something the system needs to do for the user.

As commonly taught, the user story takes a standard (user voice) form:

> As a <role>, I can <activity> so that <business value>.

In this form, user stories can be seen to incorporate elements of the problem space (the business value delivered), the user's role (or persona), and the solution space (the activity that the user does with the system). Here's an example:

> "As a Salesperson (<role>), I want to paginate my leads when I send mass e-mails (<what I do with the system>) so that I can quickly select a large number of leads (<business value I receive>)."

User stories are so important that Chapter 6 is devoted entirely to this seminal agile construct.

Tasks

To assure that the teams really understand the work to be done and to assure that they can meet their commitments, many agile teams take a very detailed approach to estimating and coordinating the individual work activities necessary to complete a story. They do this via the *task*, which we'll represent as an additional model element, as is illustrated in Figure 3–9.

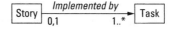

Figure 3–9 Stories are implemented by tasks.

Stories are implemented by tasks. Tasks are the lowest-granularity thing in the model and represent activities that must be performed by specific team members to accomplish the story. In our context:

A task is a small unit of work that is necessary for the completion of a story.

Tasks have an owner (the person who has taken responsibility for the task) and are estimated in hours (typically four to eight). The burndown (completion) of task hours represents one form of iteration status. As implied by the one-to-many relationship expressed in the model, there is often more than one task necessary to deliver even a small story, and it's common to see a mini life cycle coded into the tasks of a story. Here's an example:

Story 51: Select photo for upload

Task 51.1: Define acceptance test—Juha, Don, Bill

Task 51.2: Code story—Juha

Task 51.3: Code acceptance test—Bill

Task 51.4: Get it to pass—Juha and Bill

Task 51.5: Document in user help—Cindy

In most cases, tasks are "children" to their associated story (deleting the story parent deletes the task). However, for flexibility, the model also supports stand-alone tasks and tasks that support other team objectives. With this construct, a team need not create a story simply to parent an item such as "install more memory in the file server."

ACCEPTANCE TESTS

Ron Jeffries, one of the creators of XP, described what has become our favorite way to think about user stories. He used the neat alliteration *card, conversation, and confirmation*[4] to describe the three elements of a user story.

- *Card* represents the two to three sentences used to describe the intent of the story.
- *Conversation* represents fleshing out the details of the intent of the card in a conversation with the customer or product owner. In other words, the card also represents a "promise for a conversation" about the intent.

---

4. *www.xprogramming.com/xpmag/expCardConversationConfirmation.htm*

- *Confirmation* represents how the team, via the customer or customer proxy, comes to understand that the code meets the full intent of the story.

▶ **NOTE**   In XP and agile, stories are often written manually on physical index cards. More typically in the enterprise, the "card" element is captured as text and attachments in agile project management tooling, but teams often still use physical cards for planning, estimating, prioritizing, and visibility in the daily stand-up.

With this simple alliteration and agile's zealousness for "all code is tested code," we have an object lesson in how quality is achieved during, rather than after, actual code development.

In our model, we represent the confirmation function as a type of *acceptance test*, one that confirms the story has been implemented correctly. To separate it from other types of acceptance tests (an overloaded term in software), we'll call them *story acceptance tests* and treat them as an artifact distinct from the (user) story itself, as shown in Figure 3–10.

There are many reasons why we did this, which we won't belabor here. In any case, the model is explicit in its insistence on the relationship between the story and the story acceptance test as follows.

- In the one-to-many (1..*) relationship, every story has one (or more) acceptance tests.
- It's *done* when it passes. A story cannot be considered complete until it has passed the acceptance test(s).

Acceptance tests are functional tests that verify that the system implements the story as intended. To avoid creating a large volume of manual tests, which would quickly limit the velocity of the team, story acceptance tests are automated wherever possible.

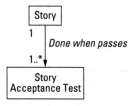

Figure 3–10   Every story has one or more story acceptance tests.

UNIT TESTS

To further assure quality, we can augment the acceptance with *unit tests*, as Figure 3–11 illustrates.

Unit tests are used to confirm that the lowest-level module of an application (a class or method in object-oriented programming; a function or procedure in procedural programming) works as intended. Unit tests are written by the developer to test that the code executes the logic of the subject module. In test-driven development (TDD), the test is written before the code. In any case, the test should be written, passed, and built into an automated testing framework before a story can be considered *done*.

Mature agile teams provide comprehensive practices for unit testing and automated functional (story acceptance) testing. Also, for those in the process of tooling their agile project, implementing this meta-model can provide inherent traceability of story-to-test, without any overhead on the part of the team.

Real Quality in Real Time

The combination of creating a lightweight story description, having a conversation about the story, elaborating the story into functional tests, augmenting the acceptance of the story with unit tests, and then automating testing is how agile teams achieve high quality in the course of each iteration. In this way:

> Quality is built in, one story at a time. Continued assurance of quality is achieved by continuous and automated execution of the aggregated functional and unit tests.

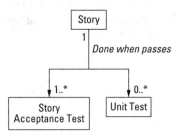

Figure 3–11   The code that implements the story should also be unit tested.

SUMMARY

In summary, we identified an organizational unit—the agile team—that eliminates functional silos and is optimized for the sole purpose of defining, building, and testing new functionality. We also described a set of requirements artifacts and relationships, including the user story, that are optimized to support the fast delivery of valuable requirements to the software baseline for release to the customers. We've also shown how agile teams achieve the highest-possible quality through comprehensive functional and unit testing and test automation.

In doing so, we've introduced a number of agile requirements artifacts. At the Team level, the requirements model isn't trivial, but it isn't that complex either, as Figure 3–12 summarizes.

In the next chapter, we'll move higher in the Big Picture and describe requirements practices for larger groups of teams, who work within agile *programs*. In later parts of this book, we'll describe how teams go about identifying, prioritizing, implementing, and delivering value using these artifacts.

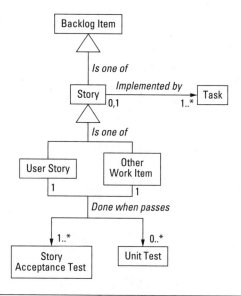

Figure 3–12   Agile team-level requirements artifacts and relationships

Chapter 4

AGILE REQUIREMENTS FOR THE PROGRAM

More relative than this—the play's the thing

—Shakespeare, *Hamlet*, Act 2, scene 2

INTRODUCTION TO THE PROGRAM LEVEL

In the previous chapter, we introduced the Team level in the Big Picture, the place where the software teams define, develop, and test the software for the solution. As illustrated in Figure 4–1, at the next higher *Program level*, we see an organizational, process, and requirements model that provides mechanisms to harness some number of agile teams to a larger enterprise purpose—the delivery of an entire product, system, or application suite to the customers.

At the Team level, teams are empowered and are largely self-organizing and self-managing. They work from a local backlog that is under the purview of the team's product owners. They have control of their local destiny and can define, build, and test their feature or component. In accordance with the principles of the Agile Manifesto, that is the optimum mechanism for incentivizing and motivating a team to produce the best possible results.

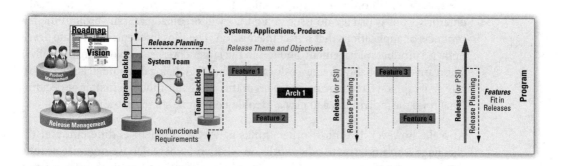

Figure 4–1　The Program level of the Big Picture

At the Program level, however, the problem changes, and the enterprise faces an additional set of challenges to successfully execute agility at this next level of scale. The objectives at this level include the following.

- *Maintaining Vision and Roadmap:* Continually defining and communicating the Vision for the program and maintaining a Roadmap so the teams are working to a common purpose.
- *Release management:* Coordinating the activities of some number of teams to build release increments on the enterprise's chosen development cadence.
- *Quality management:* Assuring that the aggregate results (the system) of the teams are routinely integrated; that performance, security, reliability requirements; and that any imposed external standards are met.
- *Deployment:* As the teams are unlikely to have the ability, purview, or authority to actually deploy systems to end users, this critical activity must be managed at the Program level.
- *Resource management:* Adjusting resources as necessary to address constraints and bottlenecks in the program's ability to deliver the needed value in a timely manner.
- *Eliminating impediments:* Program leaders and managers are also responsible for eliminating impediments that bubble up from the teams—those critical issues that are outside the team's control.

So, at this level, we'll need to deploy some additional resources and processes to accomplish this larger purpose. We'll describe these practices in this chapter.

ORGANIZING AGILE TEAMS AT SCALE

One of the first questions that arises at this level seems like a basic one: how to organize the agile teams in order to optimize value delivery of requirements. For the smaller enterprise, this is usually no issue at all; they will organize naturally around the few products or applications that reflect the mission. The silos that tend to separate development, product management, and test in the larger enterprise do not exist (ideally!). The teams are probably already co-located, rather than being distributed across disparate geographies. Creating an agile team in this context is mostly a matter of deciding what roles the individuals will play and rolling out some standard training.

At scale, however, like most other things agile, the problem is different, and the challenge is to understand who works on what and where. Do we organize around features, components, product lines, services, or what? Although there is no easy answer to this question, the question must be explored because so many agile practices—how many backlogs there are and who manages them, how the vision and features are communicated to groups of teams, and how the teams coordinate their activities to produce a larger solution—must be reflected in that decision.

Feature and Component Teams

This section compares and contrasts the feature and component approaches to organizing teams.

Component Teams

In *Scaling Software Agility* [Leffingwell 2007], we described a typical organizational model whereby many of the agile teams are organized around the architecture of a larger-scale system. There, they leverage their technical skills and interest and focus on building robust components, making them as reliable and extensible as possible, leveraging common technologies and usage models, and facilitating reuse. We even called the team's define/build/test "component" teams, which is (perhaps) an unfortunate label. However, we also noted the following:

> *We use the word component as an organizing and labeling metaphor.... Other agile methods ... stress that the team may be oriented around features....*

We weren't particularly emphatic about it but noted that a component-based organization is likely to already exist in the enterprise, and that isn't such a bad thing, given the critical role of architecture in these largest, enterprise-class systems. In any case, in a component-based approach, the development of a new feature is implemented by the affected component teams, as Figure 4–2 illustrates.

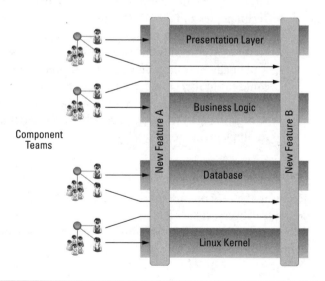

Figure 4–2   Component teams often have responsibility for a single layer in an architectural stack.

In this case, a new feature requires the creation of new backlog items for each team that contributes to the feature. Component teams minimize multiplexing across features by implementing them in series, rather than parallel. Some advantages are obvious, because each team is able to aggregate the needs of multiple features into the architecture for their component and can focus on building the best-possible, long-lived component or service for their layer. Their component does not get "sliced and diced" by each new feature; rather, it evolves as a set of services to implement current and, ideally, future features.

This approach may be reflective of an architecture-centric bias when building these largest-of-all-known software systems. That is because if you don't get the architecture reasonably right, you are unlikely to achieve the reliability, performance, and longer-term feature velocity delivery goals of the enterprise.

In addition, there are other reasons why component-based organizations can be effective in the agile enterprise.

- Based on its past successes, the enterprise may already organized that way, with specialists who know large-scale databases, web services, embedded operating systems, and the like, working together. Individuals—their skills, interests, residency, friendships, cultures, and lifestyles—are not interchangeable.
- These teams may already be co-located, simplifying communication and reducing the batch handoff of requirements, design, and test data.
- Technologies and programming languages may differ across components, making it difficult for feature teams to do pairing, collective ownership, continuous integration, test automation, and other factors.
- And finally, at scale, a single user feature can be an awfully big thing that could easily affect hundreds of practitioners. For example, a feature like "share my new phone video to YouTube" could affect dozens of agile teams, so organizing by feature can be nebulous when multiple teams are required for implementation.

Feature Teams

However, the very premise of this book, that agile teams do a better job of focusing on value delivery, creates a contrary vector on this topic. Indeed, the almost universally accepted approach for organizing agile teams is to organize around features, as Figure 4–3 illustrates.

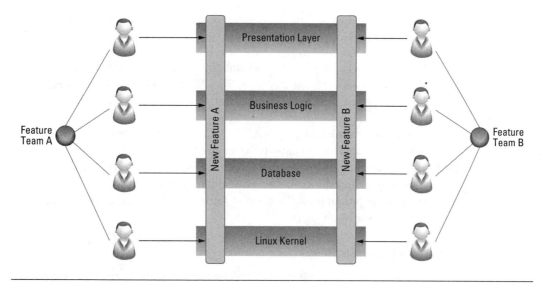

Figure 4–3   Feature team approach across an architectural stack

The advantages to a feature team approach are also obvious: Teams build expertise in the actual domain and usage mode of the system and can typically accelerate value delivery of any one feature. There is less overhead, because teams don't have to pass backlog items back and forth to see that a feature is implemented; there are far fewer interdependencies across teams. Planning and execution are leaner.

The team's core competence becomes the feature (or set of features), as opposed to one element of the technology stack. The team's backlog is simplified, just one or two features at a time. That has to promote the fast delivery of high value-added features!

Other authors support the feature-focused approach as well. For example, Highsmith [2004] states this:

> Feature-based delivery means that the engineering teams build features of the final product.

Of course, that doesn't mean to say that the teams themselves must be "organized by feature," because all engineering teams in the end build features for the final product, though perhaps that is a logical inference. Others, including Larman and Vodde

[2009], have more directly (and adamantly) promoted the concept of feature teams as the best way to organize agile teams. They note the following:

> A feature team is a long-lived, cross-functional team that completes many end-to-end customer features, one by one. Advantages include increased value throughput, increased learning, simplified planning, reduced waste....

Larman and Vodde state that you should "avoid component teams."[1] However, they also point out several challenges with the feature team approach, including the need for broader skills and product knowledge, concurrent access to code, shared responsibility for design, and difficulties in achieving reuse and infrastructure work, not to mention the potential for dislocation of some team members as the organization aligns around these boundaries.

Sometimes the Line Is Blurry

Even in light of this advice, we must also recognize that features and components are both abstractions, and the line is not so clear. One person's feature may be another's component. And sometimes a single feature may best be implemented as a stand-alone, service-oriented component.

For example, TradeStation Securities builds an online trading system where "charting" is a key capability for the trader. A few co-located agile teams work together on the charting function. On the surface, that looks like an excellent example of a feature team, because charting certainly is a major feature of the system.

When new online trading capabilities are developed, such as "trading foreign exchange currencies (Forex)," new chart functionality must be added. However, driving this new chart functionality are major components such as streaming data, account management, and interfaces with Forex exchanges. Is the new feature value stream described as "trading Forex all the way through the specialty chart function?" If so, that would make an obvious vertical feature stream, and the teams might reorganize by taking some members of each component team and creating a new vertical feature team for Forex trading. Or is the feature "trading of Forex" plus "charting Forex," in which case the charting team is *already* organized

---

1. In comments on the author's blog, Craig Larman noted: "We did not intend to write that feature teams are the only rational way to organize teams. Rather, the choice of any organizational design (including team structure) can be evaluated in terms of the global goal for optimization...early/fast delivery of value to real customers. In the context of that measure, if [organizational] design 1 has more delay and handoff and design 2 has less, design 2 is 'better'—with respect to that particular measure. The ideal cross-functional cross-component feature team minimizes delay and handoff, whereas component teams have more delay and handoff and create mini-waterfalls with single-specialist groups passing WIP items to each other."

appropriately? Is the charting capability a feature set or a component? Both? Does it matter what you call it?

Even in the case where it is clear what you call it, is a feature team always the best choice? Keith Black, VP of TradeStation Technologies, notes this:

> Online trading requires a great depth of technical expertise and industry knowledge at many different levels. We could not reasonably form feature teams that included members from every component area.

> Therefore, for our transition to agile, we organized around component teams and, through maturity, we are now in special cases putting together feature teams where it makes sense. While feature teams are excellent at driving an initiative through completion, in some cases they simply don't make sense. For example, if you have twenty feature teams and they all rely on a common component, such as a time-critical online transactional processing engine, it may be unadvisable to have 20 different teams sticking their hands into this critical component. Rather, you might choose to have these changes controlled by a single team that can broker the needs of the 20 teams and make sure they don't jeopardize areas they don't understand by making changes for their particular features.

Lean Toward Feature Teams

Given the advantages and disadvantages to each approach, the answer is not always obvious. But with agile's focus on immediate value delivery, there is an appropriate leaning toward feature teams. Mike Cottmeyer[2] points out this:

> I tend to start with the feature team approach and only move toward components if I have to...but the decision is situation-specific.

> To make this decision, you'll have to explore the diversity of your technology...how well your system is designed...what tools you have to manage your code base...the size and competence of your team...how and where your teams are distributed...and the quality of your infrastructure automation.

> You need to take a hard look at what scale your feature teams WILL break down...at some scale they WILL break down. Is scaling to this level something we need to address now or can it wait?

---

2. *www.leadingagile.com*

The Best Answer Is Likely a Mix

In the larger enterprise where there are *many* teams and *many, many* features, one should consider the previous factors and then select the best strategy for your specific context. In most cases, as you can see, the answer will likely be a mix of feature teams *and* component teams.

Indeed, even in the modest-sized agile shop, a mix is likely to be appropriate. Ryan Martens, founder and CTO of Rally Software, sketched a five-team agile org chart and its "feature paths" for us, as shown in Figure 4–4.

Ryan noted the following:

> While we don't think of it in these terms as such, three of these teams (ALM1, ALM2, and PPM in the top) would be readily identifiable as feature teams. One (I&O on the bottom) is clearly a component team. I don't know what you'd call the one (Platform and Integration) in the middle, because it sometimes originates its own features and sometimes is simply a supportive component for other features.

Given that a mix is most likely appropriate, there are two main factors that drive the mix: the practical limitation of the degree of specialization required and the economics of potential reuse. Figure 4–5 illustrates these parameters and the decision points that drive the choice of one over another.

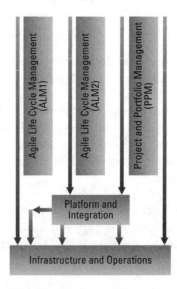

Figure 4–4   Five-team agile organization with various feature paths noted

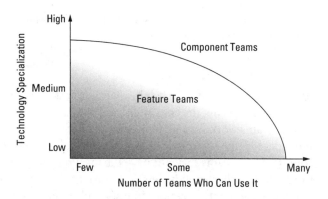

Figure 4–5   Organizing around feature and component teams

Consider Co-location

If it still isn't obvious which way you might want to organize, then you may want to optimize around *co-location*, because the communication, team dynamics, and velocity benefits of co-location may well exceed the benefits of the perfect component or feature organization. First, apply feature teams if *they* are, or can readily become, co-located. If not, and you find yourselves on the outer edges of the curve in Figure 4–5, then apply component teams, especially since it is likely that the teams are already organized that way.

As the organization evolves, you'll have lots of opportunity to inspect and adapt your model and evolve your organization in a way that makes sense to you. But, in the meantime, maybe nobody will have to move.

The System Team

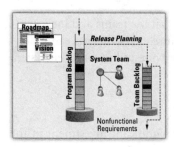

As we have described, agile teams are the software production engines that create and test the code. Each team should have the requisite skills and assets necessary to specify, design, code, and test the component or feature of their domain.

At the Program level, however, these individual teams may not have all the capabilities to integrate, test, and deploy a full solution. Therefore, we often observe an additional team that complements the feature/component teams. The name of the team varies; it could be called *system integration*, *QA and deployment*, *release team*, or, perhaps generically, a *system team* as our chosen label describes. No matter the name, this team shares the same mission, works on the same release train cadence, and typically has a set of specific, system-level set of responsibilities, highlighted in the following sections.

System-Level Testing

Ideally, each team would have the ability to test all the features at the system level. Many feature teams do have such capabilities, and that's one of the reasons why feature teams work so well. However, the fact is that it is often not practical for an individual feature or component team to be able to test a feature in its full system context. Many teams may not have the local resources (test bed, hardware configuration items, other applications, access to third-party data feeds, production simulation environment) necessary to test a full system. Moreover, at scale, many teams are developing interfaces, infrastructure components, drivers, and the like, and they may not even have an understanding of the full scope of the system feature that drove their new functionality to exist. In this case, the system team builds the skills and capabilities to perform the more extensive end-to-end behavior of the larger features and use cases that deliver the ultimate value.

System Quality Assurance

Similarly, many teams do not have the specialty skills and resources necessary to test some of the nonfunctional and other quality requirements for the system. This may include load and performance testing, reliability testing, conformance to industry compliance standards, and so on. Indeed, simply running a full validation suite on a large-scale system may even require a small but dedicated team who constantly updates the full system verification and test platforms and runs the validation. The system team may also be the only practical means to test against the "matrix of death"—the umpteen odd variants that occur in the customer's various, supported platform and application environments.

System-Level Continuous Integration

In addition, the larger the system, the less likely it is that the teams and their existing build and configuration management infrastructure environments can pull *all* aspects of the solution into place on their own to provide utility for a full system build on a daily basis.

Building Development Infrastructure

The transition to agile methods typically involves a significant investment in the environment to support configuration management, automated builds and deployment, and automated build verification tests (faster feedback). This may involve analysis, procurement of tools and systems, deployment, scripting, ongoing maintenance, and so on. This is a complicated and technical set of tasks that takes time and dedicated software development–capable resources. Building an initial infrastructure (system) team that is integral to the system release train process is one way to assure the commitment, visibility, and accountability of those resources. More importantly, it helps assure that the job will actually get done, because the program depends upon its success.

The Release Management Team

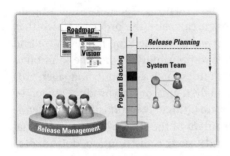

In addition to the agile teams and the system team, there is typically another significant organizational unit. Again, there is no standard convention for its name, but it takes on a *release management team* or *steering committee* function [Leffingwell 2007].

This team exists because, even though empowered, the agile teams do not necessarily have the requisite visibility, quality assurance, or release governance authority to decide when and how the solution should be delivered to the end users. Members of this team may include key stakeholders of the Program level of the enterprise, such as the following:

- Line-of-business owners and product managers who focus on the content and market impact of the release
- Senior representatives from sales and marketing
- Senior line managers who have responsibility for the teams and are typically ultimately accountable for developing the solution for the marketplace
- Internal IT and production deployment resources
- Senior and system-level QA personnel who are responsible for the final assessment of the solution's system-level quality, performance, and suitability for use
- System architects, CTOs, and others who oversee architectural integrity

In many agile enterprises, this team meets weekly to address the following questions.

- Do the teams still clearly understand their mission?
- Do we understand what they are building?
- What is the status of the current release?
- What impediments must we address to facilitate progress?
- Are we likely to meet the release schedule, and if not, how do we adjust the scope to assure that we can meet the release dates?

This forum provides weekly senior management visibility into the release status. This team also has the requisite authority to make any scope, timing, or resource adjustments necessary to help assure the release. In this manner, the release management team represents the final authority on all release governance issues and is an integral part of the agile enterprise.

Product Management

In the prior chapter, we introduced the product owner as the individual responsible for defining what stories the team implements, and the order in which they are implemented, in order to deliver end-user value. At the Program level, we find another set of stakeholders who have the same responsibility, but for the solution as a whole. These stakeholders may have different titles, such as product manager, program manager, solution manager, business analyst, area or line product owner, or whatever, but the responsibility is clear: They are ultimately responsible for the end-to-end solution. This includes not only the content of the release but the additional requirements for the "whole-product surrounds" such as distribution, documentation, support, messaging, release governance, and so on. In this book, we'll use the generic term *product manager* for this role, and we'll define these responsibilities, as well as their relationship to the product owners, in Chapters 11 and 14.

VISION

With the organizational questions behind us, we can move on to describing the requirements-specific artifacts and activities that are specific to the Program level. The first of these is *Vision*. Generally, the Vision addresses the larger questions, including the following.

- What is the strategic intent of this program?
- What problem will the application, product, or system solve?
- What features and benefits will it provide?
- For whom does it provide it?
- What performance, reliability, and so on, will it deliver?
- What platforms, standards, applications, and so on, will it support?

Since the product requirements and software requirements specification documents and the like are unlikely to exist, directly communicating the Vision for the program must take on a different form. Agile teams take a variety of approaches to communicating the Vision [Leffingwell 2007]. These include the following:

- Vision document
- Draft press release

- Preliminary data sheet
- Backlog and Vision briefing

Since the Vision plays such a critical role in defining what is to be built and aligning the teams to a common objective, we'll describe the Vision further in Chapter 13.

FEATURES

No matter the form, the primary content of the Vision is a set of features that describe what new things the system will do for its users and the benefits the user will derive.

In describing the features of a product or system, we take a more abstract and higher-level view of the system of interest. In so doing, we have the security of returning to a more traditional description of system behavior, the *feature*.

In Leffingwell [2003], features were described in the following way:

Features are services provided by the system that fulfill stakeholder needs.

Features live at a level above software requirements and bridge the gap from the problem domain (understanding the needs of the users and stakeholders in the target market) to the solution domain (specific requirements intended to address the user needs), as Figure 4–6 shows.

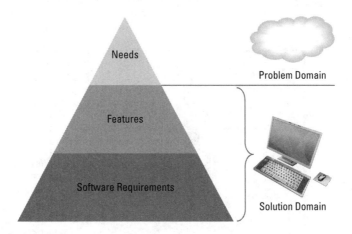

Figure 4–6   Traditional requirements pyramid

We also posited in that text that a system of arbitrary complexity can be described with a list of 25 to 50 features (just like a program backlog). This simple rule of thumb allows us to keep our high-level descriptions exactly that—high level—and simplifies our attempts to describe complex systems in a short form while still communicating the full scope and intent of the proposed solution.

And as we just described, features also give us the ability to organize agile teams in a way that optimizes value delivery.

New Features Build the Program Backlog

Features, then, are first-class citizens of our agile requirements model. They are a "kind of backlog item," and the list of proposed features constitutes the program backlog, as we illustrate in Figure 4–7.

Features are *realized* by stories. At release planning time, features are decomposed into stories, which the teams use to implement the functionality of the feature.

Features are typically expressed in bullet form or, at most, in a sentence or two. For example, you might describe a few features of an online e-mail service something like this:

Provide "Stars" for special conversations or messages, as a visual reminder that you need to follow up on a message or conversation later.

Introduce "Labels" as a "folder-like" conversation-organizing metaphor.

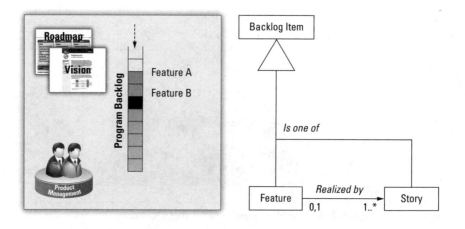

Figure 4–7   Features are program backlog items.

Testing Features

In the previous chapter, we also introduced the agile mantra "all code is tested code" and noted a story cannot be considered *done* until it has passed one or more acceptance tests.

At the Program level, the question arises as to whether features also deserve (or require) acceptance tests. The answer is, most typically, yes. Although story level testing should assure that the methods and classes are reliable (unit testing) and the stories suit their intended purpose (functional testing), the feature may span multiple teams and tens to hundreds of stories. As such, it is as important to test feature functionality as it is to test story implementation.

In addition, there are also a myriad of system-level "what if" considerations (think alternate use-case scenarios) that must be tested to assure the overall system reliability. Some of these can be tested only at the full system level. So indeed, features, like stories, require acceptance tests as well, as we illustrate in Figure 4–8.

In this manner, we see that every feature requires one or more acceptance tests, and a feature can also not be considered *done* until it passes.

NONFUNCTIONAL REQUIREMENTS

From a requirements perspective so far, we've used the feature and user story forms of expression to describe the functional requirements of the system—those system behaviors whereby some combination of inputs produces a meaningful output (result) for the user. However, we have yet to describe how to capture and express the nonfunctional requirements (NFRs) for the system.

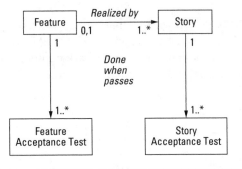

Figure 4–8   Features are acceptance tested.

Traditionally, these were often described as the system qualities—quality, reliability, scalability, and so on—and they are critical elements of system behavior. Indeed, they are as important as the sum total of all the other functionality. If a system isn't reliable (crashes) or marketable (failure to meet some imposed regulatory standard) or scalable (doesn't support the number of users required), then, agile or not, we will fail just as badly as if we forgot some critical functional requirement.

This is an important topic that we will cover thoroughly in Chapter 17, but for now, let's see how NFRs affect our requirements model.

Nonfunctional Requirements as Backlog Constraints

From a requirements modeling perspective, we could just throw the NFRs into the program backlog, but they tend to behave a little differently. New *features* tend to enter the backlog, get implemented and tested, and then are simply deleted (though persistent functional tests serve to assure the features remain working well into the future). *NFRs constrain* new development, thereby eliminating some degree of design freedom that the teams might otherwise have. Here's an example:

> For partner compatibility, implement SAML-based single-sign-on (NFR) for all products in the suite.

In other cases, when new features are implemented, existing NFRs must be revisited, and system tests that were previously adequate may need to be extended. Here's an example:

> The new touch UI (new feature) must still meet our accessibility standards (NFR).

So, in the requirements model, we modeled NFRs as backlog constraints, as illustrated in Figure 4–9.

In Figure 4–9, we see first that some backlog items may be constrained by nonfunctional requirements, and some are not. We also see also that some nonfunctional requirements may apply to no backlog items, meaning that they stand independently and apply to the system as a whole.

Figure 4-9   Relationship between backlog items and nonfunctional requirements

No matter how we think about them, nonfunctional requirements must be captured and communicated to the affected teams. Some NFRs apply to the system as a whole, and others apply only to the feature or component of the team's domain, as illustrated in Figure 4–10.

Testing Nonfunctional Requirements

These types of requirements—usability, reliability, performance, supportability, and so on—are often described as the "ilities" or *qualities* of a system. It should be obvious that these requirements must also be tested, as illustrated with the simple model extension of Figure 4–11.

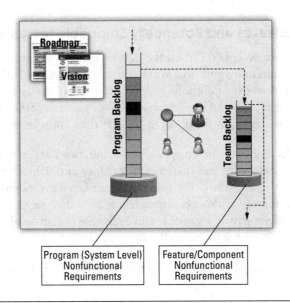

Figure 4–10 Nonfunctional requirements at the system and feature/component levels

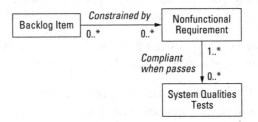

Figure 4–11 Nonfunctional requirements are tested with system "qualities" tests.

Most nonfunctional (0...*) requirements require one more or more tests. Rather than calling these tests another type of acceptance tests and further overloading that term, we've called them *system qualities tests*. This term indicates that these tests must be run at periodic intervals to validate that the system still exhibits the qualities expressed by the nonfunctional requirements.

THE AGILE RELEASE TRAIN

Now that we have discussed the organization of the program teams and the Vision, features, and nonfunctional requirements that define the strategic intent of the program, we can move on to a discussion about how the Vision is implemented over time.

Releases and Potentially Shippable Increments

As we described earlier, the development of system functionality is accomplished via multiple teams in a synchronized *Agile Release Train* (ART), a standard cadence of timeboxed iterations and milestones that are date- and quality-fixed but scope-variable. The ART produces *releases* or *potentially shippable increments* (PSIs) at frequent, typically fixed, 60- to 120-day time boundaries.

The *PSI* is to the enterprise what iterations are to the team, in other words, the basic iterative and incremental cadence and delivery mechanism for the program (an "ubersprint"). For many programs, release increments can be released to the customers at this chosen cadence; for other programs, the milestone represents achievement of a valuable and evaluable system-level increment. These increments can then be delivered to the customer, or not, based on the business context.

Designing and implementing an Agile Release Train is the topic of Chapter 15.

Release Planning

Release planning is the periodic program activity that aligns the teams to a common mission. During release planning, teams translate the Vision into the features and stories they will need to accomplish the objectives.

However, as we approach release planning, with its cost and overhead, we are reminded of some Agile Manifesto[3] principles.

- *The most efficient form of communication is face-to-face.*
- *The best requirements, architecture, and designs emerge from self-organizing teams.*

---

3. *www.agilemanifesto.org*

> - *At regular intervals, the team reflects on how to become more effective and then tunes and adjusts its behavior accordingly.*

These principles, plus the need to assure that the teams are on a common mission, drive enterprises to engage in periodic, face-to-face release planning events. These events gather the stakeholders to address the following objectives.

- Build and share a common Vision.
- Communicate market expectations, features, and relative priorities for the next release.
- Plan and commit to the content of the next release.
- Adjust resources to match current program priorities.
- Evolve the product Roadmap.
- Reflect and apply lessons learned from prior releases.

The frequency of the event depends upon the company's required responsiveness to market conditions and the iteration and release cadence it has adopted. In most enterprises, it occurs every 60 to 120 days with a 90-day cadence being typical.

Release planning will be covered in depth in Chapter 16.

ROADMAP

When we described the Vision, it was presented as time-independent; in other words, the Vision describes the objectives of the product or system without any binding to time. This is appropriate when the objective is to communicate the gestalt of "what this thing is we are about to build." Overloading that discussion of timelines, the "when," will likely derail the discussion of the "what."

However, to set priorities and plan for implementation, we need a perspective that includes time. This is the purpose of the Roadmap. The Roadmap is not a particularly complicated thing, nor is the mechanical maintenance of it difficult. For example, a typical Roadmap might be communicated in a single graphic such as Figure 4–12.

The Roadmap consists of a series of planned release dates, each of which has a theme and a prioritized feature set. Although it is a simple thing mechanically to represent the Roadmap, figuring out the content is another matter entirely and we'll cover that also in Chapter 16.

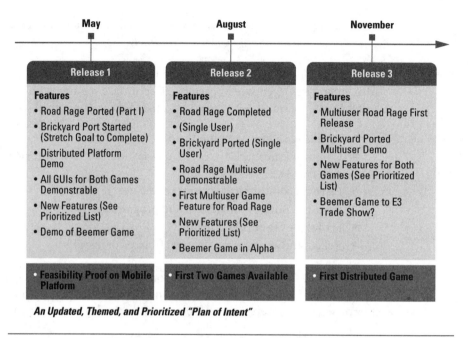

Figure 4–12   Example product roadmap for a hypothetical gaming company

SUMMARY

In this chapter, we introduced new requirements roles, artifacts, and processes that are necessary to apply agile development in programs that require many teams. We described how to organize the teams to optimize value delivery. We introduced a number of new requirements artifacts—*Vision, features, nonfunctional require-ments*, and *Roadmap*—and described how teams use these artifacts to communicate the larger purpose of the product, system, or application they are developing. We also described how teams aggregate a series of iterations to build *PSIs*, or incre-mental *releases*, via an *Agile Release Train*, which incrementally delivers value to the users and customers. In the next and final chapter of Part I, we'll increase our level of abstraction one last time and introduce a set of requirements practices suited to building a portfolio of products and services suitable to the needs of the larger enterprise.

Chapter 5

AGILE REQUIREMENTS FOR THE PORTFOLIO

At enterprise scale, things get a little more complicated.

INTRODUCTION TO THE PORTFOLIO LEVEL

For many software enterprises, including those of modest scope of 100 or so practitioners and those that develop and manage only one or two products, the team model (with its user stories, tasks, and acceptance tests) plus the program model (adding features and nonfunctional requirements) may be all that the teams need to manage system requirements in an agile manner. In this context, *driving releases with a feature-based vision* and *driving iterations with stories created by the teams* may be all that is required.

However, there is another class of enterprises—enterprises employing hundreds to thousands of practitioners and those that have many products—wherein the governance and management model for new software asset development needs additional artifacts and still higher levels of abstraction. In the Big Picture, this is the *Portfolio* level, as Figure 5–1 illustrates.

Of course, we also note that the Team, Program, and Portfolio "level" boundaries we defined here are arbitrary and are intended to serve more as a mental model—a way to reason about things at higher and higher levels of abstraction, scope, and scale—rather than a particular prescription for a particular enterprise. Having said that,

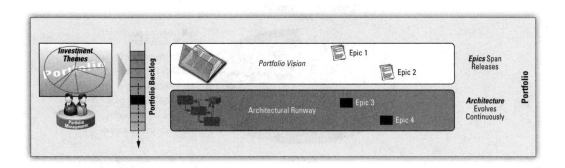

Figure 5–1   The Portfolio level of the Big Picture

however, this level does mimic some actual large and very large-scale agile implementations that have applied the model in variants of the form described here.[1]

The Portfolio level introduces two new artifact types: *investment themes* and *epics*, a new backlog (the *portfolio backlog*), a new team (the *portfolio management team*), and the container concepts of *portfolio vision* and *architectural runway*.

We'll start by describing investment themes, because that's where everything starts.

INVESTMENT THEMES

Investment themes (or product themes) represent the set of initiatives that drive the enterprise's investment in systems, products, applications, and services.

> *Investment themes represent key product or service value propositions that provide marketplace differentiation and competitive advantage.*

The set of strategic investment themes for an enterprise, or business unit within an enterprise, establishes the relative investment objectives for the entity, as the example in Figure 5–2 illustrates.

Each "partition" in the graphic represents a specific development initiative and an associated budget. Within the partition (budget allocation), managers are empowered to develop the initiative in whatever way makes the most economic and business sense for the enterprise. However, they generally may not exceed the budget or borrow resources from other themes without agreement with those stakeholders. With this process, the enterprise exercises its fiduciary responsibility by driving investment to the agreed-to business priorities.

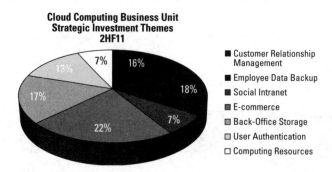

Figure 5–2   A set of strategic investment themes for an enterprise

1. The requirements model in the Big Picture was developed with the help of Juha-Markus Aalto of Nokia Corporation.

PORTFOLIO MANAGEMENT TEAM

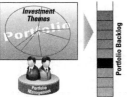 The derivation of these decisions is the responsibility of the *portfolio management function*, those individuals who have ultimate responsibility for the individual lines of business. In larger enterprises, this typically happens at the business unit level based on an annual or twice-annual budgeting process.[2]

The portfolio management team makes its decisions based on some combination of the following:

- Investment in *existing* product offerings—enhancements, support, and maintenance
- Investment in *new* products and services—products that will enhance revenue and/or gain new market share in the current or near-term budget period
- Investment in *futures*—advanced product and service offerings that *require* investment today but will not contribute to revenue until outlying years
- Reducing investment (sunset strategy) for existing offers that are nearing the end of their useful life

Themes have a much longer life span than epics, and a set of investment themes may be largely unchanged for up to a year or more. To provide ongoing governance and visibility into the investments, the portfolio management team may be assisted by a project management office (PMO).

The role and activities of the portfolio management team and PMO are explored in depth in Chapter 22, Moving to Agile Portfolio Management.

EPICS AND THE PORTFOLIO BACKLOG

The set of strategic investment themes drive all new development, and requirements *epics* are derived from these decisions.

> *Epics are large-scale development initiatives that realize the value of investment themes.*

Epics are the highest-level requirements artifact that we will use to coordinate development. In the requirements model, they sit between investment themes and features, as Figure 5–3 shows.

---

2. It's important to note here that this "traditional budgeting process" can be one of the impediments to enterprise agility. We'll discuss that in Chapter 22, Moving to Agile Portfolio Management.

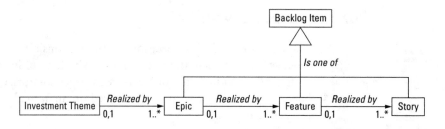

Figure 5–3 Investment themes and epics in the requirements information model

A number of observations can be derived from the figure.

- Epics are typically driven (parented by) investment themes. But some epics can be independent (they do not require a parent in order to exist).
- Epics are not implemented directly. Instead, they are broken into features, which, in turn, are broken into user stories, which are the primitives used by the teams for actual coding and testing.
- Epics are not directly testable. Instead, they are tested by the acceptance tests associated with the features and stories that implement them.

Portfolio Backlog

Epics deliver the value implied by the theme, and they are identified, prioritized, estimated, and maintained in the *portfolio backlog*. Prior to release planning, epics are decomposed into features, which in turn drive release planning, as we illustrate in Figure 5–4.

Epics may be expressed in bullet form, as a sentence or two, in video, in a prototype, in user interface mock-ups, or indeed in *any form* of expression suitable to express

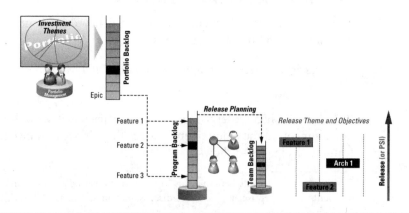

Figure 5–4 Epics are split into features prior to release planning.

the intent of the product initiative. With epics, the objective is *vision, not specificity*. In other words, the epic need only be described in detail sufficient to *initiate a further discussion* about what types of features an epic implies.

EPICS, FEATURES, AND STORIES

It's apparent by now that epics, features, and stories are all forms of expressing user need and implied benefit but at different levels of abstraction, as the hierarchical representation in Figure 5–5 illustrates.

This reduces the level of too-early specificity and decreases the overhead of managing these artifacts for larger systems. (Imagine a program or product manager attempting to maintain, estimate, and prioritize a single-level backlog of 5,000 requirements...it has happened!)

Even more importantly, the reduced specificity of the features and epics increase the team's agility by allowing them to interpret requirements in ways that are the easiest to implement and most consistent with the current constructs of the implementation.

Returning to our e-mail example from the previous chapter, we might find the following epic-feature story hierarchy.

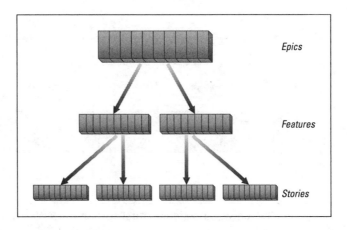

Figure 5–5   Hierarchical view of epics, features, and stories

ARCHITECTURAL RUNWAY AND ARCHITECTURAL EPICS

At the Portfolio level, we also find a last big block of interesting things to talk about, *architectural runway* and *architectural epics*, as illustrated in Figure 5–6.

In *Scaling Software Agility* [Leffingwell 2007], we defined architectural runway as following:

> *A system that has architectural runway contains existing or planned infrastructure sufficient to allow incorporation of current and anticipated requirements without excessive refactoring.*

In the context of the enterprise's portfolio of products and in the face of a series of shorter, incremental releases, architectural runway is the answer to a *big* question:

> *What technology initiatives need to be underway now so that we can reliably deliver a new class of features in the next year or so?*

Here, we are not talking about side R&D projects that an enterprise may use to determine technology strategies, establish feasibility, and so on. Those are localized efforts and can be managed fairly easily by the teams or the system architects. Rather, we are talking about large-scale changes to the code base that will be necessary to support features on the current roadmap and changes that could affect most, or even all, of the development teams. Here are some examples.

- Implement a common install, licensing, and user authentication model across each product in the suite.
- Convert the transaction server to a SOA-based architecture.
- Redesign the operating system to support symmetrical multiprocessing.

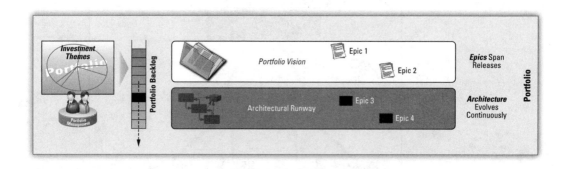

Figure 5–6   Architectural runway and architectural epics in the Big Picture

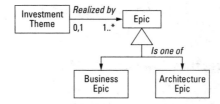

Figure 5–7 Business and architecture epics

Clearly, these are not simple refactors. These changes will involve significant, structural changes that could affect millions of line of code and require tens (or even hundreds) of man-years. And, if the enterprise wants to see it accomplished next year, or even the year after, they have to start now.

To start now, this work has to be defined and communicated to the team, like any other major initiative, even though the end-user value may be a year or so down the road.

So, in Figure 5–7, we see two kinds of epics: *business epics*, which are functional or user-experience epics such as those we have already described, and *architecture epics*, which are used to implement the technological changes that must be made to significant elements of the portfolio.

Within the enterprise, such initiatives must be elevated to the Portfolio level so that the appropriate teams can start laying in the foundation now. After all, they require significant investment. A simple "We'll refactor it later" approach is not economically viable. No enterprise wants to "do over" the last x00 man-years of work, particularly when they always knew they needed to evolve certain core technologies, platforms, security models, and so on, in a coordinated fashion.

Implementing Architectural Epics

However, since the agile enterprise no longer has the big bang, waterfall, "branch-merge-and-crash-next-year" strategies to fall back on, what's an enterprise to do? The answer is easy to say and hard to do, but it is a key agile enterprise ability:

> *Architectural epics will be implemented in the main code line, incrementally, just like any other epic.*

In so doing, development teams commit to a "do no harm" refactoring approach. In other words, they implement these large-scale refactors in small increments. At each PSI, they commit to "do no harm" to the systems or its users, and they roll out the architectural changes piecemeal and surface the new capabilities to the users only whenever there is sufficient infrastructure to do so. It isn't easy. It is agile. And it does work.[3]

Architectural Runway: Portfolio, Program, and Team

The continuous build out and maintenance of new architectural runway is the responsibility of all mature agile teams. Failing to do so will cause one of two bad things to happen.

- Release dates will be missed because large-scale, just-in-time, infrastructure refactoring adds unacceptable risk to scheduling.
- Failure to extend the architecture systematically means that the teams will eventually run out of runway. New features cannot be added without major refactoring. Velocity slows. The system eventually becomes so brittle and unstable that it has to be entirely rewritten.

This work must happen *continuously* at each of the Portfolio, Program, and Team levels.

- *Portfolio:* Portfolio-level architectural runway is achieved by defining, communicating, and implementing architecture epics that drive the company's technology vision. Some will require significant levels of investment and consume substantial resources. In the near term, some may even reduce the velocity of current and new feature implementations. Because failing to implement them will eventually compromise the company's position in the market, *architectural epics* must be visible, estimated, and planned just like any other epic.
- *Program:* At the Program level, product managers, system teams, project teams, and architects translate the architectural epics into *architectural features* that are relevant to each release. They are prioritized, estimated, and resourced like any other feature. And, like features, each architectural initiative must also be conceptually complete at each release boundary so as to not compromise the new release.
- *Team:* At the Team level, refactors and design spikes are often necessary to extend the runway, and they are prioritized along with user stories. In this way, architectural work is visible, accountable, and demonstrable at every

---

3. As an example, Rally Software Development built and launched a successful software as a service (SaaS) application but decided a year later that they had picked the wrong choice of underlying platform technology. They had built in a dependency on a vendor that was slow to develop the new features they needed to build a richer experience for their users, and licensing costs were an issue as well. They refactored their application, one module and one feature at a time, in the course of eight to ten releases over a two-year period, gradually decreasing their usage of the underlying platform. At the end, they just "switched off" the vendor's product. Their users experienced no usage paradigm change at any point. *Patience is still a virtue* in agile development.

iteration boundary. This is accomplished by agreement and collaboration with the system architects, product owners, and agile tech leads that determine what spikes need to happen and when.

Strategies for accomplishing incremental "rearchitecting" of larger-scale systems in an agile manner are a primary topic of Chapters 21 and 22.

SUMMARY

In this chapter, we described the highest, *Portfolio* level of the Big Picture. We introduced *strategic investment themes*, *epics*, the *portfolio backlog*, and the concept of *architectural runway* as necessary elements of managing agile requirements at scale. We also introduced the *portfolio management team* as the functional unit that establishes the strategic direction of the products and services the enterprise develops. Of course, we've only touched the surface of these important topics, and that is why Part IV of the book is dedicated to agile requirements for the portfolio.

SUMMARY OF THE FULL ENTERPRISE REQUIREMENTS INFORMATION MODEL

As we conclude Part I of this book, we note that we've introduced a fairly extensive requirements model in an incremental fashion. We've introduced each requirements element—user stories, features, and the like—at the appropriate time based on the team, project, or portfolio context. Perhaps now is the time to take a broader look at the totality of the model we have built incrementally. So, in summary, the full lean and scalable requirements model for the agile enterprise appears in Figure 5–8.

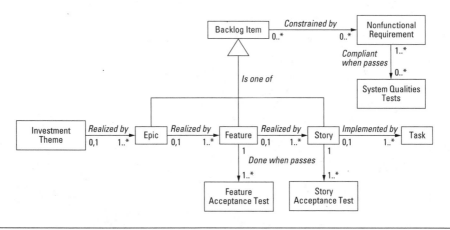

Figure 5–8   Full enterprise requirements model

Although this model may appear to be more complex than most agilists have typically applied to date, it scales directly to the needs of the full enterprise without burdening the agile teams or adding unnecessary administrative, tracking, or reporting overhead. In this manner, the enterprise can extend the benefits of agility—from the Team to the Program to the Portfolio level—and thereby achieve the full productivity and quality benefits available to the increasingly agile enterprise.

Besides, your enterprise can and should use only what it needs from this model; otherwise, it isn't *the simplest thing that can possibly work.*

Case Study: Tendril Platform

Managing requirements in a significant agile development project is a complex task, and the requirements concepts, practices, and artifacts have to scale to the task at hand.

We introduce this case study, Tendril, as an example of a company that is actively applying agile in the development of an innovative and complex hardware and software system. As the book progresses, we'll use some real artifacts from this case study to help illustrate the practices we are describing.

Background for the Case Study

The green revolution is upon us in many varied fields. For our case study, we have selected a Boulder, Colorado, company that is one of the leaders in the green energy field. Tendril has embraced the emerging technologies of the "smart grid" movement as its basis for the development of new energy-saving products for commercial and home use.

The nation's electricity grid was built and regulated for reliability and ubiquitous availability. Those were admirable goals for 20th-century infrastructure, but as we move into the 21st century, electricity and energy needs have gone beyond mere reliability and ubiquity. We now need to *reduce/eliminate global warming* and to use energy efficiency to *increase our energy independence*. Enter the smart grid.

The term *smart grid* covers a range of initiatives, including upgrades to the following:

- The long-haul transmission grid to enable movement of renewable and non-renewable energy to places that can consume them
- The short-haul distribution grids so that they are more efficient with energy delivery
- Electricity meters with two-way communications infrastructure between the customer and the generator/provider

As it is currently defined, the smart grid solves only part of the problem. It is meant to reach consumer's homes, but the existing infrastructure falls short, ending at the meter. The Tendril technology infrastructure moves inside the home and completes the smart grid in the new Information Age.

By using networking technology, the end-consuming devices can know the following:

- When environmental friendliness is high
- When grid reliability is low
- When the price is cheap
- When and where energy is needed more or less and the overall consumption "profile" that each consumer desires

Similarly, the points between the generation and consuming devices can know the following:

- Where demand is high versus low
- Where outages may have occurred and the nature of the outage
- Whether meters ought to be connected or disconnected
- Where renewable supply is and how to route it to the right demand locations
- When the long-haul or short-haul grids are inefficient (and why)

Of the many smart grid components, the consumer-oriented elements deserve as much attention as the alternatives. After all, it is only when consumers *use* renewable energy or cheap energy, or when distributed generation in their homes can be effectively sold, that our nation will achieve the results it seeks—true 21st-century energy efficiency.

As a contributing part of the smart grid solutions, Tendril offers a comprehensive line of residential energy management products, collectively known as the *Tendril end-to-end solution*. These products combine a significant array of firmware and software engineering challenges and are the focal point of a large-scale series of agile development efforts both on the firmware side and on the software side. As this book progresses, we will be examining various artifacts of these engineering projects as part of our case study.

In some cases, it will also be necessary to look at agile lean requirements that fall outside the practices used by Tendril. Never fear, these practices will also be discussed with other artifacts of other case studies.

SYSTEM CONTEXT DIAGRAM

Tendril offers a variety of products that further the smart grid initiative. For our purposes, we will consider only a representative selection of the product offerings, Tendril Vantage. This subset will typify many of the agile development techniques and challenges that are used for the entire range of product offerings.

Tendril Vantage is a browser-based Internet application that provides consumers with the tools and information they need to better understand, manage, and control their energy consumption and each of the smart devices in their homes. With Tendril Vantage, users can register their home, electric appliances, and devices. Users can also set rules, personal alerts, and notifications; track their consumption in real time; review historical usage patterns; and compare their household energy expenditure against other homes in their area with similar demographics.

As Figure I–1 illustrates, the Tendril platform consists of three major subsystems:

- The electric utility
- The energy management servers
- The consumer's home and devices

We will describe the use of agile requirements techniques in support of development of the Tendril Vantage application, as well as other products in the Tendril platform and end-to-end solution. We will start by using the case study in the context of the next chapter, User Stories.

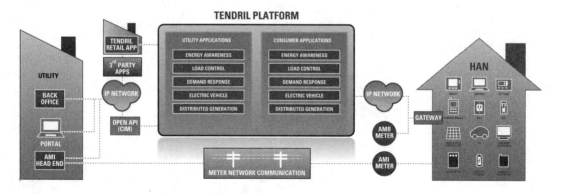

Figure I–1 Tendril platform simplified system diagram

PART II

AGILE REQUIREMENTS FOR THE TEAM

Eliminate numerical quotas, including Management by Objectives.

—W. Edwards Deming

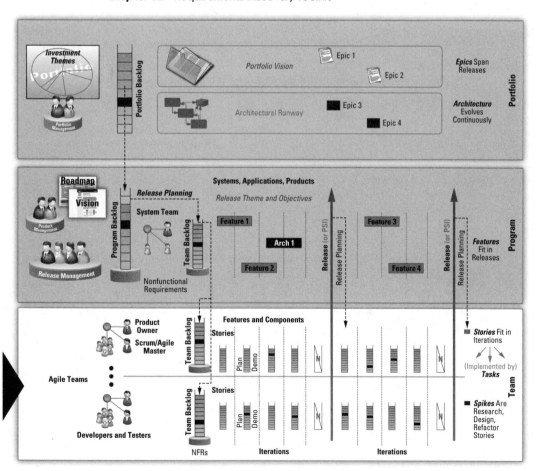

Chapter 6

USER STORIES

They have been at a great feast of languages, and stol'n the scraps.

—Shakespeare, *Love's Labour's Lost*, Act 5, scene 1

INTRODUCTION

In Chapter 3, Agile Requirements for the Team, we introduced the concepts and relationships among the key artifacts—backlogs, user stories, tasks, and so on—used by agile teams to define, build, and test the system of interest. We noted that the user story is the workhorse of agile development, and it is the container that carries the value stream to the user. It also serves as a metaphor for our entire incremental value delivery approach, that is:

Define a user value story, implement and test it in a short iteration, demonstrate/and or deliver it to the user, repeat forever!

We summarize the requirements artifacts involved in fulfilling this mission in Figure 6–1.

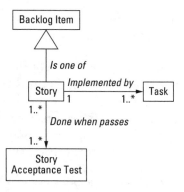

Figure 6–1 Requirements model for teams

99

From the figure, we see that stories come from the backlog and are implemented via whatever design, coding, and testing tasks are needed to complete the story. Further, stories cannot be considered to be *done* until they pass an associated acceptance test.

In this chapter, we'll describe the user story in more detail, because it is there that we will find the agile practices that help us conform our solution directly to the user's specific needs and help assure quality at the same time.

User Story Overview

We have noted many of the contributions of Scrum to enterprise agile practices, including, for example, the definition of the product owner role, which is integral to our requirements practices. But it is to XP that we owe the invention of the user story, and it is the proponents of XP who have developed the breadth and depth of this artifact. As Beck and Fowler [2005] explain:

> *The story is the unit of functionality in an XP project. We demonstrate progress by delivering tested, integrated code that implements a story. A story should be understandable to customers, developer-testable, valuable to the customer, and small enough that the programmers can build half a dozen in an iteration.*

However, though the user story originated in XP, this is less of a "methodological fork in the road" than it might appear, because user stories are now routinely taught within the constructs of Scrum training as a tool for building product backlogs and defining Sprint content. We have Mike Cohn to thank for much of this integration; he has developed user stories extensively in his book *User Stories Applied* [Cohn 2004], and he has been very active in the Scrum community.

For our purposes, we'll define a user story simply as follows:

> A user story is a brief statement of intent that describes something the system needs to do for the user.

In XP, user stories are often written by the customer, thus integrating the customer directly in the development process. In Scrum, the product owner often writes the user stories, with input from the customers, the stakeholders, and the team. However, in actual practice, any team member with sufficient domain knowledge can write user stories, but it is up to the product owner to accept and prioritize these potential stories into the product backlog.

User stories are a tool for defining a system's behavior in a way that is understandable to both the developers and the users. User stories focus the work on the value defined by the user rather than a functional breakdown structure, which is the way work has traditionally been tasked. They provide a lightweight and effective approach to managing requirements for a system.

A user story captures a short statement of function on an index card or perhaps with an online tool. In simple backlog form, stories can just be a list of things the system needs to do for the user. Here's an example:

Log in to my web energy-monitoring portal.

See my daily energy usage.

Check my current electricity billing rate.

Details of system behavior do not appear in the brief statement; these are left to be developed later through conversations and acceptance criteria between the team and the product owner.

User Stories Help Bridge the Developer–Customer Communication Gap

In agile development, it is the developer's job to speak the language of the user, not the user's job to speak the language of developers. Effective communication is the key, and we need a common language. The user story provides the common language to build understanding between the user and the technical team.

Bill Wake, one of the creators of XP, describes it this way:[1]

> A pidgin language is a simplified language, usually used for trade that allows people who can't communicate in their native language to nonetheless work together. User stories act like this. We don't expect customers or users to view the system the same way that programmers do; stories act as a pidgin language where both sides can agree enough to work together effectively.

With user stories, we don't have to understand each other's language with the degree of proficiency necessary to craft a sonnet; we just need to understand each other enough to know when we have struck a proper bargain!

User Stories Are Not Requirements

Although user stories do most of the work previously done by software requirements specifications, use cases, and the like, they are *materially different* in a number of subtle yet critical ways.

- They are not detailed requirements specifications (something a system shall do) but are rather negotiable expressions of intent (it needs to do something about like this).

1. *xp123.com/xplor/xp0308/index.shtml*

- They are short, easy to read, and understandable to developers, stakeholders, and users.
- They represent small increments of valued functionality that can be developed in a period of days to weeks.
- They are relatively easy to estimate, so effort to implement the functionality can be rapidly determined.
- They are not carried in large, unwieldy documents but rather organized in lists that can be more easily arranged and rearranged as new information is discovered.
- They are not detailed at the outset of the project but are elaborated on a just-in-time basis, thereby avoiding too-early specificity, delays in development, requirements inventory, and an over-constrained statement of the solution
- They need little or no maintenance and can be safely discarded after implementation.[2,3]
- User stories, and the code that is created quickly thereafter, serve as inputs to documentation, which is then developed incrementally as well.

USER STORY FORM

This section addresses formats for user stories.

Card, Conversation, and Confirmation

> As a *<role>*,
> I can *<activity>*
> So that *<business value>*

> Details in discussion
> between PO and team

> ▪ A list of what will make
> the story acceptable
> to the product owner

Ron Jeffries, another creator of XP, described what has become our favorite way to think about user stories. He used the alliteration *card, conversation, and confirmation* to describe the three elements of a user story.[4]

Card represents two to three sentences used to describe the intent of the story. The card serves as a memorable token, which summarizes intent and represents a more detailed requirement, whose details remain to be determined.

---

2. This is subject to the development and persistence of acceptance tests, which define the behavior of the system in regression-testable detail.
3. There can be a negative psychological effect to simply discarding the paper cards. One reviewer commented: "Sometimes when we look back at what we'd achieved recently, we don't see visually anything if all the done stories are discarded. So we actually keep all of them, piling them up in the "done" section. It's a bit messy but still it gives a good feeling, we did achieve quite a lot actually...."
4. *xprogramming.com/xpmag/expcardconversationconfirmation/*

▶ **NOTE** In XP and agile, stories are often written manually on physical index cards. More typically in the enterprise, the "card" element is captured as text and attachments in a spreadsheet or agile project management tooling, but teams often still use cards for early planning and brainstorming, as we will see later.

Conversation represents a discussion between the team, customer, product owner, and other stakeholders, which is necessary to determine the more detailed behavior required to implement the intent. In other words, the *card* also represents a "promise for a conversation" about the intent.

Confirmation represents the *acceptance test*, which is how the customer or product owner will confirm that the story has been implemented to their satisfaction. In other words, confirmation represents the *conditions of satisfaction* that will be applied to determine whether the story fulfills the intent as well as the more detailed requirements.

With this simple alliteration, we have an object lesson in how quality in agile is achieved during, rather than after, actual code development. We do that by simply making sure that every new user story is discussed and refined in whatever detail is necessary and is tested to the satisfaction of the key stakeholders.

User Story Voice

In the last few years, a newer, fairly standardized form has been applied that strengthens the user story construct significantly. The form is as follows:

> As a <role>, I can <activity> so that <business value>.

where:

- <role> represents who is performing the action or perhaps one who is receiving the value from the activity. It may even be another system, if that is what is initiating the activity.
- <activity> represents the action to be performed by the system.
- <business value> represents the value achieved by the activity.

We call this the *user voice* form of user story expression and find it an exceedingly useful construct[5] because it spans the problem space (<business value> delivered) and the solution space (<activity> the user performs with the system). It also

---

5. While looking for the origin of this form, I received the following note from Mike Cohn: "It started with a team at Connextra in London and was mentioned at XP2003. I started using it then and wrote about it in my 2004 book, *User Stories Applied*."

provides a user-first (<role>) perspective to the team, which keeps them focused on business value and solving real problems for real people.

This user story form greatly enhances the "why" and "how" understanding that developers need to implement a system that truly meets the needs of the users.

For example, a user of a home energy-management system might want to do the following:

> As a Consumer (<role>), I want to be able to see my daily energy usage (<what I do with the system>) so that I can lower my energy costs and usage (<business value I receive>)."

Each element provides important expansionary context. The *role* allows a segmentation of the product functionality and typically draws out other role-based needs and context for the activity. The *activity* typically represents the "system requirement" needed by the role. And the *value* communicates why the activity is needed, which can often lead the team to finding possible alternative activities that could provide the same value for less effort.

User Story Detail

The details for user stories are conveyed primarily through conversations between the product owner and the team, keeping the team involved from the outset. However, if more details are needed about the story, they can be provided in the form of an attachment (mock-up, spreadsheet, algorithm, or whatever), which is attached to the user story. In that case, the user story serves as the "token" that also carries the more specific behavior to the team. The additional user story detail should be collected over time (just-in-time) through discussions and collaboration with the team and other stakeholders before and during development.

User Story Acceptance Criteria

In addition to the statement of the user story, additional notes, assumptions, and acceptance criteria can be kept with a user story. *Many* discussions about a story between the team and customers will likely take place while the story is being coded. The alternate flows in the activity, acceptance boundaries, and other clarifications should be captured along with the story. Many of these can be turned into acceptance test cases, or other functional test cases, for the story.

Here's an example:

> As a consumer, I want to be able to see my daily energy usage so that I can lower my energy costs and usage.

Acceptance Criteria:

- Read DecaWatt meter data every 10 seconds and display on portal in 15-minute increments and display on in-home display every read.
- Read KiloWatt meters for new data as available and display on the portal every hour and on the in-home display after every read.
- No multiday trending for now (another story).

Etc....

Acceptance criteria are not functional or unit tests; rather, they are the conditions of satisfaction being placed on the system. Functional and unit tests go much deeper in testing all functional flows, exception flows, boundary conditions, and related functionality associated with the story.

INVEST IN GOOD USER STORIES

Agile teams spend a significant amount of time in discovering, elaborating, and understanding user stories and writing acceptance tests for them. This is as it should be, because it represents the following conclusion:

> Writing the code for an understood objective is not necessarily the hardest part of software development; rather, it is understanding what the real objective for the code *is*.

Therefore, *investing* in good user stories, albeit at the last responsible moment, is a worthy effort for the team. Bill Wake coined the acronym INVEST[6] to describe the attributes of a good user story.

Independent
Negotiable
Valuable
Estimable
Small
Testable

The INVEST model is now fairly ubiquitous, and many agile teams evaluate their stories with respect to these attributes. Here's our view of the value of the team's INVESTment.

---

6. Bill Wake. *www.XP123.org*.

Independent

Independence means that a story can be developed, tested, and potentially even delivered on its own. Therefore, it can also be independently *valued*.

Many stories will have some natural sequential dependencies as the product functionality builds, and yet each piece can deliver value independently. For example, a product might display a single record and then a list, then sort the list, filter the list, prepare a multipage list, export the list, edit items in the list, and so on. Many of these items have sequential dependencies, yet each item provides independent value, and the product can be potentially shipped through any stopping point of development.

However, many nonvalued dependencies, either technical or functional, also tend to find their way into backlogs, and these we need to find and eliminate. For example, the following might be a nonvalued functional dependency:

> As an administrator, I can set the consumer's password security rules so that users are required to create and retain secure passwords, keeping the system secure.

> As a consumer, I am required to follow the password security rules set by the administrator so that I can maintain high security to my account.

In this example, the consumer story depends on the administrator story. The administrator story is testable only in setting, clearing, and preserving the policy, but it is not testable as enforced on the consumer. In addition, completing the administrator story does not leave the product in a potentially shippable state—therefore, it's not independently valuable.

By reconsidering the stories (and the design of the system), we can remove the dependency by splitting the stories in a different manner, in this case through the types of security policies applied and by combining the setup with enforcement in each story:

> As an administrator, I can set the password expiration period so that users are forced to change their passwords periodically.

> As an administrator, I can set the password strength characteristics so that users are required to create difficult-to-hack passwords.

Now, each story can stand on its own and can be developed, tested, and delivered independently.

Negotiable . . . and Negotiated

Unlike traditional requirements, a user story is not a contract for specific functionality but rather a placeholder for requirements to be discussed, developed, tested, and accepted. This process of negotiation between the business and the team recognizes the legitimacy and primacy of the business inputs but allows for discovery through collaboration and feedback.

In our prior, siloed organizations, written requirements were generally required to facilitate the limited communication bandwidth between departments and to serve as a record of past agreements. Agile, however, is founded on the concept that a team-based approach is more effective at solving problems in a dynamic collaborative environment. A user story is real-time and structured to leverage this effective and direct communication and collaboration approach.

Finally, the negotiability of user stories helps teams achieve predictability. The lack of overly constraining and too-detailed requirements enhances the team's and business's ability to make trade-offs between functionality and delivery dates. Because each story has flexibility, the team has more flexibility to meet release objectives, which increases dependability and fosters trust.

Valuable

An agile team's goal is simple: to deliver the most value given their existing time and resource constraints. Therefore, value is the most important attribute in the INVEST model, and every user story must provide some value to the user, customer, or stakeholder of the product. Backlogs are prioritized by value, and businesses succeed or fail based on the value the teams can deliver.

A typical challenge facing teams is learning how to write small, incremental user stories that can effectively deliver value. Traditional approaches have taught us to create functional breakdown structures based on technical components. This technical layering approach to building software delays the value delivery until all the layers are brought together after multiple iterations. Wake[7] provides his perspective of vertical, rather than technical, layering:

> Think of a whole story as a multi-layer cake, e.g., a network layer, a persistence layer, a logic layer, and a presentation layer. When we split a story [horizontally], we're serving up only part of that cake. We want to give the customer the essence of the whole cake, and the best way is to slice vertically through the layers. Developers often have an inclination to work on only one layer at a time (and get it "right"); but a full database layer (for example) has little value to the customer if there's no presentation layer.

---

7. Bill Wake. *www.XP123.org.*

Creating valuable stories requires us to reorient our functional breakdown structures from a horizontal to a vertical approach. We create stories that slice through the architecture so that we can present value to the user and seek their feedback as early and often as possible.

Although normally the value is focused on the user interacting with the system, sometimes the value is more appropriately focused on a customer representative or key stakeholder. For example, perhaps a marketing director is requesting a higher click-through rate on ads presented on the Web site. Although the story could be written from the perspective of the end user...

> *As a consumer, I can see other energy pricing programs that appeal to me so that I can enroll in a program that better suits my lifestyle.*

...to provide a clearer perspective on the real value, it would be more appropriately written from the marketing director's perspective:

> *As a utility marketing director, I can present users with new pricing programs so that they are more likely to continue purchasing energy from me.*

Another challenge faced by teams is to articulate value from technical stories such as code refactoring, component upgrades, and so on. For example, how would the product owner determine the value of the following?

> *Refactor the error logging system.*

Articulating the value of a technical solution as a user story will help communicate to the business its relative importance. Here's an example:

> *As a consumer, I can receive a consistent and clear error message anywhere in the product so that I know how to address the issue. OR*

> *As a technical support member, I want the user to receive a consistent and clear message anywhere in the application so they can fix the issue without calling support.*

In these latter examples, the value is clear to the user, to the product owner, to the stakeholders, and to the team.

Estimable

A good user story is estimable. Although a story of any size can be in the backlog, in order for it to be developed and tested in an iteration, the team should be able to provide an approximate estimation of its complexity and amount of work required to complete it. The minimal investment in estimation is to determine whether it can be completed within a single iteration. Additional estimation accuracy will increase the team's predictability.

If the team is unable to estimate a user story, it generally indicates that the story is too large or uncertain. If it is *too large* to estimate, it should be split into smaller stories. If the story is *too uncertain* to estimate, then a technical or functional spike story can be used to reduce uncertainty so that one or more estimable user stories result. (Each of these topics is discussed in more detail in the following sections.)

One of the primary benefits of estimating user stories is not simply to derive a precise size but rather to draw out any hidden assumptions and missing acceptance criteria and to clarify the team's shared understanding of the story. Thus, the conversation surrounding the estimation process is as (or more) important than the actual estimate. The ability to estimate a user story is highly influenced by the size of the story, as we'll see shortly.

Small

User stories should be small enough to be able to be completed in an iteration. Otherwise, they can't provide any value or be considered *done* at that point. However, even smaller user stories provide more agility and productivity. There are two primary reasons for this: *increased throughput* and *decreased complexity*.

Increased Throughput

From queuing theory, we know that smaller batch sizes go through a system faster. This is one of the primary principles of lean flow and is captured in Little's law:

$$\text{Cycle Time} = \frac{\text{Work In Process}}{\text{Throughput}}$$

In a stable system (where throughput, the amount of work that can be done in a unit of time, is constant), we have to decrease work in process (the amount of things we are working on) in order to decrease cycle time (the time elapsed between the beginning and end of the process). In our case, that means *fewer, smaller stories in process will come out faster.*

Moreover, when a system is loaded to capacity, it can become unstable, and the problem is compounded. In heavily loaded systems, larger batches move disproportionately slower (throughput decreases) through the system. (Think of a highway system at rush hour. Motorcycles and bicycles have a much higher throughput than do cars and trucks. There is more space to maneuver smaller things through a loaded system.) Because development teams are typically fully allocated at or above capacity (80% to 120%), they fall in the "rush-hour highway" category.

When utilization hits 80% or so, larger objects increase cycle time (slow down) much more than smaller objects. Worse, the *variation* in cycle time increases, meaning that it becomes harder to predict when a batch might actually exit the system, as shown in Figure 6–2. In turn, this lower predictability wreaks havoc with schedules, commitments, and the credibility of the team.

Decreased Complexity

Smaller stories not only go through faster because of their raw, proportional size, but they go through faster yet because of their *decreased complexity*, and complexity has a *nonlinear relationship* to size. This is seen most readily in testing, where the permutations of tests required to validate the functionality increase at an exponential rate with the complexity of the function itself. This correlates to the advice we receive about developing clean code, as Robert Martin [2009] notes on his rules for writing software functions.

- Rule 1: Do one thing.
- Rule 2: Keep them small.
- Rule 3: Make them smaller than that.

This is one of the primary reasons that the Fibonacci estimating sequence (that is, 1, 2, 3, 5, 8, 13, 21…) is so effective in estimating user stories. The effort estimate grows nonlinearly with increasing story size.

On the Relationship of Size and Independence

A fair question arises as to the relationship between size and independence, because it seems logical that smaller stories increase the number of dependencies. However, smaller stories, even with some increased dependency, deliver higher value through-

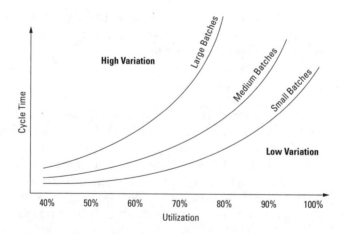

Figure 6–2 Large batches have higher cycle times and higher cycle time variability [Poppendieck and Poppendieck 2007].

put and provide faster user feedback than larger stories. So, the agilist always leans to smaller stories *and then makes them smaller still.*

Testable

In proper agile, *all code is tested code*, so it follows that stories must be testable. If a story does not appear to be testable, then the story is probably ill-formed, overly complex, or perhaps dependent on other stories in the backlog.

To assure that *stories don't get into an iteration if they can't get out* (be successfully tested), many agile teams today take a "write-the-test-first" approach. This started in the XP community using test-driven development, a practice of writing automated unit tests prior to writing the code to pass the test.

Since then, this philosophy of approach is being applied to development of story acceptance criteria and the necessary functional tests prior to coding the story itself. If a team really knows how to test a story, then they likely know how to code it as well.

To assure testability, user stories share some common testability pitfalls with requirements. Vague words such as *quickly, manage, nice, clean,* and so on, are easy to write but very difficult to test because they mean different things to different people and therefore should be avoided. And although these words do provide negotiability, framing them with some clear boundaries will help the team and the business share expectations of the output and avoid big surprises.

SPLITTING USER STORIES

Compound Problem

Split Story

User stories are often driven by epics and features—a large, vague concept of something we want to do for a user. We often find these big-value stories during our discovery process and capture them in the backlog. However, these are *compound stories,* as pictured on the left, and are usually far too big to be implemented within an iteration. To prepare the work for iterations, a team must break them down into smaller stories.

There is no set routine for splitting user stories into iteration-sized bites, other than the general guidance to make each story provide a vertical slice, some piece of user value, through the system. However, we recommend applying an appropriate selection of *ten common patterns to split a user story*, as Table 6–1 indicates.[8]

---

8. Adapted from Richard Lawrence, *www.richardlawrence.info/2009/10/28/patterns-for-splitting-user-stories/*

Table 6–1   Ten Patterns for Splitting a User Story

---

1. Workflow Steps

Identify specific steps that a user takes to accomplish a specific workflow, and then implement the workflow in incremental stages.

As a utility, I want to update and publish pricing programs to my customer.	...I can publish pricing programs to the customer's in-home display.
	...I can send a message to the customer's web portal.
	...I can publish the pricing table to a customer's smart thermostat.

---

2. Business Rule Variations

At first glance, some stories seem fairly simple. However, sometimes the business rules are more complex or extensive than the first glance revealed. In this case, it might be useful to break the story into several stories to handle the business rule complexity.

As a utility, I can sort customers by different demographics.	...sort by ZIP code.
	...sort by home demographics.
	...sort by energy consumption.

---

3. Major Effort

Sometimes a story can be split into several parts where most of the effort will go toward implementing the first one. In the example shown next, processing infrastructure should be built to support the first story; adding more functionality should be relatively trivial later.

As a user, I want to be able to select/change my pricing program with my utility through my web portal.	...I want to use time-of-use pricing.
	...I want to prepay for my energy.
	...I want to enroll in critical-peak pricing.

---

4. Simple/Complex

When the team is discussing a story and the story seems to be getting larger and larger ("What about x? Have you considered y?"), stop and ask, "What's the simplest version that can possibly work?" Capture that simple version as its own story, and then break out all the variations and complexities into their own stories.

As a user, I basically want a fixed price, but I also want to be notified of critical-peak pricing events.	...respond to the time and the duration of the critical-peak pricing event.
	...respond to emergency events.

---

5. Variations in Data

Data variations and data sources are another source of scope and complexity. Consider adding stories just-in-time after building the simplest version. A localization example is shown here:

As a utility, I can send messages to customers.	...customers who want their messages:
	...in Spanish
	...in Arabic, and so on.

6. Data Entry Methods

Sometimes complexity is in the user interface rather than the functionality itself. In that case, split the story to build it with the simplest possible UI, and then build the richer UI later.

As a user, I can view my energy consumption in various graphs.	...using bar charts that compare weekly consumption.
	...in a comparison chart, so I can compare my usage to those who have the same or similar household demographics.

7. Defer System Qualities

Sometimes, the initial implementation isn't all that hard, and the major part of the effort is in making it fast or reliable or more precise or more scalable. However, the team can learn a lot from the base implementation, and it should have some value to a user, who wouldn't otherwise be able to do it all. In this case, break the story into successive "ilities."

As a user, I want to see real-time consumption from my meter.	...interpolate data from the last known reading.
	...display real-time data from the meter.

8. Operations (Example: Create Read Update Delete (CRUD))

Words like *manage* or *control* are a giveaway that the story covers multiple operations, which can offer a natural way to split the story.

As a user, I can manage my account.	...I can sign up for an account.
	...I can edit my account settings.
	...I can cancel my account.
	...I can add more devices to my account.

9. Use-Case Scenarios

If use cases have been developed to represent complex user-to-system or system-to-system interaction, then the story can often be split according to the individual scenarios of the use case.[*]

I want to enroll in the energy savings program through a retail distributor.	Use case/story #1 (happy path): Notify utility that consumer has equipment.
	Use case/story #2: Utility provisions equipment and data and notifies consumer.
	Use case/story #3 (alternate scenario): Handle data validation errors.

10. Break Out a Spike

In some cases, a story may be too large or overly complex, or perhaps the implementation is poorly understood. In that case, build a technical or functional spike to figure it out; then split the stories based on that result. (See the "Spikes" section.)

---

[*]The application of use cases in agile development is the entire topic of Chapter 19.

When splitting stories, the team should use an appropriate combination of the previous techniques to consider means of decomposition or multiple patterns in combination. With this skill, the team will be able to move forward at a more rapid pace, splitting user stories at release- and iteration-planning boundaries into bite-size chunks for implementation.

SPIKES

Spikes, another invention of XP, are a special type of story used to drive out risk and uncertainty in a user story or other project facet. Spikes may be used for a number of reasons.

- Spikes may be used for basic research to familiarize the team with a new technology or domain.
- The story may be too big to be estimated appropriately, and the team may use a spike to analyze the implied behavior so they can split the story into estimable pieces.
- The story may contain significant technical risk, and the team may have to do some research or prototyping to gain confidence in a technological approach that will allow them to commit the user story to some future timebox.
- The story may contain significant functional risk, in that although the intent of the story may be understood, it's not clear how the system needs to interact with the user to achieve the benefit implied.

Technical Spikes and Functional Spikes

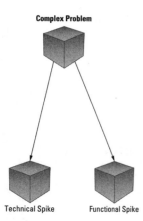

Complex Problem

Technical Spike   Functional Spike

Technical spikes are used to research various technical approaches in the solution domain. For example, a technical spike may be used to determine a build-versus-buy decision, to evaluate potential performance or load impact of a new user story, to evaluate specific implementation technologies that can be applied to a solution, or for any reason when the team needs to develop a more confident understanding of a desired approach before committing new functionality to a timebox.

Functional spikes are used whenever there is significant uncertainty as to how a user might interact with the system. Functional spikes are often best evaluated through some level of prototyping, whether it be user interface mock-ups, wireframes, page flows, or whatever techniques are best suited to get feedback from the customer or stakeholders. Some user stories may require both types of spikes. Here's an example:

As a consumer, I want to see my daily energy use in a histogram so that I can quickly understand my past, current, and projected energy consumption.

In this case, a team might create two spikes:

Technical spike: Research how long it takes to update a customer display to current usage, determining communication requirements, bandwidth, and whether to push or pull the data.

Functional spike: Prototype a histogram in the web portal and get some user feedback on presentation size, style, and charting attributes.

Guidelines for Spikes

Since spikes do not directly deliver user value, they should be used sparingly and with caution. The following are some guidelines for applying user spikes.

Estimable, Demonstrable, and Acceptable

Like other stories, spikes are put in the backlog, estimated, and sized to fit in an iteration. Spike results are different from a story, because they generally produce information, rather than working code. A spike may result in a decision, prototype, storyboard, proof of concept, or some other partial solution to help drive the final results. In any case, the spike should develop just the information sufficient to resolve the uncertainty in being able to identify and size the stories hidden beneath the spike.

The output of a spike is demonstrable, both to the team and to any other stakeholders. This brings visibility to the research and architectural efforts and also helps build collective ownership and shared responsibility for the key decisions that are being taken.

And, like any other story, spikes are accepted by the product owner when the acceptance criteria for the spike have been fulfilled.

The Exception, Not the Rule

Every user story has uncertainty and risk—this is the nature of agile development. The team discovers the right solution through discussion, collaboration, experimentation, and negotiation. Thus, in one sense, every user story contains spike-level activities to flush out the technical and functional risk. The goal of an agile team is to learn how to embrace and effectively address this uncertainty in each iteration. A spike story, on the other hand, should be reserved for the more critical and larger unknowns.

When considering a spike for future work, first consider ways to split the story through the strategies discussed earlier. Use a spike as a last option.

Implement the Spike in a Separate Iteration from the Resulting Stories

Since a spike represents uncertainty in one or more potential stories, planning for both the spike and the resultant stories in the same iteration is risky and should generally be avoided. However, if the spike is small and straightforward and a quick solution is likely to be found, there is nothing wrong with completing the stories in the same iteration. Just be careful.

STORY MODELING WITH INDEX CARDS

Writing and modeling user stories using physical index cards provides a powerful visual and kinesthetic means for engaging the entire team in backlog development. This interactive approach has a number of advantages.

- The physical size of index cards forces a text length limit, requiring the writer to articulate their ideas in just a sentence or two. This helps keep user stories small and focused, which is a key attribute. Also, the tangible and physical nature of the cards gives teams the ability to visually and spatially arrange them in various configurations to help define the backlog.
- Cards may be arranged by feature (or epic) and may be written on the same colored cards as the feature for visual differentiation.
- Cards can also be arranged by size to help developers "see" the size relationships between different stories.
- Cards can be arranged by time or iteration to help evaluate dependencies, understand logical sequencing, see the impact on team velocity, and better align and communicate differing stakeholder priorities.
- The more cards you have, the more work you see, so scoping is a more natural process.

Any team member can write a story card, and the physical act of moving these small, tangible "value objects" around the table creates an interactive learning setting where participants "see and touch" the value they are about to create for their stakeholders.

Experience has shown that teams with a shared vision are more committed to implementing that vision. Modeling value delivery with physical story cards provides a natural engagement model for all team members and stakeholders—one that results in a shared, tangible vision for all to see and experience.

SUMMARY

In this chapter, we provided an overview of the derivation and application of user stories as the primary requirements proxy used by agile teams. Along with background and history, we described the alliteration *card, conversation, and confirmation,* which defines the key elements of a user story. We provided some recommendations for developing good user stories in accordance with the INVEST model and specifically described how *small* stories increase throughput and quality. We also described a set of patterns for splitting large stories into smaller stories so that each resultant story can independently deliver value in an iteration. We also provided guidelines for creating spikes as story-like backlog items for understanding and managing development risk. In conclusion, we suggested that teams apply visual modeling using physical index cards for developing user stories and create a shared vision for implementing user value using this uniquely agile requirements construct.

In the next chapter, we'll strive for a deeper understanding of the users and user personas for whom these user stories are intended.

Chapter 7

STAKEHOLDERS, USER PERSONAS, AND USER EXPERIENCES

WITH PETE BEHRENS

Simple things should be simple, complex things should be possible.
—Ward Cunningham, XP contributor and inventor of the wiki

In the previous chapter, we introduced the user story as the primary artifact for identifying system behaviors that deliver value to the customer. We implied that engaging a user in a dialogue about how they use the system, and what benefit they derive, is a straightforward process. And it certainly can be if your solution is already in use and you have access to those users.

But what if you are building a new application or service? Who are the users then? And what about those key stakeholders who use the results of a system but don't actually use the system themselves? How do we know who they are, and how do we design for them? And if we design a system that works for our direct and indirect users, are there still other stakeholders whose needs must be met?

And what about the project sponsors? If we develop a system that meets the needs of those mentioned, are we on solid footing? What about these other stakeholders who have a material interest in how the system is developed, what it costs, and how and when it is deployed?

STAKEHOLDERS

Although it is clear that users are indeed key project stakeholders and we must, in large part, design for them, the issues are much deeper than that. To help assure success, we will have to take a much broader look at who all the stakeholders of our proposed system are. In so doing, we find it helpful to think about two different classes of stakeholders: *system stakeholders* and *project stakeholders*.

System Stakeholders

If the system is to be successful, the development teams must be certain to address the needs of the direct users, as well as the needs of the indirect users and other stakeholders who will be affected by the system. These are the *system stakeholders:*

> *A system stakeholder is anyone who*
> *—directly uses the system*
> *—works with the results of those who use the system*
> *—will be impacted by the deployment and operation of a system*

These stakeholders include users and operators, as well as users of reports, data, signals, and other outputs of the system; managers, purchasers, and administrators for those users; support and help-desk staff; developers working on other systems that integrate or interact with the system; installation and maintenance professionals; and more.

These system stakeholders will be the primary drivers for the requirements of the system, and, as such, they will be the main subjects of our requirements discovery activities, as we'll describe in Chapter 12.

Project Stakeholders

In addition to the system stakeholders, we'll also need to identify everyone who may have substantial, vested interest in the *project that is developing the system*. These include the project sponsors, project management, portfolio management, executives, financial governance staff, and so on.

> *A project stakeholder is anyone who*
> *—has a vested interest in the budget and schedule*
> *—has a vested interest in understanding how the product/system/solution is developed*
> *—will be involved in marketing, selling, installing, or maintaining the system*

From this definition, you can see that direct and indirect users aren't the only stakeholders of a project. Indeed, there is an even wider range of people potentially affected by a new system. In order to succeed, the team must first understand, and then synthesize, their requirements into one cohesive vision.

Voice of the Stakeholder: Product Owner

Each project stakeholder will have their own vision, requirements, and priorities. As the primary representative to all those stakeholders, this provides a particular challenge to product owners—because all those requirements must be *aligned* and expectations must be *managed* toward a single solution.

The product owner's primary job is to merge these diverse stakeholder voices into a single prioritized backlog for the team. They can do this by *facilitating* or *leading*, or some appropriate mix of each.

- *Facilitating:* Oftentimes, the product owner is the facilitator of a process intended to converge diverse opinions into a single product vision. There are often no clear-cut, black-and-white answers as to which potential solution is more valued or important than the other; each has pros and cons. The product owner works to help each stakeholder find common ground so they can accept a combined—and from each individual perspective, a potentially compromised—solution.
- *Leading:* Other times, the product owner makes decisions for stakeholders based on their personal, expert knowledge or experience in the industry. These decisions may not be advocated by any particular stakeholder but rather are driven from a move in markets, a change in competition, or other trends that the product owner feels are material to the solution requirements.

Levels of Stakeholder Involvement

Like the earlier example, most projects have a fairly diverse set of stakeholders, all of whose needs must be met at some level. Understanding the degree of their involvement is one key to building consensus, while still making fast, agile, forward progress. For example, the following list applies to some stakeholders.

- *They should be kept informed:* Some stakeholders simply need to know the status of the project and be informed of decisions that impact it. They may or may not have input on those decisions but may influence those that do.
- *They should be consulted:* Some stakeholders, such as subject-matter experts, marketing analysts, architects, and user-interface designers, have a specific area of expertise that aids in the definition or building of the product. They should be involved in decisions within their area of expertise.
- *They are partners in development:* Some stakeholders are partners in the process. These may include other product or business owners, other development teams, business or requirements analysts, and providers of solutions that the system interacts with.
- *They are in control of outcomes:* Some stakeholders make final decisions for the solution. These may include executives, release managers, business owners, and key customers who will be using the solution.

Building Stakeholder Trust

Projects run a lot smoother when the stakeholders trust the product owners and the teams and when that trust is reciprocated. The easiest way to build trust is to communicate all aspects of the project, clearly and without prejudice, to all stakeholders. Visibility and transparency are key. When different stakeholders understand the competing demands on the systems and the development resources, they can better judge *what is most important to them* and where they are able to compromise to allow some other stakeholder to get *what is most important to them* as well.

In addition, the product owner should describe the rationale behind any key decisions, should explain any weightings or factors used to arrive at a decision, and should conduct all activities in an open and honest manner. No hidden agendas—just the current facts of the market, system, and development context.

Stakeholder Interactions

To be successful, all project stakeholders must actively work with the team to achieve the team's goals. This creates a number of expectations and implications.

- *Timely decisions are needed:* Stakeholders must to be prepared to share business knowledge with the team and to make both pertinent and timely decisions regarding project scope and requirement priorities.
- *Active participation is needed:* Stakeholders must be included in initial solution-modeling efforts to achieve alignment across their diverse needs and gain their buy-in.
- *Teams must take an enterprise view:* Teams may also need to work with other teams to integrate their system with other systems. Integration will go much smoother with the active participation of these co-developers.
- *Production and support staff should be involved from the start:* Operations and support organizations must invest the resources required to understand the system and its new technologies. Teams may even choose to include one or two operations engineers on the development team or to invest project resources to train operations staff as required.
- *Plan for system maintenance:* If the intention is to eventually have software maintenance done by another team, it will be useful to engage them in the development process. The development team must allow time to work with these people so they can take eventual ownership.

IDENTIFYING STAKEHOLDERS

Identifying all the stakeholders and understanding their respective needs is clearly one key to success.

Identifying Project Stakeholders

One of the first steps is to make sure we understand the *internal* project stakeholders. Many times, these are obvious to the teams, but the following questions can be used to help identify them.

- Who needs to be consulted on the scope of this project?
- Who has input to the budget and schedule?
- Who ultimately manages the business relationship between the teams and the customer?
- Who will determine how and when the system is released to customers?
- Who can support or harm this project politically?
- What partners are dependent on our system?
- Who cares about the process we use to develop the system?

Once they have been identified, it can be helpful to understand their expectations for the system as well as for the project being used to develop the system. Table 7–1 provides some guidelines for considering the needs of the various project stakeholders.

Table 7–1   Guidelines for Understanding Project Stakeholder Needs

Project Stakeholder	Product Characteristics	Project Characteristics
Partner	Expects the product interfaces will remain the same or as agreed to	Wants input in the prioritization of features
	Expects a stable product integration	Expects to be notified with changes in the project schedule or prioritization changes that impact their product
	Expects backward compatibility	
Sales/marketing	Expects new features to be available as promised	Wants input in the prioritization of features
	Wants to have many new checks to select on request for proposal (RFP) responses	Expects to be notified when prioritization changes, especially when it impacts their customers
	Wants an understanding of the roadmap	
	Wants input into when and how the system will be released	Wants to know whether there any delays in the project schedule
	Wants to be able to intelligently articulate product benefits	
Operations	Expects detailed documentation about how to install the product and dependencies on the product	Wants to be informed about the project status
	Has clear expectations for system reliability and performance	Wants to be more involved toward the end of the project as details of the installation and dependencies are known

Continues

Table 7–1 Guidelines for Understanding Project Stakeholder Needs (Continued)

Project Stakeholder	Product Characteristics	Project Characteristics
Support	Expects a high-quality product that can be easily supported Wants the error management system to help the customer resolve their own problem Wants to be able to resolve issues quickly when there is a problem	Wants to be informed about project status, especially when it relates to support Expects to have input in prioritization of support issues
Sponsor	Wants to understand the team has effective processes for understanding requirements	Wants to be continually apprised of schedule, budget, and status Wants to know development is in accordance with governance
Development management	Wants to know system will be fit for intended purpose	Expects system to be developed in accordance with budget and schedule guidelines Wants to know resources stay in line with strategic investment themes
Security	Expects the system to be secure through following security coding and testing practices Expects all relevant security standards to be adhered to	Consulted about security issues Reviews designs for security flaws Expects to have input in security prioritization

Identifying System Stakeholders

Although understanding the set of project stakeholders is important, most of the requirements for the system will be driven by the people who actually use the system in their environment. The following questions can help the team understand who all these system stakeholders are.

- Who will be directly using the system?
- Who will be using the results of those who use the system?
- Who will be responsible for supporting the system?
- What other systems will our system interact with?
- What interfaces must it provide?
- Who can provide guidance on the functionality and system qualities (usability, reliability, performance, and supportability) for the system?

Classifying System Stakeholders

It can also be helpful to categorize system stakeholders in one of three categories:

- *First degree:* Direct users of the system
- *Second degree:* People who work with the results of those who work with the system
- *Third degree:* People who install, deploy, or support the system

This categorization gives the product owner and team a way to reason about who uses the system the most, and for what purpose, as well as what other stakeholder needs must be accommodated in the solution.

For example, we can see in Figure 7–1 that the Tendril system has a broad group of stakeholders and users, each of whose needs must be considered.

Understanding System Stakeholder Needs

Once the stakeholders have been identified and classified, we need to establish the high-level *expectations* for the system and to start to identify some of the *activities* they will be doing with the system. By way of illustration, Table 7–2 demonstrates a few such considerations from our case study.

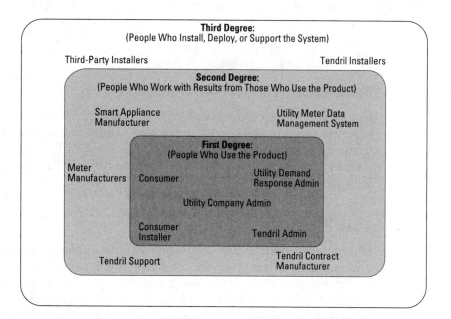

Figure 7–1   Tendril system stakeholders

Table 7–2   Case Study System Stakeholder Needs

Stakeholder Role	System Characteristics (What Do They Expect from the System?)	System Activities (What Do They Need to Do with the System?)
Consumer (user)	I want to have daily visibility into my energy consumption so I can lower the cost of my electric bill and help save the planet.	View daily/hourly consumption. Respond to demand response events. View my consumption history.
Utility	I want to notify customers of pending demand response events so I can free up load to the grid.	Sort customers by grid demographics. Communicate with customers via their in-home devices.
Appliance Manufacturer	I want to develop appliances that are smart energy–compliant so that I can integrate with open smart grid applications that utilities will use.	Integrate with smart energy modules. Provide consumer with easy-to-use UI. Respond to demand response events by shedding load (reducing consumption).
Utility meter vendor	I want to provide consumers with smart meters that will interact with smart devices in the home so they can have real-time visibility into their energy consumption.	Communicate price changes to the meter and home devices through the backhaul. Update firmware via backhaul. Provide reporting on consumer usage.
Electric vehicle manufacturer	I want to provide the consumer with convenient charging stations so that I can sell more electric vehicles.	Track consumer usage information. Provide the utility and the consumer with billing information.

Stakeholder/Product Owner Team?

Given the diversity of inputs and the need to gain continuous agreement on the priorities, the product owner may even want to build a small team (product owner team or product council) to help guide the solution. We'll describe this further in Chapter 12, Requirements Discovery Toolkit, and Chapter 22, Moving to Agile Portfolio Management.

USER PERSONAS

Designing systems that make *simple things simple and complex things possible* is an important skill for any teams whose systems have significant interaction with users. In addition to thinking of the user generically ("As a user, I can…"), user *personas* provide a means of further refining the approach to the user to make sure that the needs of different types of users are met.

Primary and Secondary User Personas

In Alan Cooper's human factors/computer interface design book, *The Inmates are Running the Asylum* [1999], he describes two primary types of personas to consider.

- *Primary personas* represent users with specific needs that can be satisfied only with a user interface designed specifically for them.
- *Secondary personas* are people who also use the system but can use an interface that was designed for a primary persona.

Identifying personas helps development teams create user experiences that are optimum for a certain class of user. User stories provide clues as to where we might find them.

Finding Personas with User Story Role Modeling

In the user voice form of expression that we described in the previous chapter ("As a <role>, I can <activity> so that <benefit>."), the <role> element identifies the role the user is playing as they interact with the system. In some systems, there is only one role (for example, a laser pointer likely has just one generic user, the person doing the pointing), and the role element of this form doesn't add much value.

In other systems, many user roles can interact with a system, or a subsystem of a larger system. Developing a set of user stories helps us identify roles, which in turn helps identify personas. For example, our case study system has a plethora of user roles, as illustrated in Figure 7–2.

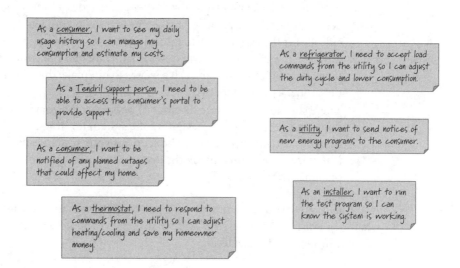

Figure 7–2   Examples of user stories and roles for the case study

Analyzing the roles and the stories give us clues as to where the personas might lie.

For example, *consumer* and *utility* use the system for totally different types of activities, so these are *primary* personas. We'll have to design and implement different user interfaces for each of these.

However, if *Tendril support person* and *installer* can use the same portal presentation as the *consumer*, then although we need to be aware of their needs, we should focus the design for ease of use by the consumer, our primary persona. In that case, we consider the needs of the installer and Tendril support person as secondary. They can use the system we design for the consumer.

Personas simply provide a finer discrimination of users and their needs, and we needn't go overboard in trying to understand them. Cooper provides a number of additional guidelines for thinking about personas.

- Don't "make up" personas out of thin air. Rather, discover them as a byproduct of your requirements discovery and user story writing process.
- Develop a specific, individual persona—an actual person who you can interview, interact with, and come to understand. Understand their abilities, background, environment, and usage of the system.
- Identify the persona's goals so that you can see what your system needs to do and not do.
- Design your system to make it easy for *that one person* to use your system. If you've defined your primary personas well, that individual will be a specific "representative of a class." However, they will be more tangible, and their needs more understandable, than attempting to design for the general case.
- Secondary personas are just that, secondary. You do not have to design specifically for them. They will bend and stretch to use the system. Even then, however, the goal should be to develop software *that bends and stretches to them*. But you must do it in such a way as to not make the system harder for the primary persona to use.
- There shouldn't be a large number of personas; the goal is to narrow down the people you are designing the system for. If you identify more than three primary personas, the scope of your system is likely too large. If that is the case, then break the system it into subsystems, and identify personas from there.

And finally, after you've identified each persona, attempt to first understand both what *they expect from the system* and what *they need to do with the system*, as the example in Table 7–3 indicates.

Table 7–3 User and Device Personas from the Case Study

Primary Persona	Category	Expect from the System	Do with the System
Consumer	Primary persona (user)	Interact and establish energy management.	Control and shed load. Be informed of pending events.
Tendril support person	Secondary persona (user)	Run maintenance routines. Query system status.	Support consumers via portal.
Installer	Secondary persona (user)	Installation instructions and utilities.	Install and test devices. Run system diagnostics.
Tendril-compatible energy device	Primary persona	Standard protocols and commands.	Send and receive commands.
Refrigerator	Secondary persona (device)	Relevant protocols and commands.	Implement energy management policies.
Thermostat	Secondary persona (device)	Relevant protocols and commands.	Report on conditions. Allow user control.
Utility	Primary persona (other system)	Manage energy distribution via consumer interaction.	Send and receive messages.

With these primary and user personas identified and some expectations and actions identified, the team is ready to proceed with the story writing and any additional requirements discovery work. That will be the subject of Chapter 12, where we introduce a requirements discovery toolkit.

AGILE AND USER EXPERIENCE DEVELOPMENT

A common problem in agile is how to incorporate the visual design of the product into the rapid iteration structure. When teams attempt to resolve complex user interactions while trying to code and test that system at the same time, they can often end up "churning" through many iterations. Teams feel that this creates waste—thrashing through many design alternatives but doing so in code. Sure, it's OK to iterate and refactor, but why do it more than might otherwise be necessary?

The User Experience Problem

User experience (UX) design is further complicated when user experience testing is required. The scheduling and running of multiple experience tests typically cannot occur within an iteration that is also attempting to complete the story. The teams should assume that all usability tests will have an impact on design and implementation; otherwise, there's really no reason to do them. However, the result of this process is delayed feedback loops that complicate productivity and introduce delays in delivering the value.

Of course, this is not just a user interface or prototyping problem. This is a meta-problem with the design and architecture in agile—a result of the elimination of big up-front design (BUFD). Fortunately, teams have found a number of practices practical for addressing these design elements. The common key is to leverage the iterations to drive out uncertainty and risk through fast feedback.

Low-Fidelity Options for User Interface Development

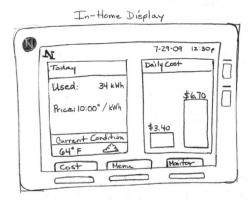

Feedback does not have to come only from writing code. Teams must also consider simpler alternatives that can generate feedback such as low-fidelity paper prototypes, simple HTML or PowerPoint prototypes, wireframes, mock objects, or coded skeletons and stubs.

Often the easiest solution is the simplest—sketch ideas on paper, and work with your users and stakeholders to determine how it should look. This can be done by working just-in-time ahead of the iteration and then by using the mock-ups as reference for story acceptance criteria in the implementation iteration. In Chapter 12, Requirements Discovery Toolkit, we'll explore this topic further.

User Experience Story Spikes

As we discussed in the previous chapter, user experience story spikes can be used to develop alternative user interfaces and test them through actual or representative users. These stories are put in the backlog, sized, developed, and tested as any other story. The only difference is that they may not end with working software. The act of scheduling them in the iteration has the effect of deferring the code development until after the tests are complete. This can improve efficiency immensely.

▶ **NOTE**   These story spikes represent risks in your backlog because they are hiding other implementation stories that may increase the scope of the plan. Consider prioritizing them ahead of other less risky items to drive out risk early in the release plan.

Centralized User Experience Development

Although it might appear attractive from the perspective of empowerment and velocity of the agile team, fully distributing UX development to the team can actually be quite problematic. Velocity may seem high at first, because the teams are able to move quickly through the initial iterations to value delivery. Later, however, problems start to occur as users use different parts of the system for similar purposes but may be presented with different style, presentation, and interaction selection paradigms. The net result is a system that has disconcertingly different implementations of like functions. User confusion and dissatisfaction are the likely results.

Repairing this work is problematic too, because many teams will then have to refactor their code to some new, common standard. Adopting common style, presentation, and user action standards can help immensely, but the devil is in the details, and that alone may still not create a comprehensive and holistic solution. This is not a very productive process.

To address this, some organizations create a central user interface design team that iterates somewhat independently from the development teams. They run a common cadence and iteration model, but their backlog will contain user experience story spikes, user experience testing, prototyping, and implementation activities that are used to define a common user experience. They typically work one or two iterations ahead to discover upcoming functionality and define how it should be implemented.

The central team implements these designs across many features and system components throughout the course of the release. While the central team has interdependencies with the feature and component teams, centralizing the activity has the advantage of increasing core competence in the UX domain and prevents "wagging" the teams as designs inevitably change. Figure 7–3 illustrates this model.

Distributed, Governed User Experience Development Model

Of course, it's not unlikely that the central team becomes a bottleneck for the development teams, and worse, the problem gets larger at scale, because there are a larger number of dependencies that must be addressed. To mitigate this problem, we've seen a hybrid model effectively applied for larger systems.

In the "distributed but governed" model, there is a small, centralized UX design authority who provides the basic design standards and preliminary mock-ups for each UI, but the teams have team-based UX implementation experts for the implementation. In this case, the UX experts are distributed among the teams, but the centralized authority provides HTML designs, CSS style sheets, brand control, mock-ups, usability guidelines, and other artifacts that provide conceptual integrity of the UX across the entire solution. The central team also typically attends iteration and PSI/release demos to see how the overall system design is progressing. Figure 7–4 illustrates this model.

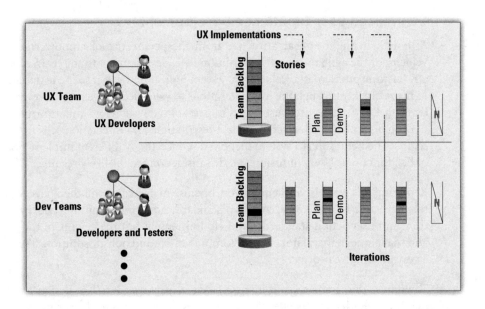

Figure 7–3   Centralized UX development

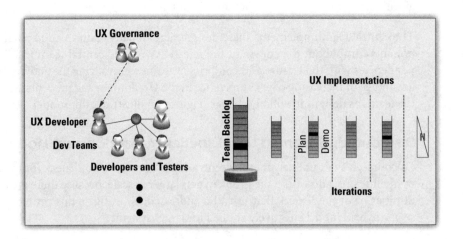

Figure 7–4   Distributed, governed UX development

This doesn't prevent refactoring, because there are still likely UX testing projects occurring on a different timeline that can alter results, but it is a fairly efficient process, and we have seen some good and consistent designs emerge in this model.

SUMMARY

In this chapter, we described how there is far more to designing a system than simply understanding user needs. We introduced *project* and *system stakeholders* and provided guidance as to how to find them, classify them, and start to get an understanding of their expectations and specific needs. Of course, we already identified users as one such important stakeholder, but in this chapter we described how to refine that further by developing *primary* and *secondary user personas*. Designing a system to these personas will help produce a system that is inherently easier and more pleasant to use.

We've concluded with a discussion of the challenge of creating effective user experience designs in rapid, iterative development. This is indeed a nontrivial problem that agile teams have evolved various means of addressing. We've provided a couple of suggestions as to how to approach this tricky problem as well.

In the next chapters, we'll move on to other important aspects of agile team requirements practices, starting with the next chapter, Estimating and Velocity.

Chapter 8

AGILE ESTIMATING AND VELOCITY

Though this be madness, yet there is method in't.

—*Hamlet*, Act 2, scene 2, Shakespeare

INTRODUCTION

One of the misperceptions about agile development is that it is a Dilbert-esque practice of software teams coding away without requirements, little or no planning, no intra-team coordination, and no documentation. Indeed, the myths of agile often prevent agile to be applied in circumstances where the benefits would otherwise be substantial. As we hope to illustrate throughout this book, nothing could be further from the truth because agile is the most disciplined and quality-driven set of development practices the industry has invented to date. But the myths remain.

When it comes to *estimating* and *scheduling* work, for example, the myth is propagated by misunderstandings of the apparent silliness (or the perceived unprofessional and unscientific nature) of the agile estimating process. Agile teams compound this because they (often rightly) refuse to make any long-term commitments about deliverables. Worse, they talk about their team's abilities in funny words such as *velocity, velocipacity, story points, modified Fibonacci series estimating,* and our all-time personal favorite *velocity in gummy bears per sprint.*

In the realm of agile mythology, agile *estimating* and its companion, *team velocity,* stand out as two of the oddest brethren. These also baffle outsiders, creating an unnecessary barrier between the language of the team and the language of the managers, executives, and other stakeholders who are dependent on the team's output. This is *not* helpful.

There's a Method to This Madness

Underneath that communication gap, however, is a proven estimating heuristic. Indeed, solid estimating skills are critical to an agile team's productivity and reliability.

This problem arose because the traditional project estimating means (use a work breakdown structure to identify every last task, estimate each task, add the tasks up, build a Gantt chart, and predict the cost and schedule) never actually worked for software projects. So, in a matter of self-defense, the teams invented something that does work, *at least for them*. By first understanding it and then extending it, we can also make it work for the enterprise.

In this chapter, we'll explore these two topics, *estimating* and *velocity*, to come to an understanding of just how useful and practical the method is. With such an understanding, we can put the enterprise on a path to higher reliability and predictability than we have ever had before.

The Goal Is the Same: More Reliable Estimates

Everyone wants more reliable estimates. Otherwise, there is no way to predict how much value a team can deliver in a time period. Plus, if an agile team can reliably predict what it can do in a short timebox, then we can more reliably predict what a few teams working together can deliver in the next month or two. Although that may seem like a modest goal, in fact it represents two breakthroughs that should set executive offices buzzing:

#1: Know where you are now: The agile project knows exactly where it is at every point in time because it is based on a subjective evaluation of working code (*really* working, as in coded, integrated, tested, evaluated, and running). Even without estimating, that is a breakthrough of significant proportions. A while back, Israel Gat commented the following:[1]

> I've spent over 30 years in the software development industry in increasingly high levels of management, and up until this (first agile) project and this very day (a sprint review), I have never ever really known exactly where my teams actually are on any significant project.

But the goodness doesn't end there, because once a team has mastered agile estimating, we can leverage another breakthrough:

#2: More accurately predict where you will be next: With effective agile estimating, teams have a fairly reliable predictor of what will be working in the next few weeks. Per the previous, they know what is working now, and they can predict what they will deliver next based on the *velocity* they have achieved in prior iterations.

---

1. Formerly of IBM Tivoli and BMC Software, now a Cutter Consortium Agile Enterprise consultant

Moreover, if we could fast-forward mentally through Part III of this book (or six months or so of agile deployment), an executive might be able to understand (exactly) where a larger program is, what software (exactly) is working today, and what software (exactly) is not, even in a program that affects dozens of teams. And, perhaps, a manager can even reliably predict where the program will be in a few weeks—perhaps even in 90 days and maybe more. But that's a subject for later chapters.

WHY ESTIMATE? THE BUSINESS VALUE OF ESTIMATING

For now, we'll get back to the first principles of agile estimating. As compared to coding and testing at least, estimating is overhead, so first we must understand why we bother to do it at all. From a lean perspective, some might even look at estimating as a form of waste. Indeed, in some kanban implementations, teams don't bother much at all with estimating. However, estimating provides substantial value added for several reasons.

- *Determining cost:* Effort is our proxy for cost. If we can't estimate effort, we can't estimate cost. If we have no way to estimate cost, then we have no reasonable basis for going about our business at all.
- *Establishing prioritization:* In Chapter 13, we'll introduce the cost of delay (CoD) as the primary prioritization factor for implementing features. Development effort predicts time, which is in turn a primary factor in cost of delay.
- *Scheduling and commitment:* It is unreasonable to ask a team to commit to delivering an unknown thing in a certain time frame, especially longer term. However, gaining commitment to near-term deliverables is important because it materially affects the planning and business objectives of our customers. It also impacts our internal customers—those who document, train, deploy, and support the system.

In other words, *estimating is the key to unlocking the ability to commit*. The ability to commit to near-term deliverables is the key to building a reliable, agile enterprise. So, there are good business reasons why we need to take a harder look at this funny agile estimating thing.

To do so, we'll take a more experiential approach in this chapter, because that is the best way to understand what the *method in't actually is*.

ESTIMATING SCOPE WITH STORY POINTS

We'll start with understanding how teams estimate the work they do in an iteration. Fortunately, we have small, independent "objects" to estimate—the user story—and we know they deliver value because we designed them that way. If a team can estimate stories, then they can estimate the things of value they can deliver to a customer and about when they can deliver it.

There are a number of approaches to agile estimating, some of which we'll describe later in this chapter, but we'll start our discussion with the most common method, the one recommended by most agile trainers. This is the art of *relative estimating with story points.*

A *story point* is an integer number that represents an aggregation of a number of aspects, each of which contributes to the potential "bigness" of a story.

- *Knowledge:* Do we understand what the story does?
- *Complexity:* How hard is it to implement?
- *Volume:* How much of it is there? How long is it likely to take?
- *Uncertainty:* What isn't known, and how might that affect our estimate?

A story point estimate combines all these facets into one number, which estimates the size of a story compared to other stories of a similar type. Story points are unitless but numerically relevant (that is, a two-point story should expect to take twice as long as a one-point story).

▶ **NOTE:** This method is largely derived from Mike Cohn's *Agile Estimating and Planning* [2006], and we recommend that book as the best source for readers who want to know about this topic. Also, because of the popularity of the text and Mike's involvement with the Scrum community, much of his work has made its way into various Scrum courses. This has been beneficial because it provides a fairly common estimating baseline for many agile teams.

UNDERSTANDING STORY POINTS: AN EXERCISE

In the following sections, we'll describe this method from the perspective of a team being newly trained, in the hope that their training experience will help us understand this abstract concept in more concrete terms.

Exercise Part 1: Relative Estimating

During training, many Scrum/agile trainers run a simple exercise with their teams to get them thinking about the relative "bigness of things." The exercise itself, along with the results from one team, appears in Figure 8–1.

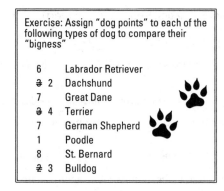

Figure 8–1   A simple relative estimating exercise, with results from one agile team

In this deceptively simple exercise, teams immediately struggle with ambiguity.

- What does the instructor mean by bigness? Height, weight, mass, muscle, bite, attitude?
- What the heck kind of poodle is it? Standard poodle? Toy poodle? "Hey, it makes a big difference!"
- What scale should we use?

The instructor can either remain silent through this process, illustrating to the team that there will *always be ambiguity* in the estimating process, or act as the product owner and answer any questions, illustrating that *when in doubt, ask the product owner for clarification*. Either way, it's a fun exercise, and it takes only a few minutes.

Exercise Part 2: Estimating Real Work with Planning Poker

With this somewhat trivial, *relative estimating experience* in hand, the teams might then be given a more meaningful "class backlog" to estimate, like the one I have used in Table 8–1.

Table 8–1   Sample Class Estimating Backlog

Example Sprint Backlog
1. Estimate the pages in the student workbook.
2. Accurately count the pages in the workbook.
3. Calculate the square root of 54289 without a computer or calculator.
4. Add the following ten numbers with a calculator and be certain the answer is correct: 1, 2, 3, 5, 8, 13, 21, 34, 55, 89.

Continues

Table 8–1   Sample Class Estimating Backlog (Continued)

Example Sprint Backlog
5.   Add the following ten numbers without a calculator and be certain the answer is correct: 1, 2, 3, 5, 8, 13, 20, 50, 100.
6.   Introduce yourself to every person in your team, and write down their children's names.
7.   Write a program, without Excel, that accepts 10 numbers from a user and displays the total as each number is entered.
8.   Estimate the cubic volume of the room to within approximately 30%.
9.   Estimate the cubic volume of the room to within approximately 5%.
10.   Estimate the snowfall in Oulu this winter in centimeters, inches, meters, and feet.
11.   Estimate the snowfall in Oulu this winter in centimeters.
12.   Estimate the number of words in the workbook.
13.   Estimate the cubic meters of snowfall in Oulu this winter.
14.   Obtain an accurate count of the number of words in the workbook.

The teams may then be introduced to the rules of an agile method called *planning poker*,[2] with a set of rules, as shown in Table 8–2.

Table 8–2   Rules for Planning Poker

Rules for Planning Poker
Participants include all agile team members.
The product owner participates but does not estimate (the product owner is briefed on role and content prior to exercise).
Each estimator is given a deck of cards with 0, 1, 2, 3, 5, 8, 13, 20, 40, and 100 as their "value." (Note: some instructors coach an optional calibrations step: calibrate *size*, such as pick one story that is agreed to be small and agree that the story would be say of size 2 and perhaps pick one more, such as a larger one that would be of size 8.)
For each story, the product owner reads the description.
Questions are asked and answered.
Each estimator privately selects a card representing his or her estimate.
All cards are simultaneously turned over so that all participants can see each estimate.
High and low estimators explain their estimates.
After discussion, each estimator reestimates, and the cards are turned over for a second time.
The estimates will likely converge. If not, the process for that story is repeated until it does.
Repeat until all stories are estimated.

---

2. Seems like "Estimating Poker" would be a better name. As we'll see in later chapters, planning is another kind of poker altogether!

Some amount of preliminary design discussion is appropriate. However, spending too much time on design discussions is often wasted effort.

The teams will be given a short timebox (maybe 30 minutes) and are instructed to estimate all the items on the list within the timebox.

Although apparently simple on the surface, there are a number of subtle aspects built into this estimating technique.

- The estimate comes from the *team as a whole*. The product owner explains the stories to the team, which commits to a *group* estimate. This prevents the product owner from biasing the estimates and also provides the best estimate possible, based on the *collective* judgment of the team.

  Since the team includes developers and testers, the estimate is a mix of efforts from these two perspectives. Teams quickly discover that some things are fairly easy to code but really hard to test, and the reverse can also be true.

- The range of numbers (Cohn's modified Fibonacci series, that is, 0, 1, 3, 5, 8, 13, 20, 40, 100) is cleverly designed. The lower range (0, 1, 2, 3, 5, 8) is designed to help teams more precisely estimate small things they understand well. However, the gaps in the sequence become larger as the size of the estimate increases, reflecting greater uncertainty.

- The expanded range (20, 40, 100) at the end of the series indicates that even larger items have even greater uncertainty. If the estimates reach this range, the story is too big for an iteration anyway and probably represents a feature or epic. If the item is that big, it represents substantial risk and needs to be split.

- Zero gives the teams a way to ignore small stories that can be implemented in just a few hours. Although they represent important things, they aren't material to the team's scoping efforts unless there are a lot of them.

- A consensus must be achieved before a final estimate is reached. By discussing only the high and low estimates, teams discover assumptions behind the estimates. For example, "It's a 20, I've built histogram software before, and it is a tedious job with lots of back and forth on the graphic images" versus "It's a 3; I just used the Open Flash Chart library, and it has built-in histograms with animated tips."

- Since the cards are turned over all at once, this prevents individual estimators from being biased by the opinions of others prior to "showing their card."

- It happens pretty fast. Guidance is to allow at most two to five minutes of discussion per item, so a team should be able to estimate ten to twenty stories in an hour or so, which is about the maximum amount of time a team should spend estimating. (If an iteration is two weeks, even one hour represents 1.25% of the total available time!)

Returning to our training exercise, once estimated, the teams spend a few moments to reflect on their estimating process and results. One such set of results appears in Figure 8–2.

In this case, given comparable instructions, the teams tended to estimate the total work to be fairly similar. This correlates with other practical experiences as well. *If the teams are given comparable starting instructions, teams tend to estimate like things in like ways.* However, it is also the case that other teams may estimate bigness quite differently, and that is a factor we will need to take into account a little later.

How Much Time Should We Spend Estimating?

In our experience, there is a rapidly diminishing value in the time spent estimating a backlog, as Figure 8–3 illustrates.

S. No.	Sprint Exercise Team 1 Estimates	Estimates
1.	Estimate workbook page count.	1
2.	Accurately count workbook pages.	2
3.	Calculate square root of 54289.	5
4.	Add ten numbers with a calculator.	1
5.	Add ten numbers without a calculator.	3
6.	Introduce yourself.	1
7.	Write a program.	5
8.	Estimate cubic volume (within 30%).	5
9.	Estimate cubic volume (within 5%).	8
10.	Estimate snowfall in centimeters, inches, meters, and feet.	3
11.	Estimate snowfall in centimeters.	3
12.	Estimate workbook word count.	3
13.	Estimate the cubic meters of snowfall.	5
14.	Accurately count workbook words.	2
	Totals	**47**

S. No.	Sprint Exercise Team 2 Estimates	Estimates
1.	Estimate workbook page count.	1
2.	Accurately count workbook pages.	3
3.	Calculate square root of 54289.	5
4.	Add ten numbers with a calculator.	1
5.	Add ten numbers without a calculator.	2
6.	Introduce yourself.	1
7.	Write a program.	5
8.	Estimate cubic volume (within 30%).	4
9.	Estimate cubic volume (within 5%).	9
10.	Estimate snowfall in centimeters, inches, meters, and feet.	3
11.	Estimate snowfall in centimeters.	3
12.	Estimate workbook word count.	8
13.	Estimate the cubic meters of snowfall.	3
14.	Accurately count workbook words.	2
	Totals	**50**

Figure 8–2 Teams 1 and 2 sprint estimates

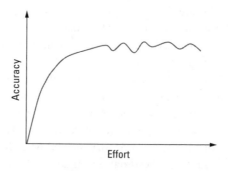

Figure 8–3 A little effort in estimating produces the most accurate results.

Spending too much time does not generally increase the accuracy of the estimates (and it bores the team!). Indeed, given too much time, the team may start to talk themselves out of the original estimates as the stories become seemingly more familiar. And yet, oftentimes, the first estimates were better because they reflected a healthier respect for the unknowns.

In addition, more investment in estimating time rarely has a material effect on the actual estimates. For example, in one short experiment,[3] a team estimated the same backlog repeatedly in three equal timeboxes. The results appear in Table 8–3.

Table 8–3 A Single Team's Estimates After Three Iterations

Example Sprint Worklist After 3 Rounds of Estimating	Round 1 Estimates	Round 2 Estimates	Round 3 Estimates
1. Estimate workbook page count.	1	1	1
2. Accurately count workbook pages.	2	2.5	2
3. Calculate square root of 54289.	9	10	9
4. Add ten numbers with a calculator.	2	2	1
5. Add ten numbers without a calculator.	3	2	2
6. Introduce yourself.	1	1	1
7. Write a program.	5	5	6
8. Estimate cubic volume (within 30%).	7	6	6
9. Estimate cubic volume (within 5%).	40	40	40
10. Estimate snowfall in centimeters, inches, meters, and feet.	4	5	3
11. Estimate snowfall in centimeters.	3	4	3
12. Estimate workbook word count.	3.5	3.5	4
13. Estimate the cubic meters of snowfall.	4	3	3
14. Accurately count workbook words.	2	2	2
Totals	86.5	87	83

---

3. This was not a statistically significant experiment. But I learned enough to not ask another team to do it.

The results indicate that all three estimates were within a few percentage points of each other. Spending too much time estimating is truly a form of waste—additional effort expended with no more meaningful output—so teams must be careful to time-box their estimating and not attempt to turn this heuristic into a pseudoscience.

A Parable of Estimating Caution: A Story within a Story

What's up with the estimates for "estimate the cubic volume of the room"?

A careful reader might note that the first two team's estimates (see Figure 8–2) for measuring the cubic volume of the room were very close to each other (5/8, 4/9). However, the third team's estimate was 40 (which in planning poker really means too big to be estimated at all!).

They were given the same normalized estimating instructions from the same instructor. Why the big difference?

Simply, the three teams were in two different rooms. Teams 1 and 2 were in a modest-sized, cubic conference room with low ceilings. Team 3 was in a much larger space with high vaulted ceilings and a very complex geometry. Without a ladder, it wasn't even clear how they could come up with the 30% estimate, much less 5%.

The lesson learned in this example is that when it comes to comparing "apparently" like things from "apparently like teams," one must fully understand the context of that team. The moral is as follows:

> Before you compare team estimates for theoretically comparable user stories, you must first understand what kind of room (software platform, programming languages, new team versus experienced team, computing resources, legacy versus green-field development, and so on) each team is in.

Distributed Estimating with Online Planning Poker

The estimating exercise we described earlier assumes the team is together. However, when face-to-face isn't practical, there are online tools that support planning poker with distributed teams. Teams log into a planning poker Web site[4] and play the game from their own desktop, no matter where they are located. A moderator (usually the product owner) facilitates the session and presents the stories to the team. The team has a separate teleconference or chat session set up for collaboration and discussion. After discussion, which can be timeboxed with a timer from the Web site, the teams vote independently, and the results of all votes are displayed simultaneously.

---

4. For an example, see *www.planningpoker.com*, from Mountain Goat Software (Mike Cohn).

After each vote converges, the moderator presents the next story, and the process continues until the backlog has been estimated. Results are easily exported for use by the teams.

AN ALTERNATE TECHNIQUE: TABLETOP RELATIVE ESTIMATION

Planning poker is but one of a number of techniques used by agile teams to estimate size in relative story points. An alternate technique, one that drives to a similar result in a different way, is *tabletop relative estimation*.[5] Like planning poker, this technique involves the entire team but clearly requires face-to-face communication.

In tabletop estimation, the team discusses each story in the backlog and places the story on the table in a size position relative to other stories—small stories to the left, bigger stories to the right. Stories of about the same size are stacked in columns. As the stories accumulate, the tabletop appears as shown in Figure 8–4.

As the stories are discussed, it's likely that there will be some second thoughts and shuffling of stories. That is to be expected. The process is fast and visual; each story can be seen with respect to all the other stories. As the prospective iteration unfolds, the team gains a sense of the work ahead.

Of course, the stories aren't really estimated yet; they are just placed in relative sizes. To create the actual estimates, points can be assigned to columns, as shown in Figure 8–5.

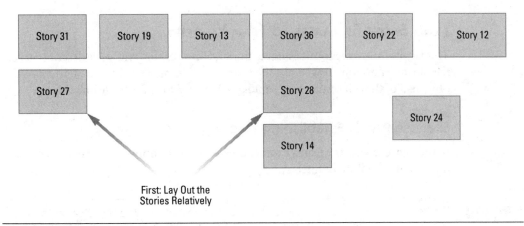

Figure 8–4   Stories placed on the tabletop in order

5. Thanks to Pete Behrens for describing this model.

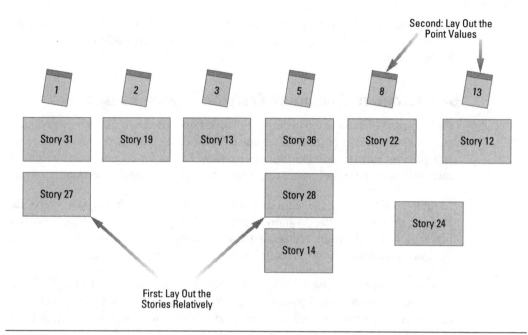

Figure 8–5 Assigning point values to columns of stories

Proponents of this technique note that it can be faster than planning poker. In addition, visualization of the entire iteration enhances the team's understanding of the work ahead.

FROM SCOPE ESTIMATES TO TEAM VELOCITY

This is how most agile teams estimate stories. However, nothing we've described so far tells anyone how long it will take the team to deliver anything. For that, we need the other half of the agile estimating paradigm. We need to know the team's *velocity*.

Exercise Part 3: Establishing Velocity

In the final exercise, the teams execute the iteration by completing as many stories as they can in the allotted timebox.

> ▶ **NOTE** The exercise is not intended solely to understand estimating and velocity but rather to experience an example sprint, replete with planning, breaking stories into tasks, taking responsibility, implementing and testing, demo, acceptance, and retrospective—all within a few hours. Feel free to "try this at home."

Figure 8–6 illustrates the result of one such exercise.

S. No.	Sprint Exercise Team 1 Actuals	Actuals
1.	Estimate workbook page count.	1
2.	Accurately count workbook pages.	2
3.	Calculate square root of 54289.	-
4.	Add ten numbers with a calculator.	1
5.	Add ten numbers without a calculator.	3
6.	Introduce yourself.	1
7.	Write a program.	5
8.	Estimate cubic volume (within 30%).	5
9.	Estimate cubic volume (within 5%).	-
10.	Estimate snowfall in centimeters, inches, meters, and feet.	-
11.	Estimate snowfall in centimeters.	-
12.	Estimate workbook word count.	3
13.	Estimate the cubic meters of snowfall.	5
14.	Accurately count workbook words.	2
	Totals	**28**

S. No.	Sprint Exercise Team 2 Actuals	Actuals
1.	Estimate workbook page count.	1
2.	Accurately count workbook pages.	3
3.	Calculate square root of 54289.	5
4.	Add ten numbers with a calculator.	1
5.	Add ten numbers without a calculator.	2
6.	Introduce yourself.	1
7.	Write a program.	-
8.	Estimate cubic volume (within 30%).	-
9.	Estimate cubic volume (within 5%).	-
10.	Estimate snowfall in centimeters, inches, meters, and feet.	3
11.	Estimate snowfall in centimeters.	3
12.	Estimate workbook word count.	8
13.	Estimate the cubic meters of snowfall.	3
14.	Accurately count workbook words.	2
	Totals	**32**

Figure 8–6 Team accomplishments during the iteration

The shaded areas represent stories that the team was unable to complete in the time-box. Team 1 completed 28 story points in their iteration, and team 2 completed 32. In other words, team 1's *velocity* is 28 points/iteration, and team 2's *velocity* is 32 points per iteration.

A team's velocity is simply how many points that team can complete in a standard iteration.

Given a team's known historical velocity in a given domain, they can now predict how long it will take them (how many iterations) to complete an arbitrary amount of work. It is also a valuable calibration that will help them bid the next round of stories more accurately.

CAVEATS ON THE RELATIVE ESTIMATING MODEL

This is a simple and reliable process that works quite well, subject to some serious caveats.

- It is based on historical data and is predictive only to the extent that the future (new stories) looks like the past (stories already completed).
- It is valid only to the extent that the team continues to have the same individuals. If you change the team members (imagine, for example, if we doubled the size of team 2 in the exercise), velocity will change dramatically, but it should stabilize after a few iterations.
- A team's velocity cannot be compared to any other team. (Imagine if team 1 had used 2 as the smallest story and compared everything to that. Their apparent velocity would be twice as large, but the actual productivity would be the same.)

Another Parable: Increasing Velocity, Be Careful What You Ask For

The goal of every agile team is the same—to continuously increase velocity while improving quality at the same time. However, even though it is predictive and even though it measures the team's ability to achieve a certain amount of functionality in a time period, it is not a true (or at least complete) measure of productivity.

As such, velocity can be a fairly reliable predictor of short-term future events, but it is not a tool for managing teams. It is only a tool by which teams manage and measure themselves. If management attempts to use velocity as a measure of team performance, the team will respond in one of three ways.

- Continuously improve the team's true productivity and agility in all aspects: apply retrospection, problem solving, corrective action, implement advanced agile practices, improve technical practices (continuous integration, unit testing, test automation, test-driven development, coding standards), increase individual performance and productivity, move less productive members into different roles on (or off) the team, adopt better technologies, and so on and so on.

  Or, for more immediate impact:

- Cut back on quality, building technical debt for a future period. This will increase the apparent measured velocity for implementing functionality (maybe earn a current MBO) but will *decrease* the actual productivity (which is a product of quality and functionality).
- Simply increase the size of the estimates.[6]

If you were a team member facing a management challenge to "increase your velocity" and if failing to do so could affect the team's standing within the organization, your incentives, or perhaps even your job security, what would you do? So, be careful what you ask for.

FROM VELOCITY TO SCHEDULE AND COST

Next we make the connections between velocity, estimating schedule, and estimating cost.

---

6. In the previous exercise, I often do an "abusive manager" role play with the team that has the lowest velocity. I give them two minutes to tell me what they are going to do to dramatically increase their velocity for the next exercise. Within about one minute, they tell me, "We'll double the size of our estimates."

Figure 8–7 Converting story points to time

Estimating Schedule

Given a team's velocity, determining a schedule to achieve some amount of functionality is straightforward. If we know size and velocity, we can calculate how long it will take to do something, as Figure 8–7 shows.

First, teams estimate each individual story in the backlog they are trying to schedule. Then they add those estimates together. Then, since they also know the length of their iterations, they use the following simple formula to estimate how many days it might take to work an arbitrary backlog:

days to do the work = # days per iteration * (backlog size estimate/velocity)

As we'll see in Part III, this even scales to the Program level, as long as each team estimates their own backlog items. (What else would be sensible? Well we won't go into that now.)

Estimating Cost

At this point, estimating cost to work down a backlog is also fairly readily calculable; simply take the average burdened cost for a team and divide it by their velocity. That provides the cost per story point *for that team*. Then when the team estimates an arbitrary backlog, just multiply the cost per story point for that team by the total estimate for the backlog.

ESTIMATING WITH IDEAL DEVELOPER DAYS

Although we hope we have effectively described the relative estimating method to your satisfaction, to those with a background in traditional project estimating, this may seem to be quite a roundabout approach (at best). Indeed, as we struggled to explain it as simply as we could in this chapter, it took quite a few pages to do so, and there were some not-so-obvious twists and turns. Although the model works quite well and is the most generally applied, it isn't the only model that agile teams use.

The next model we'll describe estimates stories in ideal developer days (IDDs), which is a fancy way of saying that the story is simply estimated based on the number of total person days, including development and test, that the team thinks they will need to accomplish the story. IDDs are conceptually simpler than story points, and they bring into focus some problems with the story point method we just described.

- It isn't so easy to understand by the team, and it's even less easy to understand by their outside stakeholders, including those who provide project management assistance and financial governance.
- It's hard to get started. Until teams have done a few iterations, they have no idea how to predict what they can accomplish. That gets even trickier at the Program level, where we need to aggregate these estimates to attempt to predict when some larger functionality will be available.
- Getting to schedule and cost estimates is very indirect. You have to work through relative estimates, establish velocity, and so on, and you have to understand the burden cost of each individual team, before you can translate a story point into a cost.
- Teams occasionally struggle to adjust their velocity based on the availability of team members. For example, if a team member is only part-time for a sprint or a key resource is not available for a period, what is the anticipated velocity then?
- Team velocities are not normalized. It's not unusual for one small team to have a velocity of 40 points per iteration, while a team twice that size has a velocity of half that. That makes for some pretty uncomfortable discussions.

Instead, with IDDs, the team returns to a more traditional way to estimate their work. In this technique, the team looks at each story, discusses it with respect to the same complexity factors we described earlier, and then estimates how many IDDs it will take to do the story. The reason the estimates are called "ideal" developer days is that the team typically deprecates their capacity for planning, demos, management meetings, and other team and company overhead items. There are many advantages to this method.

- Teams have always done it that way.
- Management needs schedule and cost estimates anyway.
- It's far easier to understand and explain.
- It's easy to adjust velocity for sick leave, vacations, training, and so on.

However, before we rush to attempt to retrain any story point teams to IDDs, we have to mention the serious disadvantages as well.

- Teams tend to get caught up when estimating in times. It's too tangible and too meaningful. They feel they have to get it right, and they don't have the law of large relative numbers to average each story into a total velocity for them.
- It's far more personal and can be politically loaded. One developer might say a story takes two days, another four. Either could be correct—for them— but again, more interesting discussions result. And these discussions are not likely to be supportive of the team spirit we work so hard to achieve. That's because they tend to highlight the lower velocity contribution of new team members, as well as other valuable team members, who are simply slower. That's just reality. But it's not a reality we want to shove in people's faces every sprint. Worse, if this information finds its way to personnel reviews, then you have *major* problems.
- It's the way we used to do it, and heaven knows, that didn't work very well.

Given these disadvantages, in balance, we prefer the relative estimating model, and that's why we described it first. Besides, the point may be moot anyway because if your team has already rolled out agile training, they are already off and running with story points. Try to change that, and you'll look like a cog in their newly agile works, and an ossified one at that. You may even be promoted to "impediment."

However, there is a third way—a way to blend these worlds—and one way we have found to be quite effective. That's because it has many advantages of both and far fewer disadvantages.

A Hybrid Model

The third model is a hybrid model. With this model, teams can proceed in large part with the relative estimating model. But we add two simple rules.

- Each team is guided to estimate the smallest story, one that can be done by one person in about a day, as a 1.
- Each team is also guided to initially estimate that they have eight IDDS per team member per two-week iteration (or adjust accordingly). This leaves about 20% for planning, demoing, company functions, training, and other overhead.

Thereafter, they do everything else in relative fashion just like they were likely taught with Scrum. There are many advantages to this approach.

- The teams can still use planning poker, as well as the modified Fibonacci series, and gain most all those tangible benefits.
- The estimate is still a consensus, and it doesn't say who is doing it. It's not so political.
- They can start immediately. They have their first velocity estimate (8 * team members) on day one.
- The relative methods still avoid any tendency to overinvest in estimating; if your choices are only 1, 2, 3, 5, and 8, you can't be breaking things down into hours. So, it goes just as fast.
- The translation to cost is obvious. Average the daily cost across all practitioners, including burden. The cost for one point is equal to that number, multiplied by 1.25 (because we also have to pay for the days that are not included in the IDD).

Normalizing Velocity

Perhaps most importantly, this technique has the effect of normalizing all teams to a common model. This means that a team of X people has a definitive, starting velocity of Y points, and so does every other team of the same size. Bigger and smaller teams have more or less velocity accordingly. We can create new teams and not be blind to estimating. While they will wander off fairly quickly from the model (some teams estimate better than others, some are newer, and some are simply more productive), they don't typically wander too far, and we again remind our management selves that these numbers are meaningful *only in the context of that one team*. But more broadly, we have estimates in units of measure that have meaning throughout the enterprise.

We've used this hybrid model to good effect in teams that are new to agile, as well as teams that have some degree of maturity. It usually works quite well. With this approach, you can have the advantage of both models, with fewer of the downsides. Generally, we recommend this approach, especially as we start to discuss teams developing software for larger programs, as we'll see in Part III.

SUMMARY

In this chapter, we introduced the models for agile estimating and how to use those models to estimate cost and schedule and to improve the team's ability to make and meet commitments. We described the story point–based relative model first, because it is the most common and it works. We also described an alternate in ideal developer days and pointed out many of the advantages and disadvantages to this approach. Generally, if given the choice of the two, we lean toward the story point approach, because there is absolutely "a solid method to that apparent madness."

However, we don't have to choose from just those two, so finally, we introduced a third, hybrid model, which combines the best of the two approaches. We leave this chapter with that as our primary recommendation.

With the overhead of estimating and velocity behind us, we can now have those tools as part of our newfound agile software "work physics." With that, we can move on to challenges and opportunities of other areas of our agile requirements practice, continuing with the next chapter, Iterating, Backlog, Throughput, and Kanban.

Chapter 9

ITERATING, BACKLOG, THROUGHPUT, AND KANBAN

We place the highest value on actual implementation and taking action. There are many things one doesn't understand; therefore, we ask them, why don't you just go ahead and take action?

—Fuijo Cho, Chairman, Toyota Motor Corporation

Apply fast feedback. . . . Control queue size.

—Don Reinertsen

In the previous chapters, we introduced the user story as the primary carrier of requirements through the value stream; described sources of requirements through understanding project and system stakeholders, user needs, and user personas; and described the estimating and velocity mechanisms teams use to plan their work.

In this chapter, we'll cover the closely related topics of iterating, backlog, throughput, and kanban systems. These describe the way teams go about managing those requirements, stories, and ideas and how they convert them to code. We'll start by describing the basic iteration pattern, discuss product backlogs for a bit, and then move on to a discussion of some of the interesting perspectives that come into play when we think about product backlogs from a lean perspective as a queue of work for the teams. We'll conclude with a brief introduction to software kanban systems, which provide another organized way to manage the sequencing and flow of work.

ITERATING: THE HEARTBEAT OF AGILITY

The basic unit of agile development is the iteration—the ability to take a set of user stories from the backlog and refine, code, test, and accept those stories into a new integrated baseline within a fixed timebox. The goal of each iteration is the same: to build an increment of potentially shippable code that is of value to the users. This is a significant challenge for the team, and mastering the process takes time. Figure 9–1 illustrates the basic iteration framework.

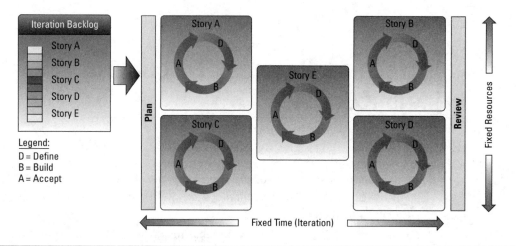

Figure 9–1   The basic iteration framework

Iteration Length

Before we begin, however, we must first entertain another small debate—the optimal iteration length. Most agree that iterations are a fixed, constant length, but the length of the iteration in the literature is a variable.

In practice, however, most teams have come to a common conclusion: *a week is too short and 30 days is too long,*[1] so they standardize on two weeks. This choice has a number of advantages.

- Two weeks is enough time to create meaningful incremental value.
- It is the fastest feedback they feel they can afford given the transaction costs of planning and other overhead.
- Short iterations force breaking stories into bite-size chunks, and define/ build/test has to be concurrent, avoiding the tendency to "waterfall" the iteration.

To facilitate coordination with other teams and larger releases, we also recommend that all teams on a project apply this same iteration timebox. (We'll see more of this in Chapter 15, The Agile Release Train).

▶ **NOTE**   In support of our recommendation and for simplicity, we'll assume a two-week iteration length in this book, but the requirements practices are independent of iteration length.

---

1. In our current experience, about 90% of the teams use two weeks. A few use one week, and a few use three weeks.

Iteration Pattern: Plan, Execute, Review, and Retrospective

No matter the length, all iterations have the same pattern: plan, execute, review, and retrospective, as Figure 9–2 illustrates.

The first phase is a short *planning session* (two to four hours) during which the backlog is reviewed and prioritized, estimates are established, and the team commits to an amount of work for the upcoming iteration. The second is the *execution phase*, when the iteration backlog items are implemented in code and tests. The final phase involves *review and evaluation* of the new system increment followed by a *retrospective* on the iteration process and results.

Team Backlog

The team's backlog serves as a "to-do" list for the team. It references or contains the identified new stories that must be done in order to release the product.

Unlike a traditional product or software requirements specification, the backlog is not designed to contain all the elaborated requirements for the solution. Rather, it contains a list of reminders of what must be done in order to complete the project. Prior to implementing a backlog item, more detailed requirements will likely be

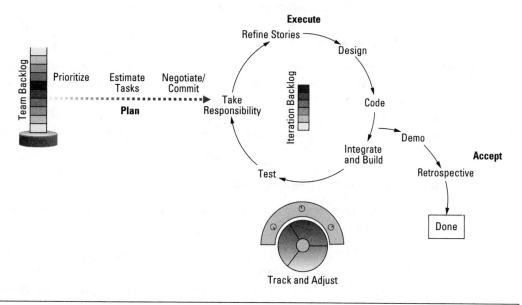

Figure 9–2   Iteration pattern

required. They may be detailed by elaborating the item itself, they may be detailed by providing attachments referenced by the backlog, or they may be developed as more detailed acceptance criteria for the backlog item.

Backlog items can take on many forms, but most are represented as user stories. However, the backlog may contain items of any size; it may even include larger-grained objects such as features and/or epics that will be done some time in the future. However, these larger items are placeholders only; they will eventually need to be split into smaller stories prior to implementation.

Backlog items should be focused on user functionality. More detailed requirements and acceptance criteria are typically not elaborated until just prior to, or within, the iterations in which they are implemented.

The backlog may also contain other *to-do* items, including defects, infrastructure work, and the like.

Planning the Iteration

The team begins the iteration with a planning session during which it reviews the backlog, selects and reviews the stories for the current iteration, and defines and estimates the tasks necessary to deliver the stories. When complete, the team makes a commitment to deliver a certain number of user stories and other backlog items to the baseline; that set of things is the team's *iteration backlog*.

Refining Backlog Stories

For mature teams, stories will likely have been elaborated, estimated, and prioritized prior to the planning meeting. However, the items may be a few weeks old, or even older, so it is likely that the stories must be reconsidered in light of the current project state and current project priorities, so some reestimating and reprioritization may occur. In addition, stories will be split as necessary, and new stories may be discovered.

Preparation for the Iteration Planning Meeting

Because the planning meeting is short and timeboxed, team members must be prepared as summarized in Table 9–1.

Everyone who will be involved in the iteration should attend. Required attendees typically include the Agile/Scrum Master, product owner, developers, test, QA, documentation personnel, and maybe a tech lead or architect. Other project stakeholders may also attend, but the meeting is for the team.

Table 9–1 Iteration Planning Meeting Preparation Responsibilities

Product Owner Responsibilities	Development Team Responsibilities
Review the release plan to make sure the Vision and goals are still appropriate.	Review the top-priority items in the backlog and prepare any questions.
Review and reprioritize items in the backlog, including stories that (a) were already there, (b) failed acceptance in a prior iteration, and (c) are newly generated from defects or other stories.	Consider technical issues, constraints, and dependencies, and be prepared to share these concerns.
Understand how the reprioritization may affect other teams who are dependent on commitments made during release planning.	Think about the work involved in delivering the functionality in the stories in order to be better prepared to make estimates in the meeting.
Understand the customer needs and the business value that each story is to deliver.	Understand what the team's capacity should be for the upcoming iteration, based on team discussions at the last review.
Be prepared to further elaborate the story.	

The objective of planning is to define and accept a reasonable scope for the iteration. The product owner and the development team may add or reduce stories, defects, and other infrastructure work on the basis of the current project context. Stories may be split, combined, estimated, and reestimated as necessary. The product owner then reranks the work items, and the team selects an initial scope of work based on the estimates and the team's velocity. The product owner may adjust certain backlog items in ways that make them less costly to develop or trade out entire backlog items for others.

The final scope of the iteration, on which the commitment is based, is the result of a negotiation between product owners and the development team. At the end of the iteration planning meeting, the product owners and development team jointly commit to the iteration plan. After that, the scope of the work must remain fixed; otherwise, the commitment cannot remain meaningful.

Iteration Commitment

Perhaps surprisingly, whether a team makes a commitment to the objectives of an iteration is a topic of some debate. Some argue that making commitments and then allowing the team the freedom to fail fast are incompatible objectives. Some argue that, in the absence of enlightened management, a team's commitments will just be a big, self-imposed stick with which they will be beaten about the head every time they fail to meet the objective. Some argue that a team will take whatever shortcuts it takes to meet commitments, cutting quality as necessary.

We, and many others, however, argue differently. The ability to make and meet one's own commitments is as much an element of professionalism as it ever was. Even though this is R&D, our new agile tools, our maturity, and our willingness to admit that not every iteration can, or even should, be a success allows us to make the majority of our commitments to each other, to the other teams, and to the enterprise. So, we are in the camp of those who believe that small, tangible objectives—that the teams *commit themselves* to—are an important building block of the agile enterprise.

If we have problems with management maturity in our new model, we *should fix that*. If we have problems with teams cutting quality corners, the team should self-correct itself to define objectives that can be met *with* quality.

Even more importantly, we'll use the team's ability to meet their iteration commitments as an important building block of a new organizational ability to meet near-term release objectives, as we will see in later chapters. And we can guess how critical that is to the enterprise.

Is This a Return of the Iron Triangle, Albeit a Little One?

If we are reasoned in our approach, we needn't fear a return to the iron triangle (fixed scope/schedule/resources) in iteration.

- This commitment is made *by* the teams, not *for* the teams.
- The objectives should allow a degree of freedom as to how to meet them and can also include a few *stretch objectives* (goals beyond the commitment) in case things go really well.
- Understand that not *every* commitment can be met. A good team may miss committing to an occasional stretch goal or fall into a short-lived technical abyss. Even then, we didn't lose two weeks; we gained two weeks of knowledge.

This is one of the main reasons why we keep our iterations short. So, we continue to coach teams and enterprises to these "commitments-in-the-small" so that our agile enterprises can start to achieve reliability in the large. It is still software R&D, but we can be masters of our own destiny.

There are a variety of ways in which teams commit to the content of an iteration. There isn't one right way, though there are many entertaining debates about which model is best.

Velocity-Based Commitment

Some teams simply pull stories into the iteration backlog in priority order (as adjusted for sequencing, dependencies, and so on) and then stop when the estimate reaches their target velocity. This is a *broad brushstroke approach*, because the teams know only that "it is about the right amount of work," but the work is not further analyzed with respect to available resources, task breakouts, and assignments. In this model, teams are counting on their experience, constant communication, tag-teaming stories, and, where necessary, "covering each other's backsides," for stories that may overload some individuals.

The commitment, then, is just the set of stories in the iteration backlog. Many teams assign a *chief engineer* to each story, whose job is to wrangle the story to completion, independent of their particular role in that particular story. In this way, every story has an owner whose job is to understand status, eliminate impediments, and, to generally, *just help get the job done* for that story.

Objective-Based Commitment

In an even *broader brushstroke* approach, some teams who have been working together for some time make their commitment based on the broader objectives negotiated with the product owner. In this model, the stories themselves are just a means to the end, and the statement of the objective trumps all. Thereafter, some teams use a pull/kanban style approach, whereby they pull items from the backlog and complete them serially. Few stories, if any, are committed up front. The team simply starts work, pulls stories from the backlog, creates new stories where necessary, communicates vociferously, and attempts to meet the objectives of the iteration "on the fly." Figure 9–3 shows an example of an *objective-based commitment*.

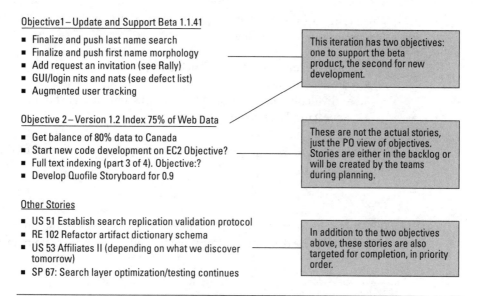

Figure 9–3 Objective-based commitment

Task-Based Commitment

Story ─ *Implemented by* ─ Task
1   1..*

At a much finer-grained scale, many XP and Scrum teams are rigorous in their use of task-based commitments. XP, in particular, tends to task stories in fine-grained detail. In this case, each story is broken into tasks that individual team members take responsibility for.

Tasks have an owner (the person who is going to do the task) and are estimated in hours (not points). The *burndown* chart of task hours applied versus task hours remaining represents one form of iteration status. As implied by the one-to-many relationship expressed in the model, there is often more than one task necessary to deliver even a small story.

It's common to see a mini life cycle coded into the tasks of a story. Here's an example:

Story 51: Select photo for upload

Task 51.1: Define acceptance test	Juha, Don, Bill
Task 51.2: Code story	Juha
Task 51.3: Code acceptance test	Bill
Task 51.4: Get it to pass	Juha and Bill
Task 51.5: Document in user help	Cindy

When teams use the task-based commitment model, the flow for achieving an iteration commitment is as follows:

1. Take the top story from the backlog.
2. Break it into tasks.
3. Individuals take responsibilities for tasks and estimate hours.
4. Repeat until teams run out of hours.

The team then makes the commitment to the stories that fit and to the objectives the stories imply.

Tasks

Bill Wake (the inventor of INVEST for user stories) uses the acronym SMART[2] to describe tasks. He describes the meaning behind each letter acronym in Table 9–2.

---

2. *http://xp123.com/xplor/xp0308/*

Table 9–2   SMART Tasks Elaborated

Specific	A task needs to be specific enough that everyone can understand what's involved in it. This helps keep other tasks from overlapping and helps people understand whether the tasks add up to the full story.
Measurable	The key measure is, "Can we mark it as done?" The team needs to agree on what that means, but it should include "Does what it is intended to," "Tests are included," and "The code has been refactored."
Achievable	The task owner should expect to be able to achieve a task. XP teams have a rule that anybody can ask for help whenever they need it; this certainly includes ensuring that task owners are up to the job.
Relevant	Every task should be relevant, contributing to the story at hand. Stories are broken into tasks for the benefit of developers, but a customer should still be able to expect that every task can be explained and justified.
Timeboxed	A task should be timeboxed (limited to a specific duration). This doesn't need to be a formal estimate in hours or days, but there should be an expectation so people know when they should seek help. If a task is harder than expected, the team needs to know it must split the task, change players, or do something to help the task get done.

In this task-based approach to commitment, individuals are accountable to complete their tasks, communicate with others when their task is complete or impeded, and then move on to the next task without additional supervision. It is highly granular and highly accountable. If the tasks are all completed, the stories will be accepted, and the goals of the iteration will be met.

Result: The Iteration Plan

No matter the approach to the commitment, the result of the planning meeting is an iteration plan that contains a number of key elements:

- An objective—a statement of what the iteration is intended to accomplish
- A prioritized list of stories to work on for the iteration
- The stories' estimated tasks and owners
- A commitment by the team to the objectives of the iteration
- Documentation of the plan in a visible place or in a widely accessible tool

Planning with Distributed Teams

It is far preferable to bring the team together in one location for planning sessions. However, if this isn't always feasible, teams can use shared agile project management tools to host their discussions and persist the stories, tasks, commitments, and so on.

Executing the Iteration

Having committed to the iteration plan, the team is faced with the question of how to allocate and adjust work for the members of the development team. The preferred approach is that developers simply pick the work they would like to do.

> When things are happening quickly, there is not enough time for information to travel up the chain of command and then come back down as directives [Poppendieck and Poppendieck 2003].

Taking responsibility for work must be supported by a visible indicator showing who is responsible for what work and by the daily status meetings during which status and issues can be discussed.

Each developer (or perhaps developer pair or developer/tester pair) will follow the same basic process repeatedly throughout the iteration:

1. *Take responsibility* for an assigned backlog item (for example, user story, defect fix, other).
2. *Develop* (refine, design, code, integrate, and test) the backlog item.
3. *Deliver* the backlog item by integrating it into a system build.
4. *Declare* the backlog item as developed, signaling that it is ready for acceptance testing.
5. Get the backlog item *accepted* by the product owner.

This cycle repeats as someone ultimately takes responsibility for all the backlog items in the queue. In most organizations, developers also support management of the process by estimating effort expended so far and remaining effort for the backlog items that they are responsible for. This creates a *burndown* chart that the teams use to track the overall status of the iteration.

As described earlier, because the story is pliable, these activities happen in parallel, and the objective is to deliver a working story (as it evolves) into the baseline. (Definition affects design, design affects test, test affects design, and so on.)

Tracking and Adjustment

Even within the course of a short iteration, scope must be managed, and deviations from the plan will occur, so tracking status and adjusting course is necessary.

Tracking Progress with the Big Visible Information Radiator

Tracking progress requires having visibility into the status of the stories, defects, and other tasks that are being worked on during the iteration.

Most teams use a *big visible information radiator* (BVIR, or sprint status board) on a wall in the team room for this purpose. Figure 9–4 shows an example.

In the deceptively simple radiator shown in Figure 9–4, the team simply moves the ribbon to the current day before each daily stand-up. This gives the entire team an instant assessment of where they are in the iteration (note how you can tell that the iteration in Figure 9–4 is at risk) and, more importantly, what they need to do to complete it successfully. If a manager or remote participant needs status information, all the team needs to do is to snap a picture and send it off!

Tracking in Daily Stand-Ups

One of the key rhythms of agile development is the practice of daily, 15-minute stand-up meetings, an event that all team members attend. The stand-up's purpose is to share information about the progress, to communicate, and to coordinate activities daily. Ideally, the team performs the daily stand-up in front of the BVIR. A typical round-robin format is as follows:[3]

- What stories I worked on yesterday and their status
- What stories I will be able to complete today
- What is getting in my way (am I blocked?)

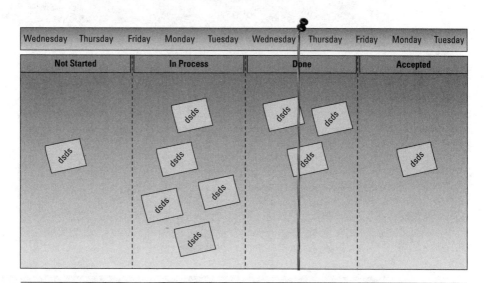

Figure 9–4   Example of an iteration BVIR

---

3. Note: This differs slightly from the standard "What I did yesterday," "What I'm doing today," and "Am I blocked" Scrum training and is more focused on the team communicating about how to get the user value to the finish line.

The Meet After

Daily stand-ups often trigger meaningful design discussions and discussions between developers, testers, and product owners about the objective of a piece of code or a test. To keep the meetings short, the Scrum Master simply notes those discussion items on a *meet after board*, and the involved parties are free to stay afterward as long as needed to complete their discussion, while the uninterested team members are free to leave the meeting on time.

Tracking with Agile Project Management Tooling

For larger and distributed teams, status is usually tracked using an automated agile project management tool, as Figure 9–5 illustrates.

With a tool like this, any stakeholder can see the current status of the iteration including the state of each story (an example of such a state model is as follows: Backlog, Defined, In-Progress, Completed, Accepted, Blocked), the remaining task-based work estimates (to-do hours remaining), and the overall burndown for the iteration.

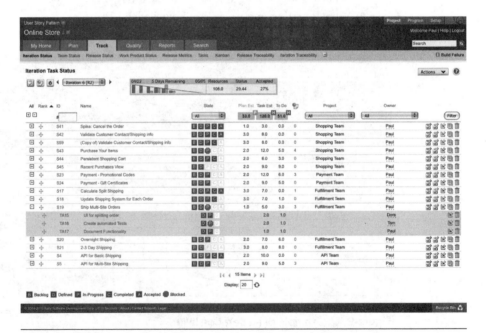

Figure 9–5   Iteration status in an agile project management tool

Courtesy of Rally Software Development Corp.

Many teams use both. The agile project management tool is the information master for stories and story state and also contains attachments and acceptance criteria that further define the detailed requirements for the story. This creates the "one central version of the truth" that is so valuable when multiple teams must cooperate on a project. Even then, however, many teams use the BVIR for visual status, but the story card on the wall is then just a token representing the real object in the tool or repository.

Completing the Iteration

This part is simple. When the timebox is over, the iteration is done, no matter the actual status of the stories in the iteration! From there, the team moves into the review and retrospective. These are conducted on time, and as scheduled, no matter the actual accomplishments of the team in the timebox.

Review and Retrospective

The final activity has two parts, the product demonstration and review and the iteration retrospective.

Review and Demonstration

The reality of software development is that the customer's understanding of the requirements for a system evolves as they see and use the software. Every iteration is an opportunity for the team to get feedback and guidance from the customer or product owner (customer proxy) about how to make the system more valuable. This feedback is typically structured as a somewhat formal, one-hour demonstration of new functionality.

Attendees include the key stakeholders, such as product managers, business owners, executive sponsors, other teams, customers, and, of course, the product owner and team. The format for this meeting is as follows:

- Demonstration of each story that was committed to be delivered at the iteration planning by the responsible party
- Discussion and feedback of each with stakeholders

Afterward, the teams review the results of the iteration from two perspectives.

- Did we accomplish the objectives for the iteration?
- If so, or if not, how might that impact the upcoming release?

Iteration Retrospective

The goal of the retrospective assessment is to mine the lessons learned during the iteration and then adapt the development process accordingly. The assessment allows the team to continually improve the throughput of the development process and the quality of the resulting system. Typically, the team conducts the retrospective in two parts.

- *Quantitative (metrics) review:* The team assesses whether the team met the objectives of the sprint (yes or no). They also collect any metrics they have agreed to analyze, which must include velocity—both the portion that is available for new development and the portion devoted to maintenance.
- *Subjective (process) review:* In the subjective review, the team analyzes its own process, with a focus on finding one or two things they can do better in the next iteration. A simple whiteboard format is often used:

What Went Well?	What Didn't?	What (One Thing) Can We Do Better Next Time?

The whole team participates, and the Scrum Master facilitates the retrospective, which is timeboxed to about 30 to 45 minutes.

Iteration Calendar

As part of establishing a rhythm of agile development timeboxes, meetings, and checkpoints, teams typically establish a standard "cadence calendar" at the start of each program. The cadence calendar (an example of which is shown in Figure 9-6) helps the team set its schedules so that members can set aside time for planning meetings, daily stand-ups, demos, reviews, and retrospectives. Thereafter, no meeting notices are required, because the schedule for each day is fixed.

	Day 1		Day 2–9		Day 10
8:00		8:00		8:00	
9:00	Iteration Planning (PO Presents Stories)	9:00	Daily Stand-up (15 min)	9:00	Daily Stand-up (15 min)
10:00		10:00		10:00	
	Planning: Team Breakouts, Elaborate, Task, and Estimate Stories	11:00		11:00	
		12:00		12:00	
		1:00		1:00	
		2:00		2:00	Demo
		3:00		3:00	Retrospective
4:00	Reconvene, Negotiate Scope, Commit	4:00	(Mid-Iteration Only) Feature Preview	4:00	

Figure 9–6 Sample iteration calendar

Feature Preview

One challenging aspect of agile is what we call the "tyranny of the urgent iteration." The team's commitment to the current iteration causes an intensity of focus that is unparalleled in prior development models. That is mostly good, because focus increases productivity and quality, in part by eliminating task switching and overhead. Moreover, working in a highly productive team, coupled with peer pressure, drives the team to new levels of performance. During this process, the teams tend to operate in a "heads-down" mode, and there is a danger that they could make tactical, near-term decisions in the code that could complicate future stories.

One way to address this is with a weekly (or every other week) meeting where the product owner discusses upcoming features or user stories (this meeting is sometimes called *story time* or *backlog grooming*). The meeting can include brainstorming new ideas, having short implementation discussions, and refining and estimating backlog items.

This scheduled meeting gives the team a "timeout" from the current iteration and time to think a bit about the future. It also gives the product owner a way to meet with the team and discuss upcoming stories and perhaps estimate some features that a new customer is requesting, without interfering with the team's cadence or velocity.

Backlog, Lean, and Throughput

The invention of the simple backlog construct in agile is one of those deceivingly simple constructs that can radically improve the performance of a software team. Indeed, it's hard to overstate the importance of this construct in organizing and unifying the mission of the team. Benefits include the following.

- It prevents the team from getting instructions from a variety of sources.
- Since the backlog has a single owner, teams always know what the current priorities are and who to ask for clarification.
- The fact that "if it isn't in there, it isn't going to happen," communicates to all the stakeholders how the team does their work. It also informs stakeholders how to influence that work (that is, by working with the product owner to get their item in the backlog).
- The fact that the backlog is prioritized at iteration boundaries (and as we will see later, the feature backlog is prioritized at release boundaries) means that priorities are current and local.

Therefore, agile software teams spend a significant portion of their time identifying, estimating, and elaborating items in their backlog. Indeed, it isn't too much of an oversimplification to say that managing the team's *backlog* is their basic requirements management process.

For some teams, a nice, well-formed, and deep backlog gives them a sense of control of their destiny. They can see the work ahead, they can plan for current and future work, and they have a sense of comfort in knowing that they are always working on the next higher-prioritized thing.

Before we conclude, however, that a deep, well-considered, estimated, and elaborated backlog is our silver bullet for managing development, we must take a look at the backlog from another perspective—the perspective of lean and how backlogs affect time to market for new ideas and initiatives. After all, a backlog is nothing less than a queue of work, and long queues of work, well, are not so good.

▶ **NOTE**   Although the discussion here focuses on the team's local backlog, it describes a general set of principles that we'll also apply to the program and portfolio backlogs in Parts III and IV of the book.

Backlog Maturity, Lean, and Little's Law

We'll introduce this discussion in the form of an author's blog thread, because it tells the story in the (somewhat exaggerated[4]) perspective from which it developed.

A Blog Story: Is That Well-Formed Product Backlog Decreasing Your Team's Agility?

I was sitting at a Starbucks in Munich—a rainy, snowy Saturday morning—watching the queue of people looking for their caffeine kick-start (the same reason I was there). For some reason, the queue of people ordering coffee reminded me of the question teams ask about "how big" and "how well formed" (or how well elaborated) their product backlog needs to be.

The size of the team's backlog, the rate of backlog processing, and the ultimate rate of value delivery is really a problem of queuing theory, just like at Starbucks. At Starbucks, I was trying to do Little's law in my head, but to not very good effect, so I had to write it out when I came back to my hotel. Little's law, the general-purpose theory for queuing and processing problems, is one of the fundamental laws of lean. It states the following:

$$W_q = \frac{L_q}{\lambda}$$

---

4. As is sometimes the case with such blogs, this blog thread represents a somewhat exaggerated view of the problem, in part as an attention-getting device.

where the following is true.

- *Wq* is the average waiting time in the queue for a standard job.
- *Lq* is the average number of things in the queue to be processed.
- *Lambda* is the average processing rate for jobs in the queue.

While I was drinking my latte, I noticed that the queue at the ordering counter varied from 0 to as many as 12 people in line. With my iPhone timer, I was methodically trying to time the average time that it took the single barista to serve each customer. However, when the queue got long, as if by magic, another barista appeared from the back somewhere (Starbucks likely understands queuing theory). That confused my timing, and I lost track.

However, let's assume it takes about 45 seconds on average to serve a customer (a service rate of 1.33 customers per minute). We can use Little's law to calculate the average wait of someone in the queue on this particular Saturday morning as follows:

$$W_q = \frac{6 \text{ (Average Queue Length)}}{1.33 \text{ (\# Customers Processed per Minute)}}$$

So, the average wait time is 4.5 minutes in this case (not too bad, even if you do need that quick fix).

It's important to note that this is the average case, and your wait could be shorter (I was the third person when I went in, and I had to wait only a minute or two to order) or longer (the person at the back of the 12-person queue had to wait about 9 minutes; yikes, he could easily go somewhere else).

Little's Law and an Agile Team's Backlog

Fair enough, but what does the line at Starbucks have to do with agile development and the team's requirements backlog? *They are similar problems of queuing theory.*

For example, let's assume the following.

- A single agile/Scrum team, working in two-week iterations.
- The team averages about 25 to 30 story points per iteration, or a story completion rate of about 8 stories per iteration.
- The team is justifiably proud of how well they are maintaining their backlog, and the backlog averages about 100 stories, most of which are committed to near-term releases.

The question is, how agile is this team? In other words, how long does it take, on average, for a new requirement (story) to get to the end of an iteration, where it can start to deliver value (assuming no additional waiting time for the release, a topic for later)?

We simply plug this data into Little's law:

$$W_q = \frac{100 \text{ Stories}}{\left(\dfrac{8 \text{ Stories}}{1 \text{ Iteration}}\right)} = 12.5 \text{ Iterations}$$

The answer is 12.5 iterations to get into the sprint, plus 2 weeks to get out, or 27 weeks on the average. More than half of a year! And, if your item is in the back of the backlog, it could take even longer (remember the guy who had to wait 9 minutes).

Wow. If it takes a team *on average* half a year to deliver a new requirement to the customer, that doesn't seem very responsive.

Plus, in the enterprise, there are multiple teams with interdependencies, and the individual results of the teams have to be aggregated, packaged, and validated in some kind of release envelope before distribution, so it can take longer still. Therefore, it's understandable when we see an enterprise with 20, 50, or even 100 reasonably agile teams that it still takes 300 to 500 days to move a new requirement from customer request to delivery.

So although this may be an exaggerated case (as we'll see in the comments shortly), it is not at all unusual to see these types of delays in the enterprise. So yes, it may be understandable, but no, it's not acceptable. Let's see what we can do about it.

Applying Little's Law to Increase Agility and Decrease Time to Market

The formula is not complicated. If we are going to improve (decrease) time to market, we have to either increase the denominator or decrease the numerator (or both). And of course, if we can do both, we will achieve even better results. Let's look at each opportunity.

Increasing Lambda, the Rate of Story Completion

Increasing the rate of story completion, and thereby the overall rate of value delivery, is the legitimate goal of every agile team. Of course, if we could simply add resources, we could probably increase Lambda, but for the purpose of this discussion, let's assume that is impractical. Besides, although it's the easy way out of the argument, it increases the cost of the value created and decreases return on investment (ROI).

So although you might get there faster, you may not make any money when you do. Let's work within the fixed resource constraints of our archetypical team and see what we can do.

The primary mechanism for increasing the rate of story completion is the team's inspect and adapt process, whereby the teams review the results of each iteration and pick one or two things they can do to improve the velocity of the next. This is the long-term mission; it is a journey measured in small steps, and there is no easy mathematical substitute for such improvements. These improvements include better coding practices, unit testing and unit testing coverage, functional test automation, continuous integration, and other enhanced agile project management and software engineering practices.

In my experience, however, two primary areas stand out as the place where teams can get the *fastest* increase in Lambda: first, *gaining a better understanding of the story itself* before coding begins, and second, *decreasing the size of the user stories* contained in the backlog.

Gaining a Better Understanding of the Story: Acceptance Test-Driven Development

The fact is that the overall velocity of the team is not typically limited by the team's ability to write, or even integrate, code. Instead, it is gated by the team's ability to understand what specific code they need to write, as well as to avoid code they do not need to write. Doing so involves having a better understanding of the requirements of the story, before coding it.

However, this must be done on a just-in-time basis, just prior to the iteration boundary, or else the team's backlog will get wider, and the team will have too much requirements inventory. Some of it will likely decay before they get to it. However, a wider backlog (small numbers of well-elaborated stories) is not nearly as bad as a deeper backlog (larger numbers). The worst case is that a few team members have gone too far, too early, in elaborating a few backlog items, but it won't slow value delivery nearly so badly as would a deeper backlog. It's a bit of waste, but it doesn't really drive Little's law.

Therefore, once a story has reached a priority whereby it will be implemented in the next iteration or two, time spent in elaborating the story will pay dividends. Often, this is described as Acceptance Test-Driven Development (ATDD), and, fortunately, it's a little easier for teams to intellectualize and adopt than code-level TDD. ATDD involves two things: writing better stories and establishing the acceptance tests for the story before coding begins. We'll cover that in the next chapter.

Increasing Lambda with Smaller Stories

If all the people ordering at Starbucks had ordered a tall, black coffee, rather than a Venti, nonfat, double shot, half-caff, no foam, vanilla latte, with a heated bagel on the side, the length of the queue and the wait from the back of the line would have been much shorter. Small jobs just go through a system faster than large ones.

In Chapter 6, we described the benefits of smaller user stories at length, and I won't repeat them here. However, it's worth pointing out that decreasing the size of user stories has both a linear and exponential effect on Lambda, both of which are positive.

- *Linear effect:* Smaller user stories are just that, smaller. They go through the iteration faster so teams can implement and test more small user stories in an iteration than large ones. And, although the total value of a small story can't be as big as a large story, the incremental delivery hastens the feedback loop, improving quality and fitness for use.
- *Exponential effect:* Because they are smaller and less complex, small user stories decrease the coding and testing implementation effort. The coded functions are smaller and less complex, and the number of new paths that must be tested also decreases exponentially with story size. (However, some of this is offset by the additional overhead of managing more stories.)

So, even if the length of the backlog remains the same, a combination of better-defined and smaller user stories has a very positive effect on value delivery time.

Clearly, increasing Lambda, the denominator of Little's law, is a prime opportunity for the team to increase agility and time to market. Every truly agile team continuously commits to doing so.

Decreasing Lq, the Length of the Queue

Now that we've seen two ways to decrease time to market (Wq) by increasing the denominator (Lambda) of our equation, let's look at the other half of our equation and see what opportunities we find there.

Fortunately, there are even faster ways to decrease time to market while the team is working on continuously improving development practices. That is by *forcing a limit on the length of the queue.*

Decreasing queue size causes a directly proportional decrease in the wait time. Therefore, if we cut our queue size in half, we can halve our time to market without taking any further action. As if this weren't enough motivation, Reinertsen [2009] points out that there are a number of additional reasons why long queues are fundamentally bad in the product development process.

- *Increased risk:* While a story is in the queue, there is some probability that the market or customer has changed their mind and the story is no longer valuable. The longer the queue, the higher the probability. When we invest in an unneeded story, we waste valuable resources. Worse, the unneeded story has displaced some other story that would have had economic benefit.
- *Increased variability:* With a long queue, there is always way more than enough work to do, so the team takes on everything they possibly can. Management supports this by driving teams to high utilizations (95% or better). In turn, high utilization drives thrashing and high variability, as we saw in Chapter 6. High variability decreases reliability, causes stress in the organization, and, perversely, drives even higher utilization because of fire fighting—a deadly spiral.
- *Increased costs:* Every story in the team's queue was put in there somehow by someone. That takes labor. Once it's in there, the team has to continue to account for it, prioritize it, and rearrange it as higher-priority items come into the queue.
- *Reduced quality:* The longer the queue, the longer it is before we get feedback on new items from the customer (or product owner proxy). The longer the feedback, the more other developers may have invested in the nonconforming story, and the more expensive it is to rework.
- *Reduced motivation and initiative:* If it's going to be a long time before a customer sees a story in the middle of the queue, there is little sense of urgency. But if the customer is going to see it soon, we better worry about getting it right, right now.

This summarized the initial blog post on the topic. Prior to this discussion, I suspect that many teams believe that a lengthy, well-articulated product backlog was an asset that increased, rather than decreased, the team's agility and the rate of value delivery to the customer. Common sense and intuition may have led us to believe that was the case.

But the economics and math behind queuing theory and lean product development teach us otherwise. Instead, we've learned that agile teams need short backlogs of small items, a number of which are quite well-articulated and socialized, but only just prior to the iteration boundary in which they will be implemented.

Readers React

Of course, agile teams are proud of their backlogs, and the post generated some interesting reactions—some supportive, some critical, but all pretty perceptive. Here are a few samples:

Lengthy backlog is not a disease. It shows that there's lots of work waiting to be prioritized and worked on! This is all about prioritizing. Either customer or the team—they have to decide what to implement first. You can't force release time with the single aim to make your backlog shorter. Backlog is a tool for work, not the absolute indicator of team's agility or capability.

—Olga Kouzina, Product Specialist at TargetProcess, Inc.

All of your suggestions are good. However, the underlying assumption that the entire backlog must be completed is flawed. People do indeed halve their time to market (or better) by having a reasonably long backlog, and producing a viable release after less than half that backlog has been completed.

—Bjorn Gustafsson

I agree: managing requirements and increasing throughput and value on agile projects means having a dynamic, yet sparse—or at least reasonably-populated—backlog (one containing items in varying sizes; including MMF-sized items—minimal marketable features—is fine). It's crucial to analyze the requirements/stories to derive very slim/right-sized stories with sharply and clearly defined "doneness" criteria. Exploring the requirements—doing this "work ahead"—gets you what Jeff Sutherland calls "ready" backlog items.

—Ellen Gottesdiener

I wholly agree that the length of a product Backlog is an indication of how agile a team really is. Even if you are able to release every day, an item that is on the backlog for months carries risk and cost. Fortunately, unlike at Starbucks, features can push to the front of the queue. But this is just Class of Service, which should be made explicit, and can sometimes be a smell in itself (e.g. too much expediting).

—Karl Scotland

The Product Backlog is NOT scope. Although some organizations and teams treat it as scope, that is not a healthy way to manage a backlog. This approach asserts that we can think of the most important items in order of their

*importance over time. Prioritization is key in product backlog management
and therefore 6 months to deliver an item should not be part of the equation.*

—Chris Sterling

Managing Throughput by Controlling Backlog Queue Length

Given these comments and many more, coming from both camps, I reflected on
what drove me to write that lengthy post (and to include it in this book). It wasn't
the boredom of the wait at Starbucks on that dreary Saturday. Rather, I wanted to
make a few, fundamental points about agile and lean and address a few things I have
seen in practice that inhibit team agility and program responsiveness.

Point #1: Little's Law Doesn't Lie

Little's law[5] tells a fundamental truth: The longer the queue and the slower the processing time, the longer the (mathematically predictable) wait. This core law of
queuing theory is irrefutable.

From lean, we also understand that long queues of work in process are fundamentally bad. Whether it be elaborated user stories in a backlog that won't see the light
of day, code that has been written but not tested, hundreds of manual tests awaiting
automation, blobs of new code that haven't been checked back into the baseline, a
long set of Portfolio-level projects awaiting resources, and so on, they are *all* universally bad, because they all decrease agility and time to market. (It's hard to respond
quickly to an order for fenders with a metallic finish if you have stacks of fenders
primed for regular finish in front of the paint shop.)

However, we also understand that, at least when it comes to backlog, Little's law isn't
a perfect analogy because a story can jump the queue in agile (I recommend that
you do not try that at Starbucks, because those people in front of you likely really
need that caffeine), and a system can decide not to process all items in the queue
(Starbucks could do that to decrease queue length, but the long-term economics
would be unfavorable).

So when it comes to the backlog post, as some readers pointed out, we are not forced
to assume that all backlog items will make their way into processing in an orderly
fashion. We are smarter than that. And therefore Little's law cannot be blindly and
universally applied. However, the fact that we are smarter than that does not prevent
some undesirable behaviors that we often see in practice. This brings me to points
#2 and #3.

---

5. Actually, Little did the formal proof, rather than inventing the law.

#2: Don't Be Hostage to Your Own Backlog

In many sprint reviews, I ask teams how they are doing with respect to the release objectives. Surprise, many times they are behind (and that's one of the reasons we like agile—we are likely behind less than we would have been, we actually know it, and it's not too late to take corrective action).

When I ask them how they can "jump the queue" and meet the release objectives though they are behind, they often say, "Well, we have all these backlog items we have to finish first. We have elaborated them, we understand them, we have invested in them, we have committed them to others, they are important, and they are ready to go."

However, I then comment, "As true as that may be, those are sunk costs, and that doesn't make those backlog items necessary per se. If the backlog you have isn't the one you need to meet the release objectives, ignore the sunk costs and flush it!"

#3: The Enterprise Can't Be Held Hostage to the Team's Backlog Either

As we'll see in Parts II and III of this book, at enterprise scale this problem is badly compounded. Often, we approach release-planning boundaries with 10 to 20 agile teams having detailed and well-structured backlogs for the existing work in process, 3 to 6 months of committed customer work. In that case, the enterprise has little or no agility, because nothing can really be changed. After all, if the teams must first work through their committed backlog, then Little's law is in your face, and the result is immutable. You can't do much of anything quickly at the enterprise level unless you do the following.

- You wait the (potentially) infinite amount of time it takes teams to work their local backlogs down to near zero. It's (potentially) infinite because other laws—the law of "teams don't like having empty backlogs," the law of "we have too much technical debt," and the law of "our current users will drive us to expand our work to consume the time allotted to it"—come into play.
- The enterprise must override the teams—or kill entire projects—or abrogate commitments in order to move forward with more globally aligned objectives.

Either choice will be painful and suboptimal. Wouldn't it be far better if the system were leaner, if the team's backlogs were really short and lightweight, and if the backlogs didn't represent fixed commitments based on too-long-a-term thinking?

Backlogs are great, as long as you keep them short, lightweight, and negotiable. Remember, never overinvest in some stories you may just not do.

And never, ever be held hostage by your own backlog.

SOFTWARE KANBAN SYSTEMS

For these reasons, driven by lean thinking, many teams have decided to place work-in-process limits on the size of the backlog, which are sized and adjusted as necessary to create the desired time to market, response time, or internal feedback loop. Once the queue is full, they quit even thinking about new stories until there is room for more stories in the queue.

Indeed, the negative effect of long software queue sizes is a primary economic and philosophical principle that drives the current lean software Kanban movement, which we introduced briefly in Chapter 1.

The Limited WIP Society[6] describes the following.

- Kanban manages the flow of units of value through the use of work-in-process (WIP) limits.
- Kanban manages these units of value through the whole system, from when they enter until they leave.
- By limiting WIP, kanban creates a sustainable pipeline of value flow.
- Further, limiting WIP provides a mechanism to demonstrate when there is capacity for new work to be added, thereby creating a pull system.
- Finally, the WIP limits can be adjusted and their effect measured as the kanban system is continuously improved.

Kanban System Properties

David Anderson, one of the thought leaders behind the movement, further describes five core properties of a kanban implementation as follows.[7]

- *Visualize workflow:* Highlights the mechanisms, interactions, handoffs, queues, buffers, waiting, and delays that are involved in the production of a piece of valuable software.
- *Limit work in progress:* Implies the introduction of a pull system from a family of possible solutions.
- *Measure and manage flow:* Highlights a focus on keeping work moving and using the need for flow as the driver for improvement. A focus on flow rather

---

6. *www.limitedwipsociety.org*
7. *www.limitedwipsociety.org/2010/04/11/five-core-properties-of-a-kanban-implementation*

than on waste removal is a higher mastery of lean and much less likely to lead to "Lean and Mean" antipatterns and dysfunction.

- *Make process policies explicit:* It's about holding up a mirror to the working reality and encouraging the whole team and its leadership to reflect on its effectiveness. Thinking of a process as a set of policies rather than a workflow is a very powerful technique.
- *Use models to recognize improvement opportunities:* Kanban is quantitative and takes a scientific approach to improvements. Focus on the theory of constraints, an understanding of variation and the system of profound knowledge, and the lean models of waste and flow.

Classes of Service in Kanban

To assure that a kanban system is responsive to the business needs, Anderson[8] describes utilizing various classes of service, which allow flexibility and enhanced velocity of delivery based on the cost of delay for each backlog item. For example, he recommends four classes of service to help manage the queuing problem:

- *Expedite:* Unacceptable cost of delay
- *Fixed delivery date:* Step function cost of delay
- *Standard class:* Linear cost of delay
- *Intangible:* Intangible cost of delay

Each class of service has its own work-in-process limits, which can be adjusted based on current context and associated with different management policies. With a kanban system, teams have a structurally sound basis for decreasing L_q, the length of the backlog, and can thereby reap the throughput benefits accordingly.

We'll see kanban systems such as this at work later, in Chapters 21 and 23.

SUMMARY

In this chapter, we first described the iteration, the basic, time-based building block of agile development whereby the teams build an increment of user functionality in a short timebox. Each iteration delivers some new requirements into the new baseline. With this mechanism, we have a reliable and predictable way to address building larger and larger amounts of user value in these small, demonstrable increments, thereby mitigating technical risk while also assuring that the users come along with us for the ride.

---

8. *www.agilemanagement.net*

We also discussed the unique role the product backlog (and by extension program and portfolio backlogs) play in managing work in process and controlling the rate of value delivery. We found a little controversy here—some weighted on the side of "well-formed backlogs increase throughput" and others on the side of "the bigger the backlog, the slower the team." Neither side is right or wrong. Instead, we must strive for a sense of balance—right-sized backlogs with near-term items elaborated and implementation ready. Everything else is just a "notion" held in a low-cost holding pattern.

Perhaps most importantly, however, as the programs and epics get bigger in the later chapters, we'll have to keep in mind that simply stacking all these well-formed backlogs end to end will create a large and unresponsive system, even if we think we are agile. We will have to be much smarter than that. One way to address this is by introducing a kanban system, which many have adopted ether stand-alone or in combination with Scrum (see Kniberg and Skarin [2010] and Ladas [2008]). We'll also see an implementation of a kanban system for architectural and business epics in Chapters 21 and 23.

But for now we can move on to a more tactical consideration—how can we know that backlog item is actually *done* so we can move our attention to the next one. To understand whether the requirements we've just implemented *really* meet the needs of our users, we'll need to make sure that each passes an acceptance test. That is the subject of the next chapter, Acceptance Testing.

Chapter 10

ACCEPTANCE TESTING

What's done, is done.

—Shakespeare, *Macbeth*, Act 3, scene 2

If it isn't tested, it doesn't exist.

—Anonymous agile master

We recently transitioned to agile. But all our testers quit.

—Vignette from Crispin and Gregory [2009]

WHY WRITE ABOUT TESTING IN AN AGILE REQUIREMENTS BOOK?

As a sanity check in preparing for this chapter, I went to my bookshelf and looked at a number of texts on software requirements management, including my own [Leffingwell and Widrig 2003], for guidance on testing whether an application meets its requirements. Of course, I knew I wouldn't find much on testing there, if for no other reason than I knew I hadn't written much. I wasn't surprised that other requirements authors haven't written much of anything on testing either.

So, the question naturally arises: Why do we feel compelled to write about testing now, in a book on agile requirements? The question itself reflects a traditional view, that historically, software requirements were somehow independent of their implementation. They lived a separate life—you could get them (reasonably right) at some point, mostly up front; the developers could actually implement them as intended; they would be tested somewhat independently to assure the system worked as intended; and the customers and users would be happy with the result. Of course, it never really worked that way, but it sure was easier to write about it.

In thinking in lean and agile terms, however, we must take a much more systemic and holistic view. We understand that stories (requirements), implementation (code), and validation (acceptance tests, unit tests, and others) are not separate activities but a continuous refinement of a much deeper understanding; therefore, our thinking is different:

> No matter what we thought earlier in the project, *this* functionality is what the user really needs, and it's now implemented, working, and tested in accordance with the continuous discussions and agreements we have forged during development.

> Just as importantly, we have instrumented the system (with automated regression tests) such that we can assure this functionality will continue to work as we make future changes and enhancements to the system. Then, and only then, can we declare that our work is complete for this increment.

That is the reason that we have taken a much more systemic view of "requirements" in this book—discussing users, agile teams, agile process, roles, product owners, and whatever else is necessary for a team to develop an application that, in the end, actually solves the user's problem.

However, when describing requirements in book form, the subject is fuzzier and more tangible at the same time. It's *fuzzier* because you can't really tell where a story ends and its acceptance test begins. Are the data elements in a user entry field included in the story, or are they implied requirements attached to the story? Are they really details left for the acceptance test? Or are they perhaps so fine-grained that they may be covered solely in the unit tests for the method that implements it?

And yet, the subject is *more tangible*, because the precise answers to these questions aren't so important. What is important is that we worked through a cycle of incremental information discovery; we collaborated, we negotiated, we refined, we compromised, and we ended up with something that actually works. In addition, we have captured the details of system behavior in a set of tests that will persist for all the time the software continues to provide value to its users. So, the requirements are implemented, complete, and tested.

In this chapter, we'll provide guidance to these questions and an overview of how we achieve quality in our agile requirements practices. In agile, we simply can't do that without a discussion of testing.

AGILE TESTING OVERVIEW

Given that we are taking a systemic view to requirements, across the team, program, and portfolio, we must also take a broader view of agile testing in general, so we'll know the context in which a discussion of acceptance testing can make sense.

Brian Marick, an early XP proponent (and a signer of the Agile Manifesto), has provided much of the thought leadership in this area and has developed a framework that many agilists use to think about testing in an agile paradigm. His philosophy of agile testing is as follows:[1]

> Agile testing is a style of testing, one with lessened reliance on documentation, increased acceptance of change, and the notion that a project is an ongoing conversation about quality.

He goes on to describe two main categories of testing: *business-facing* and *technology-facing* tests:[2]

> A **business-facing** test is one you could describe to a business expert in terms that would (or should) interest her.... You use words drawn from the business domain: "If you withdraw more money than you have in your account, does the system automatically extend you a loan?"

> A **technology-facing** test is one you describe with words drawn from the domain of the programmers: "Different browsers implement JavaScript differently, so we test whether our product works with the most important ones."

He further categorizes tests, whether business-facing or technology-facing, as being used primarily to either *support programming* or to *critique the product*.

> Tests that **support programming** mean that the programmers use them as an integral part...of programming. For example, some programmers write a test to tell them what code to write next.... Running the test after the [code] change reassures them that they changed what they wanted. Running all the other tests reassures them that they didn't change behavior they intended to leave alone.

> Tests that **critique the product** are not focused on the act of programming. Instead, they look at a finished product with the intent of discovering inadequacies.

In *Agile Testing*, Crispin and Gregory developed these concepts further [2009]. With a few minor adaptations for our context, we find an agile testing matrix in Figure 10–1.

---

1. *agilemanifesto.org/authors.html*
2. *www.exampler.com/old-blog/2003/08/21/*

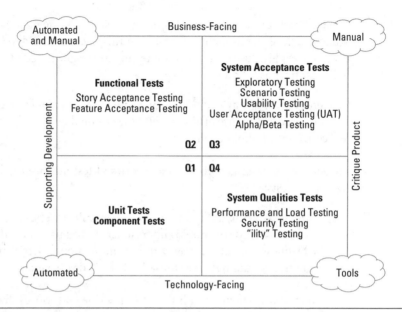

Figure 10–1   The agile testing matrix

In quadrant 1, we find *unit tests* and *component tests*, which are the tests written by developers to test whether the system does what they intended it to do. As indicated on the matrix, these tests are primarily *automated*, because there will be a very large number of them, and they can be implemented in the unit testing environment of choice.

In quadrant 2, we find *functional tests*. In our case, these consist primarily of the story-level acceptance tests that the teams use to validate that each new story works the way the product owner (customer, user) intended. Feature-level acceptance testing is referenced in this quadrant as well. Many of these tests can be automated, as we'll see later, but some of these tests are likely to be manual.

In quadrant 3, we find *system acceptance tests*, which are system-level tests to determine whether the aggregate behavior of the system meets its usability and functionality requirements, including the many variations (scenarios) that may be encountered in actual use. These tests are largely manual in nature, because they involve users and testers using the system in actual or simulated deployment and usage scenarios.

In quadrant 4, we find *system qualities tests*, which are used to determine whether the system meets its nonfunctional requirements. Such tests are typically supported by a class of testing tools, such as load and performance testing tools, which are designed specifically for this purpose.

With this perspective, we have a way to think about the different types of testing we'll need to do to assure that a system performs as expected.

WHAT IS ACCEPTANCE TESTING?

The language around testing is as overloaded as any other domain in software development, so the words *acceptance testing* mean different things to different people. Indeed, there are two different uses of the term in the agile testing matrix. In Figure 10–1, quadrant 2, we see *functional* and *story and feature acceptance tests*, and in quadrant 3, we see *system-level acceptance tests*. In this chapter, we'll focus on two of these quadrants, Q2 and Q1. In Chapter 17, Nonfunctional Requirements, we'll revisit the testing process to look at testing practices that support the tests indicated in quadrants 3 and 4.

In quadrant 2, we find both feature and story acceptance tests, which are used to assure that features and stories, respectively, are *done*, as we illustrate in our model in Figure 10–2.

Story Acceptance Tests

The majority of the testing work done by agile teams is in the development, execution, and regression testing of story acceptance tests (SATs), so we will focus on those first. Story acceptance tests are functional tests intended to assure that the implementation of each new user story (or other story type) delivers the intended

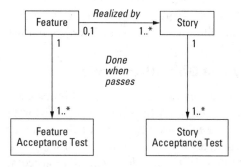

Figure 10–2 Features and stories cannot be considered done until they pass one or more acceptance tests.

behavior. If all the new stories work as intended, then each new increment of software is delivering value and provides assurances that the project is progressing in a way that will ultimately satisfy the needs of the users and business owners. Generally, the following is true.

- They are written in the language of the business domain (they are business-facing tests from quadrant 2).
- They are developed in a conversation between the developers, testers, and product owner.
- Although anyone can write tests, the product owner, as business owner/customer proxy, is the primary owner of the tests.
- They are black-box tests in that they verify only that the outputs of the system meet the conditions of satisfaction, without concern for how the result is achieved.
- They are implemented during the course of the iteration in which the story itself is implemented.

This means that new acceptance tests are developed for every new story. If a story does not pass its test, the teams get no credit for the story, and the story is carried over into the next iteration, where the code or the test, or both, are reworked until the test passes.

CHARACTERISTICS OF GOOD STORY ACCEPTANCE TESTS

If stories are the workhorse of agile development—the key proxy artifact that carries the value stream to the customer—then story acceptance tests are the workhorse of agile testing, so teams spend much time defining, refining, and negotiating the details of these tests. That's because, in the end, *it is the details of these tests that define the final, agreed-to behavior of the system.* Therefore, writing good story acceptance tests is a prime factor in delivering a quality system. Good story acceptance tests exhibit the characteristics described in the following sections.

They Test Good User Stories

An attribute of a good SAT is that it is associated with a good user story. In Chapter 6, we described the INVEST model for user stories and the quality of our acceptance tests are fully dependent on the native quality of the story itself. In particular, the user story to which a test is associated has to be independent, small, and testable. If the development of an acceptance test illustrates that the story is otherwise, then the story itself must be refactored until it meets these criteria. To get a good acceptance test, we may need to refactor the story first. For example, the following:

> As a consumer, I am always aware of my current energy costs.

becomes this:

> As a consumer, I always see current energy pricing reflected on my portal and on-premise devices so that I know that my energy usage costs are accurate and reflect any utility pricing changes.

They Are Relatively Unambiguous and Test All the Scenarios

Since the story itself is a lightweight (even potentially throwaway) expression of intent, the acceptance test carries the detailed requirements for the story, now and into the future. As such, there can be little ambiguity about the details in the story acceptance test. In addition, the acceptance test must test all the scenarios implied by the story. Otherwise, the team won't know when the story is sufficiently complete in order to be able to be presented to the product owner for acceptance. Here's an example:

Story:

> As a consumer, I always see current energy pricing reflected on my portal and on-premise devices so that I know that my energy usage costs are accurate and reflect any utility pricing changes.

Acceptance test:

1. Verify the current pricing is always used and the calculated numbers are displayed correctly on the portal and each on-premise device (see attachment for formats).

2. Verify the pricing and the calculated numbers are updated correctly when the price changes.

3. Verify the "current price" field itself is updated according to the scheduled time.

4. Verify the info/error messages when there is a fault in the pricing (see approved error messages attached).

They Persist

One of the mysteries about agile, and indeed a key impediment to adoption, is a commonsense question: "If developers don't document much and there are no software requirements specifications as such, how are we supposed to keep track of what the system actually does? After all, we are the ones responsible for assuring that it actually works, now and in the future. Isn't that something we have to know, not just once, but in perpetuity?"

The answer is yes, indeed, we do have to know how it works, and we have to routinely regression test it to make sure it continues to work. We do that primarily by persisting and automating (wherever possible) acceptance tests and unit tests (discussed later).

User stories can be safely thrown away after implementation. That keeps them lightweight, keeps them team friendly, and fosters negotiation, but acceptance tests persist for the life of the application. We have to know that the current price field didn't just get updated once when we tested it but that it gets updated every time the price changes, even when the application itself has been modified.

ACCEPTANCE TEST-DRIVEN DEVELOPMENT

Beck [2003] and others have defined a set of XP practices for agility described under the umbrella label of test-driven development (TDD). In TDD, the focus is on writing the unit test before writing the code. For many, TDD is an assumed part of agile development and is straightforward in principle.

1. Write the test first. Writing the test first forces the developer to understand the required behavior of the new code.
2. Run the test, and watch it fail. Because there is as yet no code to be tested, this may seem silly initially, but this accomplishes two useful objectives: it tests the test itself and any test harnesses that hold the test in place, and it illustrates how the system will fail if the code is incorrect.
3. Write the minimum amount of code that is necessary to pass the test. If the test fails, rework the code or the test as necessary until a module is created that routinely passes the test.

In XP, this practice was primarily designed to operate in the context of unit tests, which are developer-written tests (also code) that test the classes and methods that are used. These are a form of "white-box testing" because they test the internals of the system and the various code paths that may be executed.

However, the philosophy of TDD applies equally well to story acceptance testing as it does to unit testing. This is called *acceptance test-driven development*, and whether it is adopted formally or informally, many teams write the story acceptance test first, before developing the code. The acceptance tests serve to record the decisions made in the conversation (card, conversation, confirmation) so that the team understands the specifics of the behavior the card represents. The code follows logically thereafter.

Proponents argue (correctly, we believe) that writing the acceptance test first is lean thinking that reduces waste and substantially increases the productivity of the team. This was illustrated best in the simple equation that Amir Kolsky, of NetObjectives, showed on a whiteboard. As shown in Figure 10–3, Amir wrote this:[3]

If R_t is 0, of course, then there is no savings. However, we all know that R_t isn't always zero, and since finalizing the test finalizes our understanding of the required behavior, why not write the test first, just to be sure?

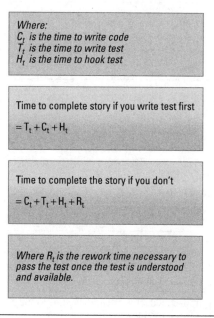

Where:
C_t *is the time to write code*
T_t *is the time to write test*
H_t *is the time to hook test*

Time to complete story if you write test first

$= T_t + C_t + H_t$

Time to complete the story if you don't

$= C_t + T_t + H_t + R_t$

Where R_t is the rework time necessary to pass the test once the test is understood and available.

Figure 10–3   The simple math behind acceptance test-driven development

---

3. Personal interaction between Kolsky and Leffingwell

ACCEPTANCE TEST TEMPLATE

At each iteration boundary or whenever a story is to be implemented, it comes as no surprise to the team that they need to create an acceptance test that further refines the details of a new story and defines the conditions of satisfaction that will tell the team when the story is ready for acceptance by the product owner. In addition, in the context of a team and a current iteration, the domain of the story is pretty well-established, and certain patterns of activities result, which can guide the team to the work necessary to get the story accepted into the baseline.

To assist in this process, it can be convenient to the team to have a checklist—a simple list of things to consider—to fill out, review, and discuss each time a new story appears. Crispin and Gregory [2009] provide an example of such a story acceptance testing checklist in their book. Based on our experience using this checklist, we provide an example from the case study in Table 10–1.

Table 10–1   An Acceptance Testing Example from the Case Study

Story	
Story ID: US123	As a consumer, I always see current energy pricing reflected on my portal and on-premise devices so that I know that my energy usage costs are accurate and reflect any utility pricing changes.

Conditions of Satisfaction
1. Verify the current pricing is always used and the calculated numbers are displayed correctly on the portal and other on-premise devices (see attachment for formats).
2. Verify the pricing and the calculated numbers are updated correctly when the price changes.
3. Verify the "current price" field itself is updated according the scheduled time.
4. Verify the info/error messages when there is a fault in the pricing (see approved error messages attached).

Modules Impacted	
Pricing RESTlet API	Impact: Amend protocol to allow pricing data.
In-home display	Impact: Refactor pricing schedule to support pricing programs to display on the in-home display.
Portal	Impact: Refactor pricing schedule to support pricing programs to display on the portal.

Documents Impacted	
User guide	Impact: Add new section on pricing.
Online help	Impact: Update online help to reflect pricing programs.
Release notes	Impact: Document defects in release notes.
Utility guide	Impact: Document pricing schedule changes.

Test Case Outline	

Test ID:
☒ **Manual**
☐ Automatic
	Outline:
	1. Check pricing: When there is no pricing info for a user:
	2. Change of pricing:
	   • When there is a pricing change in all allowed ways.
	   • Effective in the future.
	   • Effective in the past before the current pricing.
	   • Effective in the past but later than the current pricing.
	3. Our current release does not support pricing change in the middle of a billing cycle.
	4. Check the dashboard billing period consumption and the current bill to date.

Communications		
Internal	Involved parties: marketing, sales, product management.	Message: This is a new marketable feature.
External	Involved parties: utilities.	Message: This is a new feature to support new programs.

Since each team is in a different context, their templates will differ, but the simple act of creating a template as a reminder of all the things to think about benefits the team and increases the velocity with which they can further elaborate and acceptance test a new story.

AUTOMATED ACCEPTANCE TESTING

Because acceptance tests run at a level above the code, there are a variety of approaches to executing these tests, including manual tests. However, manual tests pile up very quickly (the faster you go, the faster they grow), and eventually, the number of manual tests required to run a regression slows down the team and introduces delays in the value stream.

To avoid this problem, most teams know that they have to automate most of their acceptance tests. They use a variety of tools to do so, including database-driven tests, Web UI testing tools, and automated tools for record and playback.[4] However, many agile teams have discovered that some of these methods are labor-intensive and can be somewhat brittle and difficult to maintain because they often couple so tightly to the specific implementation.

A better approach is to take a higher level of abstraction that works directly against the business logic of the application and one that is not encumbered by the presentation layer or other implementation details.

Automated Acceptance Testing Example: The FIT Approach

One such method is the Framework for Integrated Tests (FIT) method created by Ward Cunningham [Mugridge and Cunningham 2005]. This open source framework was designed to help with the automation of acceptance testing in a fast-moving agile context.

The FIT approach mirrors the unit testing approach in that the tests are created and run against the system under test, but they are not part of the system itself. FIT is a scriptable framework that supports tests being written in table form (any text tool will work) and saved for input as HTML. Therefore, these tests can be constructed in the business language (input and expected results) and can be written by developers, product owners, testers, or anyone on the team capable of building the necessary scripts.

Another open source component, FitNesse, is a wiki/web-based front end for creating text tables for FIT that also provides some test management capability. FIT uses data-driven tables for individual tests, coupled with fixtures or methods written by the developers to drive the system under test, as Figure 10–4 illustrates.

During the course of each iteration, new acceptance tests are developed and validated for each new story in the iteration, and these tests are then added to the regression test suite. These suites of acceptance tests can be run automatically against the system under test at any time to assure that the build is not broken by the new code.

---

4. Many agilists consider the record and playback model obsolete. Elizabeth Hendrickson notes three key reasons why traditional record and playback test automation solutions are not agile: "(1) The test-last workflow encouraged by such tools is all wrong for agile teams. (2) The unmaintainable scripts created with such tools become an impediment to change. (3) Such specialized tools create a need for Test Automation Specialists and thus foster silos." *www.infoq.com/news/2008/05/testobsessed-agile-auto-testing*

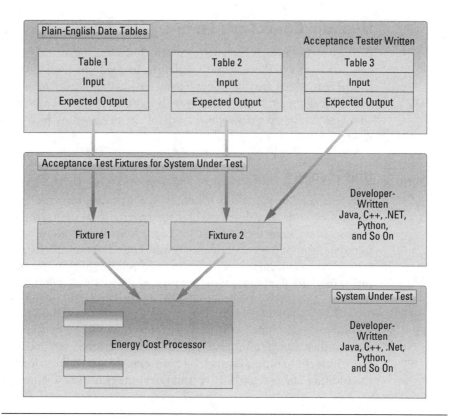

Figure 10–4   Acceptance test framework for the costing processor

As with unit tests, the FIT approach requires continuous involvement by the developers in establishing the acceptance test strategy and then writing the fixtures to support the test, illustrating yet again that the define/build/test team is the necessary structure for effective agile development. As always, the team's goal is to develop and automate tests within the course of the iteration in which the new functionality is introduced.

In some application domains, FIT does not provide an appropriately configurable framework. Sometimes, teams must build custom frameworks that mirror this approach but work in the technologies of their implementation.

In any case, whatever can't be automated eventually slows the team down, so continuous investments in testing automation infrastructure are routine items on a team's backlog, and like any other backlog item, they must be appropriately prioritized by the product owner to achieve sustainable high velocity.

UNIT AND COMPONENT TESTING

Before we leave this chapter, we must drill down one more level into testing and discuss quadrant 1 in the agile testing picture. In quadrant 1, we see *unit tests* and *component tests*, which are technology-facing tests as they are implemented and executed by the development team. Together with feature and story acceptance tests, they also complete the *support development* side of the agile testing picture, as Figure 10–5 illustrates.

Unit Testing

Unit testing is the white-box testing whereby developers write test code to test the production code they developed for the system. In so doing, the understanding of the user story is further refined, and additional details about a user story can be found in the unit tests that accompany the code. For example, the presentation syntax and range of legal values for *current price field* can likely be found in the unit tests, rather than the acceptance tests, because otherwise the acceptance tests are long, are unwieldy, and cause attention to the wrong level of detail.

A comprehensive unit test strategy prevents QA and test personnel from spending most of their time finding and reporting on code-level bugs and allows the team to move its focus to more system-level testing challenges. Indeed, for many agile teams, the addition of a comprehensive unit test strategy is a key pivot point in their move

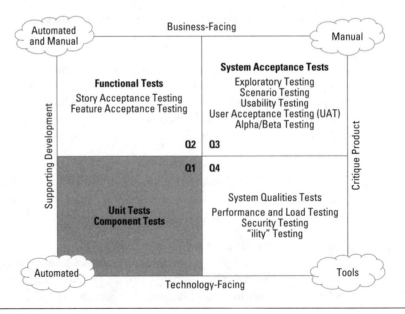

Figure 10–5   Unit testing in quadrant 1

toward true agility—and one that delivers the "best bang for the buck" in determining overall system quality.

The history of agile unit testing closely follows the development of XP, because XP's test-first practices drove developers to create low-level tests for their code prior to, or concurrent with, the development of the code itself. The open source community has built unit testing frameworks to cover most forms of testing, including Java, C, C++, XML, HTTP, and Python, so there are unit testing frameworks for most languages and coding constructs an agile developer is likely to encounter.

These frameworks provide a harness for the development and maintenance of unit tests and for automatically executing unit tests against the system under development. Unit testing the energy cost calculator might be a matter of writing unit tests against every object in the component, as Figure 10–6 illustrates.

The unit tests themselves are not part of the system under test and therefore do not affect the performance of the system at runtime.

Unit Testing in the Course of the Iteration

Because the unit tests are written before or concurrently with the code and because the unit testing frameworks include test execution automation, all unit testing can be accomplished within the iteration. Moreover, the unit test frameworks hold and manage the accumulated unit tests, so regression testing automation for unit tests is largely free for the team. Unit testing is a cornerstone practice of software agility, and any investments a team makes toward more comprehensive unit testing will be well rewarded in quality and productivity.

Figure 10–7 shows an example of a unit test for Tendril's energy costing module that takes the consumer's time-based pricing structure and runs a small sample that will exercise many of the costing module's pathways. This test ensures that the costing

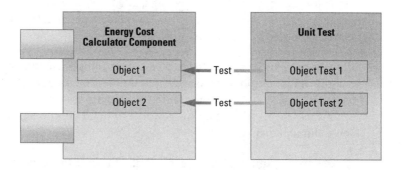

Figure 10–6   Unit testing the energy cost calculator

```
@Test
public void testDailyCost_MultiplePrices() {
    List<ConsumptionValue> consumptionValues = new ArrayList<ConsumptionValue>();
    consumptionValues.add(new ConsumptionValue(TUESDAY_NOON, new Double(100)));
    consumptionValues.add(new ConsumptionValue(THURSDAY_NOON, new Double(200)));

    List<TemporalPrice> prices = new ArrayList<TemporalPrice>();
    prices.add(new TemporalPrice(new BigDecimal(".10"), SUNDAY, FIXED_PRICE));
    prices.add(new TemporalPrice(new BigDecimal(".25"), WEDNESDAY_NOON, FIXED_PRICE));

    DailyConsumptionHistory dailyConsumptionHistory =
        new DailyConsumptionHistory(new DayRange(SUNDAY, 7), consumptionValues, prices);

    DailyCost dailyCost = dailyConsumptionHistory.getDailyCost(new Day(WEDNESDAY_NOON));
    assertNotNull(dailyCost);

    /* First half of Wednesday is .10 / kWh, second half is .25 / kWh */
    /* 50 kWh burned that day = 25 * .10 + 25 * .25 = 2.50 + 6.25 = 8.75 */
    assertEquals(new BigDecimal("8.75"), dailyCost.getCost());
}
```

Figure 10–7   A sample unit test from the case study

Thanks to Ben Hoyt of Tendril for this example.

algorithm effectively accommodates price changes that may occur at times other than standard day boundaries. Note that many more unit tests will be required before the costing module can be considered *done*. This is just one of many unit tests using the JUnit testing platform. This unit test example is one of many associated with calculating current costing, but it is automated and is an integral part of the regression testing package. The sample shows another useful feature in that there are comments embedded in the test to explain what the test results are supposed to be.

Component Testing

In a like manner, component testing is used to test larger-scale components of the system. Many of these are present in various architectural layers, where they provide services needed by features or other components.

Testing tools and practices for implementing component tests vary according to the nature of the component. For example, unit testing frameworks can hold arbitrarily complex tests written in the framework language (Java, C, and so on), so many teams use their unit testing frameworks to build component tests. They may not even think of them differently.

Acceptance testing frameworks, especially those at the level of *http Unit* and *XML Unit*, are also employed. In other cases, developers may use testing tools or write fully custom tests in any language or environment that is most productive for them.

SUMMARY

In this chapter, we described acceptance testing as an integral part of agile requirements management. If a requirement (feature or story) is not tested, unless it's simply work in process, which we indeed try to minimize, it doesn't really have any value to the team or to the user. With this discussion, we described the agile testing approach to assure that each new story works as intended, as it is implemented. This covers quadrant 2, functional testing of the agile testing matrix.

We also described the testing necessary to assure systematic quality from the perspective of quadrant 1, unit and component tests. Unit tests are the lowest level of tests written by the developer to assure that the actual code (methods, classes, and functions) works as intended. Component tests are higher-level tests that are written by the team to assure that the larger components of the system, which aggregate functionality along architectural boundaries, also work as intended. We also described how the team must endeavor to automate all the testing that is possible or else they will simply build a pile of manual regression tests that will eventually decrease velocity and slow down value delivery.

In Chapter 17, Nonfunctional Requirements, we'll describe acceptance testing practices associated with quadrant 4—system qualities tests.

Chapter 11

ROLE OF THE PRODUCT OWNER

What's in a name? That which we call a rose, by any other name would smell as sweet.

—Shakespeare, *Romeo and Juliet*, Act 2, scene 2

IS THIS A NEW ROLE?

In Chapter 1, we described the evolution of agile methods over the past decade or so, noting that when it comes to market share at least, the market is currently dominated by Scrum, followed by a Scrum/XP hybrid, then XP, then custom methods, then agile unified process, and so on. We are also seeing a growing influence of lean-agile hybrids and lean-kanban (and Scrum+Kanban) implementations. So, while the market is maturing, agile methods continue to flourish. That has both positives (advancing practices, new methods, increasing scale) and negatives (differing practices hinder standardized adoption) for the industry.

In all these methods, as well as in traditional requirements practices, it has always been clear that *someone*, or some small *group of someones*, must have a definitive say as to what the relative priorities for the solution requirements are. This focuses the team on the highest-value work and minimizes thrashing, wherein team members receive conflicting inputs from multiple sources.[1] In that case, they can't possibly satisfy all the stakeholders, so frustration and dissatisfaction are the likely outcomes.

In Scrum, the responsibility for these activities falls on the role of the *product owner*, and these responsibilities are well articulated in Scrum trainings. However, we also recognize there are various other titles ascribed to this role. For example, it has been called a *product champion* [Leffingwell and Widrig 2000, 2003, Shalloway 2010]. In XP, the role is the responsibility of the *on-site customer*. In IT shops, it's typically the *business analyst* who has those responsibilities.

The product owner title and responsibilities, as largely defined by Scrum, are emerging as the default standard for the role and function in many agile implementations.

---

1. In one pre-agile implementation, we asked a developer where they got their input for what to do. The answer was, the project manager, tech lead, system architect, engineering manager, product manager, and program manager. Six sources, one developer. What's wrong with this picture?

This is a healthy trend because it simplifies agile adoption. Also, the availability of specialty training for that role improves the team's skills in prioritizing and elaborating requirements. In turn, this empowers teams to take stronger control of their destiny and ultimately increases the velocity of the team by accelerating local decision making. However, as agile scales to larger programs and to the enterprise, there are some challenges with the role as defined in Scrum, and some modifications are typically necessary.

PERSPECTIVES ON DUAL ROLES OF PRODUCT OWNER AND PRODUCT MANAGER

As we described, the Scrum product owner is responsible for the following:

> Representing the interests of everyone with a stake in the resulting project...achieves initial and ongoing funding by creating the initial requirements, return on investment objectives and release plans [Schwaber 2007].

But the product owner's responsibilities don't end with the previous broad statement. At the same time, the product owner is a resident of the ideal Scrum team, as Figure 11–1 illustrates.

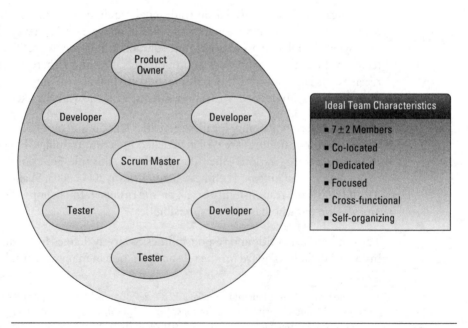

Figure 11–1   An ideal Scrum team

As shown in the figure and as it follows in support of Agile Manifesto principle #4 (*Businesspeople and developers must work together daily throughout the project*),[2] the product owner is ideally co-located with the team and participates *daily* with the team and its activities.

We also note the "7 ± 2 members" recommendation for the ideal team. Having experimented with larger teams, mostly unsuccessfully, we support this recommendation as well. Further, the Scrum product owner has additional tactical activities:

- Setting objectives for the sprint (or iteration)
- Prioritizing and maintaining the backlog
- Participating in the sprint planning meeting
- Elaborating stories on a just-in-time basis with the team
- Accepting stories into the baseline
- Accepting the sprint
- Driving release planning

In summary, there are two primary sets of responsibilities that can be implied from the previous.

- *Responsibility set #1:* The product owner sets the Vision and product objectives, manages the ROI, defines pricing and licensing policies (which can impact the implementation), and works with marketing to position the product in the marketplace.
- *Responsibility set #2:* The product owner is a member of the team and works daily with developers and testers to elaborate stories and help the team meet its objectives.

Given these responsibilities, when Scrum is introduced into a larger enterprise context, there often occurs a *role and paradigm mismatch* between the Scrum teachings and the existing organization's structure. Specifically, the enterprise is certain to already employ product managers or business analysts who have the requisite skills, training, and existing responsibilities for responsibility #1.

- They work directly with customers; their responsibilities include product definition, and their reward system may contain an ROI element.
- They are trained professionals.[3] They have experience in the broader domain of defining and launching successful products.
- They have extensive domain and marketing knowledge.
- They have influence and authority over what gets built and why.

---

2. Agile Manifesto, *http://agilemanifesto.org*
3. See, for example, the Pragmatic Marketing Institute: *www.pragmaticmarketing.com.*

This can create a significant conflict with a Scrum rollout, a conundrum that is now being addressed by both sides.

- *From the Scrum community:* As Scrum advances into enterprise settings, the Scrum community is expanding its view of Scrum to include more of the outbound nature of the role, including market research, defining pricing and licensing policies, and so on. This can be seen in books such as Pichler's *Agile Product Management with Scrum* [2010] and the newer Scrum Certified Product Owner courses. There, we are also seeing the introduction of a new Scrum *product owner hierarchy*, including the newly invented roles of *product line owner* and *chief product owner*.
- *From the professional software product management community:* To those in the independent software vendor (ISV) product management and product marketing community, this looks like a new version of "barbarians at the gate," whereby the development community is attempting to extend their control into areas where they lack competence, background, and training. To them, Scrum is a process, built by developers for developers. Who says that these processes and new roles will now be used to drive product definition and policy? In one pointed article, for example, Rich Mironov says this:[4]

Product Managers are responsible for the overall market success of their products, not just delivery of software. In the agile world, a new title is emerging—the Product Owner—which covers a small subset of the Product Management role. While this makes sense for internal IT groups that have traditionally gone without Product Management....agile product companies need full-fledged Product Managers to drive strategic activities and manage organizational/external participation.

Given this dichotomy, the enterprise appears to have two choices: Option #1 is that product management will pick up the additional, tactical responsibilities of the Scrum product owner, and option #2 is that individuals from the development teams will be trained to become product owners and assume ROI and product definition of responsibilities. Experience has shown that neither of these is options particularly effective.

- *Option #1:* When product managers assume the roles of product owners, there are many issues.

    - It doesn't scale. There may be a significant number of agile teams that now require this intense, daily tactical support. There are typically not

---

4. *www.enthiosys.com/insights-tools/pm-prod-owner/*

nearly enough product managers to go around.[5] And they were quite busy *before* agile came to their enterprise. Current Scrum guidance is "one team-one product owner" [Cohn 2010], so where would all these new product owners come from?

- Even if you had enough product managers to fill the roles, they may be ill-suited, ill-inclined, and downright uninterested in these increasingly technical and development team-bound responsibilities. For those with a thicker skin, see the footnote from the Cranky Product Manager blog (but remember, we did say "cranky").[6]
- Product managers often have insufficient technical depth and interest to add significant value to the team's highly technical language, activities, and responsibilities.

In summary, option #1 doesn't always work, so let's try option #2.

- *Option #2:* Newly provisioned team-based product owners assume some of the responsibilities of the product managers. Again, there are issues.

  - There is now an overlapping set of responsibilities, including the most important one, "Who decides what the product is supposed to do?" What a fun place to foster more conflict in the enterprise!
  - Team-based product owners are unlikely to be trained or skilled in the other aspects of the traditional product manager role. What makes us think they would be very good at it? If they wanted to live with marketing and customers, wouldn't they already be in another role?

- *Option #3:* Fortunately, there is another choice: dual agile roles. Many enterprises take a more refined approach, one that supports *dual roles* of agile product manager *and* agile product owner, as Figure 11–2 illustrates.

---

5. In one project, prior to agile, there were six product managers supporting approximately 250 developers, which became about 30 agile teams. That didn't work very well to begin with. Then, when one of the most talented product managers went on maternity leave, *it didn't work at all.*

6. "[Some] argue that in Scrum the product manager is the same as the Product Owner, and therefore the Cranky Product Manager needs to be constantly available to the team in order to make on-the-spot decisions within minutes of the asking. Ergo, you demand the Cranky Product Manager sit in that sticky-note-encrusted, windowless tomb with you all…day. Uh, no way. Not gonna happen. Why not? Because the Cranky Product Manager needs to be the Voice of the Customer and the Voice of the Market. How is she to do that without actually VISITING some customers and prospects? And VISITING means that she actually needs to leave the office, hop on airplanes, and fly far, far away." *http://crankypm.com/category/agile-scrum/*

Figure 11–2   Dual roles of product owner and product manager

- The *market/customer-facing* product managers continue in their role along with most of their existing responsibilities, but they also evolve a far more agile set of practices, including *taking on a tighter relationship with the development teams.*
- The *solution/product/technology-facing* product owner role is assumed either by the more technically inclined product managers or business analysts or by development team members who are interested in that new role; they assume the agile team product owner responsibilities but also *take on a tighter relationship with product management.*

We strongly advocate option #3. We believe that this puts the right people in the right roles—team-based product owners who work their wonders with the technology; market-based product managers who work their wonders in the market—and it does so with minimum disruption to the enterprise's existing organization.

The Name Game: Experimenting with the Product Owner Role/Title

Given this bit of confusion, the loaded role/title and implied responsibilities of a new "product owner" can portend a small crisis in the prospective agile enterprise adopting Scrum. One way to address this problem is by changing the title of the person assuming the role. For example, the product owner role may be assumed by the existing role and title of the *business systems analyst.* Or, the historical title of *requirements analyst* may be assigned to the role. In another case, a new title/role of *requirements architect* was invented, primarily to avoid conflict with existing titles role and responsibilities. In still other cases, a small product owner *team* may be created.

Of course, none of these fits every context perfectly, and changing the title of the product owner role is probably more trouble than it's worth, since it isn't reflected in agile literature or trainings.

Table 11–1   Agile Product Manager and Product Owner Roles and Responsibilities

Agile Product Owner	Agile Product Manager
Product/technology-facing	Market/customer-facing
Co-located and reports into development/technology	Co-located and reports into marketing/business
Focuses on product and implementation technology	Focuses on market segments, portfolio, ROI
Owns the implementation	Owns the Vision and Roadmap
Drives the iterations	Drives the release

Our Conclusion: Apply the Dual Roles

Throughout this book, we'll operate under the "option #3, dual role" assumption, and we'll use the generic term *product owner* for the development team–based role and ascribe a subset of the Scrum product owner responsibilities to it.

We'll also use the generic, traditional role and title of *product manager* (you can substitute *business analyst* for IT shops), but we'll also describe how this traditional role has to assume a new set of responsibilities to enable the agile enterprise.

However, no matter the choice of labels, enterprises should assign the people they think will be most effective in fulfilling the responsibilities and call them whatever makes the most sense in their context.

Given our assumption, we suggest that Table 11–1 is a reasonable division of responsibilities for the dual roles to support the agile development.

In this fashion, the agile product manager assumes (or continues) most of the outbound and ROI responsibilities; the agile product owner assumes the product/technology/development team-facing responsibilities.

In this chapter, we'll describe the responsibilities and activities of our generic *product owner*. In Chapter 14, we'll do the same for the *product manager* role.

RESPONSIBILITIES OF THE PRODUCT OWNER IN THE ENTERPRISE

Within this context, the responsibilities of the product owner can be divided into five primary areas:

- Managing the backlog
- Performing just-in-time story elaboration

- Driving the iteration
- Co-planning the release
- Collaborating with product management

We'll describe each of these in the following sections.

Managing the Backlog

In Chapter 3, we described the team's (project) backlog as the primary organizing technique for all the to-do work. Because it is the primary artifact that helps the team control and prioritize their work, it's hard to overstate the value of this simple construct. Although the backlog primarily contains user stories, it also contains other work that the team needs to do to complete the current release as well as build architectural runway for future releases.

Building the Backlog

With input from the stakeholders (Chapter 7), the product owner has the primary responsibility to build, prune, and maintain the backlog. Since teams use the backlog to capture and manage all their work, any team member can put something in the backlog, so the resultant backlog is likely to include a number of different types of things.

- *User stories:* The primary content consists of the user stories that have been defined to deliver value. As such, the user story content constitutes the product definition, and it can be sourced a number of ways:

  - Teams work directly with stakeholders to understand solution requirements. Product owners and product managers use a variety of discovery techniques to determine these requirements; that is the subject of the next chapter.
  - User stories will be defined during release planning. Features are presented at release planning boundaries; teams decompose features into the various stories they will need so that the feature, in aggregate, can be implemented.

- *Defects:* Defects are generally obvious to the team; they may have found the defects themselves in their testing, or they may have been reported from support or from the customers. They are kept in the backlog so as to be prioritized with all the other work.
- *Refactors and technical debt:* The backlog will also typically contain a list of refactors (rework) items that need to be done to improve the quality, maintainability, and extensibility.
- *Infrastructure work:* The teams may also have responsibility for building the internal tooling and infrastructure they need for their agile development practices. Since this takes capacity, this work must also be visible in the backlog.

Prioritizing the Backlog

In general, the topic of prioritizing the backlog is a tricky one, because many nonquantitative and (many times, arguable) factors potentially enter into determining priorities. These can include the *user value* of a thing, the *penalty for not doing* the thing, the *risk of doing* the thing, the *cost of doing* the thing, and the *potential financial return* for doing the thing. When it comes to prioritizing the program-level *features* that drive the project teams and ultimately determine the overall fitness for use, we'll need a way to prioritize features based on economic value. We'll provide a method for doing so in Chapter 13.

However, in the context of a product owner facing a near-term iteration boundary, the problem of prioritizing stories for an iteration is less daunting. This is because there is current context to help in the decision making.

- The goals for the next iteration should be clear (from the release plan).
- The results of the last iteration are known.
- The backlog contains things that are roughly the same size (that is, small enough to fit a few of them into an iteration). Therefore, we don't have to prioritize huge things against small things (in other words, the size of the story doesn't really matter in this context).
- The scope of the prioritization problem is limited to just the next iteration; the team doesn't have to be right forever, just right enough for the next iteration.

In other words, the team has localized, current context in which to make priority decisions. The product owner can probably set these priorities fairly easily with knowledge of this context and a Vision of where the team needs to be a few iterations later.

For example, as is illustrated in Figure 11–3, we see a backlog that has defects at a high priority, user stories ranked on a relative basis, and then more defects, and so on, further down the priorities list.

All	Rank ▲	ID	Name	State	Plan Est P 43.18	Task Est H 55.0	To Do H 15.0	🐝	Project
⊞ ⊟		#		All ▼					All ▼
	0.001	DE2763	Unable to register IHD with new 3.5 stack against tree broadband	D P C A		0.0	0.0	0	EMS
	0.001	DE2760	No Price displayed on Backhaul IHD	D P C A	0.5	0.0	0.0	0	EMS
	0.001	DE2765	Cancel All on the DRLC Portal Manage Events page does not cancel any event	D P C A	0.25	0.0	0.0	0	EMS
	0.001	US3093	SW - Tunnel True-Up to IHD via Backhaul	D P C A	2.0	0.0	0.0	0	EMS
⊞	0.01	US2929	Backhaul consumer portal reflects device registration status	D P C A	6.0	10.0	0.0	0	EMS
	0.06	US2971	[SPIKE breakdown on BH] User turns on previously provisioned device - DR	D P C A	1.0	0.0	0.0	0	EMS
	0.07	US2972	SW - User views Price on PCT	D P C A	0.25	0.0	0.0	0	EMS

Figure 11–3   A prioritized iteration backlog

A Richer Scheme for Prioritizing the Backlog

However, when the situation is a little more complex and the decisions are not so obvious, we suggest a simple rating system that rates each backlog story on three factors.[7]

- *Independent user value:* This attribute rates the value of the story to the user, relative to other stories in the backlog. The product owner can usually just set this from domain knowledge.
- *Iteration/(time) value:* Another consideration is how the story will help the team meet its objectives for the current iteration. Also, because program commitments are dependent on individual teams meeting their iteration objectives and there are interdependencies among teams, this value is important both to the team and to the program.
- *Risk reduction:* The final factor is the value of the information that may be discovered—information that reduces risk in future development activities.

With this system, coming up with the total value (weighted priority) of a backlog item can be as simple as, for example, adding the values assigned to each of these factors, as Table 11–2 shows (the scale is 1 to 9).[8]

Table 11–2   Rated, unsorted, and sorted backlog items

Unsorted	Independent	Iteration	Risk Reduction	Weight
Story US17	6	4	2	12
Story US32	8	2	1	11
Spike 43	2	5	7	14
Defect DE311	6	2	1	9
Story US53	5	5	6	16
Sorted				
Story US53	5	5	6	16
Spike S43	2	5	7	14
Story US17	6	4	2	12
Story US32	8	2	1	11
Defect DE311	6	2	1	9

---

7. These are all elements of the "cost of delay," which we'll introduce more formally when we prioritize features in Chapter 13.
8. We used a simple sum, but each attribute can be weighted as well.

From the table, we can see that story US53, which was lowest on the ordinal list, became the highest-ranked story for the next iteration. Spike S43, which doesn't deliver much user value, was elevated to the second position, based on the high value the team placed on risk reduction.

Just-in-Time Story Elaboration

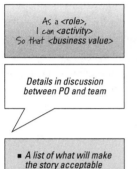

As a <role>,
I can <activity>
So that <business value>

Details in discussion
between PO and team

- A list of what will make
  the story acceptable
  to the product owner

In the context of an iteration timebox with a set of priorities and an iteration objective, developers and testers take their objectives seriously, and they do not like it when they fail to meet them. In practice, countless iteration retrospectives have surfaced this common feedback:

> We failed to deliver the stories that weren't understood before we committed.[9]

Therefore, once the priorities are clear, it's likely that some of the stories in the backlog are going to need additional work before the team is comfortable putting them in the iteration. In other words, it's time for the *conversation* and *confirmation* parts of our *card, conversation, and confirmation* metaphor.

From a timing perspective, there are three opportunities to do this.

- *Prior to the iteration:* These can often be discussed during a regular *feature preview meeting* (see Chapter 9) wherein the product owner discusses stories that are anticipated for upcoming iterations.
- *During the iteration planning meeting:* The team can take the time during planning to discuss the story itself and to understand the acceptance criteria. Some teams spend significant time in order to do this. If a team cannot be comfortable enough to commit to the story before the meeting is over, then there are two options: postpone the story and have the product owner take the action to clarify the story before the next iteration, or put in a spike to "figure out the story" in the current iteration so that the story can be implemented in a later iteration.
- *During the iteration:* Lastly, if the team is sufficiently confident that the story can be implemented within the iteration or if the story is a relatively lower priority, then the conversation can happen during the iteration. Of course,

---

9. We once had the experience of working with a proud and capable developer, new to agile, who took his personal commitments seriously. In one iteration, he wrote a detailed, *four-page narrative* of how an apparently simple story blew up on him to take most of an entire iteration. His point was, "I couldn't possibly have anticipated this; how am I supposed to estimate anything?"

at that point, the risk of not completing the story is material; however, that is often an acceptable case for teams that have good knowledge of the domain.

In any case, how the team addresses story maturity on a just-in-time basis depends on the risk of the particular story and how the team addresses risk, as shown in Figure 11–4.

You can see from this figure that the probability of completing a story is proportional to how well the story is understood by the team prior to including the story in an iteration commitment. However, the story can't be too well elaborated prior to meeting a likely iteration boundary, since the team can't be certain it will actually be implemented. Instead, it could be "trumped" by a higher-priority story, or the nature of the story itself may have evolved after it was elaborated, which creates waste. In this case, just-in-time is just agile common sense.

Driving the Iteration

In Chapter 9, we described the iteration itself at length. For context, the basic iteration pattern is repeated here in Figure 11–5.

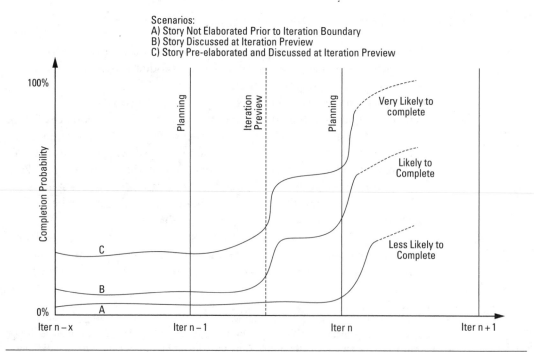

Figure 11–4   Probability of completion as a function of story maturity

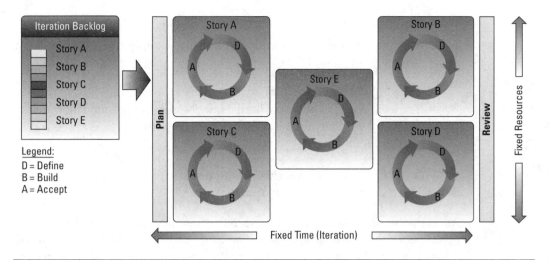

Figure 11–5   Basic iteration pattern

Since every iteration delivers some incremental value and value is in the eye of the beholder (in this case, the product owner), the product owner will be integrally involved in this process.

Preparation for Iteration Planning

The planning meeting is an important ceremony for the team. Given that the objective is to *agree on the content for the upcoming iteration*, some preparation is required.

- Further elaborate higher-priority stories as necessary.
- Prepare a draft objective.
- Coordinate any common objectives and dependencies with other product owners and product managers.
- Review and reprioritize the backlog. This includes stories that
  - Were already in the backlog
  - Failed acceptance in the prior iteration
  - Are generated from defects or bugs
- Consider necessary refactorings, defects, constraints, and dependencies.
- Understand the team's velocity for the upcoming iteration.

With this preparation in hand, the product owner is ready to participate in an intense, productive, and timeboxed planning meeting.

The Planning Meeting

The product owner begins the meeting by reviewing the objective for the iteration. Thereafter, the process is as follows.

- The product owner presents a backlog item for discussion.
- The team discusses each item until it is well enough understood for the development team to detail and estimate the engineering tasks necessary to implement the story.

As we described in the previous chapter, this process is repeated for each story on the backlog until the team runs out of capacity.

At that point, the team reviews the stories against the objectives and revises the objectives or the stories as necessary. Therefore, the final, agreed-to scope of the iteration is typically the result of some negotiation between the product owner and the development team.

Iteration Commitment

The result of the meeting is an iteration plan that contains the following:

- A committed iteration objective
- A prioritized list of stories with estimated tasks and owners

In any case, however, the product owner's primary role and goal is to *help position the development team for success in the iteration*. For if they fail, *they fail together*.

Executing the Iteration

Thereafter, the primary responsibility for successfully executing ("landing") the iteration lies with the development team. The team members deliver the stories to the code baseline in *priority* order.

1. *Define:* Elaborate the story and its acceptance test.
2. *Build:* Build the code and the test.
3. *Test:* Get the code to pass the test and ready for final acceptance.
4. *Accept:* As soon as a story is ready, it should be reviewed by the product owner. If accepted, the story is *done*. If not, the story definition, code, or acceptance test must be revised, and then the story is presented again.

▶ **NOTE**   Whenever possible, do this serially; otherwise, the entire acceptance process is deferred until the end of the iteration. The result is that the team may tend to "waterfall" the iteration, leaving all stories for acceptance on the last day, and nasty surprises are a likely result. Occasionally, however, there are stakeholders in addition to the product owner who may need to provide final acceptance of the story, so this is not always practical.

This cycle repeats until the end of the timebox, with an objective of getting all stories completed and accepted. During this time, the primary responsibility for completing all the stories rests with the development team members. As a member of the team, the product owner has a critical daily role as well.

- Work with developers and testers to elaborate each story.
- Re-scope where necessary to better meet the iteration objectives.
- Attend the daily stand-ups.
- Review stories that are ready for acceptance.
- Accept those stories that pass the acceptance criteria.

Iteration Review

At the end of the iteration, a demo of the working, integrated software is held for all interested stakeholders. The format is as follows:

- Presentation of each story by the responsible party
- Discussion and feedback with stakeholders

Based on stakeholder review and team feedback, the product owner may move the story to "accepted state" (if it wasn't already) or leave the story in the backlog if incomplete.

At the end of the review process, the product owner reviews the objectives of the iteration and decides whether to accept the iteration or not based on how well the team (inclusive of the product owner) did against the stated objectives.

Retrospective

The final activity is the retrospective, where the team takes the time to reflect on and assess the results and then adapts the development process accordingly. The product owner participates, just like every other team member.

A Product Owner's Iteration Calendar

Taken together, the activities and meeting commitments can fill up a product owner's daily diary pretty well, as Figure 11–6 indicates.

Iteration N – 1	Iteration N (Two Weeks)		
	Day 1	**Day 2–9**	**Day 10**
Prioritize and Elaborate the Backlog	Iteration Planning Commitment	Daily Stand-up Collaborate: Define and Accept Stories	Daily Stand-up Demo Retrospective

Day 6 Feature Preview

Figure 11–6   A product owner's typical schedule

The Problem of Technical Debt and the Value Stream

Agile is an empowering software development model, and it often creates a sense of excitement and reward for rapidly delivering value. However, this energy level—coupled with an "insane focus on value delivery"—can become problematic over time. This can happen when the team feels intense pressure to continually meet new value delivery commitments. In doing so, they may slip (or fail to improve) their quality engineering practices. This is the "tyranny of the urgent, iteration style." In the process, the team may accumulate *technical debt*, as illustrated in Figure 11–7.

For example, some new code may not have automated test coverage or adequate documentation. Perhaps it is more complex than it needs to be because the team couldn't afford the time to clean it up.

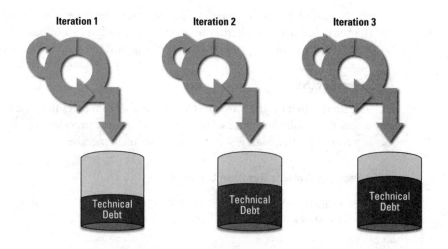

Figure 11–7   Accruing technical debt from iteration to iteration

Now, because it's inadequately documented and complex, it's going to be harder to maintain. It's also hard to refactor without introducing bugs because there aren't automated tests to determine whether the system still works as required. Systemically, the development process will become less lean as more time is spent on overhead, defects, and other forms of development waste.

Just like credit card debt, if you keep racking it up, it could eventually cause the project to default.[10] Because the team is now working slower, the team may be falling further and further behind. And if they are not able to finish everything by the end of the iteration, they rack up even more debt. Product owners see this as the team getting less done in each iteration than they were earlier, even though they may have had fewer people back then.

Paying Down the Debt

Reducing technical debt is similar to getting out of credit card debt and is psychologically just as hard. The first step is cut up the credit cards—*simply refuse to accrue any more technical debt from this time forward*. Instead, demo only things that meet the *real definition of done*, even if this means the team can't claim credit for everything they thought they would. This takes a certain degree of courage and is probably something to do right after a major release, rather than just in front of one.

What's a Product Owner to Do?

Since the product owner sets the priorities, they must be part of the solution. When a team pushes back on getting stories done "right," the product owner has to listen and adapt. After all, velocity may now be decreasing—so it is in the product owner's best interests to take corrective action and start allowing additional investment in defects, infrastructure, refactors, and so on.

When the team says "We could do it the fast way, or we could do it the right way," *listen*. Discuss what it means in terms of building more technical debt. Generally, a team should be able to devote *as much as 15%* of its ongoing capacity to work that accelerates future, rather than current, velocity.

Co-planning the Release

Of course, the iterations serve a larger purpose—frequent, reliable, and continuous *release* of value-added software to the customer or marketplace, as Figure 11–8 indicates.

---

10. Thanks to Pete Behrens for the credit card analogy.

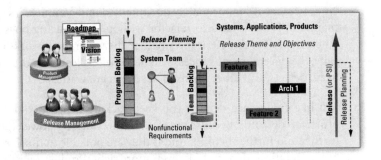

Figure 11–8   The objective is to "release"

As we will discuss in Chapter 16, *release planning* is the seminal enterprise event that regularly aligns the teams to a common Vision. The product owner must be well prepared for that event by

- Updating the team's local backlog
- Meeting with other product owners to understand overall system status
- Meeting with product managers to understand the Vision for the upcoming release
- Briefing the team on the upcoming release objectives

During the release planning event, the product owner will typically

- Help identify, prioritize, and estimate stories that will be necessary to achieve the release objectives
- Help design the release plan by laying the stories into iterations
- Participate in the team's discussion, impediment, and risk identification
- Identify and coordinate dependencies to ensure a cohesive solution
- Participate in refining the release objectives and making a commitment to the release

Once the release plan is committed, the product owner assumes the responsibility with the team to deliver on each iteration's objectives. If all teams meet their iteration objectives, then the release will go out on time.

FIVE ESSENTIAL ATTRIBUTES OF A GOOD PRODUCT OWNER

In this chapter, we've seen that the product owner, whether as applied in Scrum per se or as we have applied it more generically, is a key figure in our agile requirements process. While the ultimate velocity of the team depends on many factors, the ability for the team to quickly determine what the system is supposed to do hinges on this important role. Given that importance, we'll take a moment to characterize the key skills and attributes of someone who is likely to be successful in this role.[11]

- *Communication skills:* The product owner is the "glue" that binds the product management function and all the other project stakeholders to the development team. Doing so requires good communication skills because the product owner translates user and business objectives into the level of detail suitable for implementation. Moreover, the product owner will almost certainly be involved in customer demonstrations, sales support, and other outbound activities, so customer skills are beneficial.

- *Good business sense:* Agile's focus on value delivery also demands that product owners have working knowledge of the business domain. In this way, the product owner can better understand and define user stories that deliver real value to the end users and establish priorities and appropriate trade-offs for system functionality and performance. In addition, they have their own business's best interests at heart, and with this knowledge, they can make decisions that balance the customers' and business's needs.

- *Technical foundation:* Effective scope triage requires the constant evaluation of technical, functional, performance, and user-value trade-offs. In turn, this requires a degree of technical competence, because the foundation for effective decision making is an understanding of the technology. In addition, the ability to intelligently prioritize refactors, defects, and technical debt versus new value stories requires empathy and respect for the technical challenges the team faces.

- *Decisive:* At the pace of agile development, *no* decision (even if the decision is a clear "no decision for now") is worse than any other kind. The product owner must be able to make decisions, every day, in the presence of far-from-perfect knowledge. This requires empowerment, courage, and the ability to admit when one is wrong. This is agile after all—you'll get another whack at it if you need it.

- *Trustworthy:* Since the primary responsibility for prioritizing and managing the backlog (that is, what *will* and *will not* be done) falls to this role, the most essential attribute of the product owner is *trustworthiness*. The teams have to

---

11. In *Succeeding with Agile: Software Development Using Scrum* [Cohn 2010], Mike describes a similar set of five attributes as "ABCDE": available, business-savvy, communicative, decisive, and empowered. We've assumed *availability* and *empowerment* throughout, by virtue of the one product owner–one team design.

trust the product owner to make the hard calls on scope triage and to defend their interest in quality *and* functionality; the product managers have to *trust* the product owner to faithfully represent their feature priorities to the teams. The keys to building trust in this role include transparency, honesty, meeting commitments, and admitting when you are wrong.

COLLABORATION WITH PRODUCT MANAGERS

Although the release planning event is one structured and routine collaboration opportunity, enterprise agility is most effective when product owners have a far more closely coupled relationship with product management. To help address this problem, we often recommend that product owners "report on a fat dotted line" into the product management team, even if they are in the development line organization.

From a line-management perspective, product owners

- Are co-located with the team
- Share managers, incentives, and culture with development
- Should be rewarded based on how the team as a whole performs

But they are also honorary members of the product management organization. Here, they

- Receive overall product direction
- Attend most relevant PM meetings, functions, and planning sessions
- Receive input with respect to career growth and performance

In fact, product owners live in *two* teams—the development team and the extended product management team. Neither team is less or more important than the other. And for either to succeed, they must both succeed, so there can be little or no political infighting within the system. It's not an easy job.

Making this work fairly seamlessly creates its own set of challenges but is a worthy endeavor for the enterprise. Jennifer Fawcett notes this:[12]

> Creating the ultimate product team does not come without emotional challenges of adopting, coaching, and nurturing this high-performing team. Past processes, roles, and behaviors do not change overnight.

---

12. *www.agileproductowner.com*

PRODUCT OWNER BOTTLENECKS: PART-TIME PRODUCT OWNERS, PRODUCT OWNER PROXIES, PRODUCT OWNER TEAMS

The product owner is the linchpin to the timely flow of value, the overall productivity of the team, and the overall quality of the solution. If a story can't be elaborated, then implementation will be poor or delayed. If it is elaborated badly, then it will need to be reworked before it fulfills the real user need. If the product owner is unavailable, then stories can't be reviewed and accepted into the baseline.

In situation after situation, we've discovered a common, limiting factor, a root cause of agile development challenges: *insufficient depth and competence in the critical product owner role.*

Product Owner Proxies

In these situations, we often find a single product owner supporting as many as three to five teams, a line manager as a product owner proxy (and sometimes, unfortunately, telling people both *what* to do and *how* to do it), product managers flexing "down" to the technical details of the role (often doing a poor job because of interest, experience, or inclination, and sometimes failing in their other responsibilities at the same time), and a variety of other workarounds.

Product Owner Teams

In some organizations, the bottleneck is so severe or the decision-making process is so broken that a *product owner team* is formed. This can help, because it adds capacity, but it can hurt just as easily—decisions bounce from team member to team member, or individual developers get different answers from different members. As Schwaber and Beedle [2002] pointed out, "The product owner is one person, not a committee."

As an industry, I believe we have concluded that none of these ad hoc approaches work very well. So, as Cohn [2010] points out, our objective is clear:

> Each team needs exactly one product owner.

It's not that these other solutions don't work at all, and in some cases, they are necessary as an initial means to an end. But the interim results will be mixed at best, and the teams should evolve, with few exceptions, as quickly as possible to *one product owner per team.*[13]

---

13. In the case of smaller teams, teams of three to five total members, we have seen a single product owner support two, or even three teams, with some success.

SEEDING THE PRODUCT OWNER ROLE IN THE ENTERPRISE

Of course, the product owner role probably didn't exist prior to the agile rollout. But in the smaller project context, finding someone for the role is usually not too hard. Indeed, someone has probably already been playing the role, if not the title; management and the team will likely recognize them fairly quickly. Throw in some product owner training and coaching, and you should be well on your way.

However, in the larger organizations, finding and growing some number of individuals (5 or 10 or 20, even up to 100 in the largest cases) to assume this key, but previously underserved and undeclared, role is a significant challenge unto itself. Moreover, since the enterprise has probably grown into various silos, the solution requirements may have been historically "handed off" from product management to development, and there may be no natural interpreter on each team to gravitate to the role. But find them we must, because if the product owners aren't there, the requirements won't *flow*, and if the requirements don't flow, value delivery will suffer. It's not a trivial undertaking, so in the following sections, we'll describe how some real enterprises have handled it.

TradeStation Technologies

TradeStation is a premier brokerage-trading platform for rule-based securities trading. At TradeStation, Keith Black, John Bartleman, and their teams have been driving a comprehensive, all-in agile transformation that affects 100+ practitioners. John described their approach to filling the product owner role as follows:

> Before transitioning to agile, our product management team was made up of ten product managers who reported into development. When we transitioned to agile, seven of the ten product managers became full-time product owners; the other three now focus on the market-facing product manager role. This separation of labor and concerns has helped us bring additional focus to both the market and technical aspects of our solution.

John then comments on the staffing challenge:

> When staffing the product owner role, I would have preferred to use a few lead developers and/or testers, since they have the domain knowledge and technical expertise; however, we are reluctant to do this because of the impact on development resources. Therefore, we hired a few additional product owners from outside the company. These people need to be technical but also need to have good industry-specific experience, and that is a difficult combination to find. So far, former developers/tech leads with business sense and good project management skills seem to be the

best fit…in my view at least, technical skills are mandatory, and domain experience is a plus whenever I can get it.

CSG Systems

CSG Systems is a customer interaction management company that provides software and services-based solutions that help clients engage and transact with their customers. In 2007, CSG began transforming its ACPx product development (more than 100 practitioners) efforts using enterprise agility best practices. Mauricio Zamora noted that they established product owners through a series of phases:

> We first had to leverage a combination of product analysts originally responsible for waterfall requirements, architects originally responsible for designing our software, and a few product owners already experienced in agile execution. Over the course of a few releases, we used the really good product owners to set the standard for others. In the process, we discovered candidate product owners that weren't a good fit for the role, moved them to other slots, and replaced them with more appropriate internal resources and a few additional external hires.

Mauricio went on to note that the transformation wasn't easy, and it took time to help people see all that needed to change:

> We first educated everyone on the differences between the traditional product management, agile product owner, and architect roles. We had to convince management that the product owner role required dedicated focus. The visibility agile provides made the increasingly obvious gaps in product ownership easier to see and address. Finally, we had to revisit and revise organizational titles and compensation, because the new product owner role didn't map well into our existing organization.

Symbian Software Limited

When it comes to embedded systems and an even much larger enterprise scale, Symbian Software (now part of Nokia) develops and licenses Symbian OS, the market-leading open operating system for mobile phones. Symbian initiated an agile transformation in 2008 that affected thousands of practitioners. The development of a mobile phone operating system is a highly technical endeavor and one where the ultimate user (mobile device user) is fairly far removed from the major technologies (OS, device drivers, media players, and so on), which are the primary focus of the implementation. As such, the development process does not lend itself quite so easily to the traditional customer/user-facing agile product manager/product owner roles.

Mathew Balchin described their approach this way:

> We identified the product owner role as a pivotal role for success. We recruited them primarily from the ranks of engineering teams, and most are senior engineers with product or customer experience. We typically have a mapping of one PO to every 1–2 teams. We also identified the need for soft skills training in addition to the standard agile training.

Discount Tire

Discount Tire is America's largest independent tire dealer. Chris Chapman and his teams develop the internal software that keeps Discount Tire's corporate and store operations (more than 750 stores in 21 states) running. In 2008, they implemented an agile transformation that affected the entire information systems team. Chris noted how they addressed the product owner challenge:

> Our Business Systems Analysts in IT are filling the role of product owner. They are the liaison to the business and in many cases speak for the business. Their previous responsibility of documenting detailed business requirements and rules now falls to the entire team in the form of user stories and acceptance tests (which is still a major "cheese moving" event for us).

SUMMARY

In this chapter, we described the product owner, the individual who has the highest impact on the flow of value stream to and through an agile team. We described how, at least on the context of the larger program or enterprise, the role of the product owner, as originally defined by Scrum, is more likely to be shared between some number of product owners and product managers, whose activities and behaviors will also have to adapt to the new agile paradigm.

We described the responsibilities and activities of the product owner in driving the content and priorities of the iteration and the role they play there in helping the team build small increments of value in a timebox. We also described the problem of technical debt and the role the product owner can play in increasing *or* decreasing it.

Since it is such a critical role, we also described the essential attributes of an individual who can effectively fill the role and the part they play in building an effective product owner and product manager team. Finally, since the role is likely to be new to a team and enterprise, we provided some case studies of how a number of agile enterprises have found the right people they need to fill the role.

In so doing, we've elaborated on the "how" (the activities and role the product owner plays in the agile process) but not the "what" (the requirements content that the product owner feeds into the system). In the next chapter, Requirements Discovery Toolkit, we'll describe a set of tools that the product owner and team can use to discover the "what."

Chapter 12

REQUIREMENTS DISCOVERY TOOLKIT

WITH DON WIDRIG[1]

So, ummm, how many undiscovered ruins are there?

—Anonymous tourist, winner of the
"stupidest question asked by a tourist award,"
Mesa Verde, Colorado tour guides

In Chapter 6, we introduced the user story as the primary carrier of customer requirements through the value stream. Assuming your system is already in use and you have access to users, that may be all you need. If you don't know what the system needs to do next, you can always just ask them.

However, that simple explanation makes light of a significant challenge in software development, which is how teams should go about understanding—on a more systematic basis—what problems their solution is intended to address, what markets or types of customers it is intended to serve, and what the functional and nonfunctional requirements for such a system need to be. Agile or not, most teams face this challenge at one or more stages of a project's life cycle.

This is the challenge of *requirements discovery*, and it represents one of the most critical competences required in the industry. Get it right, and you can be a winner; get it wrong, and you won't be successful no matter how good your skills at writing user stories or coding and testing the implementation.

Given the variety of circumstances, markets, consumers, uses, products, systems, services, and so on, that many teams face, they will likely need a variety of tech-

---

1. Don Widrig was instrumental in reformulating and updating this chapter, in part from our earlier works [Leffingwell and Widrig 2000, 2003].

niques to discover requirements, each suited for one or more types, times, or aspects of the discovery process. And they'll need to be good at applying them, too.

In this chapter, we'll introduce techniques that teams can use to discover requirements. We'll describe a variety of techniques that teams can use for this purpose:

- Requirements workshops
- Brainstorming
- Interviews and questionnaires
- User experience mock-ups
- Product council
- Competitive analysis
- Customer change request systems
- Use-case modeling

Of course, there is no "one-size-fits-all" approach to this critical front-end challenge, and development teams will likely find that a combination of these techniques may be required for any particular circumstance. In the following sections, we'll describe each of these techniques so that a team can have them available in their *requirements discovery toolkit.*

THE REQUIREMENTS WORKSHOP

The requirements workshop is one such tool. Its purpose is to drive consensus on the requirements of the system or application and to gain rapid agreement on a course of action from the key stakeholders, in a very short time. Key stakeholders of the project are gathered together for a short, intensive period, typically no more than a day or two. The workshop may be facilitated by a product owner, product manager, team member, or outside facilitator.

A properly run requirements workshop has many benefits:

- It forges an agreement between the stakeholders, the product owners, and the development team as to what the application must do.
- It assists in building an effective team of these stakeholders, all committed to a common vision.
- All stakeholders get their say; no one is left out.
- It can expose and resolve political issues that may otherwise interfere with project success.

In the following sections, we'll provide some guidelines as to how to plan and run a successful requirements workshop.

Preparing for the Workshop

These sections lay out the steps to follow to prepare for the workshop.

Selling the Concept

First, it may be necessary to sell the concept by communicating the benefits of the workshop to prospective participants. This is typically not a difficult process, but surprisingly it's not unusual to encounter resistance: "We can't possibly get all these critical people together for one day." "You'll never get [name your favorite stakeholder] to attend." Don't be discouraged; if you hold it, they will come.

Ensuring the Participation of the Right Stakeholders

Second, preparation involves identifying the particular stakeholders who can contribute to the process and whose needs must be met in order to ensure a successful outcome. Although we described how to identify these key stakeholders in Chapter 7 (Stakeholders, User Personas, and User Experiences), now is the time for one last review to make sure that all critical stakeholders have been identified.

As we described, the team should consider the following.

- Who needs to be consulted on the scope of this project?
- Who has an input to the budget?
- Who can provide guidance on the functionality and required qualities (reliability, safety, lifetime, maintainability, and so on) of the new system?
- Who will use it?
- Who can support or harm this project politically?
- Who else could be impacted by the new system?

Attending to Logistics

Third, a conscientious approach to logistics is necessary. Logistics involve everything from reserving proper facilities to arranging travel to managing breaks and refreshments. Murphy's law—"Whatever can go wrong will go wrong"—should be your guideline, because the team may have only one chance to get it right. If you approach logistics with a high degree of professionalism, it will be obvious to the attendees that this is an important event, and they will act accordingly. You'll also have a more successful workshop.

Providing Warm-up Materials

Fourth, send warm-up materials in advance to prepare the attendees and to increase productivity of the actual session. These materials set each attendee's frame of mind and context for the session. We recommend that you provide two types of warm-up materials.

- *Project-specific information:* This might include lists of suggested features, results of interviews with prospective users, analysts' reports on trends in the industry, material from the product council (covered later in this chapter), new management directives, new marketing data, and so on. Although it's important not to bury the prospective attendees in data, it's also important to make sure they have context.
- *Out-of-the-box thinking information:* This can include thought-provoking and stimulating articles about the process of creativity, rules for brainstorming, requirements management, managing scope, and so on.

▶ **TIP**   Do not send the data out too far in advance. You don't want the attendees to read it and forget it, and you don't want an extended planning cycle to decrease the sense of urgency. Send the data out anywhere from two days to one week in advance.

Role of the Facilitator

You may want to have the workshop run by an outside facilitator, one who has experience with the unique challenges and charged atmosphere of the requirements scoping process. However, if this is not practical, the workshop could be facilitated by the product owner or other team member *if* that person has the following characteristics:

- Has solid consensus-building or team-building skills
- Is personable and respected by the internal and external team members
- Is strong enough to chair a challenging meeting

Generally, however, if the workshop is to be facilitated by a team member, that person should *not* contribute to the ideas and issues at the meeting. Otherwise, the workshop is in danger of losing the objectivity that is necessary to foster an open environment in which a new consensus can emerge. This can be especially challenging for a product owner, who, after all, is supposed to have strong opinions about what the system is supposed to do.

In any case, the facilitator plays a pivotal role in making the workshop a success. After all, the team has all the key stakeholders gathered together, perhaps for the first and last time on the project, and they cannot afford a misfire. Some of the responsibilities of the facilitator include the following:

- Establishing a professional and objective tone
- Starting and stopping the meeting on time
- Establishing and enforcing the meeting "rules"
- Introducing the goals and agenda
- Managing the meeting and keeping the team "on track"
- Facilitating decision and consensus making
- Managing any facilities and logistics issues to ensure that the focus remains on the agenda
- Making certain that all stakeholders participate and their input is heard
- Controlling disruptive or unproductive behavior

Setting the Agenda

The agenda for the workshop will be based on the length, the needs of the particular project, and the content that needs to be developed. However, we provide a sample starting agenda in Table 12–1.

Table 12–1   Sample Agenda for the Requirements Workshop

Time	Agenda Item	Description
8–8:30	Introduction	Review agenda, facilities, and rules.
8:30–10	Context	Present project status, market needs, results of user interviews, and so on.
10–12	Brainstorming	Brainstorm features of the application.
12–1	Lunch	(Some work though lunch to avoid loss of momentum. Other times a break is sorely needed.)
1–2	Brainstorming	Continue brainstorming.
2–3	Feature definition	Write two- or three-sentence definitions for features.
3–4	Idea reduction and prioritization	Consolidate and prioritize features.
4–5	Wrap-up	Summarize and assign action items; address "parking lot" items.

Running the Workshop

These decision-making workshops are often characterized by a highly charged atmosphere. In fact, there are reasons why it can be difficult to get consensus, including differing opinions and expectations for the solution requirements and the impact on resources and budgets; nearly all these reasons will be present at the workshop.

So, the setting may be politically charged, confrontational, or both. This is yet another reason for having a facilitator who is not a team member. Let the facilitator take the heat and manage the meeting so as to not exacerbate any problems—past, present, or future—among key stakeholders.

Brainstorming and Idea Reduction

The most important part of the workshop is the brainstorming process. This technique is ideally suited for the workshop setting. It fosters a creative and positive atmosphere and gets input from all stakeholders. We'll cover brainstorming below.

Production and Follow-Up

After the workshop, the facilitator records conclusions and distributes them after the meeting. Then the facilitator's job is over, and responsibility for success is again in the hands of the development team.

Typically, it's the product owner's job to follow up on any open action items that were recorded at the meeting. Often, the output of the meeting will be a simple list of ideas or suggested product features that can be turned over to the development team for user story development and implementation. In some cases, additional workshops with other stakeholders will be scheduled, or additional research or other efforts will be necessary to gain a better understanding of the ideas fostered at the workshop.

So far, we've primarily described the mechanics of the workshop, yet it is the creative part of the workshop that delivers the real value. There, new ideas are generated, and a clearer vision for the new project begins to emerge.

BRAINSTORMING

Whether you are in the workshop setting, whether you are in an informal setting with some team members or stakeholders, or indeed whenever you find yourself needing new ideas or creative solutions to problems, brainstorming is a simple, fun, and easy way to get stakeholders to contribute.

In the requirements workshop setting, you probably already have a pretty good idea of the features of the new product. After all, few projects begin with a totally clean slate. However, in addition to reviewing the suggested features for the product, the workshop provides the opportunity to solicit new input and to mutate and combine these new features with those already under consideration. This process will also help in the goal of "finding the undiscovered ruins" and thereby making sure that you have sufficient input and that all stakeholder needs are addressed, or at least understood. Typically, a major portion of the workshop is devoted to brainstorming new ideas and features for the application. Brainstorming does the following:

- Encourages participation by all parties present
- Allows participants to "piggyback" on one another's ideas
- Has high bandwidth—many ideas can be generated in a short period
- Identifies multiple potential solutions to whatever problem is posed
- Encourages out-of-the-box thinking—unlimited by the usual constraints

Brainstorming has two phases: idea generation and idea reduction. Idea generation identifies as many ideas as possible, focusing on breadth of ideas, not depth. The goal during idea reduction is to analyze and reduce the ideas generated. This includes pruning, organizing, ranking, expanding, grouping, refining, and so on.

Idea Generation

The first objective is the generation of as many ideas as possible in a short time frame. Typically, the facilitator first explains the rules for brainstorming, as illustrated in Figure 12–1.

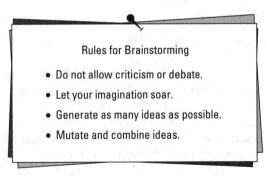

Rules for Brainstorming

- Do not allow criticism or debate.
- Let your imagination soar.
- Generate as many ideas as possible.
- Mutate and combine ideas.

Figure 12–1   Rules for brainstorming

The facilitator also explains the objective of the process. For example, the following questions may be used for this purpose.

- What features would you like to see in the product?
- What services should the product provide?
- What opportunities are we missing in the product or the market?

After stating the objective of the process, the facilitator asks participants to share their ideas aloud and to also write them down, one per card. Ideas are spoken out loud to enable others in the room to piggyback on the ideas, that is, to think of related ideas and to mutate and combine ideas. In this process, however, the first rule—no criticism or debate—must be foremost. If this rule is not enforced, the process will be squelched, and people who are sensitive to criticism may not feel comfortable putting forth more ideas.

▶ **TIP** In our experience, the most creative and innovative ideas (those that truly revolutionized the product concept) did not result from any one person's idea but, instead, from the combination of multiple and perhaps even seemingly unrelated ideas. Any process that fosters these types of breakthroughs in ideation is a worthy process.

When a person comes up with an idea, he or she writes also writes it down in order to assure the following:

- Ideas are not lost
- Ideas are captured in that person's own words
- Ideas can be posted for later piggybacking
- There are no stalls in the creative process that could be caused by a single scribe trying to capture all ideas

As ideas are generated, the facilitator collects them and posts them on a wall. Idea generation should proceed until all parties feel it has reached a natural end.

It is common for lulls to occur during idea generation. These are not necessarily times to stop the process. Lulls tend to correct themselves as soon as the next idea is generated. Longer lulls might be cause for the facilitator to state the objective again or to ask stimulating questions. Most idea generation sessions last around an hour, but some last two to three hours. The number of ideas generated will be a function of how fertile the subject being discussed is, but it is common to generate 50 to 100 ideas.

The process tends to have a natural end; at some point, the stakeholders will simply run out of ideas. This is typified by longer and longer gaps between idea submissions. At this point, the facilitator ends that portion of the session.

Idea Reduction

Of course, not all ideas are worthy of consideration for the solution. (If they were, the idea generation process was deficient; see the following tip). When the idea generation phase ends with a sufficiently large number of ideas, it is time to initiate idea reduction and to bring focus on a set of ideas that can drive the next increment of solution development. Several steps are involved in idea reduction.

Pruning Ideas

The first step is to "prune" those ideas that are not worthy of further investment by the group. The facilitator starts by visiting each idea briefly and asking for concurrence from the group that the idea is basically valid. There is no reason for any participant to be defensive or to claim authorship for any idea; any participant may support or refute any idea.

▶ **TIP**   The presence of ideas that can be easily pruned is an indicator of a quality process. The absence of a fair number of wild and crazy ideas indicates that the participants were not thinking far enough "out of the box."

The facilitator asks the participants whether each idea is worthy of further consideration and then removes an invalid idea, but if there is any disagreement among the participants, the idea stays on the list. If participants find two sheets with the same idea, group them together on the wall.

Grouping Ideas

It may be helpful during this process to start grouping similar ideas. Doing so is most effective when participants go to the wall and do the grouping themselves. Grouping might be as follows:

- New features
- Enhancements to current features
- Usability, user interface, and ease-of-use issues
- Reliability, performance, and supportability issues

Idea generation can be reinitiated now for any one of these groups if the participants think the grouping process has spurred development of new ideas or that some area of key functionality has been left out.

Defining Features

At this point, ideas can be converted to prospective feature descriptions by drafting a short description of what the idea means. This gives the contributor the opportunity to further describe the feature and helps ensure that the participants have a common understanding. This way, everyone understands what was meant by the idea, thus avoiding a fundamentally flawed prioritization. In this process, the facilitator walks through each idea that has not been pruned and asks the submitter to provide a one-sentence description.

Idea Prioritization

In some situations, the generation of ideas is the only goal, and the process is then complete. However, it is often useful to prioritize the remaining ideas. After all, no development team can do "everything that anybody can think of," and the key stakeholders are still present. A variety of techniques can be used for prioritization; we'll describe two.

Cumulative Voting: The $100 Test

This simple test is fun, fair, and easy to do. Each person is given $100 of "virtual idea money" to be spent on "purchasing ideas." Each participant decides how much money to spend on each idea. Then votes are tabulated, and the results are rank ordered. A quick histogram of the result can help participants see the visual impact of their decisions.

This process is straightforward and usually works quite well. However, there are a few caveats.

First, it may work only once, because once the results are known, participants may bias their input for the second vote.

Similarly, it may be necessary to limit the amount anyone spends on one feature. Otherwise, a participant, knowing that other important features will make the cut to the top of the list, might put all of their money on a single feature in order to elevate it to a higher priority.

"Critical, Important, Useful" Categorization

Another technique is prioritization by value category. Each participant is given a number of votes equal to the number of ideas, but each vote must be categorized "critical," "important," or "useful." The trick is that each stakeholder is given only one-third of the votes from each category.

- Critical features are mandatory; a system deployed without this feature could not fulfill its primary mission or meet the market need.
- Important means that failure to include the feature could cause a loss of customer utility, market share, or revenue.
- Useful means nice to have. Useful features make the system more appealing to use or deliver higher utility to some class of users.

After voting, each feature will probably have a mix of categories. Simply multiply "critical" votes times 9, "important" by 3, and "useful" by 1; then add up the score. This tends to spread the results to heavily favor the "critical" votes, and thus every stakeholder's "critical" need will tend to bubble toward the top.

Online Brainstorming

The process we described works effectively when all stakeholders can be gathered together at the same time, the participants are proactive, and the facilitator is experienced. Indeed, there is no substitute for the developers and outside stakeholders spending this time together.[2] Each will remember the various priorities, concerns, and issues raised by the others, and perspective and mutual respect are often by-products of the process. Therefore, the face-to-face requirements workshop and brainstorming are the preferred approaches.

However, sometimes face-to-face brainstorming is simply not possible. In these situations, an alternative is to facilitate the process in a collaborative online environment. This technique may be particularly suited for developing advanced applications for which research is required or a long-term view is critical, the concept is initially fuzzy, and a wide variety and significant number of user and other stakeholders inputs are involved.

With this technique, the product owner sponsors an online service for recording and commenting on product features. An advantage of this technique is its persistence; ideas and comments can be circulated over a long period of time, with full recording of all threads for each idea. Perhaps most importantly, ideas can grow and mature with the passage of time.

On the other hand, it may be the case that there is no time to contemplate the issues, and the team needs resolution now! In such cases, distributive, immediate collaboration is still possible through any number of online meeting/collaboration tools.

Summary of Requirements Workshop and Brainstorming

The goal of these techniques is to maximize the contribution of each team member in harmony with the objectives of the project and its mission. We are constantly impressed by the unique and creative talents our local and extended team members exhibit in these forums. We encourage your teams to try them.

INTERVIEWS AND QUESTIONNAIRES

Another requirements-gathering technique is the *user/stakeholder interview*, a simple and direct technique that can be used in virtually every situation. This section

---

2. Agile Manifesto principle # 6—*The most efficient and effective method of conveying information to and within a development team is face-to-face conversation.*

describes the interviewing process and provides a generic template for conducting interviews.

One of the key goals of interviewing is to make sure that the biases and predispositions of the interviewer do not interfere with a free exchange of information. This is a subtle and pernicious problem. Sociology (a class most of our developers missed) teaches us that it is *extremely difficult* to truly understand others because we are all biased by our own conceptual filter, one that results from our own environment and cumulative experiences.

In addition, as solution providers, we rarely find ourselves in a situation in which we have no idea what types of potential solutions would address the problem. Indeed, in most cases, we operate within a repetitive domain or context in which certain elements of the solution are, or at least appear to be, obvious. We may even be experts. ("We have solved this type of problem before, and we fully expect that our experience will apply in this new case.") Of course, this is not all bad because having context is part of what we get paid for. However, we must not let our current context interfere with a better understanding of a new problem to be solved.

Context-Free Questions

How do we avoid prejudicing the user's responses to our questions? We do so by asking questions about the nature of the user's problem without context for a potential solution. In a classical requirements text, *Exploring Requirements: Quality Before Design*, Gause and Weinberg [1989] introduced the concept of the "context-free question." Examples of such questions include the following.

- Who is the user?
- Who is the customer?
- Are their needs different?
- What other stakeholders will be impacted by this product or project?
- Where else can a solution to this problem be found?

These questions force us to listen before attempting to invent or describe a potential solution. Listening gives us a better understanding of the customer's problem and any problems behind the problem.

Solutions-Context Questions

After the context-free questions have been asked and answered, it may be appropriate to begin exploring solutions. After all, we are not generally rewarded for simply understanding the problem but rather for providing solutions. The solution context may also give the interviewee new insights. And, of course, our users depend on us to have context; otherwise, they would have to teach us everything they know about the subject.

As an aid to building this skill within the development team, we have combined these techniques into a "generic, almost context-free interview," a structured interview that can be used to elicit user or stakeholder requirements. Appendix A provides the template for this interview. The interview consists of both context-free and context-rich sections. It also provides questions designed to make certain that all aspects of requirements, including nonfunctional requirements, such as usability, reliability, supportability, and so on, are explored.

The Moment of Truth: The Interview

With a little preparation and the structured interview template, the product owner (or any other member of the team) can do an adequate job of interviewing a user or customer. Here are some tips for a successful interview.

- Prepare an appropriate context-free interview.
- Understand the background of the stakeholder to be interviewed.
- During the interview, jot down answers in your notebook (don't attempt to capture the data electronically at this time).
- Refer to the template during the interview to make certain you're asking the right questions and that you have covered all you intended.

Make sure that the script is not overly constraining. Once rapport has been established, the interview is likely to take on a life of its own. The customer may well launch into a stream-of-consciousness dialogue, describing in detail the horrors of the current situation. *This is exactly the behavior you are looking for.* If this happens, do not cut it off prematurely with another question; rather, write down everything as quickly as you can, letting the user exhaust that particular stream of thought. Ask follow-up questions about the information that has just been provided. Then, after this thread has run to its logical end, get back to other questions on the list.

After even a couple of such interviews, the product owner/developer/analyst will have gained some knowledge of the problem domain and will have an enhanced understanding of both the problem being solved and the user's insights on the characteristics of a successful solution.

Compiling the Needs Data

Your problem analysis will have identified the key stakeholders and users you will need to interview to gain an understanding of the stakeholder's needs. Typically, it does not take many interviews to get a convergent understanding of the issues.

The Analyst's Summary

The last section of the interview form in the appendix, the Analyst's Summary, is used for recording the three most important needs or problems uncovered in the interview. In many cases, after just a few interviews, these highest-priority needs will start to be repeated. This means you may be starting to get convergence on some common needs. This is the start of your feature backlog, a set of assets you will build and use to good advantage over the course of your project.

A Note on Questionnaires

We are sometimes asked whether the team can substitute a questionnaire for this interviewing process. In some cases, the need expressed is perhaps a simple desire for efficiency ("I could do 100 questionnaires in the time it takes to do one interview"). In other cases, the need may come under suspicion ("Do I really have to talk to these people? Couldn't I just send them a letter?").

No matter the motivation, the answer is generally no. Although questionnaires are often used and appear scientific because of the opportunity for statistical analysis, a questionnaire is not a substitute for interviewing in the requirements discovery context because it has some fundamental problems.

- Relevant questions cannot all be decided in advance.
- The assumptions behind the questions bias the answers.
- It is difficult to explore new domains ("What you really should be asking about is…").
- It is difficult to follow up on ambiguous user responses.

Indeed, some have concluded that the questionnaire technique suppresses almost everything good about requirements discovery, and we do not generally recommend it for this purpose.

There is no substitute for the personal contact, rapport building, and free-form interaction of the interview. After one or two interviews, your worldview will probably change, and the vision for the solution will change along with it. Our advice is, do the interview first and do it for every new class of problem.

However, questionnaires can be applied as a corroborating technique after the initial interviewing and analysis activity. For example, if the application has a large number of existing or potential users and if the goal is to provide statistical input about user or customer preferences among a limited set of choices, a questionnaire can gather a significant amount of focused data in a short period of time. In short, the questionnaire technique, like all elicitation techniques, is suited to a subset of the requirements challenges that an organization may face.

When all is said and done, one of the easiest ways to find out what a system needs to do is to simply ask the prospective stakeholders! If we approach this requirements-gathering activity in a structured way—that is, we know who the stakeholders are likely to be and what questions we need to ask of them—then we are likely to discover the real requirements.

USER EXPERIENCE MOCK-UPS

As we described Chapter 7, developing user experience interfaces in agile (or nonagile for that matter) is always a challenge. In some ways, agile makes it easier; teams have lots of chances at it, iteration by iteration. But in other ways, agile makes it harder because it's unlikely that much big, up-front design (BUFD) has happened. So, all the aspects of the presentations, dialogues, and flows that make a user interface easy to navigate are likely to be largely unexplored prior to beginning implementation. That can make for a lot of churn—and real frustration often results. In that chapter, we also described various organizational approaches, including a dedicated UX team that can mitigate the churns.

In any case, the lighter the representation, the quicker the feedback, and the lower the churn in code, so we'll look at some lighter-weight approaches to defining user interfaces here.

Of course, a "picture is indeed worth a thousand words," so a soft and fuzzy, easy-to-change drawing or mock-up is an early and effective means of communicating elements of user presentation. Mock-ups can cover a wide spectrum of techniques and sophistication. At the low end, we can simply make a quick pencil sketch of what we want, as Figure 12–2 illustrates.

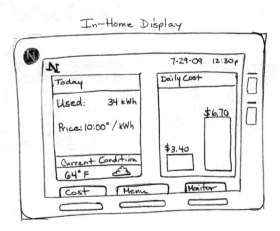

Figure 12–2   A simple sketch

A step up from there is to use a simple drawing tool to illustrate preliminary page design and also flow between pages, as is illustrated in Figure 12–3.

A further step up in sophistication is the use of tools to create wireframe models of the desired story. Wireframes usually start as a static drawing using any number of drawing tools, like we illustrated in Figure 12–3. Once the general shape of the story begins to jell, it is helpful to animate the model to illustrate the important interactions with the user. Figure 12–4 illustrates a wireframe model for a fairly complex web interface. This model was animated in HTML so it was interactive with the user. This gives a semblance of life to the UI and the users' interaction, all before the code was cut.

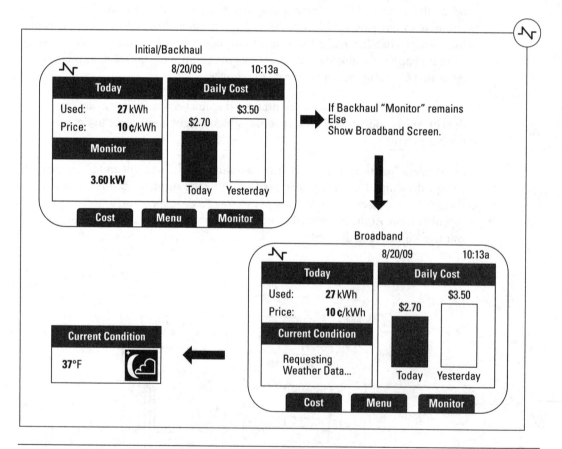

Figure 12–3   Preliminary flow design

Figure 12–4 A web wireframe model animated with HTML design tools

FORMING A PRODUCT COUNCIL

In some circumstances, the challenge is less one of building a backlog of prospective requirements than it is to understand how to prioritize a long list of existing requirements (or even whole projects). In the next chapter, we'll provide concrete suggestions for prioritizing features based on the cost of implementation and the cost of delay. Even that method, however, doesn't necessarily tell a product owner which business segments deserve the most attention from limited IT resources or how to align a diverse set of stakeholders around an agreement to a common set of objectives.

Often, the product owner is in a tough situation. It all can't be done, but each executive stakeholder thinks their stuff should (or must) be done. So, *any* decision the product owner makes is likely to be criticized, and some of the executives carry a pretty heavy club with their criticism. It can be a hazardous job.

In these cases, we recommend that the product owner organize a *product council*, which is empowered to act as the approval body on the key decisions. The product council should consist of the key stakeholders in the enterprise or business unit. If the constitution of the group is not obvious, the product owner may need to do a stakeholder analysis (as described in Chapter 7). For example, in one IT shop that served a large retail organization, a product council was formed that included representatives from each line of business, the CFO, a CTO, a few enterprise business analysts, and the most senior development manager. This group meets periodically to review the backlog of projects and decide what projects get funded and how many resources they deserve.

In Chapter 22, we'll describe the product council's big brother, the *portfolio management team*, in more detail. For now, it's sufficient to understand that such a group can help the product owner make the hard decisions and stand up to each other as necessary to defend and support the decisions that the group has made ("Yes, there were multiple opinions on the topic, but these are the decision we have agreed to in product council").

COMPETITIVE ANALYSIS

Product companies always face the question, "Who is our competition, and what features are they offering?" It is possible to hire market survey companies that will research a domain and produce reports outlining prospective benefits of a product proposition. But most companies do their own competitive analysis; that way, they gain the knowledge directly, and it helps create their own distinctive competence over time.

In its simplest form, a competitive analysis consists of the following:

- Refining the domain of interest/product category
- Identifying competitors
- Studying competitive offerings
- Preparing an analysis of the finding for evaluation

A competitive analysis is usually presented as a matrix. The columns on the top of the matrix provide a listing of the various features that are important to the product. The rows of the matrix list the potential (perhaps "top ten") competitors. The first row of the matrix is dedicated to the features offered by the company's own proposed product.

Table 12–2 shows an example of competitive analysis for a company offering a new product in the web search and browsing domain.

Table 12–2 A Sample Competitive Analysis Comparison Matrix

Product	Web Approach	Content Transparency	Page Commenting	"Stumbling"
Our product plans	Collects every page visited.	Toolbar tags give "flavor" of a page; embedded tags in search pages allow users to jump to selected pages.	Instant messaging, "sticky notes" on pages	Based on similar useful pages.
Search Engines				
Google, MSN, Yahoo	Finds "all" pages based on search.	Short abstract of discovered pages.	None	The user must supply topic.
Social Networks				
YouLicit	The user must bookmark page.	Poor.	None	Based on similar pages.
StumbleUpon	The user must bookmark page.	Embedded categories (not actually a tag); rating into Google search pages.	Offline comments	Stumbling on category of interest.
Del.icio.us	The user must bookmark page.	Click bookmark button to see community tags.	Offline comments	No.
Yoono	The user must bookmark page.	No tagging.	None	User-suggested links.

In more complete analyses, such as those generated using the technique of Quality Function Deployment,[3] analysts assign weights to each of the features, assign numerical values to each competitor's features, and then sum the weighted values to figure out which features provide the best competitive differentiation.

CUSTOMER CHANGE REQUEST SYSTEMS

In addition, as our industry has matured and our users' online access has become ubiquitous, our customer's expectations for direct and unfiltered input have grown as well. To this end, many companies maintain a customer-facing enhancement request system for just this purpose. For example, Rally Software provides one such system, as is illustrated in Figure 12–5.

---

3. For more on Quality Function Deployment, see, for example, *www.qfdi.org/index.htm.*

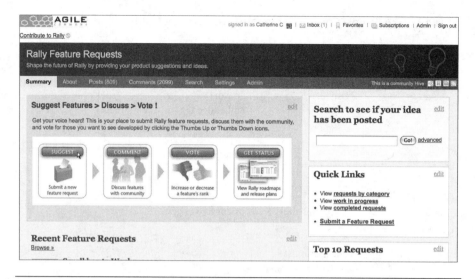

Figure 12–5   Example customer-facing feature request system
Source: Rally Software © 2010

Here's how Rally describes its system:

> Customers provide feedback on our roadmaps and generate new concepts for products and features. Members can build on ideas and crowd-source priorities through voting. Product managers pull ideas from the community into their life-cycle management system. They weave customer-created concepts directly into their real-time roadmap—without having to run traditional focus groups, use off-line surveys, or wait for an annual user conference. It all happens 24x7. Developers can then more efficiently develop the right features, already vetted by customers. In fact, by last count, nearly half of the features recently released were attributed entirely to community participation. Customers can participate through the entire process—they track the features they care about, and are notified when they are released. Full cycle.

Defect Logs

Also, lest we forget, defect logs provide a rich source of product requirements, because typically many of the reported "defects" are really enhancement requests. A high number of enhancement requests for a particular capability item is a relatively unbiased form of prioritization (at least from the perspective of *existing* customers).

USE-CASE MODELING

In Chapter 6, we introduced and described the *user story* as the primary technique used by agile teams to understand and communicate customer requirements. It's certainly a handy construct, and small user stories help us drive the extreme instrumentalism that characterizes agile development.

However, when it comes to systems of complexity—systems that are composed of other systems, systems that contain hardware devices and software components, and suites of applications that work together to provide even higher value to the user—we have overstated the case. Here, neither features nor user stories are sufficiently capable constructs to describe this complex, *aggregate* behavior. For these systems, we need a construct that describes the interplay among the actors (users, devices, subsystems) and the various systems that work together to deliver this behavior. Here we suggest applying *use cases* and *use case modeling* as a primary requirements discovery technique. It's such an important tool that we'll devote Chapter 19 entirely to this method.

We mention the topic here because when building complex systems or systems of serious scale, our requirements discovery toolkit cannot be complete without it.

SUMMARY

Agile development is often characterized, rightly or wrongly, as an entirely "heads-down," immediate value-driven process that delivers value in small increments. The user story is the primary tool agile teams use to capture the behavior, and value is achieved one user story at a time. However, we all understand that the systems we are building with agile methods today are more and more complex. In many circumstances, we need to take a step back and do a little more up-front (yes, we said *up-front*) analysis to better understand what we are about to build and why. To this end, this chapter provided a variety of requirements discovery techniques that teams can use to address this larger challenge. No one tool is perfect or comprehensive in itself. But no intelligent agile team would settle for any one tool anyway. That's why we have provided a more complete *requirements discovery toolkit*.

Part III

AGILE REQUIREMENTS FOR THE PROGRAM

I mean that everybody, every team, every platform, every division, every component is there, not for individual competitive profit or recognition, but for contribution to the system as a whole on a win-win basis.

—W. Edwards Deming

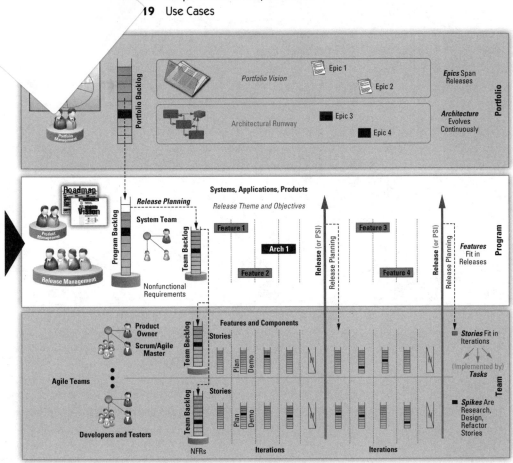

Chapter 13

Vision, Features, and Roadmap

The best way to predict the future is to invent it.

—Alan Kay, American computer scientist

In this chapter, we'll introduce three different but closely related topics—the Vision, features, and the Roadmap. First, we'll describe how the *Vision* is used to continuously communicate the strategic intent of the program, and we'll describe a number of approaches for communicating and documenting this critical information. Then, as the primary content of the Vision is a set of *features*, we'll describe how to formulate, estimate, and prioritize features to deliver the maximum value to our users. Lastly, we'll discuss the *product Roadmap*, which is a tool we'll use to communicate how we see the future of the program unfolding, at least insofar as we can predict it.

Vision

Traditionally, the intended requirements for a product, system, or application were captured and communicated in document form. And, when properly applied, the good news is that documents still work great, even in agile, and we can continue to use them for this purpose.

As we have noted, however, the investment in up-front requirements analysis is greatly reduced in agile, and therefore the traditional marketing requirements documents (MRDs), product requirements documents (PRDs), software requirements specifications (SRSs), and the like are unlikely to appear. In their place, agile enterprises take a leaner approach better suited to the last-responsible-moment, delayed decision-making, and artifact-light development practices. This prevents overinvestment in things we are unlikely to understand very well anyway and prevents the too-early binding of resources to a set of fixed commitments that are likely to haunt us later. In turn, this keeps the program agile and light on its feet.

However, since the MRD, PRD, and SRS documents may no longer exist to specify intended system behavior, communicating the *Vision* directly to the agile development teams is even more critical. Otherwise, how would they know what it is they are supposed to build?

This is generally executive's and product management's responsibility, because the Vision is an outcome of the company's business and portfolio investment strategy.

Generally, the Vision communicates the strategic intent for the program and answers some of the big questions.

- Why are we building this product, system, or application?
- What problem will it solve?
- What features and benefits will it provide?
- For whom does it provide these features and benefits?
- What performance, reliability, and scalability must it deliver?
- What platforms, standards, applications, and so on, will it support?

EXPRESSING THE VISION

How the Vision is communicated to the teams is a matter of the organization's preference, and the mechanisms vary greatly. In the next section, we'll look at a number of options agile teams are using for this purpose.

A Vision Document

Writing things down is still the best way to communicate when face-to-face is impractical and when key decisions and discoveries need to persist over time. For example, in the Rational Unified Process (RUP), the Vision document is a key, well-defined artifact that teams used to communicate the components of the Vision. Many teams have had good success with this document in their RUP-based practices, and it is an easy carryover to a team's agile practices. Indeed, we've seen this approach used to good effect on relatively small teams of 10 to 15 team members. Their belief is that "We document the Vision to test our own understanding of what we think we know."

No matter the form of approach, this template should serve as a prompt of the things that need to be described to the teams to gain an understanding of what they are about to build, who uses it, and how they use it to do their jobs.

Often, it is developed in parallel with the advanced data sheet (discussed next), which provides a summary from a more market-based perspective.

In larger programs, the Vision document plays an even greater role, serving as the "umbrella" document for a large system initiative. With respect to agility, it is important to note that typically only one such document of 5 to 10 pages (20 maximum for a large system) is needed, even for a large green-field program, so developing and updating this document is not a burdensome overhead.

A generic template can serve as a starting point; such a template appears in Appendix B of this book.

The Advanced Data Sheet Approach

Source: Ping Identity, Ping Federate Data Sheet

For product-oriented companies, the development of the business case for a new product requires an understanding of the user's needs; the key benefits a proposed solution is to provide; the platforms and operating environments that must be supported in the user's environment; and the key labeling claims for performance, compatibility, and so on.

Moreover, the need for the product team to be able to articulate the business case in a concise manner to prospective buyers is also imperative: If this cannot be done effectively, the product value proposition is likely to be lost on the marketplace, regardless of the team's ability to produce a worthy offering.

Also, since the role of product management is well understood by these teams, one or more individuals on that team will eventually need to communicate the product boundaries and features, so why not start now?[1]

One way to do that is with the development of a "very preliminary, advanced data sheet," which isn't an actual data sheet per se, but it uses a data sheet template to start to define, at a high level, what the product does and for whom it is intended to do it.

Since the data sheet, by definition, is an extremely concise document (two pages front and back are typical), it must focus on what is critical to communicate. Figure 13–1 provides a template for such a two-page data sheet that has been used to good effect by a number of teams.

Although this data sheet appears to be very simple on the surface, teams will quickly discover that drafting the data sheet is, in fact, a fairly difficult exercise but one that forces development of an early and concise common Vision for the team.

---

1. Some agilists might argue that starting a data sheet at this point violates the principle of last responsible moment (LRM), but when making the business case, that LRM may need to occur before the substantive investment in the product begins.

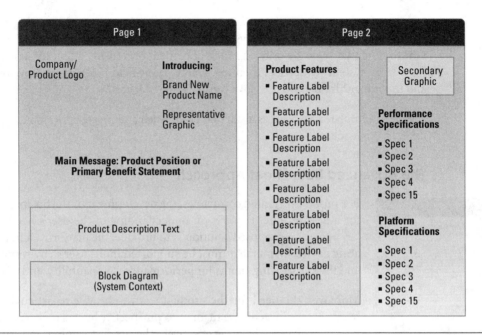

Figure 13–1   Template for a product data sheet

The Preliminary Press Release Approach

In a manner similar to the advanced data sheet, some teams have found that drafting a preliminary, hypothetical press release causes them to think through the Vision from the standpoint of the way the solution will be described to the market. Teams understand that a press release has to tell a complex story in a simple and compelling way, a way that clearly articulates the benefits to the prospective customers, and they also know that they have only two pages to do it in.

Having the team work with their marketing partners to draft a preliminary press release is a way to foster early collaboration, illustrate that the development team can speak in the language of the customer community, and also paint the Vision in the minds of those key internal stakeholders who will become involved as the product approaches market readiness.

Source: Ping Identity, Ping Federate Data Sheet

The "Feature Backlog with Briefing" Approach

In even lighter-weight approaches, the backlog alone may be sufficient to communicate much or all of the Vision to the team. In this case, product managers elaborate far enough ahead to show the team where the project is headed, while simultaneously laying in priorities and estimates for future scoping of work.

A reasonably well-formed and maintained backlog—in conjunction with a face-to-face Vision briefing by the product managers or other business stakeholders to the development team—can be an adequate way to communicate the Vision. We'll see more of that approach in Chapter 16, Release Planning.

Communicating Nonfunctional Requirements (System Qualities)

Before we leave this topic, however, we note that many nonfunctional requirements, which are qualities of the system in use—as opposed to specific functional behaviors—may be equally important to the Vision. These NFRs communicate attributes such as the usability, performance, reliability and supportability requirements, imposed standards, compatibility requirements, and so on. In some fashion, these items must also be communicated to the teams as part of the Vision and captured for future consideration. Chapter 17 is devoted exclusively to the topic of these nonfunctional requirements, or *systems qualities*.

FEATURES

No matter the form, the primary content of the Vision is a set of prioritized features, which describe what new things the system will do for its users, and the benefits the user will derive from them.

In describing the features of a product or system, we take a more abstract and higher-level view of the system of interest. In so doing, we have the security of returning to a more traditional description of system behavior, the feature.

In *Managing Software Requirements, Second Edition: A Use Case Approach* [Leffingwell and Widrig 2003], features were described as follows:

> Services provided by the system that fulfill one or more stakeholder needs.

They lived at a level above software requirements and bridged the gap from the problem domain (understanding the needs of the users and stakeholders in the target market) to the solution domain (specific requirements intended to address the user needs), as Figure 13–2 shows.

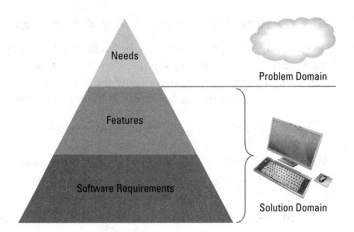

Figure 13–2 Requirements pyramid

We also posited in that text that a system of arbitrary complexity can be described with a list of 25 to 50 such features. That simple rule of thumb allowed us to keep our high-level descriptions exactly that—high level—and simplified our attempts to describe complex systems in a shorter form while still communicating the full scope and intent of the proposed solution.

Of course, in so doing, we didn't invent either the word *feature* or the usage of the word in that text. Rather, we simply fell back on industry-standard norms to describe products in terms of *features and benefits*, the language typically used by marketing to describe the capabilities and benefits provided by a new system.

By applying this familiar construct in agile development, we also bridge the language gap from the agile project team/product owner to the system/program/product manager level and give those who have traditionally operated outside our agile teams a traditional label (feature) to use to do their traditional work (describe the thing they'd like us to build).

Of course, features also provide a focus to organize agile teams around—as the feature team, as we described in Chapter 4. The ability to describe a system in terms of its proposed features and the ability to organize agile teams around those same features gives us a straightforward method to approach building systems with a value delivery focus.

▶ **NOTE** In some agile usage, the things that a story is grouped under, that is, the higher-level value statement, is often called a *theme*. In other texts, such as *Lean-Agile Software Development: Achieving Enterprise Agility* [Shalloway 2010], they are called *features* as we use the word here.

We used the word *feature* in the requirements model and in this text for two reasons: first, we didn't see any reason to invent a new term, and second, it is in common use, and people have a natural affinity to the word. Users know that a feature of a word processor is *spell checking as you type*.

Expressing Features in User Voice Form

It is also natural for an agilist to want to express a feature in user story voice form, so a feature such as *automatic spell checking* becomes the following:

> *As a writer, I can get automatic notification of spelling errors as I write so that I can correct them immediately.*

There is nothing right or wrong about this. There is certainly an advantage in this approach, because the user role and benefit are more clearly described. However, in that form, they do look just like user stories, although they are written at a higher level of abstraction—but in a sense, that's what they really are!

ESTIMATING FEATURES

In Chapter 8, Estimating and Velocity, we described how teams estimate user stories. Since we'll build on that model to help us estimate features here, a brief recap may be useful.

- Teams typically estimate user stories using an abstract, relative estimating model based on *story points*. Story points can be measured in the abstract (unit-less but numerically relevant) or as ideal developer days (IDDs), with the abstract measure being the most common.
- The aggregate amount of story points that a team can deliver in the course of an iteration is the team's *velocity*.
- When a team's size changes or vacations or holidays occur, the team adjusts the expected velocity accordingly.

If the system (no large-scale architectural refactoring at work) and organizations are largely stable (no large-scale personnel changes in process), after some number of iterations, teams will generally have a fairly reliable velocity. That allows them to make intelligent commitments for each iteration. It also provides the basic mechanism we need for estimating at the program/release level.

Depending on where the item is in the program backlog and how important the estimate is, the estimate for a feature may go through a series of preliminary, refined, and final estimates, as Figure 13–3 shows.

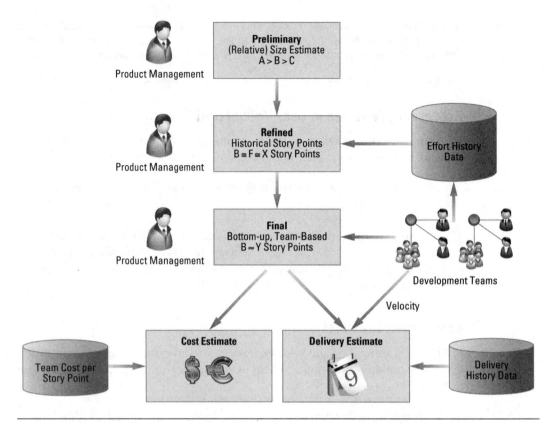

Figure 13–3   Feature estimate refinement and conversion to cost and schedule estimates

We'll describe this process further in the following sections.

Estimating Effort

Estimating the amount of effort needed to implement a feature typically goes through a series of successive refinements, as we describe in the following sections.

Preliminary: Gross, Relative Estimating

For initial backlog prioritization, the product management team may simply need a rough estimate of the effort to implement a feature, even before discussion with the teams. If so, they can simply use the same, relative estimating model—the "bigness" of each backlog item is simply estimated relative to others of the same type. This provides a simple and fast estimating heuristic that can be used for the initial (but again, only *relative*) scoping and prioritization of work.

Refined: Estimate in Story Points

At some point, it may be useful to refine the effort estimate by converting the feature effort estimate into story points. With story points, the teams can start to reason about potential cost and schedule impact. For this, we need tracking information that allows us to convert the effort estimate for features into story points. Fortunately, many agile project management tools support the feature-to-story hierarchy, and the teams can leverage this to build some historical data. A simple comparison of the new feature to the expended story points for a similar size feature provides this first refinement. This is still a fairly gross estimate, because it depends on comparing the new feature to like features for which there is historical data, but at least it's in a currency that can be used for further analysis.

Final: Bottom-up, Team-Based Estimating

The estimates so far require only a minor time investment and can be done by the product management team in isolation. That can be appropriate, based on the stage of the feature. However, for any meaningful estimate, the fidelity of the estimate can be significantly improved by having the estimating done by the teams. In any material program, there will be multiple teams, and they may or may not be affected by the new feature. Sometimes, only they know whether their module, feature, or component is impacted. Therefore, only they can actually determine a more responsible estimate. They will typically have their own history of like features—and the story points required to complete them—in their project management repository.

However, since ad hoc requests for estimating interrupts the team from their daily iteration activities, the estimating task is most efficiently done on a cadence. In Chapter 9 (Iterating, Backlog, Throughput, and Kanban), we described the semi-weekly *feature preview* meeting, which is designed, in part, for just this purpose.

Estimating Cost

Once the feature has been estimated in the currency of story points, a cost estimate can be quickly derived. Although the development teams themselves may not have ready knowledge of the *cost* of a story point, at the Program level it is fairly straightforward to calculate one. Simply look at the burdened cost per iteration timebox for the teams that provided the estimates, and divide that by their velocity. This gives an estimate of the *cost per story point* for the subject teams affected by the new feature.

Additional work may be necessary when teams are distributed in differing geographic locations, because that can result in a highly varying cost per story point for individual teams.

Estimating Development Time

Finally, given an understanding of what percentage of the team's time the program is willing to devote to the new feature, we can also use historical data to predict how long it will take to deliver. For example, if feature A was implemented in about 1,000 story points and took three months and feature B is a little bigger, then feature B will take a little more than three months, assuming similar resource allocations and availability.

As a further refinement, the program can also look at the *current* available velocity of the affected teams, make some assumptions about percentage time allocation, and derive a better time and schedule estimate from there.

TESTING FEATURES

As we described in Chapters 4 and 10, features, like stories, are business-facing behaviors that are subject to functional testing to assure that the aggregate behavior of the system is in accordance with the objectives. Feature testing is referenced in quadrant 2 of the agile testing matrix, and features cannot be considered *done* until they pass an acceptance test, as Figure 13–4 illustrates.

For teams that are organized by feature, this testing can be done by the team that implements the feature. If the teams are organized around components, then much of this testing is likely to be done by the system team. In either case, however, there are likely to be some spanning features that touch multiple feature and component teams; testing of those features is often done under the purview of the system team.

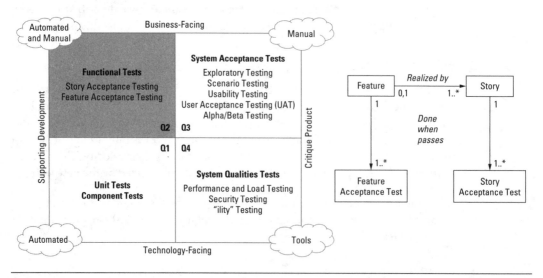

Figure 13–4   Feature testing in the agile testing matrix and the agile requirements model

As with stories, feature tests may be manual or automated, with automation being the preferred approach.

PRIORITIZING FEATURES

One of the biggest challenges that all software teams face is prioritizing requirements for implementation and delivery to the customers. This is certainly a challenge for every agile team at iteration boundaries, and it rises to even greater importance when prioritizing features at the Program level. Here, small decisions can have big impacts on implementation cost and timeliness of value delivery.

There are a number of reasons why prioritization is such a hard problem.

- Customers are seemingly reluctant to prioritize features. Perhaps this is because they simply "want them all," which is understandable; or perhaps they are uncertain as to what the relative priorities are; or perhaps they cannot gain internal agreement.
- Product managers are often even more reluctant. Perhaps this is because that if they could only *get them all*, they wouldn't have to prioritize anything, and more importantly, they would be assured of receiving all the ultimate value.[2]
- Quantifying value is extremely difficult. Some features are simple "must haves" to remain competitive or keep market share. How does one quantify the impact of keeping market share, one feature at a time?

  It is often necessary to compare and prioritize very unlike things. For example, how does one prioritize a entirely new initiative that could take many months against a minor feature that can be delivered in just a few weeks?

To assist us, we often attempt to provide a return on investment (ROI) per feature, by predicting the likely increase in revenue if a feature is available. Of course, determining feature ROI is most likely a false science, because no one's crystal ball is an adequate predictor of future revenue, especially when you attempt to allocate revenue on a per-feature basis. This is compounded because the analyst who does the work is likely to develop a vested, personal interest in seeing that the feature is developed. Plus, any product manager or business analyst worth their salt can probably make a case for a great ROI for their feature; otherwise, they wouldn't have worked on it to begin with.

In agile, however, the challenge of prioritization is immutable. We admit up front that we can't implement (nor even *discover*) all potential requirements. After all, we

---

2. I once saw a cartoon on this topic. The developer says to the product manager, "Please tell me what your priorities are so I'll know what I don't have to work on."

typically have fixed quality, resources, and delivery schedules. Therefore, the only variable we have is scope. Effective prioritization becomes a mandatory practice and art—one that must be mastered by every agile team and program.

Of course, prioritizing requirements is not a new problem. A number of authors have described reasonable mechanisms for prioritization. Our favorites include the following:

- *Agile Estimating and Planning* [Cohn 2006]
- *Software Requirements* [Wiegers 1999]
- *Software by Numbers* [Denne and Cleland-Huang 2004]

For those for whom this topic is potentially a determinant of program success or failure of the program, we refer you to these bodies of work. Although we will take a different approach in this book, there is certainly no one right way to prioritize, and teams will benefit from differing perspectives on this unique problem.

Value/Effort as an ROI Proxy: A First Approximation

As we alluded to earlier, we have traditionally prioritized work by trying to understand the relative ROI, which is the relationship between potential return (value) divided by the effort (cost to implement) for a feature. At least the model was simple.

$$\text{Relative Priority} = \text{Relative ROI} = \text{Relative } \frac{\text{Value}}{\text{Cost}}$$

If we could simply establish value and cost (if not in absolute terms, then at least relative to other features), then we have a way to prioritize based on economics. After all, who wouldn't want to deliver a higher ROI feature before a lower ROI feature? That seemed to make totally intuitive and (apparently) economical common sense.

What's Wrong with Our Value/Effort ROI Proxy?

However, based on more complete economic framework, it turns out that relative ROI (as we've too simply defined it earlier) is not an adequate proxy for prioritizing value delivery. Recently, one of the more thoughtful and rigorous economic views to prioritizing value delivery (*sequencing work* in flow terms) is Reinertsen's *Principles of Product Development Flow* [2009], which we introduced in Chapter 1. These principles describe methods of sequencing work based on the mathematics and underlying economics of lean product development.

We'll use those principles to describe an enhanced method for prioritizing features. As we do so, we'll discover a deeply seated flaw in our first assumption—the assumption that a high relative ROI feature should naturally have precedence over a lower ROI feature.

Instead, what we need to understand is the way in which the economics of our program may be dramatically affected by *sequence*. For example, the potential profit for a particular high ROI feature could be less sensitive to a schedule delay than a lower ROI feature. In this case, *the lower ROI feature should be implemented first*, followed by the higher ROI feature. This may not make intuitive sense, but we'll see that it does make economic sense.

Prioritizing Features Based on the Cost of Delay

Since prioritizing value delivery is the key economic driver for a program, we'll need a more sophisticated model to produce better returns. As we described in Chapter 9 (Iterating, Backlog, Throughput, and Kanban), prioritizing value delivery in software development is an application of queuing theory. Applying those principles will create a solid economic foundation for critical decision making around feature priorities.

Introducing Cost of Delay (CoD)

As Reinertsen points out, "If you only quantify one thing, quantify the cost of delay,"[3] so we'll need to be able to estimate the CoD as part of our more economically grounded approach (more on that shortly). Fortunately, however, we don't have to quantify *only* one thing, and because we have already outlined an estimating strategy, we'll actually be able to quantify *two* things, the *feature effort estimate*, as we have described earlier, and the *cost of delay*. Together, we should have what we need.

Reinertsen describes three methods for prioritizing work based on the economics of CoD.

Shortest Job First

When the cost of delay for two features is equal, doing the *Shortest* (in our case, *smallest*[4]) *Job First*, produces the best economic returns, as is illustrated in Figure 13–5.

---

3. Principle of Product Development Flow E3—*If you only quantify one thing, quantify the CoD.*
4. Although duration (the time to do a job in Reinertsen's term) is not the same as effort (the size estimate for the feature in our terms), all else being equal, a bigger feature will take longer to implement than a smaller one. If, for whatever reason, a bigger feature can go through the system faster (availability of resources, or whatever), then the rating system must be adjusted accordingly.

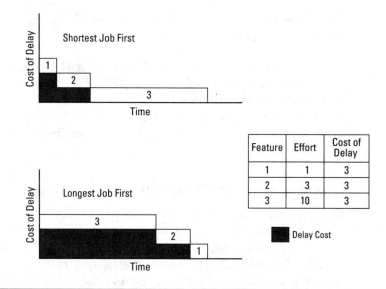

Figure 13–5   Shortest Job First. When the cost of delays are the same, do the smallest feature first.

Source: Donald G. Reinertsen, *The Principles of Product Development Flow*, Celeritas Publishing, 2009

In Figure 13–5, the black area represents the total cost of delay of the two scenarios. The impact can be dramatic, as we can see that delivering the smallest feature first substantially decreases the overall cost of delay in this case. So, we arrive at our first conclusion:

If two features have the same CoD, do the smallest feature first.

High Delay Cost First

If the effort to do two new features is about the same, then the second approach, *High Delay Cost First*, illustrates the effect of prioritizing the features with the highest cost of delay. Again, the economics can be compelling, as Figure 13–6 illustrates.

Of course, this makes intuitive sense in this case as well (not that intuition has always led us to the correct conclusion). In other words, if CoD is a proxy for value and if one feature has more value than another and if it's the same effort (and takes the same amount of time), we do the higher value feature first; we knew that already from our ROI value/effort proxy. So, we have our second conclusion:

If two features have the same effort, do the feature with the highest CoD first.

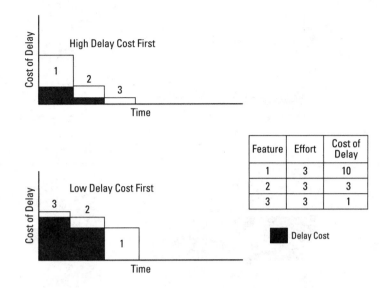

Figure 13–6 High Delay Cost First. When effort is the same, do the high delay cost feature first.

Source: Donald G. Reinertsen, *The Principles of Product Development Flow,* Celeritas Publishing, 2009

Weighted Shortest Job First

Now that we have seen the impact, we understand that these two conclusions are quite sensible when the effort or CoD of two features are comparable. Of course, we are not manufacturing widgets here. The CoD and implementation effort for different software features are likely to be highly variable. Plus, they often have weak or no correlations (that is, some valuable jobs are easy to do, and some are hard); that's just the way it is with software. In the case where the CoD and effort for a feature are highly variable, then the best economics are achieved when we implement them in order of the *Weighted Shortest Job First.*

In this case, we calculate the relative priority weighting by dividing the CoD by the effort (time proxy) estimate. This favors the jobs with the best ratio of value to delivery time. If the CoD and job sizes vary greatly, then the differential economics can be even more dramatic, as is illustrated in Figure 13–7.

This, then, is our preferred approach for software development:

If two features have different efforts and CoD (and they almost always do), do the weighted, smallest effort feature first.

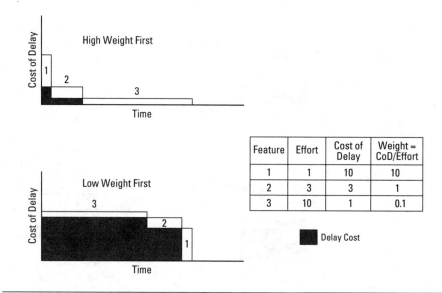

Figure 13–7 Weighted Shortest Job First. When job effort and delay costs differ, prioritize by dividing the job's cost of delay by its effort.

Source: Donald G. Reinertsen, *The Principles of Product Development Flow*, Celeritas Publishing, 2009

We'll apply this prioritization scheme, Weighted Shorted Job First (WSJF), throughout this book, and we'll see it again when prioritizing architectural (Chapter 21) and business (Chapter 23) epics.

Estimating the Cost of Delay

This seems like a promising decision model for prioritizing features. It is based on solid economics and is quite rational once you understand it. However, we have excluded one small item: How does one go about calculating the cost of delay for a feature? If we aren't careful, we could fall into the analysis trap we mentioned earlier; overinvestment in calculating size estimates for features plus overinvestment in calculating CoD could lead to too much overhead plus a potential bias by those doing the work. We need something simpler.

We suggest that CoD—so critical to our decision-making criteria—is, in turn, an aggregation of three attributes of a feature, each of which can be estimated fairly readily, when compared to other features. They are *user value*, *time value*, and *risk reduction value*.

- *User value* is simply the potential *value* of the feature in the eyes of the user. Product managers often have a good sense of the relative value of a feature ("they prefer this over that"), even when it is impossible to determine the absolute value. And since we are prioritizing like things, relative user value is all we need.

- *Time value* is another relative estimate, one based on how the user value *decays* over time. Many features provide higher value when they are delivered early and differentiated in the market and provide lower value as features become commoditized. In some cases, time value is modest at best (implement the new UI standard with new corporate branding). In other cases, time value is extreme (implement the new testing protocol prior to the school year buying season), and of course there are in-between cases as well (support 64-bit architectures as soon as our competitors do).

- *Risk reduction/opportunity enablement* value adds a final dimension—one that acknowledges that what we are really doing is software *research and development*. Our world is laden with both risk and opportunity. Some features are more or less valuable to us based on how they help us unlock these mysteries, mitigate risk, and help us exploit new opportunities. For example, move user authentication to a new web service could be a risky effort for a shrink-wrapped software provider that has done nothing like that in the past, but imagine the opportunities that such a new feature could engender.

With these three value factors—user value, time value, and risk reduction value—we have the final pieces to our prioritization puzzle.

Feature Prioritization Evaluation Matrix

Now, we can integrate all this information into an evaluation spreadsheet that we can use to establish the relative priorities for a feature, based on WSJF, which incorporates effort and CoD. Table 13–1 shows an example of such a feature prioritization matrix.

Table 13–1   WSJF Feature Prioritization Example

	Cost of Delay				Effort	WSJF
	User	*Time*	*Risk Red.*	*Total*		
Feature A	4	9	8	21	4	5.3
Feature B	8	4	3	15	6	2.5
Feature C	6	6	6	18	5	3.6

Legend:
   Scale: 10 is highest, 1 is lowest.
   Total is sum of individual CoD.
   WSJF (weighted result) is calculated as Total (Cost of Delay) divided by Effort.

In our example, it is interesting to note that feature B—the job with the highest user value (8) *and* the highest feature/effort (raw ROI) rating (8/6 =1.3)—is actually the job that has the *lowest* WSJF and therefore should be implemented *last*, not first. The job that has the lowest feature value (feature A) actually produces the *highest* actual return on investment, so long as it is implemented *first* (because it has an extremely high time value). So much for our intuition!

▶ **NOTE**   In this simple example, the individual attributes are not weighted relative to each other. Teams may apply a rating scale to their specific context. For example, if immediate, incremental revenue can be gained from delivering customer-specific features, then user and/or time value may be weighted higher accordingly.

All Prioritizations Are Local and Temporal

Reinertsen points out another subtle implication of WSJF scheduling. Priority should be based on delay cost, which is a *global* property of the feature, and effort, which is a *local* property of the team that is implementing the feature. In other words, a job with a lower relative feature value may require little resource from a specific team and therefore should be implemented ahead of another, higher-priority feature, if that feature requires more resources for that team. This means that all priorities are indeed inherently local.[5]

This applies to entire projects, as well as to specific features within a project. This occasionally flies in the face of the way we often do things, whereby management sets a global priority for a project, which is to be applied across all teams. In that case, a lower-priority task for a high-priority project may take precedence over a high-priority task for a lower-priority feature that could have otherwise delivered value immediately. And availability of scarce resources doesn't even enter into the equation. We see now that this approach simply doesn't make economic sense.

In addition, we note that our model is highly sensitive to the time element—*priorities change rapidly as deadlines approach*. For example, implement the new testing protocol in time for the school year buying season could have a time value of "1 to 2" in the winter prior to the next school year start but could easily be a "10" in May of the next year.

One conclusion of the previous is that priorities have to be determined locally and at the last responsible moment. That is the time when we can best assess the CoD and the resources available to work on the feature.

---

5. Principle of Product Development Flow F18—*Prioritizations are inherently local.*

Fortunately, in our Big Picture model, we prioritize features frequently on release planning boundaries. The rapid cadence we have established for our release train serves us well here, so long as we take the time to *reprioritize* at each such boundary.

When we do so, we can be confident that our priorities are current—taking into account then-current availability of resources and then-current cost of delay, as well as being based on solid economic fundamentals.

Achieving Differential Value: The Kano Model of Customer Satisfaction

Along with his colleagues, Noriaki Kano, an expert on the field of quality management and customer satisfaction, developed a model for customer satisfaction that also challenged some traditional beliefs. Specifically, the Kano model challenges the assumption that customer satisfaction is achieved by balancing investment across the various attributes of a product or service. Rather, customer satisfaction can be optimized by focusing on *differential features*, those "exciters" and "delighters" that increase customer satisfaction and loyalty beyond that which a proportional investment would otherwise merit. Figure 13–8 shows the Kano model.

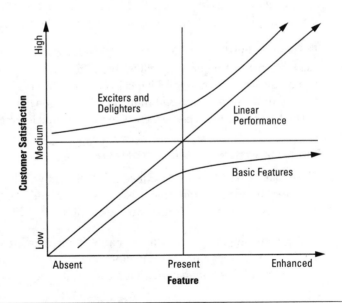

Figure 13–8 Kano model of customer satisfaction

The model illustrates three types of features.

- *Basic (must-have) features:* Features that must be present to have a viable solution. Without them, your solution cannot compete in the marketplace.
- *Linear features:* Features for which the capability of the feature is directly proportional to the result. Generally, the more you invest in those features, the higher the satisfaction.
- *Exciters and delighters:* These are the features that differentiate the solution from the competition. They provide the highest opportunity for customer satisfaction and loyalty.

The primary insight from the Kano model is the position and shape of the lower and upper curves.

The shape of the *basic* curve is telling. Until a feature is simply "present," satisfaction remains low until a threshold is achieved. Thereafter, however, enhancing the feature produces a *less* than proportional reward. The center point (the *present* line) of this basic curve gives rise to what is often described as the *minimum marketable feature* (MMF), which is the smallest set of functionality that must exist in order for the users to perceive value in that feature. For a solution to be considered viable, it must contain some requisite set of MMFs. However, enhancing or "gold plating" any MMF will not produce a proportional economic return.

The position and shape of the *exciters and delighters* curve tells the opposite story. Because these features are unique, compelling, and differentiated, even a small investment (the area on the left) still produces high customer interest and potential satisfaction. Additional investment produces still more, and proportionally more investment produces still higher satisfaction. This is where we get the greatest leverage for our investment.

Prioritizing Features for Differential Value

Given that we have already described a full-fledged Weighted Shortest Job First prioritization model, the question arises as to what additional benefit we can derive from Kano's thinking. There are three takeaways.

First, when competing on features in an existing marketplace, teams should place relatively high user value (and therefore a relatively high cost of delay) on features required to reach *minimal* parity. This leads us to rule #1:

Differential value rule #1: Invest in MMFs, but never overinvest in a feature that is already commoditized.

Thereafter, the strategic focus should move to placing higher user value on *differentiating features*—those that will excite and delight the users, those for which competitive solutions have no answer, and those for which an incremental invest-ment produces a nonlinear return. This leads us to rule #2:

Differential value rule #2: Drive innovation by having the courage to invest in exciters.

Finally and most subtly, when we are forced to engage in feature wars with competi-tors that may already be ahead of us, *it may not make sense to put all our investment into MMFs.* After all, our competitors will keep investing too; what makes us think we can catch up (they are likely becoming more agile, too)? Instead, it may be bet-ter to slight some narrow category of MMFs and, instead, focus some amount of investment on exciters, *even if we have not reached full basic feature parity.*

Experience has shown that customers can be relatively patient with suppliers when they can reasonably anticipate the appearance of adequate MMFs and see the prom-ise of the differential value of the exciters that the team is bringing forward from the backlog. This leads us to our third and final rule of feature prioritization:

Differential value rule #3: If resources do not allow you to compete on the current play-ing field, change the playing field.

THE ROADMAP

The Vision we described earlier was presented as time-independent. That was appro-priate, because the objective there was to just communicate the strategic intent of "*what* this thing is we are about to build." Overloading the Vision with prospective timelines will likely quickly derail the discussion of the "what."

However, in order to set priorities and plan for implementation, we need an additional perspective, a product *Roadmap* that provides a view we can use to communicate *future* objectives to our outside stakeholders. An agile Roadmap is not a particularly complicated artifact, nor is the mechanical maintenance of it difficult. For example, a typical Roadmap might be communicated in a single graphic, as Figure 13–9 shows.

Each vertical box represents an upcoming release (or PSI). The label at the bottom represents the theme or primary objective of the release. The features are listed in prioritized order.

The Roadmap consists of a series of *planned release dates*, each of which has a *theme* and a prioritized *feature set.* Although it is a simple thing *mechanically* to represent the Roadmap, *figuring out the content for anything beyond the next release is another matter entirely.* The topic of *what* the business *plans to ship* and *when* can be a fas-cinating and contentious topic in agile. However, the easiest way to think about the Roadmap is that it is an *output,* rather than an *input* to the release planning process, as we will describe in the next few chapters.

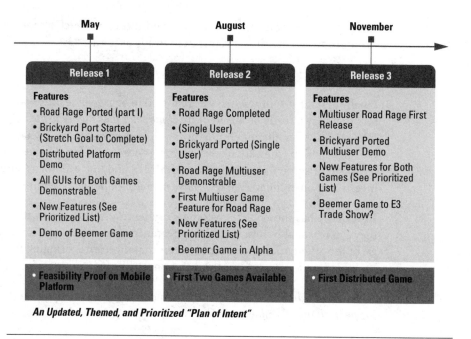

Figure 13–9   Roadmap—a themed, prioritized "plan of intent"

To avoid the iron triangle, the dates, themes, and quality for the next release are *fixed*. The features are *prioritized* and *variable*. The teams can commit only to the features in the next upcoming release. Releases beyond the next represent only a best estimate. The Roadmap, then, is a "plan of intent" and is subject to change as development facts, business context, and customer needs *change*.

With respect to the upcoming release, perhaps the most important guidance is this:

Even though the team has committed to the objectives and we have agreed that the feature set cannot be guaranteed, it is a reasonable expectation that the agile teams will

- *Meet the date*
- *Deliver on the promise of the theme*
- *Deliver most of the features, and certainly the highest-priority ones, with the requisite quality*

Anything less would be unprofessional and belie the power, discipline, and accountability of our agile model. Moreover, it will eventually threaten our own empowerment, because failure to deliver will inevitably cause the implementation of various management controls to "help us"!

On Confidence and Commitments for Release Next, Next +1, and More

As we will see in Chapter 16, Release Planning, the objectives and prioritized feature set for "Release Next" should be a high confidence plan of intent. And to be flippant for a second, it's often true that release Next +1 has a pretty clear definition as well, if for no other reason than it usually "must" contain all the stuff that didn't fit in Release Next!

Anything after that, however, is likely to be a somewhat futile attempt to predict the future. In any case, it is important to keep any such future commitments abstract so that at least the intent can be met under most normal circumstances. After all, if long-term commitments are fixed, then we have essentially reentered a waterfall model of fixed resources, time, and scope. Even worse, in so doing, the program will lose its ability to exploit any new market opportunities that present themselves in the meantime. You can't have it both ways.

We'll revisit this topic again in Chapter 15, The Agile Release Train, and Chapter 16, Release Planning.

SUMMARY

We covered three different but closely related topics in this chapter: Vision, features, and Roadmap. We described how the *Vision* is used to continuously communicate the strategic intent of the program, and we provided a number of mechanisms for documenting and communicating this critical aspect of the program.

We also described *features* as the artifact we'll use to carry the value stream from the Vision to the user. We illustrated models for estimating the amount of *effort* (work) involved in implementing a feature, as well as how to convert the effort estimate into *cost* and *schedule* estimates. We also described how to prioritize features, based on the lean-flow economics of *cost of delay*. In so doing, we illustrated how many of our prior assumptions about prioritizing work were flawed, or at least insufficient to produce the optimum economic outcomes. We concluded the estimating section with an example spreadsheet that teams or programs can use to do a better job of prioritizing features at release planning boundaries.

Finally, we included the intended delivery time element for features in a *Roadmap*, which is a statement of intent that describes how we intend to implement the features over time. We ended with a note of caution to make sure that the Roadmap is used for its intended purpose—a preliminary, general, statement of intent—and how it should not be used to make fixed, longer-term, program commitments.

In the next few chapters, we'll highlight the role of product management in defining and prioritizing features. Then we'll move on to discussion of the Agile Release Train, and its partner, release planning.

Chapter 14

ROLE OF THE PRODUCT MANAGER

It is clear to me that you need serious professional help.

—Author's ex-wife

In earlier chapters, we described why the responsibilities of the agile product owner, as primarily defined by Scrum, are more typically a set of responsibilities that are shared between a number of agile product owners and a smaller number of agile product managers in the mid- to larger software enterprise. In Chapter 11, we described the specific activities of the product owner role—a relatively new role that is tightly coupled to the team and the implementation. We also described how this modest separation of concerns and responsibilities can improve the value stream by avoiding bottlenecks in decision making relative to priorities and product definition.

In this chapter, we'll describe the other half of that equation, which is the role of the *product manager* in the agile enterprise.

In the Big Picture, product managers operate a little above the fray of the iterations and the tactical work the teams do to actually develop and deliver the code. Instead, they operate primarily at the *Program and Release* level, where they focus on vision for the overall solution, its features, and the plans for PSIs and releases, as Figure 14–1 indicates.

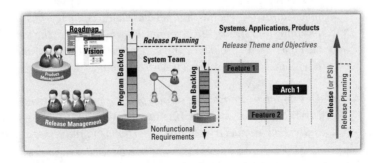

Figure 14–1 Product managers operate at the Program and Release level.

PRODUCT MANAGER, BUSINESS ANALYST?

Before we proceed, however, we pause for a second to reflect on the title of the role. In different industries and organizations, the role can be responsible for a variety of activities, from strategic to tactical. Individuals with a variety of different titles, who may come for marketing, development, or IT operations, can fulfill the role.

In addition, the titles associated with these responsibilities tend to differ based on industry segment.

- In product-oriented companies, including independent software vendors (ISVs) and product and system manufacturers, *product manager* is a common role and a title that usually has a fairly clear set of responsibilities for defining and positioning the product in the marketplace. However, we've also seen other titles carry that same responsibility within product companies, including such titles as *solutions manager* and even *program manager*.
- In information systems/information technology (IS/IT) departments, the title is most typically *business analyst*.

The function of this role varies by industry segment, which we will highlight briefly below.

RESPONSIBILITIES OF THE PRODUCT MANAGER IN A PRODUCT COMPANY

The Product Development and Management Association has published a body of knowledge, which suggests the responsibilities of those who perform the various functions of product management in a product-oriented company.[1] The body of knowledge is organized into three *lifecycle phases* and six *knowledge (competency) areas:*

The lifecycle phases are as follows.

> **Discovery Phase:** *Discovery covers the process of searching for and identifying opportunities—whether market-based or technology-based—and all of the planning and strategy to accomplish this. It requires the identification of customer needs, problems, and benefits, and the conceptual features that are envisioned for the products it wishes to build.*

> **Development Phase:** *The second phase is primarily about realization. It covers the process of converting specifications into designs—whether for an individual product or a complete portfolio of products—and all of the processes*

---

1. *http://pdmabok.arcstone.com/description.php*

to accomplish this. It usually requires detailed resource management, creative engineering and process design capabilities, and sophisticated information technology. It ends when the products or services achieve their first commercial availability.

Commercialization Phase: *The third phase is primarily about fulfillment. It covers the entire process of new product introduction and the organization's management of its product and service portfolio as it attempts to fulfill its financial potential. It ends when the products or services have reached the end of their useful life cycle and are to be considered as candidates for retirement, renewal, and regeneration. At this stage, the process begins anew with the undertaking of a new product development initiative and a return to the Discovery Phase.*

The six knowledge areas are as follows.

Customer and Market Research: *Bringing external insight into product innovation, development, and growth, especially insight about customers (buyers and end users) but also information about channels, competitors, markets, alternatives, etc.*

Technology and Intellectual Property: *The invention, development, acquisition, licensing, and management of technologies and intellectual property that enable and become part of products.*

Strategy, Planning, and Decision Making: *Strategies, plans, and decision-making around product innovation, development, and growth. These would include strategies, plans, and decision making at the business level (as relates to product innovation, development, and growth), as well as for platforms, product lines or product families, and products.*

People, Teams, and Culture: *The people side of product development across the life cycle, including organization/team structures, people management, skills development, culture, organization change management, human interaction, etc.*

Co-development and Alliances: *Innovation, development, and growth activities that take place in unison with external partners, including customers, suppliers, service providers, and channels. This would include co-development or development chain strategy, partner management, co-development execution processes, co-development teams, etc.*

Process, Execution, and Metrics (including Financial): *Pricing, positioning, promotion, channel management, financial management, the customer support* *operational dimension of product innovation, development, and growth including: processes and tools for requirements development and management, design, manufacturing, supply chain (engineering), and change management.*

Although there are many viewpoints on the role of product management in a product company, this description is generally reflective of a typical set of responsibilities for people who fill the role.[2]

BUSINESS RESPONSIBILITIES OF THE ROLE IN THE IT/IS SHOP

In the IS/IT shop, the focus is on helping the enterprise meet its business objectives through the following:

- Developing new systems for internal use
- Installing and configuring commercial, off-the-shelf software
- Integrating internal development capabilities with acquired solutions
- Supporting and maintaining these systems

The business analyst plays a product manager-like role in needs assessment, defining solutions, build-versus-buy decisions, and so on.

The International Institute of Business Analysts (IIBA) has developed a *Guide to the Business Analysis Body of Knowledge* (BABOK Guide) to guide practitioners who fulfill this role.[3] BABOK consists of six *knowledge areas* and eight underlying *competencies*. The six knowledge areas are the most relevant here, because they describe the activities of a business analyst.

> **Business Analysis Planning and Monitoring** . . . *covers how business analysts determine which activities are necessary in order to complete a business analysis effort. It covers identification of stakeholders, selection of business analysis techniques, the process that will be used to manage requirements, and how to assess the progress of the work.*

> **Elicitation** *(requirements discovery techniques) describes how business analysts work with stakeholders to identify and understand their needs and concerns, and understand the environment in which they work. The purpose of elicitation is to ensure that a stakeholder's actual underlying needs are understood, rather than their stated or superficial desires.*

---

2. Some of this language, when taken literally, reflects some of the historical mind-sets of waterfall development, a problem we'll address in later sections of this chapter.
3. *IIBA Guide to the Business Analysis Body of Knowledge*

Requirements Management and Communication describes how business analysts manage conflicts, issues, and changes in order to ensure that stakeholders and the project team remain in agreement on the solution scope, how requirements are communicated to stakeholders, and how knowledge gained by the business analyst is maintained for future use.

Enterprise Analysis describes how business analysts identify a business need, refine and clarify the definition of that need, and define a solution scope that can feasibly be implemented by the business. This knowledge area describes problem definition and analysis, business case development, feasibility studies, and the definition of solution scope.

Requirements Analysis describes how business analysts prioritize and progressively elaborate stakeholder and solution requirements in order to enable the project team to implement a solution that will meet the needs of the sponsoring organization and stakeholders. It involves analyzing stakeholder needs to define solutions that meet those needs, assessing the current state of the business to identify and recommend improvements, and the verification and validation of the resulting requirements.

Solution Assessment and Validation describes how business analysts assess proposed solutions to determine which solution best fits the business need, identify gaps and shortcomings in solutions, and determine necessary workarounds or changes to the solution. It also describes how business analysts assess deployed solutions to see how well they met the original need so that the sponsoring organization can assess the performance and effectiveness of the solution.

The underlying competencies describe the expectations for an individual's skills and abilities in analytical thinking and problem solving, behavioral characteristics, business knowledge, communication skills, interaction skills, and software applications.

RESPONSIBILITY SUMMARY

Fortunately, from the standpoint of an agile software development process, this is probably more than we need to know. However, in our agile context, the business analyst/product managers have the primary organizational responsibility to do the following:

- Understand solution needs, gaps, and opportunities
- Define products and solutions to address those needs

- Work within the organization to address all the other issues (internal and external) that are necessary for successful deployment
- Work with the development team to define requirements and help assure the solution evolves to meet the real needs of the stakeholders

Given this set of responsibilities, it is clear that—even with a staff of competent product owners—product management remains an important function in agile development and one that must be well executed to assure enterprise success. Indeed, the criticality of the relationship with development is implied directly in Agile Manifesto principle #4—*Businesspeople and developers must work together daily throughout the project.* However, the question we must address here is not the role itself—for there is a large body of work on that; rather, we'll need to describe how the role changes when the team moves to an agile development paradigm.

PHASES OF PRODUCT MANAGEMENT DISILLUSIONMENT IN THE PRE-AGILE ENTERPRISE

Before we move on to making these changes, however, it's important to set the cultural context, because the relationship between product management and development may already be quite challenging.

As we described in Chapter 1, the legacy of waterfall development still influences much of the work we have to do to successfully implement agile development. In the case of the product management organization, it's likely that the product manager's mind-set has evolved through a series of increasingly foreboding attitudes, as is illustrated in Figure 14–2.

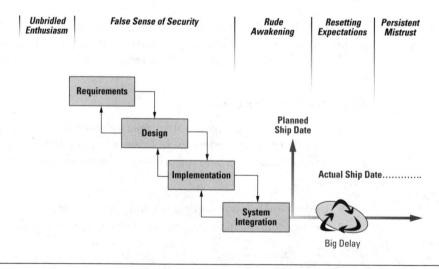

Figure 14–2   Phases of disillusionment in the pre-agile enterprise

Phase 1: Unbridled Enthusiasm

In this phase, the product manager spent time with customers, interviewing, running workshops, and using whatever other tools were available to define and document the requirements for the prospective new system. These requirements were typically captured in a marketing requirements document (MRD) or product requirements document (PRD). After that, the development team typically responded with a software requirements specification or system design specification (SDS), which further refines and documents the intent of the PRD.

At the end of this phase, which could take from three to six months to document, review, and gain the requisite approvals, the development effort was launched, and there was a *handoff to engineering*.

Phase 2: False Sense of Security

This initial, upbeat phase was followed by a period of relative calm—the *period of a false sense of security*. During this phase, development proceeded apace. The product manager was likely uninvolved or perhaps attended periodic milestone reviews where models, documents, and project plans were reviewed and inspected. Toward the end of this period, which typically lasted from 8 to 12 months, the software was declared to be 90% complete and launch plans were put into place. Customers were notified that the release was impending. External and internal release commitments were solidified.

Phase 3: Rude Awakening

Of course, as we've discussed, the next phase was a painful one. During system integration, many defects were discovered, some design-related (think: uh-oh, lots of rework...), and the dreaded defect triage process began.

Now it became obvious that the schedule would not be met, and communication of that prospect began. Worse, in the early period, the defect "find rate" exceeded the "fix rate," the schedule became *less and less certain*, and product delivery looked *further and further out*. Even worse, the customer typically now had their first opportunity to see the actual software, and they discovered that it was not exactly what they currently needed. This is because either they didn't know what they wanted back then or their needs changed in the past year. No matter the cause, substantive, additional rework would be required before it could be deployed.

This was a period of *substantial* pain for product managers and for *all* key stakeholders, including development.

Phase 4: Resetting Expectations

Fortunately, we didn't get this far in the software industry without most teams eventually figuring out how to deliver software, so a period of rework and recovery inevitably followed. The scope was typically slashed dramatically, and commitments for schedule and functionality were renegotiated. Of course, credibility was lost throughout the enterprise—the development team to its stakeholders—as well as the product managers to their external stakeholders.

Phase 5: The Season of Perpetual Mistrust

What follows was, for many, the period we are in now—an enduring, persistent period of mistrust between the development and product management organizations. This is often characterized by inter-department distance, hostility, *reduced* communication, and, occasionally, complete dysfunction.

Worse, as the product managers learn that they get only about half what they ask for in the each delivery, they often resolve to ask for twice as much in the next go-around. So, the vicious cycle feeds on itself.

Exiting the Season of Perpetual Mistrust

We describe this not to belabor the pain, but to point out that this may well be the environment in which the enterprise finds itself as we reach the threshold of the agile transformation. Oftentimes at this point, the development teams sponsor the agile change initiative and deliver a few key messages to the product management organization:

> Message 1: "We are heading down a new path, and this type of thing won't happen again."

> Message 2: "But in order for us all to be successful, you'll need to change many of your behaviors, too."

> And perhaps implicitly (and sometimes tactlessly—we are developers, after all...):

> Message 3: "With the new agile model, we are going to stop predicting what will be delivered and when, and we probably won't need those marketing requirements documents anymore, and we also won't be creating those software design specs you've been reviewing, either."

And now, finally, we ask those leading such a transformation to perform the following thought experiment:

> *If you were a product manager operating in this environment, how would you react to such a message?*

Clearly, we'll need a somewhat more mature thought process and a credible strategy to get these key stakeholders on board with our new model.

EVOLVING PRODUCT MANAGEMENT IN THE AGILE ENTERPRISE

But change they must. The reality is that the role, behaviors, and activities of the people who fill the product management function will need to undergo a substantial transformation, as we summarize in Table 14–1.

Adapting to all the behaviors in the right column in Table 14–1 is a substantial change for the newly agile product manager, so we'll discuss each of these briefly.

Table 14–1 The Product Manager's Changing Role in the Agile Enterprise

PM Responsibility	Traditional		Agile
Understand customer need	Up-front and discontinuous	→	Constant interaction
Document requirements	Fully elaborated in documents	→	Constant communication with team
Scheduling	Plan a one-time delivery, way later	→	Continuous near-term roadmap
Prioritize requirements	Not at all or one time only in PRD	→	Reprioritize every release and iteration
Validate requirements	Not applicable; QA responsibility	→	Involved with iterations and each release; smaller, more frequent releases
Manage change	Prohibit change; weekly CCB meetings	→	Adjust at every release and iteration boundary
Assess likelihood of release date	Milestone document review	→	Release dates are fixed, reliable; manage scope expectations

Understanding Customer Need

Understand Customer Need	Up-Front and Discontinuous	→	Constant Interaction
	May be developed over many months, perhaps annually. Write it all down. Hope for the best.		Continuous and incremental discovery Continuous communication to customer and team

The traditional months and months spent up front to determine customer needs are largely eliminated because they cause big delays in the value stream. Instead, we start by implementing what we do know, and we evolve the system from there. Interactions with customers are continuous. Constant, face-to-face communication—customer > product manager > product owner > development team—replaces much of the documentation.

Documenting Requirements

Document Requirements	Fully Elaborated in Documents	→	Constant Communication with Team
	Marketing requirements documents. Product requirement documents. Sign-offs, approvals, and feature "freeze." Throw over the transom to development. Hope they build something like it.		Vision statements Release planning briefings Mock-ups, screen shots, videos, lightweight tools Daily to weekly meetings

Traditional marketing requirements and product requirements documents are often eliminated, reduced in scope, or replaced by lightweight substitutes such as briefings, videos, mock-ups, and so on. Product managers communicate at the feature level, stating intent and avoiding unnecessary specificity (requirements). Intense communication with development teams occurs at iteration and release boundaries, coupled with constant, daily communication with product owners.

Scheduling

Scheduling	Plan a One-Time Delivery, Way Later →	Continuous Near-Term Roadmap
	Annual release schedule (at most)	Date and quality fixed; content variable
	Date and feature fixed	Rolling wave planning
	Quality variable	Potentially shippable increments every quarter
	Hope they meet the date but doubt they will	

Scheduling is continuous; deliverable plans are updated frequently. Quality is fixed, not variable. Teams will always have a high confidence in the current plan of intent for the next release increment. Longer-term deliverables are more vague.

Prioritizing Requirements

Prioritize Requirements	Not at All or One-Time Only in PRD →	Reprioritize Every Release and Iteration
	All features created equal.	Constant reprioritization (Weighted Shortest Job First)
	All "must haves."	Not "What is the highest priority?" but "What do you want next to see delivered next?"
	No prioritization.	

It has always been difficult to prioritize requirements in document form. Spreadsheets and requirements management tools work better mechanically, but even then, it can be difficult to get product managers to prioritize. Perhaps this is because we've taught them that what "prioritization" really means to developers is this: "Here's the stuff I really need you to do, and here's the stuff I invested all these words in that you probably will never do anyway." In agile, we break that deadlock with the availability of near-term incremental releases. It's far easier to get a product manager to commit to "what we should deliver next" than to say, "These features are not so important." Plus, we can apply Weighted Shortest Job First (WSJF) prioritization to product optimal economic outcomes. To do that, we must continually revisit the current CoD.

Validating Requirements

Validate Requirements	Not Applicable; QA responsibility	→	Involved with Iterations and Each Release; Smaller, More Frequent Releases
	Hand off to development and QA.		Attend feature demos.
	Assume system will meet requirements.		See, validate, and adjust at every iteration.
	Pretend they haven't changed in the last year or so.		Reset priorities at rolling wave release planning cadence.
	Hope for the best.		

Validating requirements was never a responsibility ascribed to the product management role. Delivery was late anyway, and we always came up short on requirements. Therefore, it was easy to hide behind "what didn't get done," so it was impossible to say if it would have satisfied the customer. Now, with rapid delivery of code increments that can be externally validated, product managers have the opportunity *and* responsibility to help the team *evolve* requirements to better meet the customer's need, no matter what we thought they were back when the project started. Everyone is accountable. Status is objective and visible.

Managing Change

Manage Change	Prohibit Change; Weekly CCB Meetings	→	Adjust at Every Release and Iteration Boundary
	Manage and try to control change.		Embrace change.
	Feature "freeze" date.		Dev team commits to continuous code quality.
	Defect and feature triage as the end game.		Can add new things up to last responsible moment.

In some ways, managing change was conceptually easier in the old days. Simply, we would freeze the requirements at some point and then minimize, or even try to eliminate, change in order to assure we could deliver something. Of course, the customer's needs were changing whether the code was changing or not, so value decayed while we rejected change. Now, we are engaged in a constant process of embracing change, refactoring code, and trusting our automated test assets to help keep us out of trouble. If it isn't right, we can still change it.

Assessing Status

Assess Likelihood of Release Date	Milestone Document Review	→	Release Dates Are Fixed, Reliable; Manage Scope Expectations
	Attend milestone reviews.		Attend iteration demos.
	Look at indirect artifacts.		See iteration goal progress.
	Pretend the data presented is understandable and can actually help predict delivery.		Evaluate working code in PSI.
			Get interim customer feedback.
	Look in crystal ball; what does 90% complete mean?		Know velocity and actual feature status.
	Lean on the project office to "get this program back on track."		Release predictability measure (RPM) improves forecasting.

Since product managers interface directly with customers, they are usually quite curious about delivery dates. Although the agile truth is to "admit what we don't know," customers ask, even demand, to know what we don't know, and that puts the product manager in the hot seat. ("Hmmm…we don't really know, but 'we don't know' is not an answer.")

So if necessary, they might even make something up. Thereafter, they hope that developers will deliver *something a lot like they said, a lot like when we said they would.* Unfortunately, however, our historical means to know—milestone reviews, status reports, documents, and the like—didn't really tell them much, except "No, it isn't done yet."

Instead, now we have real working code, and our release predictability measure (RPM; see next chapter), which improves forecasting. So, instead of making something up, we can tell our customers, "Here's what's working now, and here's what's going to be working in the next PSI." It still isn't perfect, and it isn't long range, but *it's far better than what we had before.*

RESPONSIBILITIES OF THE AGILE PRODUCT MANAGER

We must recognize that this is a lot of change for a product management organization to address, initiated just because *we* changed *our* development model. Fortunately, however, others have gone before us, and there are some fairly well-defined patterns for effective product management in the agile enterprise.

In Chapter 11, Role of the Product Owner, we suggested a responsibility split between the project manager and product owner roles. We repeat that table as Table 14–2 for context.

Table 14–2   Agile Product Manager and Product Owner Roles and Responsibilities

Agile Product Owner	Agile Product Manager
Product/technology-facing	Market/customer-facing
Co-located and reports into development/technology	Co-located and reports into marketing/business
Focuses on product and implementation technology	Focuses on market segments, portfolio, ROI
Owns the implementation	Owns the Vision and Roadmap
Drives the iterations	Drives the release

More specifically, the product manager's role evolves in agile to fulfill the following primary responsibilities:

- Own the Vision and release backlog
- Manage release content
- Maintain the product Roadmap
- Build an effective product manager/product owner team

We'll define each of these responsibilities in the following sections.

Own the Vision and Release Backlog

As was the case with traditional development, it all starts with a vision of what it is that we need to build.

The Agile Vision

Though the instantiation and delivery models (Vision versus product requirements document) are different, the responsibility for owning the product or solution vision is not new to the role. After all, if the product manager does the following, then building a *Vision*, which articulates a clear direction for addressing gaps and opportunities, is a logical outcome:

- Has a continuous, in-depth understanding of the current solution
- Stays abreast of the latest industry trends
- Understands the changing needs of the market and the customer base
- Articulates a clear direction for addressing gaps and opportunities

We described a variety of methods for documenting and communicating the Vision in Chapter 13.

Communicating the Vision Doesn't Have to be Formal

Each of the methods we described has proven their worth, but it doesn't even have to be that well structured. For example, in one release planning session, there wasn't an opportunity for the four product mangers to collaborate prior to the release planning session. Even if there was an opportunity, it's doubtful that they could have necessarily come up with a harmonized, force-ranked feature set anyway. (Question: Which product manager wants their number-one feature to be placed fourth on the release backlog?) Instead, each product manager was given 45 minutes to present. Each presented a briefing, including a list of the "top ten new" features proposed for the next PSI. Based on this context, the teams then went into the more detailed planning session.

Clearly, this was not an ideal forced-rank prioritization, and it was left up to the teams to understand how the various priorities affected their specific, local plans. But software, like life, can be a little messy. But it worked—in part because the product managers were part of the process, in part because they had visibility into what the teams could and could not achieve in the timebox, and in part because they were able to see and empathize with the other product managers' priorities.

Undelivered Features Fill the Program (Release) Backlog

In the Big Picture and in Chapter 11, Role of the Product Owner, we noted that the primary currency of requirements expressions for the agile teams is the user story, which is contained in the *team's (product) backlog*, as illustrated in Figure 14–3.

In a like manner, the program backlog contains the prioritized set of *features* that have not yet been implemented, as is illustrated in Figure 14–4.

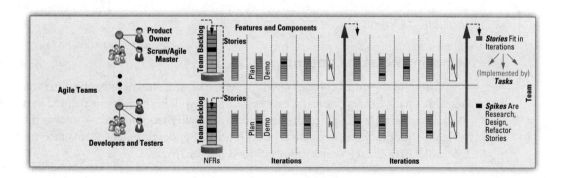

Figure 14–3   Teams and their backlog

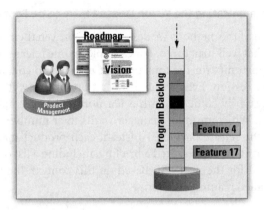

Figure 14–4 Features fill the program backlog.

Like stories, features can be *scheduled* (in a release) or *unscheduled* (waiting for future attention). They are estimated and prioritized with WSJF. Even then, estimates at this scale are coarse-grained and imprecise, which prevents any temptation to over-invest in feature elaboration and estimating.

If and when a feature reaches a priority such that it hits a release-planning boundary, it will be broken into user stories prior to implementation.

Nonfunctional Requirements

In addition, the enterprise is too large to assume that all the development teams will naturally understand the various constraints and "ilities," such as reliability, accuracy, performance, quality, and so on, that reflect system quality as a whole. Therefore, the *nonfunctional* requirements must also be known and communicated as part of the Vision.

Managing Release Content

The Vision for the product is delivered to the market in a stream of continuous and frequent small releases (typically, every 60 to 120 days). Each release is defined by a fixed date, theme, planned feature set, and fixed quality requirements—*scope* is the variable. Product managers deliver the Vision to the development teams face-to-face in the periodic release planning events (Chapter 16).

Preparing for Release Planning

We suggest that agile teams that build cooperative subsystems operate on a synchronized *Agile Release Train* model (Chapter 15). In this model, periodic release planning is the seminal event that aligns the individual teams to the overall strategy of the business unit and enterprise. As such, the release planning event is to the enterprise what iteration planning is to the team, the fixed pacemaker that drives the enterprise's delivery cadence. Therefore, release planning is the focus of much preparation, communication, and coordination by the product managers. Product managers should be well prepared for each such event by doing the following:

- Understand the status of the current (in process) release
- Update the release backlog and priorities
- Meet with other business owners and other product managers to coordinate initiatives and priorities
- Meet with product owners and discuss the preliminary Vision for the upcoming release
- Update any vision artifacts and prepare a Vision briefing

The Release Planning Event: Day 1

The event is typically a full day minimum, more likely two, and often follows a pattern as illustrated in Figure 14–5 and Figure 14–6.

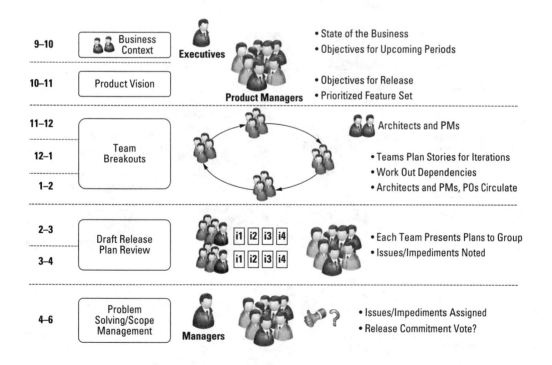

Figure 14–5 Release planning, typical day 1

Day 1 is focused on delivery of the Vision, which the product managers deliver via whatever medium suits them best, followed by initial planning by the teams. Product managers participate in this planning by answering questions, describing features in more detail, and triaging scope as the plans unfold.

Teams present their draft plans at the end of day 1.

The Release Planning Event: Day 2

In most cases, the Vision doesn't "fit" in the release time frame provided (after all, no self-respecting product manager would bring *less* Vision than the teams could likely accomplish). Thus, some day 2 scope management triage and out-of-box thinking is required.

Release Objectives and Commitment

During day 2, the process should start to converge on a set of release (or PSI) objectives, one set for each project team. As we'll describe in Chapter 16, each objective should have a business value, which is set by the business owner, typically the product manager, business analysis, or sales/marketing stakeholder. An example of such a set appears in Figure 14–7.

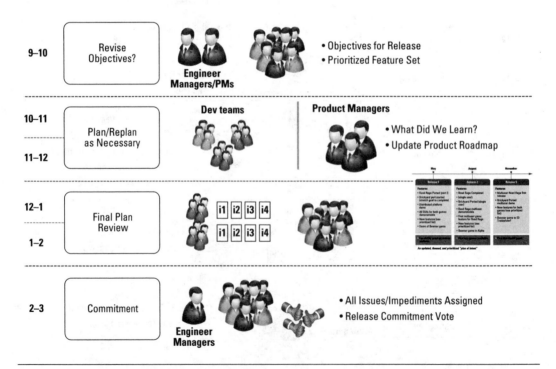

Figure 14–6   Release planning, typical day 2

Objective	Bus Value
1. Thermostat Over-the-Air Update	10
2. Next generation thermostat firmware (V300x only)	4
2. First pricing programs	10
3. Gateway Pointing Rearchitecture	6
4. Trade show demo by 3/15	10
5. Release v3.1 upgrade to channel	9
Stretch goals	
All thermostat versions	4
Pricing program 2	8

Figure 14–7   Example release objectives

The total set of goals established by each team creates a prioritized, aggregate set of objectives for the next release increment. If the release planning session converges, as it should, the goals will be defined and committed to by the teams. At this point, all teams and product managers are in alignment. They have agreed to a set of tangible set of objectives, which have been created by the teams based on their known velocity, and risks have been addressed. Now the program has a clear, common target for the next PSI.

Tracking the Release

All the hard work the enterprise has put into the agile transformation should now start paying dividends. Once a commitment is achieved, the primary responsibility for *delivering the release* in a series of short iterations resides within the project teams. After all, they write and test all the code, and in agile they are both *empowered* and *accountable* to achieve the agreed-to objectives.

Even then, however, the agile enterprise recognizes that continuous trade-offs of changing requirements and scope is inevitable, so the product manager also plays a pivotal role in *helping the teams meet the release objectives*. Doing so requires ongoing tracking and managing of the release and adjusting its content. Fortunately, the agile enterprise model is replete with visibility, so understanding the actual versus planned status of a release is no longer a crystal-ball activity. Instead, there are a number of mechanisms product managers use to keep the Agile Release Train on its rails.

- *Constant informal communication with the product owners:* The product manager has a direct liaison to the teams via the teams' product owners. The fan-out is not too extreme; a single product manager may typically interact with some small number (three to six) of product owners and thereby have ready status from all the project teams that must collaborate in meeting the release objectives.

- *Participation in the release management team:* Earlier, we introduced the release management team (RMT) that has the primary responsibility for shepherding the release to market. Product managers participate on this team. The RMT typically meets weekly to assess release status and adjust scope where necessary.

- *Attendance at iteration demos:* Agile's visibility also provides an inherent opportunity to *see the working code as it develops.* This happens in the context of the iteration review, which includes a product demo. The every-other-week demo provides product managers with objective status and progress. This one- to two-hour weekly forum is a not-to-be missed opportunity to see the product, interact with the teams, provide feedback, and make mid-course adjustments where necessary.

- *Status via agile project management tooling:* As we'll see in Chapter 15, The Agile Release Train, based on the physics of agile software development (teams' known velocities, hierarchical feature-to-story breakdown, story point estimates and burndown, and so on) the teams' agile tooling should provide a solid, quantitative basis with which to assess release progress. Product management should routinely be able to see reports that can help answer the following questions.

  - What is the overall release burndown (probability to bring the entire release in on time)?
  - What is the status of each feature of interest?
  - How are the teams tracking to the release objectives?

Together, this information gives the RMT and product managers real, objective knowledge of where they are. Even more importantly, they'll have the data they need to reason about what scope or resourcing changes might be necessary to "land" the release on time.

Maintaining the Roadmap

An Updated, Themed, and Prioritized "Plan of Intent"

In the previous chapter, we discussed the Roadmap, which consists of a series of planned release dates, each of which has a theme and a prioritized feature set.

This is the primary artifact that agile teams use to communicate the way in which the teams intend to implement the Vision over time. At the conclusion of each release planning session, the product managers typically meet to consolidate the objectives and update the Roadmap. At that time, the plan for Release *Next* is clear, and there is also good visibility into Release *Next+1*. Beyond that, however, it is, at best, an educated guess based on the relative backlog priorities and an understanding of the team's release predictability measure. The Roadmap serves as the primary communication vehicle, particularly to outside stakeholders, as to the current *plan of intent* for the program.

Building an Effective Product Manager/Product Owner Team

The product manager/product owner team provides the "steering wheel" that guides the enterprise to its solution outcomes. From a reporting standpoint, we described the typical relationship as a "fat dotted line" and noted the following:

> *Product managers typically report into marketing or business, and product owners typically report into development. However, product owners are also honorary members of the product management organization from whence they receive overall product direction.*

Of course, there is a natural tension in this relationship because the needs of the key constituents (development team capacity versus business/customers/market) are different. The product managers naturally want *more product more quickly*, and there is no upper limit to their demands. Product owners and development teams want that too but are sensitized to the inevitable technology, resource, architectural, and quality constraints endemic to every software project. And there is no upper limit to their demands.

Needed: A Sense of Balance

This natural tension is a direct delegation of the larger business-versus-technology enterprise-balancing act, as is illustrated in Figure 14–8.

If the business (product management) solely has its way, it's possible that expediency of value delivery will rule, and technology might get the short stick. After all, what business owner would not want to accelerate value delivery at every opportunity?

If technology (product owner/team) solely has its way, there can be little doubt that the product will be built on sound (and the latest!) technology without shortcuts or quality compromises. But the business value delivery may get the short stick. After all, what technologist wouldn't want to build the most extensible and reliable platform to support *future* customer needs?

So, the best we can do is to first recognize and then balance these competing interests. Occasionally we can purposefully tip it a little this way or that (refactoring versus new features) based on the current business context. Perhaps more importantly, it is in the heat of this natural friction and its constant resource constraints that the sparks of true innovation and creativity are born. If it were easy, anybody could do it.

Essential Ingredients: Collaboration, Partnership, and Trust

It is clear that building an effective relationship between these teams is critical. In a series of blog posts,[4] Jennifer Fawcett describes how to go about it, noting the

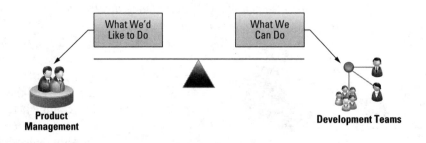

Figure 14–8   The balancing act—what we'd like to do versus what we think we can do

---

4. *www.agileproductowner.com*

essential ingredients of *collaboration*, *partnership*, and *trust*. Together, we provide a few tips for building these essential ingredients.

- *Collaboration:* Synchronize and communicate the ever-changing priorities daily. Invite product managers to attend daily stand-ups. Politely insist on attendance at most/all demos. Have an "open door" policy for all development and product management meetings. If one party cannot attend, summarize results in minutes or email.
- *Partnership:* Ask each other, "How can I help?" Create and participate in after-hour events to eliminate any "us versus them" thinking. Prepare for release planning together. Operate under the "never surprise each other in front of others" rule.
- *Trust:* Trust each other to make the right decisions. When (not if!) your product manager/product owner partner makes a decision that conflicts with yours, support that decision. Teams will know you are both empowered, will "cover each other's backside," and will also know that you can both be trusted with business decisions and authority.

SUMMARY

In this chapter, we described the role of the product manager in the agile enterprise. We started by highlighting the traditional responsibilities of product managers within software and system vendors and the similar role of the business analyst in IT shops. We then noted that, although many of the larger responsibilities are the same in the traditional and agile enterprise, the manner in which these responsibilities are fulfilled must undergo some pretty significant changes. We described a challenging organizational context for the transformation, one that is often characterized by a *season of perpetual mistrust*. We then described the specific activities of the agile product manager and how they participate in driving release content and helping assure release success. Finally, we provided some guidance as to how to build effective relationships between the product manager and product owner/ development teams. It is that relationship that will determine the ultimate velocity of value delivery, and too much friction there will slow down the gears of our lean software machine.

We also highlighted the fact that the product manager is the driving force behind the Agile Release Train and the cadence-based release planning events that drive the trains. We'll discuss these two topics in the next two chapters.

Chapter 15

THE AGILE RELEASE TRAIN

Today's development processes typically deliver information asynchronously in large batches. Flow-based processes deliver information in a regular cadence in small batches. Cadence lowers transaction costs and makes small batches more economically feasible.

—Don Reinertsen

The original title for this chapter was to be "The Release" or perhaps "Releasing" or "Release Planning and Execution." But none of these titles, nor others that I toyed with, communicated the essence of what I intended to communicate. Each of them implied a thing that was historically true—that the *release event* or the *release planning* event, or both, were a "really big deal" in the enterprise. It represented either the *beginning* (release planning) or the *end* (the release) of some significant project—a major milestone in the history of the company. But that didn't resonate for me, and it harkened back to the psychology of the waterfall, whereby achieving a release was some giant milestone—a cause for celebration, write the press releases, schedule an all-hands event, get your CEO on stage, or whatever.

None of these notions reflects life in the agile enterprise. Instead, we see a continuous *flow* of releasing value to the users in small, frequent increments—a continuous build of value added to the marketplace. Releasing often, yet typically with little fanfare. Properly done, it's a big win in the market, but it's hard to look backward and determine exactly when the successful tipping point was reached.

That's not to say that releasing a product to the market with traditional fanfare is no longer apropos, and enterprises learn how to make newsworthy events out of steady, incremental progress. But this chapter will focus primarily on how to *make each product release a successful and routine event*—an event that is indeed planned and eagerly anticipated yet one that happens almost on autopilot. We call this process the *Agile Release Train* (ART).

INTRODUCTION TO THE AGILE RELEASE TRAIN

In Part I of this book, we introduced the Program level of the Big Picture with an overview graphic and an explanation. A portion of the graphic is provided in Figure 15–1 for context.

In the figure, we see that at the Program level, teams and activities are organized around an ongoing series of incremental releases. The releases may be *internal* and used for evaluating the system as a whole (in which case we call them PSIs, or *potentially shippable increments*). The releases may be made *external*, in that they are made generally available to our customers (in which case the *Release* label is more appropriate).

In any case, the development of the software asset base occurs with a standard cadence of iterations that has been established by the enterprise. In the Big Picture, we've illustrated four *development* iterations (indicated by a full iteration backlog), followed by one *hardening* iteration (indicated by an empty backlog) prior to each release increment.

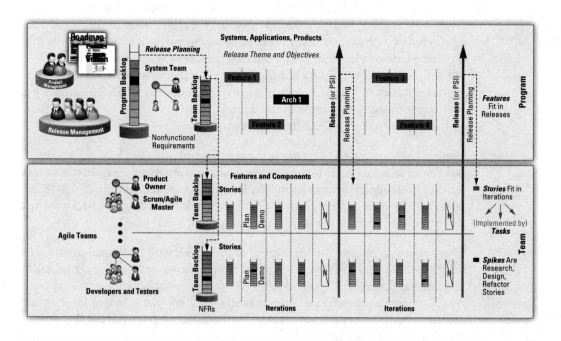

Figure 15–1   The Big Picture implying the Agile Release Train

This pattern is arbitrary, and there is no fixed rule for how many times a team iterates prior to a PSI or how much, if any, time or investment in hardening is required. However, many enterprises apply this model with a repeating pattern of 4 to 5 development iterations, followed by a hardening iteration, creating a cadence of a shippable increment about every 90 days. This is a fairly natural production rhythm that corresponds to a reasonable external release frequency for customers and also provides a nice quarterly planning cadence for the enterprise.

In any case, the length and number of iterations per release increment and the decision as to when to actually release a PSI are left to the judgment of each enterprise. However, the planning of an *external* release requires special care and attention, as we'll cover later.

Rationale for the Agile Release Train

While we introduced the Agile Release Train early in Part I of the book, we didn't take the time to justify its existence or use. We simply posited it as an answer to some set of problems or unasked questions. However, because implementing the ART is no small feat for the enterprise and because its use can be quite instrumental in achieving enterprise success, it seems reasonable to introduce the rationale before we go any further.

Like much of the guidance in this book, many of us did not start out with the ART when we headed down the agile path. More typically, we rolled out Scrum/XP/hybrid variants and focused on getting the teams successfully building small increments of working, tested functionality in a short timebox. Moreover, if we were working with only one or a few teams, releasing the product did not create many additional challenges. We could release it when we felt like it and whenever the market required it. Coordinating our efforts wasn't extraordinarily complicated either—we could do that by just talking among ourselves in the hallways, or maybe we'd have to reserve a conference room to meet with other stakeholders; quality, sales, marketing, and so on, would all be present.

This was appropriate and was the *simplest thing that could possibly work.*

However, as the number of teams engaged in agile development in the company increased, as the enterprise grew with its successes, as we acquired new teams and new products, or as our customers drove us to higher levels of integration among the various components of our solution, a *substantial* problem began to emerge. This became the problem:

How do we harness all that new, empowered, but potentially entropic, energy into a cohesive team of teams that can deliver ever larger and more integrated piles of value to our customers?

For many, the first temptation was to reimplement some of the former planning and governance models we had abandoned when we "went agile." "That should get things on track," we thought. The results of that approach are pretty obvious—the teams fought back hard against the new overhead and governance and lack of empowerment that it implied. Worse, those who attempted to implement, or reimplement, those governance practices became impediments to be avoided ("Careful, don't make eye contact with the program manager"). Simply stated, that didn't work.

That left many companies in an in-between state—improving performance of agile teams but still very hard to build an integrated solution. Whether we understood it or not, the "process model" we had implemented for larger-scale system releases was starting to look something like Figure 15–2.

Teams were iterating with some degree of success; indeed, some were now maniacally focused and committed to their specific product, feature, or component. That seemed like real progress.

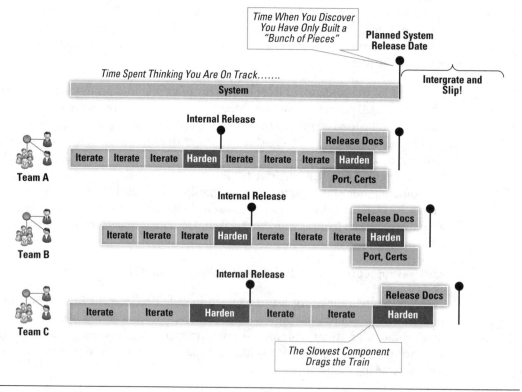

Figure 15–2   Three agile teams building a system, before the release train

Adapted from *Scaling Software Agility: Best Practices for Large Enterprises* [Leffingwell 2007]

But their iteration lengths were different; continuous integration at the system level was unachievable, and the vision for the larger system was hard to decipher or even infer. As a result, as newly agile as we believed ourselves to be, our releases and release quality still suffered from some of the same deferred risk practices as the waterfall model that we had just so recently abandoned!

To address this problem, the Agile Release Train evolved.

Principles of the Agile Release Train

The Agile Release Train provides alignment and helps manage risk by providing Program-level cadence and synchronization. It is based on agreement and adoption of a set of common operating principles (OK, rules) that are followed by *all* teams that will be placing cargo (user value) on their particular train. These rules include the following.

- Frequent, periodic planning and release (or PSI) dates for the solution are fixed (dates are fixed, quality is fixed, scope is variable).
- Teams apply common iteration lengths.
- Intermediate, global, objective milestones are established.
- Continuous system integration is implemented at the top, system level, as well as at the feature and component levels.
- Release increments (PSIs) are available at regular (60- to 120-day typical) intervals for customer preview, internal review, and system-level QA.
- System-level *hardening* iterations are used to reduce technical debt and to provide time for specialty release-level validation and testing.
- For teams to build on top of like constructs, certain infrastructure components—common interfaces, system development kits, common installs, user stores, licensing utilities, and the like—must typically track ahead.

Constraining teams to the dates and fixed quality criteria means that the systems, feature, and component functionality must be flexible (or we will quickly find ourselves back inside the iron triangle).

Although these rules may not seem that constraining, the fact is that this model requires an additional degree of agility and flexibility on all teams and stakeholders who participate.

- *From the perspective of the team*: To be assured of meeting a date, a team might need a primary plan and a fallback plan (or perhaps a set of options) they can deploy as necessary to make sure they can "get their cargo on the train." In some cases, the fallback plan can be as simple as planning to ship the old version. Even then, the team must support any new interfaces, provide backward compatibility, and be certain to not violate any other common requirements (regulatory compliance, localizations, and so on) that may be imposed on the cargo.

■ *From the perspective of product, program, and executive management:* The plan is a result of a collaboration, which weighs the input of all stakeholders and also matches input (release requirements) to capacity (development team velocities) so that flow can be achieved. Rarely, if ever, do expectations of input and output match. Compromise is required. Moreover, the result of the plan is just that, a *plan*, and the exact scope of the final achievement can still not be known for certain up front.

Although implementing the Agile Release Train is a far from trivial task, implementation is a must for the agile enterprise. It addresses two imperatives that are necessary to achieve success within the enterprise:

■ Driving strategic alignment across the teams
■ Institutionalizing product development flow

We'll look at each of these in the following sections.

DRIVING STRATEGIC ALIGNMENT

Empowering individual agile teams to truly focus on rapid value delivery typically unlocks the raw energy, motivation, and innovation that has likely been stilted by our pre-agile process and governance models. That's why we do it. However, that alone is not enough, because the teams will naturally tend toward *local optimization.* They'll do what they can to deliver requirements to their customer constituency, but they have less interest (or perhaps awareness and ability) in taking a more global view.[1] After all, having two masters is more complicated.

However, in the lean enterprise, the highest benefit is achieved when we achieve *global optimization.*[2] To do this, we must implement systems, like the ART for product programs, that purposefully drive the teams toward the global targets, as illustrated in Figure 15–3.

In this way, we can align our *mass* to a common direction and achieve far more *force* to address the targets of opportunity. We can have both local *and* global alignment to a common goal.

---

1. One VP, who had responsibility for a dozen such agile teams, called this his "12 tribes of Israel" problem—all empowered, all agile, yet each wandering independently toward their own version of the promised land.

2. Product Development Flow Principle 8.7—*There is more value created with overall alignment than with local excellence.*

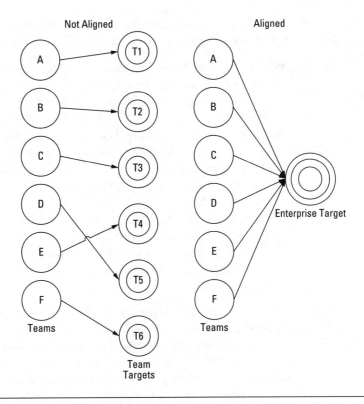

Figure 15–3 Aligning agile teams to a common target

INSTITUTIONALIZING PRODUCT DEVELOPMENT FLOW

In addition to driving alignment, the Agile Release Train is instrumental in institutionalizing *product development flow*. In so doing, the ART supports the eight primary product development flow themes that we described in Chapter 1. Understanding this mapping is the key to understanding the criticality and motivation for the ART itself.

- *Theme 1, Take an economic view:* Make trade-off decisions based on economic rationale. One such trade-off is how we frequently we release the product. Smaller releases substantially improve the ROI of software development by accelerating the release of value to the customer. This helps capture early market share and drives gross margins by delivering features to the market at the time when the market values them most highly. In addition, we can reprioritize features at every planning boundary, based on the then-current cost of delay.

- *Theme 2, Actively manage queues:* The short, frequent planning cycles of the Agile Release Train help actively manage queue lengths across the enterprise.

  - *Team backlogs:* These queues of waiting stories are generally limited to about the amount of work that can be accomplished in a single PSI. Planning much beyond that is generally not very productive for the teams, because strategic priorities could change at any release boundary.
  - *Release (Program) backlogs:* These queues of waiting features are typically limited to those features that can realistically be implemented in the next release or two. Beyond that, product managers understand that they may be overinvesting in elaboration of features that will never see the light of day.
  - *Portfolio backlogs:* These queues of waiting epics and future projects are typically limited to those epics that could likely find their way to release planning in the next six months or so. Too early, or too in-depth, investment in business cases for projects that will not be implemented is a form of waste.

- *Theme 3, Understand and exploit variability:* Since a high degree of variability is inherent in software development, frequent, cadence-based re-planning provides the opportunity to adjust and adapt to circumstances as fact patterns change. New, unanticipated opportunities can be exploited by quickly adapting plans. Critical paths and bottlenecks become clear. Resources can be adjusted to optimize throughput and better avoid unanticipated delays.

- *Theme 4, Reduce batch sizes:* Large batch sizes create unnecessary variability and cause delays in delivery and quality. ART reduces batch sizes by releasing to development only those features that are prioritized, are elaborated sufficiently for development, and are sized to fit within the next release cycle. This helps avoids overloading the development teams with multiple development projects, which otherwise causes multiplexing, thrashing, and loss of productivity. Face-to-face planning provides high-bandwidth communication and instant feedback, so the transport (handoff) batch delay between teams is minimized.

- *Theme 5, Apply WIP constraints:* Teams plan their own work and take on only the amount of features that their velocity indicates they can achieve. This forces the input rate (agreed-to, negotiated release objectives) to match capacity (what the teams can do in the release). The current release timebox prevents uncontrolled expansion of work so that the current release does not become a "feature magnet" for new ideas. The global WIP pool, consisting of features and epics in the enterprise backlog, is constrained by the local WIP pools, which reflects the team's current backlog as driven by the current PSI. Limiting WIP increases response time to new, higher-priority activities.

- *Theme 6, Control flow under uncertainty—cadence and synchronization:* Cadence and synchronization help us manage uncertainty and variability by keeping accumulated variances to single interval. In the ART, we achieve this through periodic *planning* (cadence) and *integrating* (synchronization).

  - *Planning:* The release train planning *cadence* makes planning predictable and lowers transaction costs (facilities, overhead, travel). Planning can be scheduled well in advance, allowing participation by all key stakeholders in most planning events and making face-to-face information transport reliable, efficient, and predictable. Periodic re-planning (*resynchronization*) allows us to limit variance and misalignment to a single planning interval.

  - *Integrating:* The regular, system-wide integration provides high-fidelity system tests and objective assessment of project status at regular intervals. Transaction costs are lowered as teams prioritize investment in the infrastructure necessary for continuous integration, automated testing, and more automated deployment. Since planning is bottom-up, (performed by the teams and based on team's actual known velocity) and short-term, delivery becomes predictable. Most all that has been planned should be reliably available as scheduled.

- *Theme 7, Get feedback as fast as possible:* The fast feedback of the iteration and release cycle allows us to take fast corrective action. Even within the course of a PSI, feedback is no more than two weeks (or the iteration length) away. Small incremental releases to customers allow us to track more quickly to their actual, rather than anticipated, needs. Incorrect paths can be abandoned more quickly (at worst, at the next planning cycle).

- *Theme 8, Decentralize control:* Release plans are prepared by the teams that are doing the actual implementation, rather than by a planning office or project management function. Commitments to the plans are bottom-up based on each individual's commitment to teammates and team-to-team commitments reached during the planning cycle. Once planned, the teams are responsible for execution, albeit subject to appropriate lightweight governance and release management. Agile project management tooling automates routine reporting; management does not have to slow down and annoy the teams to assess actual status.

So, as we see, the ART is fundamental in achieving strategic alignment and Program-level, product development flow. In the next sections, we'll describe how to implement and manage the Agile Release Train.

DESIGNING THE AGILE RELEASE TRAIN

One initial activity is to determine the *release train domain*, that is, who will be planning and working together and what products, services, features, or components the train will deliver. In the Big Picture, we've indicated that there is some collection (or pod) of agile teams that constitute a program. That is often the case, and in the smaller enterprise or business unit, the ART domain consists of everyone on the team who will participate in the outcome. If the assets you are building can be built with five to eight agile teams, then the planning domain *is* the program, and not much more thought is required.

However, in the larger enterprise, there may be dozens (or more) of such teams, and planning everything together is not feasible. In that case, we must first determine who will be on the train. Considerations should include the following.

- Trains should be focused on a single, primary product, solution, or value theme objective.
- Trains work best when between 50 to 100 people, including stakeholders outside the team, contribute to the train.
- Teams with features and components that have a high degree of interdependencies should plan and work together.
- Locale is a major consideration. Wherever possible, train teams should be co-located, or at least geographic distribution should be as limited as feasible, because that simplifies planning logistics and cooperation among the teams.

PLANNING THE RELEASE

Once the parameters and the cadence for the ART have been established, the teams can establish a release-planning schedule for the train. Since the dates for the PSIs are fixed, the release planning dates can be fixed as much as a year in advance. This helps lowers facility, travel, overhead, and other transaction costs associated with the event.

Given the importance of the event in driving strategic alignment, planning and executing the release event is a project unto itself. We'll cover release planning thoroughly in the next chapter.

Release Objectives

As we will see in the next chapter, one important result of the release planning process is a set of *release objectives*, which define the individual team and aggregate goals of the release. These quantitative objectives are a key artifact of the release planning session and provide us with an important baseline for release governance and tracking. Each objective will have been ranked by business value, as the example in Figure 15–4 illustrates.

Objective	Bus Value
1. Thermostat Over-the-Air Update	10
2. Next generation thermostat firmware (V300x only)	4
2. First pricing programs	10
3. Gateway Pointing Rearchitecture	6
4. Trade show demo by 3/15	10
5. Release v3.1 upgrade to channel	9
Stretch goals	
All thermostat versions	4
Pricing program 2	8

Figure 15–4   An example of release objectives, ranked by business value

Most of the objectives will be features from the backlog, and this gives us the targets we need to track and manage the release.

TRACKING AND MANAGING THE RELEASE

With the quality and date fixed, it is certain that some amount of adjustment to content will be needed during the course of the PSI. In support of this need, the enterprise will likely have implemented some form of agile requirements/project management tooling, which provides support for the higher-level status views needed by product managers and other stakeholders. Such tooling should provide hierarchical, release-level burndown so that the program can assess, *on an aggregate basis*, exactly where they stand within the release, as Figure 15–5 shows.

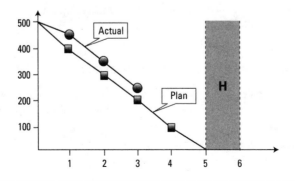

Figure 15–5   Release-level burndown

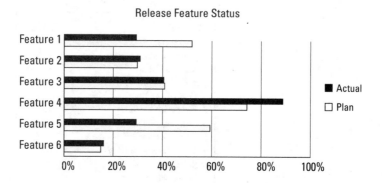

Figure 15–6   Release status by feature

This chart provides a sense of the probability of "landing" (delivering the expected value) of the release. However, by itself, it doesn't provide any information as to *which* features may or may not be delivered. For that, the tooling should also provide reports on the status of each individual feature, which is in turn based on percentage of story points completion for that feature, relative to plan. Such a chart might look something like Figure 15–6.

Together, this information provides the objective knowledge of where it is and, even more importantly, what changes might be necessary to successfully deliver the release. After all, content (scope and feature) management is continuous in agile, and an in-flight ART is no exception.

RELEASE RETROSPECTIVE

Each PSI boundary also provides the opportunity for a Program-level release retrospective, wherein the teams assess how well they did and take corrective action to increase the velocity, quality, and reliability of the next release increment. This retrospective can also include a quantitative measure of *predictability*, as we'll describe in the following section.

MEASURING RELEASE PREDICTABILITY

If you ask top executives what they would most like to see out of the software development process, many will answer "predictability." And that is one of the many challenges in agile. We can reliably predict *quality* (by fixing it and adopting effective technical practices) and *date* (by fixing it) and *cost* (by fixing the team size and the

PSI date), but we can't actually predict *functionality*, at least in the longer term. If we did, we'd be right back in the iron triangle that has served us so poorly in the past. Moreover, if we predicted and controlled functionality long term, then we'd have to temporarily ignore the new opportunities the market presents. That isn't agile.

However, as professionals, we must be able to provide our enterprise with a reasonably reliable predictor of upcoming events, at least near term, as well as some sense of the future product Roadmap that we intend to execute.

When implemented properly, the ART can provide just such a predictability measure, at least for the next PSI (or maybe two). That gives the enterprise from three to six months of visibility into upcoming release content—enough to plan, strategize, and support with market communications, release launches, and so on. The *release objectives* that we established during release planning are our primary means to do this.

During each release retrospective, the teams can meet with their business owners to self-assess the percentage of business values they achieved for each objective. This can be done both at the Team and Program levels. For example, a program might rate its accomplishments as in Figure 15–7.

Objective	Bus Value	
	(plan)	actual
1. Thermostat Over-the-Air Update	10	8
2. Next generation thermostat firmware	4	0
2. First pricing programs	10	8
3. Gateway Pointing Rearchitecture	6	4
4. Trade show demo by 3/15	10	10
5. Release v3.1 upgrade to channel	9	9
Totals	49	39
% achievement: 79%		

Figure 15–7 Plan versus actual release accomplishments

Release Objectives Process Control Band

In the example shown in Figure 15–7, the program accomplished 79% of its release objectives. The questions arises, how good, or bad, is that? To answer this, we must return to our lean principles and the context for the enterprise program.

On the surface, at least, it might appear that accomplishing 100% of release objectives is the only worthy goal. Closer analysis, however, tells us differently. For a team to routinely accomplish 100% of its release objectives, they must do either of the following:

- Drive all risk out of the plan by eliminating or curtailing innovation and risk taking
- Back off on objectives so as to assure completion

Neither of these optimizes the economic impact of our efforts. To achieve that, we need to operate successfully in some acceptable *process control band* so that the program has reasonable predictability and yet allows for the variability, "optionality," and stretch goals inherent with software development.

In our experience, a program that can reliability achieve *most* of its release objectives is a trusted program that is an extraordinary asset to the enterprise. In this case, the release predictability measure should fall in a process control band something like that in Figure 15–8 over time.

In this figure, while team B, the controlled team, does not routinely hit 100% of its release objectives—leaving room for innovation, stretch objectives, and responsible risk taking—it is still fairly predictable because it typically achieves most of its objectives. Team A, the out-of-control team, however, is all over the map. It's hard

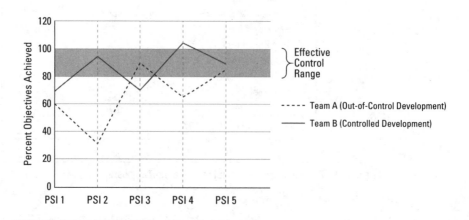

Figure 15–8   Release predictability process control band

to manage any program or enterprise with the characteristics of team A. You simply can't depend on them to do anything like they said they would and that will cause real difficulties in delivering the program.

By creating and measuring this predictability measure for the program at every PSI, the enterprise can eventually achieve the right balance of predictability and risk taking, thereby achieving the optimum economic outcomes.

RELEASING

That is all well and good, but there is still work ahead. The Agile Release Train simplifies software development by "making routine that which can be routine." Planning and team coordination are simplified. Work in process is limited. Flow is achieved. In describing it so far, however, we have oversimplified one of the more complicated challenges, which is an understanding of when to actually *release* a set of assets to the customers, distribution, or marketplace. To coordinate the ART with actual releases of products, we must consider three separate cases: *releasing on the same cadence as the ART*, *releasing less frequently*, and *releasing more frequently*. We'll look at each of these in the following sections.

Releasing on the ART Cadence

When you look simplistically at the Big Picture, it tends to imply that the planning and release cadences are identical, as Figure 15–9 illustrates.

This is the simplest case, because planning, releasing, and release retrospectives are coordinated by the same cadence and same calendar dates. In addition, the hardening iterations are timed nicely to support the more extensive release activities, which can include everything from preparation of release notes and customer documentation, standards validation, load and performance testing, built-in demos and tutorials, updating user documentation, and the like.

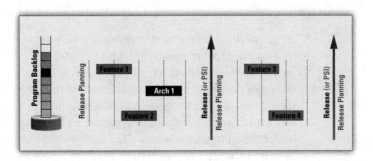

Figure 15–9   Releasing on the ART cadence

This is the model used by a number of Software as a Service (SaaS) companies. In that case, the Agile Release Train is conceptually simple because they release frequently and have only a single platform to support. All customers are migrated to the new release at the same time. There is one planning session and only one release per PSI.

This is incredibly convenient to the program because *all* activities—internal supporting functions as well as customer-facing activities—can be driven by the same cadence and synchronization as the development of the assets themselves. Program planning is harmonized. The model is conceptually simple. Life is good and lean.

However, this is not always a practical case, so other models come into play.

Releasing Less Frequently Than the ART Cadence

In many cases, releasing on a fast PSI cadence may not be possible. For example, in some enterprise settings, deployed systems constitute critical infrastructure of a customer's operating environment. Even if the customers would like to have the new software, service-level and license agreements may be prohibitive, and there is the overhead and disruption of installation. Plus, there is always the fear of regressive bugs affecting customer operations, potentially on a large scale. Scary stuff.

In other cases, the timelines of an enterprise's building systems that contain both software *and* hardware, such as mobile phones and other devices, are often driven by long-lead hardware items—displays, chipsets, keyboards, cases, and the like. Here, there are actual laws of physics involved that must be obeyed. You have to have the new hardware first, so releasing early and incrementally is not an option.

In these cases, releasing on a PSI cadence is simply not an option, and the planning and releasing activities must be decoupled.

There are other reasons to decouple the PSI cadence from the release cadence as well. For example, while the sales and marketing and development teams are headed to the same end goal—that is, more and higher-quality product released to the market more quickly—their intermediate objectives may be quite different.

- *For development*, the goal is to deliver more value to the market more quickly on a cadence that provides the highest productivity and fastest market feedback. Indeed, you often see development teams pushing for ever-shorter release cycles to put pressure on themselves to fix the major impediments in their own internal processes. Agile development practices such as concurrent testing and continuous integration are best implemented and mastered under these intense pressures. Also, the more routine the operations of daily build, release retrospectives, iteration acceptance testing, and the like, become, the easier it is to manage their daily and weekly activities and to thereby avoid the "death-march" experiences at the end of each release cycle. So, development likes to push for very fast release cycles.

- *For sales and marketing*, the goal is also to deliver more software as rapidly as possible, but they also strive to optimize the *market impact* of their efforts. This means release frequency may be limited by practicalities such as the following:

  - Not disrupting customers with too-frequent upgrades
  - Not complicating any big deals in process that are based on the current released product
  - Having worthy (bigger) news to take to the market, typically in synchronization with analyst tours, trade shows, and so on
  - Avoiding overloading internal support infrastructures for marketing communication, sales and support training, and so on

Separation of Development from Release and Marketing Concerns

Although the goals are the same, the perspectives and concerns of these two departments may be quite different. Therefore, we need to provide a model that allows for *separation of those concerns* to achieve a higher degree of flexibility and greater market impact. Figure 15–10 illustrates such a model.

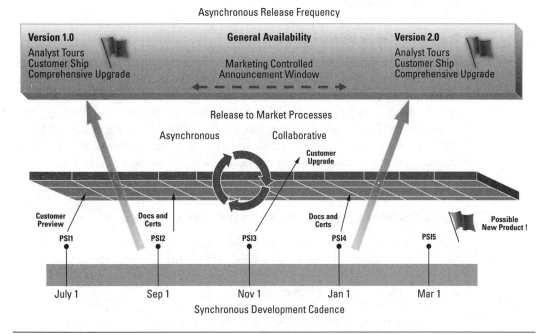

Figure 15–10   Separation of development, release, and marketing concerns

Source: *Scaling Software Agility: Best Practices for Large Enterprises* [Leffingwell 2007]

This model decouples asset development from product release via a "general availability firewall." The firewall allows "just the right number of releases" to reach the market at "just the right time."

The process is flexible, asynchronous, and collaborative among the development, operations, and sales and marketing teams. Figure 15–10 illustrates the following characteristics.

- PSI1 is an internal release, suitable for customer previews.
- PSI2 is preannounced and released to the market as version 1.0.
- PSI3 is a quiet release, perhaps just deployed to customers under maintenance, but it may not be newsworthy because it follows version 1.0 by only 60 days.
- PSI4 is positioned to the market as a major new release because it incorporates two releases of new functionality (PSI 3 and 4).
- PSI5 may even be positioned as a new product, rather than a continuum of the existing product line.

Of course, this release schedule is just an example that shows the flexibility of the model, and your train will address different objectives. There is no need to predict in advance exactly how an Agile Release Train will evolve; just build *it* and figure out what to do with *it* later.

The Firewall Can Be Opaque or Transparent

The firewall can be as opaque or transparent as the enterprise needs. In other words, the development of new functionality can be kept confidential, or customers can be told about the availability of new releases or even the product Roadmap. The development team is free to establish the best production rhythm it can master, continuously building incremental product functionality. Marketing is free to deliver external releases on an ad hoc basis, responding contemporaneously to current market conditions, competitive responses, and so on, or on a planned, programmatic basis—whatever meets their needs.

Releasing More Frequently Than the ART Cadence

For programs and enterprises that are building systems of systems, either of the previous two cases can still appear to be overly simplistic. In these cases, although the larger system may lend itself to either of these models, various components of the system may have to serve different masters.

For example, in a securities trading system, back-office transaction servers may need to be updated for ongoing securities compliance on their own independent schedule. Client-side software may be gated by availability of new types of securities to be traded or access to new securities marketplaces.

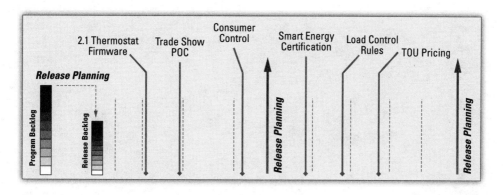

Figure 15–11   Releasing more frequently than ART cadence

In our case study example, the Tendril platform is composed of a number of different components. For various business reasons, these components often need to be released to the market at various times, as Figure 15–11 shows.

In this third case, releasing more frequently, the PSI cadence becomes a *planning* cadence, rather than a *release* cadence. The periodic planning function still provides the cadence, synchronization, and alignment the enterprise needs to manage variability, but forcing the development of all assets to the same cadence is unnecessary and over-constrains the ability to deliver value, as and where necessary.

SUMMARY

This chapter introduced the Agile Release Train as a mechanism to drive strategic alignment and institutionalize product development flow. We described the rationale behind the model, along with the mechanics for implementing a release train. We also used the ART to introduce a predictability measure the enterprise can use to help predict near-term deliverables. Finally, we showed how the ART is highly flexible and how it can be used to provide enterprise alignment, synchronization, and cadence, even if release requirements do not align perfectly with the ART cadence itself. We hope that this introduction will provide the motivation and background you need to implement a release train in your program so that you too can achieve the steady drumbeat of value delivery that characterizes truly agile programs.

In the next chapter, we'll describe a thorough approach to release planning, which you can use to put your own train firmly on the tracks.

Chapter 16

RELEASE PLANNING

Worldly affairs do not always go according to a plan and orders have to change rapidly in response to a change in circumstances. If one sticks to the idea that once set, a plan should not be changed, a business cannot exist for long.

—Taiichi Ohno, widely considered to be the father of lean manufacturing

We Plan to Re-plan.

—A T-shirt seen at the Agile Alliance Conference

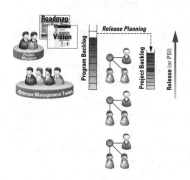

In the previous chapter, we saw how the Agile Release Train implements systemic product development flow at the Program level. This is the primary tool programs use to align the teams to a common vision and to provide cadence and synchronization of the software assets the program is developing. We also introduced release planning as the seminal event—the heartbeat—of the release train itself.

In this chapter, we'll provide a detailed description of a prototypical release planning event. Although individual program circumstances will vary, the format we are describing here has been well-tested in many such events, including some with as many as 14 teams and well over 100 attendees.

PREPARING FOR RELEASE PLANNING

Given the importance of the event, the number of attendees, the input, and the expected outcomes, planning for a successful event is a small project unto itself. For the first such event, there is typically much to do to assure that cadence and release plans are well understood, teams know what they need to plan together, solution Vision is ready for presentation, and the logistics are prepared. Over time, however, planning becomes routine as people come to better understand their roles and the necessary preparation; the program should expect that the transaction costs and preparation overhead will decrease over time.

Release Planning Domain

As we described in the previous chapter, some thought must be given to the makeup of who participates on the Agile Release Train. Trains work best when they constitute 50 to 100 team members (5 to 10 agile teams) who collaborate on a product or system. And of course, geographic co-location is a prime consideration, because that dramatically simplifies planning and execution.

Planning Attendance

Planning should be done face-to-face. This is consistent with both the Agile Manifesto and lean principles, because face-to-face communication is, *by far*, the most efficient way to make the batch transfer of information from product management to the development teams.[1] (One such planning session can replace thousands of e-mails, and it happens 10 to 20 times faster; imagine the impact on program efficiency.)

Therefore, to make it feasible for as many members as possible to plan together, program travel budgets should be optimized around release planning sessions. Generally speaking, it isn't "new travel money" anyway, because it likely replaces a host of ad hoc, asynchronous meetings that would have otherwise been necessary.

In the event that the teams that need to plan together are so widely distributed that meeting face-to-face is impossible because of travel costs or restrictions, then *it's likely that you have a highly inefficient organizational structure to support new development anyway*. In that case, the enterprise should do the following:

- Continually refactor teams and assignments to support ever higher degrees of co-location
- Move entire projects, features, components, or subsystems to locales where a critical mass already exists or can quickly be assembled

In doing so, the enterprise will continuously lower the transaction costs of the planning event as well as decrease the costs and accelerate the feedback of the ongoing, and continuous, information transfer that is vital to development.

However, in the likely event that all team members cannot be assembled in one place for release planning, then the program must make plans for communication with remote teammates so that planning is still *simultaneous*, though not to face-to-face.

Release Planning Facilitator

Release planning is a strategic event. As such, it is replete with the challenges and inherent conflicts of Vision (what we'd like to accomplish) versus reality (what we

---

1. Agile Manifesto principle # 6—*The most efficient and effective method of conveying information to and within a development team is face-to-face conversation.*

actually can accomplish). However, this potential for conflict is not bad, per se. Rather, when properly managed, the inherent mismatch of expectations engenders a creative friction between product management and development. If a team could do everything product management wanted them to do, then either product management isn't stretching far enough or the team is overcapacity. Rarely (never?) is either of these true.

And although it's true that we want absolutely need to create product flow, where input does match output, we can't simply achieve flow by just "backing off the accelerator," or fewer cars will go down the freeway than it has capacity for. Yes, it's flowing, but it's *too slow*. Rather, we want to accelerate to the point of most efficient productivity, the point just below which congestion (in this case as witnessed by a combination of overloaded, multiplexed teams *and* badly matched expectations) occurs.

We can do this by mining this creative friction during release planning and watching for those sparks where real innovation can often be found. In other words, in the midst of a potential overload, it behooves all team members to find simpler ways to achieve the maximum potential value delivery. A few animated discussions along the way are likely and appropriate.

Like we said, it's a strategic event. Experience has shown that these events are more successful when a facilitator—someone who is not bound solely in product management or development—runs the event. It can be someone from inside or outside the company.

Often, it can be a project or program manager who may well be struggling to find their role in the new agile enterprise anyway. These specialists often have many of the valuable skills necessary to plan and run such an event. However, they must not conflate that objective with the need to *plan and run the program*. The Agile Release Train largely manages itself; we don't "program manage" it. However, we do have to facilitate and manage the *process* effectively.

In any case, from here forward, we'll use the word *facilitator* to describe the person who is largely responsible for running the actual release planning event.

Release Planning Checklist

In preparing for a successful event, there are three primary areas of concern:

- Strategic alignment and organizational readiness for planning
- Management and development team preparedness for the event itself
- The actual logistics for the event

Since any one of these can interfere with the potential outcome—an actual, specific, and committed release plan—careful consideration of all three factors is warranted. In support of this, we have developed a set of checklists to assist those who are responsible for planning such an event. Since the lists are somewhat long and detailed, we have placed them in Appendix C, Release Planning Readiness Checklist.

RELEASE PLANNING NARRATIVE, DAY 1

Although the agenda for the planning event itself will, of course, vary based on the current context of the company, Table 16–1 provides a typical agenda as a starting template for a standard release planning event.

Table 16–1   Agenda for Day 1 Release Planning

Release Planning Day 1 Agenda			
Time	**Subject**	**Description**	**Presenter**
8–8:30	Opening	Introductions. Schedule and objectives for the day. Review of release cadence (iterations and PSI).	Release planning facilitator.
8:30–9	Business context	State of the business. Objectives for upcoming periods.	Executive.
9–10:30	Solution Vision	Vision for content of solution, product, or service. Vision of solution components, features, and so on.	Product management. Individual product, component, feature content managers.
10:30–10:45	Break		
10:45–11:30	Architecture Vision	Vision for architecture. New architecture epics. Common frameworks. Security, usability, performance, reliability, requirements.	Technology office, system architects.
11:30–12	Development practices	Updates on project setup, agile tooling and infrastructure, engineering practice improvements.	Development management.

Release Planning Day 1 Agenda			
Time	Subject	Description	Presenter
12–1	Lunch break		
1–4	Team planning breakouts I (Scrum of Scrums planning checkpoints every hour to assess progress, interdependencies)	Teams break out and plan iterations. Break features into stories. Plan release.	Architects and product managers circulate with teams.
4–5	Draft plan review	Each team presents plan to group: logic of plan work in process, draft objectives, identified risks, and impediments.	Individual teams.
5–6	Manager's review and problem solving	Discussion of scope, challenges to plan, impediments, and risks. Decision making. Resource and scope adjustments as necessary.	Line management, product management, architects, team representatives.

We'll describe each of these sessions in the following sections.

Opening

The release planning facilitator opens the meeting, provides any necessary introductions, reviews the objectives and agenda, reviews planning rules and expectations, and reviews amenities and other logistics items. The facilitator also presents the upcoming calendar of events, including the iteration and release cadence, future PSI/planning dates, and any scheduled releases, as well as any company holidays or other events that may affect planning objectives or team capacity.

Business Context

Next, a senior executive or line-of-business owner typically sets the business context for the planning session. This may include discussion of current business performance, revenue or market share, measures of customer satisfaction, and so on. It may also include updates to operating plans; organizational developments; strengths, weakness, opportunities, threats (SWOT) analysis; strategies; and competitive context. The presenter will typically conclude with a discussion of the current strategic investment themes and business objectives for the upcoming periods.

The meeting organizers should reach as high into the organization as possible for this opening speaker, because it is an important opportunity to align the entire development team to a common Vision for the business. It also gives the teams the opportunity to meet and interact with some of the executives who drive the business Vision.

Solution Vision

Next, the product managers, solution managers, or program managers responsible for the planning domain present the current Vision for the product and the tentative Roadmap going forward. The briefing includes the objectives (or themes) for the upcoming PSIs as well as the specific feature priorities.

If there are multiple product managers, each may need some time in this slot to present the Vision for their particular aspect (product, feature, component) of the solution, but presentation time is rigorously timeboxed.

At the conclusion of this session, product managers will often provide a handout, provide pointers to where the release backlog can be found, or otherwise make their feature priorities and descriptions fully visible to the teams, because those features are the driving elements for the breakout planning sessions.

Architecture Vision

In small to medium-sized projects, the architecture for the system is the responsibility of the development teams themselves, and no special time or consideration for architecture discussion may be necessary in planning. However, as we will discuss in Chapter 20, Agile Architecture, in the larger program or enterprise setting, system-level architecture (and system-level architects) often play an important role in defining cross-cutting aspects of the solution.

In this next session, the CTO or senior system architects typically present the Vision for architecture in this session. This may include descriptions of new architectural epics for common infrastructure, any large-scale refactors under consideration, new system-level frameworks, or emerging new technologies or platforms, and so on, that must be addressed in the solution.

In addition, any system-level nonfunctional requirements—such as operating platforms; governing regulatory or industry standards; and usability, performance, reliability, and security requirements—are also highlighted in this session.

Team Planning Breakouts

The next session is the longest and most critical session of the two-day event. In this session, the teams break out into separate meetings and draft their initial plan to achieve the objectives of the next PSI.

▶ **NOTE**   Some enterprises plan for "1+1" PSIs. The first PSI is planned in detail and is the subject of the commitment at the end of the meeting. The second PSI is a rough plan, intended primarily to help fill out the product Roadmap and to catch those priority features that did not fit the scope of the upcoming PSI. However, for most programs, time and visibility does not usually allow planning more than one PSI.

In this session, the teams iterate through a process that proceeds roughly as follows.

1. Meet with product managers to better understand features and feature priorities.
2. Estimate the capacity (velocity) the teams will have during each iteration.
3. Brainstorm and identify the user and other stories that are necessary to meet the input objectives and prioritized features of the release. Stories are kept at "backlog-level detail." The objective is to get a first, high-level feel for how the plans unfold. There is no time for story elaboration or discussion of acceptance criteria. Too much detail bogs down the process and creates false precision and excessive WIP.
4. Understand the impact of architectural initiatives on the plan, and identify stories for those initiatives as well.
5. Factor in local dependencies as well as interdependencies with other teams.
6. Estimate the stories and place them on iterations in sequenced order until capacity (velocity for each iteration, excluding maintenance allocation) is exhausted.
7. Create a backlog of things that can't be accomplished in the period and that will have to be postponed.
8. Itemize objectives of things the team can accomplish during the PSI period.

During this process, there will also be variety of interactive discussions with product managers, system architects, and other teams to understand scope, priorities, necessary infrastructure development, interdependencies, potential for common code, and so on. It is a very intense and active time.

Plans are created visually, with wall charts and story cards so that all plans are visible for all to see. Teams build their plans with one wall chart sheet per iteration, another sheet for objectives, and one final sheet to capture risks and impediments.

For example, a plan might appear as in Figure 16–1.

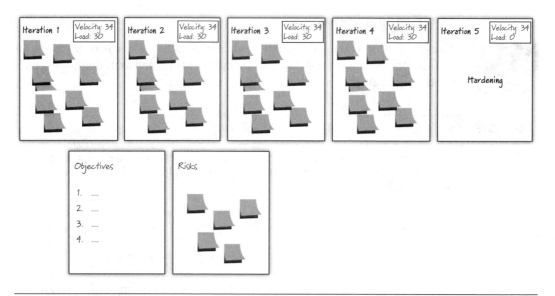

Figure 16–1   Example visual release plan

Note that the hardening iteration should not contain any user value stories, though the teams may identify some stories dedicated to special hardening activities, such as load and performance testing, system documentation, and so on.

Teams may also use color-coded story cards (sticky notes) to help identify various types of stories. These often include colors for new user value stories, maintenance stories, interdependencies, spikes, help needed, and so on.

Hourly Scrum of Scrums Planning Checkpoints

Typically, teams will have a variety of interdependencies that must be worked out with other teams during the planning process. To avoid some of the constant interruptions implied by such a process, many programs have adopted an hourly, five- to ten-minute "Scrum of Scrums" planning checkpoint. In this short stand-up meeting, Scrum Masters work out interdependencies, report status, and state any looming impediments. The facilitator uses this meeting as a clocking mechanism to keep release planning moving at an acceptable pace.

Line management, product management, and other key stakeholders typically also attend this short meeting. It will often turn into a problem-solving meeting with line managers involving themselves with resource adjustments, impediment removal, adjustments to release scope, or ad hoc modifications to the planning agenda, based on progress. Although the meeting is intended to be short and timeboxed, the time for problem solving is now—or else the plans may not converge.

Draft Plan Review

Reprinted by permission of Discount Tire Company

At the designated time, the group reconvenes in plenary session to review each of the plans. Many of the plans will not be complete; however, the preliminary review is still held on time so the groups can see the planning process and get an initial look at the assumptions, dependencies, and initial objectives that their counterpart teams are putting together. Each team presentation is strictly time-boxed, with five to ten minutes per team, based on the size of the planning domain.

▶ **NOTE**   Many executives, managers, and other key stakeholders in the company may be invited to this portion of the event. This allows for total program visibility and shared business and development context. In addition, the unfolding plans may well affect their department or area of interest, and they may have input or adjustments to the plan, based on their perspective. In turn, the development teams may also have dependencies on these functions (such as marketing, sales, customers, distribution deployment, or IT).

▶ **SPECIAL NOTE**   Teams do not worry that these key stakeholders, including executives and managers of other departments, are present while they are in the middle of the "sausage making" portion of our planning. Agile is based on trust,[2] and nothing engenders trust faster than transparency.

To keep the sessions focused and comprehensive in the team presentations, the facilitator might tell the teams to be certain to address the following items.

- Where are you in the planning process?
- Describe your plan in brief.
- Highlight any identified draft objectives.
- Highlight any major impediments and risks discovered so far.
- When do you think your plan will be complete?

There will typically be a minute or two left for Q&A. During Q&A, the facilitator has to walk a fine line between abruptly cutting off important discussions about interdependencies, trade-offs, misunderstandings, and so on, and keeping the plan review sessions within the allocated timebox.

---

2. Agile Manifesto principle #5—*Build projects around motivated individuals. Give them the environment and support they need, and trust them to get the job done.*

The session proceeds until all teams have presented their draft plans (even at the risk of slipping out of the allocated timebox a bit). For most attendees, this is often the end of day 1, and they may be dismissed from the meeting room at that time.

Managers' Review and Problem Solving Meeting

For others, however, day 1 planning is not yet over. In all likelihood, the draft plans present substantial challenges to the management team, product management, and other key stakeholders. Challenges may come from a number of directions.

- The input expectations for the PSI will likely be over-scoped. After all, what self-respecting product manager would under-scope a set of target release objectives?
- Critical paths, resource constraints, and bottlenecks should now be obvious.
- Team dynamics and inter-team dynamics are obvious as well.

To this end, line managers, Scrum Masters, product owners, and product managers will typically meet to address the larger challenges identified in the draft review session. If these issues are allowed to persist, day 2 may come out badly for either of two reasons.

- The process will not converge on agreed-to release objectives because of these unresolved issues.
- Convergence will appear to happen, but the release is at risk because underlying problems have not been addressed.

Action is necessary. This may involve cuts to scope, rethinking prior commitments, coming to understand that some critical date will not be met, or moving resources (or even entire projects) from team to team.

The facilitator plays an important role, because many of the challenges noted may be politically charged or historical in nature. The facilitator holds the key stakeholders together as long as necessary to make the decisions necessary to improve the probability of a successful outcome of the next PSI (or at least the next day's planning session). Any such decisions reached should be carefully and clearly stated, because they will serve as input to the day 2 session.

RELEASE PLANNING NARRATIVE, DAY 2

In day 2, the program must get to a committed plan of action, one that fits the team's capacity *and* that achieves the maximum value delivery possible in the next PSI timebox.

Table 16–2 describes the typical agenda for day 2.

Table 16–2   Sample Release Planning Day 2 Agenda

Release Planning Day 2 Agenda			
Time	**Subject**	**Description**	**Presenter**
8–8:15	Opening	Schedule and objectives for the day.	Release planning facilitator.
8:15–9	Planning adjustments	Managers discuss any revisions to plan, adjustment to scope, resources, and so on.	Line management and product management.
9–11	Team planning breakouts II (Scrum of Scrums planning checkpoints every hour to assess progress, interdependencies)	Teams continue planning based on status of their plan from the day before and any planning adjustments. Objectives for the PSI are finalized.	
11–12	Final plan review	All teams present plans to group. Present objectives, risks, and impediments.	Teams.
12–1	Lunch break		
1–2	Risks and impediments	Remaining risks and impediments are discussed and "ROAMed" (resolved, owned, accepted, mitigated).	Management at front of room. Facilitator presents each item.
2–2:15	Release confidence vote	Facilitator asks for fist of five "confidence factor" (commitment).	Facilitator.
2:15–??	If high confidence is achieved, continue to the planning retrospective. If not, scope is adjusted and planning continues until commitment is achieved.		
When commitment is achieved	Planning retrospective	Planning retrospective. What went well? What didn't? What can we do better next time?	Facilitator.
	Final instructions	Any final instructions, capturing release plans in project tooling, facilities cleanup, and so on.	Management/ facilitator.
	Adjournment		

Opening

In the day 2 opening session, the facilitator provides an overview of the agenda and the objectives for the final day, including the timeboxes in which the teams should complete their plan and be ready for presentation.

Planning Adjustments: A United Front

Even though management will have attempted to communicate most of the key decisions prior to the day 2 opening, it is inevitable that in this "frenzy of the last responsible moment," some of the decisions reached in the prior day will come as a surprise to some team members. Many decisions will be greeted with enthusiasm, since they often simplify scope, assign additional resources to critical bottlenecks, or resolve key impediments. Some decisions, however, may be received less enthusiastically, because many are the results of compromises among key stakeholders or even between teams.

To make management's full support for the key decisions unambiguously clear, a senior manager, or perhaps the management team as a group, takes the responsibility for describing the results of the review meeting at the end of day 1, highlighting those decisions that may affect the planning process, organization, or objectives. This presents a *united front* in support of the key decisions and changes, controversial or not. After all, we are going to need a *united effort* from the development teams to accomplish the release. The least we can do is know that management stands behind them, also united as a team.

Planning Continues: Team Planning Breakouts Session II

With planning adjustments in hand, this next session is a continuation of the prior day's team breakouts. By now the teams should be planning smoothly. The facilitator's role is the same as the day before—keep the teams moving forward; keep the business owners, product managers, engineering managers, and architects circling; watch for new developments that require additional decision making, provide assistance to the team members whose work is being refactored, are still struggling with estimating, or are still over-scoped; and so on.

And, like the day before, the planning Scrum of Scrums convenes hourly to assure that plans and timelines converge for the final review.

Establishing Release Objectives

Sometime during this second breakout session, the teams will start to finalize their individual objectives for the release. Although they do not appear in the requirements meta-model, release objectives are a key artifact of the release planning session, and they provide the primary mechanism the program will need to track and assess progress and manage scope.[3]

> Release objectives are brief summaries, in business terms, of the specific features the teams intend to deliver in the upcoming PSI.

Many of these objectives will simply be features taken directly from the backlog. As such, their importance and the value they deliver are immediately recognizable. Others may be aggregations of a set of features but stated in more convenient, and more concise, terms.

Some, however, may not represent user value delivery directly but may represent some milestone (trade show demo by 3/15) or infrastructure or architectural epic (gateway pointing rearchitecture) the team must achieve. Still others are clarifications or mitigations—perhaps things the teams will *not* be able to accomplish (the thermostat upgrade will support only model 300X).

Whatever they are, they are negotiated *outputs*, rather than inputs, to the release planning session. They represent an important commitment from the team: They understand the Vision, they understand their velocity, and they understand what the business would like to do, but *these are the things they can and will do.*

Business Owners Rank Release Objectives by Business Value

To assure alignment and to help the teams understand the relative value, objectives should be ranked by business value by the team's business owner (typically a product or solution manager, program manager, or executive). Each individual objective could be ranked on a scale of 1 to 10, as illustrated in Figure 16–2.

This is an important two-way, face-to-face dialogue between the team and their most important stakeholders. It is an opportunity to develop a personal relationship upon which a mutual commitment can be based and to better understand the business objectives and their relative value. Most importantly, it is an opportunity to extend the boundaries of the "team" to include these key stakeholders.

During the ranking process, the user-facing features (pricing programs) will typically be ranked most highly by the business owners. That's as it should be. But mature business owners know that architectural and other concerns (for example, gateway pointing rearchitecture) will also increase the velocity of the team in producing *future* business value, so placing some business value on those items helps drive ultimate velocity and is a sign of support for the team's legitimate, technical challenges.

---

3. The requirements model artifacts—epics, features, stories—define intended system behavior. They are not coupled to the dimension of "when that behavior will be implemented." Release objectives do that.

Objective	Bus Value
1. Thermostat Over-the-Air Update	10
2. Next generation thermostat firmware (V300x only)	4
2. First pricing programs	10
3. Gateway Pointing Rearchitecture	6
4. Trade show demo by 3/15	10
5. Release v3.1 upgrade to channel	9
Stretch goals	
All thermostat versions	4
Pricing program 2	8

Figure 16–2   An example of release objectives, ranked by business value

In addition, because the road after PSI planning takes its inevitable twists and turns, having objectives ranked by business value gives the teams guidance in making trade-offs and minor scope adjustments in a manner that allows the team to deliver the maximum possible business benefits.

Final Release Plans Review

This session is a repeat of the session of the prior day, but by now the teams should have completed their plans and are able to present them in final form.

Reprinted by permission of Discount Tire Company

- All iterations are planned. Hardening iterations have only hardening stories. Work fits in the time (team velocity) available.
- Out-of-scope work has been identified on a backlog sheet.
- Team has a final set of release objectives.
- Business owners have reviewed and agreed to the team's objectives and ranked them by business value.
- Teams have also identified all critical dates.
- Teams have identified the key risks and impediments that are outside of their local control but have the potential to cause the team to fail to meet the objectives.

In a manner similar to the day before, each team presents their plan to the group in the allotted timebox. While so doing, the facilitator is looking for agreement—within the teams, across the teams, and with management and other stakeholders—as to the sensibility and appropriateness of the plan. Questions from the reviewers are asked and answered.

Reprinted by permission of Discount Tire Company

Then, at the end of each team's time slot, the team states their risks and impediments. There is no attempt to resolve them in this short time slot. The facilitator captures those on a central, visible sheet.

The team also brings their release objective sheet to the front of the room so that all can see the aggregate release objectives unfold in real time.

In addition, the facilitator, or perhaps a project or program manager, often collects critical dates—releases, dependencies, milestone events, and the like—on a master schedule sheet at the front of the room.

This process continues until all teams have had a chance to present their plan.

Addressing Risks and Impediments

Even though the plans are complete, there is still work to do. During the planning, teams have been asked to identify the most critical risks and impediments—those issues they identify that could affect their ability to meet the agreed-to objectives. Addressing these is a must for the agile program, because they typically represent those things that *can* (and if not addressed, likely *would*) interfere with the success of the next PSI.

Reprinted by permission of Discount Tire Company

By now, the teams should have been coached to address those risks that are under their control; otherwise, they couldn't be responsible for their own plan. The risks and impediments that remain in the final review will need to be addressed in a broader, management context.

This is an important time for the management team and the facilitator. *Every* impediment or risk that has been identified by the team will be discussed and addressed in front of the full group as is illustrated in the figure.

Each item is discussed until the group agrees that the item can be categorized in one of the following (ROAM) categories.

- *Resolved:* The teams agree that the issue is no longer a concern, and the item moves to the *Resolved* sheet.
- *Owned:* The item cannot be resolved in the course of the meeting, but someone (usually a manager or a specific team) takes ownership of the item. Ownership means that the responsible party will take whatever action is necessary to assure that the issue will not negatively affect the release commitment. An owned item is moved to the *owned* sheet, and its ownership is recorded.
- *Accepted:* Some risks are simply facts or potential occurrences that must be understood and accepted. For example, *extraordinary support requirements* for a prior release or *late delivery of a component* from a supplier often appear on the list and could potentially cause a team to miss a future commitment. However, allocating excessive resources just to *assure* that these risks will not affect the release will lower value delivery and may not be economically prudent. Some risks just have to be *accepted*.
- *Mitigated:* However, we want to *accept* as few as possible. Often, the teams can identify a plan to mitigate the impact of a risk. This may be a workaround plan, a minor descoping, or other such actions that the teams can take to lessen the impact of a potential problem. If so, the mitigation plan is identified as notes on the back of the risk card as it is moved to the *Mitigated* sheet.

▶ **NOTE** The facilitator's role depends on the management team's strength, cohesiveness, and culture. Sometimes the facilitator must be very active in order to drive consensus between managers among themselves, teams to managers, or teams to teams. In other cases, the facilitator can step back and let management do the work. This is the preferred outcome because the teams then see that one of management's primary roles in the agile enterprise is the elimination of impediments and the mitigation of risks.

In any case, the facilitator should assure that the issues are being addressed in a clear, honest, and visible manner, or the commitment, which (ideally) follows, will be flawed.

The Commitment

At some point, the "backlog of risks and impediments" sheet is empty, because they have all been moved into a ROAM category. The consolidated statement of release objectives is apparent and visible in the front of the room. Risks have been addressed.

Now is the time to ask for a commitment.

However, a commitment, per se, is actually not quite the right thing to ask for, because no intelligent participant is going to indicate that they are not committed to the team's release objectives in front of their managers. Instead, we create a commitment by asking teams to vote on their *confidence in their team's ability to meet the release objectives.*

For example, the question is often stated as "how confident are you that you and your teams will be able to meet the objectives of this release."

A public, "show of hands, five-finger vote" is then prompted, with the meaning as follows:

1 = No confidence; will not happen

2 = Little confidence; probably will not happen

3 = Good confidence; the team should be able to meet the objectives

4 = High confidence; should happen

5 = Very high confidence; will happen

If the average is three to four fingers or more, that's about as good as it gets, and management should accept the commitment.

If the average is fewer than three fingers, then the work is not yet complete. Scope and resources are adjusted again as necessary and planning continues—that day, into the evening, or even rolling over into the next morning—until a commitment can be reached.

▶ **NOTE**   Many agile planners allocate 1.5 or 2.5 days to planning, with the final half day being reserved for continuing education, training, iteration planning, or whatever. In the case of the commitment not being achieved (which can happen), those activities are canceled in order to take a third cut at the plan.

Assuming, however, that commitment has been achieved, the facilitator and managers should thank the attendees for their participation in planning, because a commitment represents a job well done.

Planning Retrospective

The next session is a brief retrospective led by the facilitator. Figure 16–3 shows a simple format to capture such data, along with a few example comments.

What went well	What didn't	Do better next time
• Good time box management	• Key stakeholders not present	• Get key stakeholders here for plan review
• Teams collaboration	• Backlog not clear for Team A	• Pass out vision briefing ahead of meeting
• Group review of plans	• Couldn't hear well enough	• Better backlog grooming prior
• Management of interdependencies	• Not enough time for lunch	• Better audio
• Hourly Scrum of Scrums	• Scope management	• More time for lunch
• Risks being addressed	• Didn't restart on time	• Restart on time
• Scope management		

Figure 16–3   Retrospective format with example comments

This session should last no longer than about 15 to 20 minutes. Toward the end of the timebox, the facilitator may ask the teams to rank the items in the third column (what we could do better) in order to focus on the process improvement steps that can be taken before the next planning session.

Final Instructions to Teams

The last session is typically a brief set of final instructions to the teams. Such instructions often include the following:

- Capturing the objectives and stories in the agile project management tool
- Updating the Roadmap
- Cleaning up the room
- Scheduling key events and activities in the next few days

Thereafter, the meeting is (thankfully) adjourned.

STRETCH GOALS

Before we leave this chapter, there is one more topic to discuss. Gaining a meaningful *commitment* from the team is a tricky proposition culturally. Without it, no one is committed to anything, and it's all on a "best-effort" basis. Some prefer that. After all, one can argue that a fixed set of release commitments puts the team back in the iron triangle. Moreover, if teams are castigated for failing to meet commitments over time, their most natural defense is to back way down on their commitments. From the team's perspective, it *beats a beating*, but from the enterprise's perspective, it drives undesirable economics because the teams are not motivated to stretch to their maximum potential.

To this end, mature programs have learned to make commitments meaningful in two ways.

- As we discussed in the previous chapter, the expectation is that teams will meet "most" of their objectives. A yield of anywhere greater than 80% should be acceptable. This gives the teams the flex they need to stretch and commit, without negative consequences.[4]
- Mature teams will soon learn that they need a set of committed goals (because the enterprise has to depend on something), but given the variability of R&D, the teams will also establish a set of *stretch goals*. These goals are also ranked by business value, as illustrated in Figure 16–4.

This latter case is usually the best case. This gives the teams the opportunity to meet or exceed 100%, without fear of being in the penalty box for stretching their objectives to the maximum. In addition, if we want teams to operate reliability in the 80% plus process control range as we described in the previous chapter, then the ability to achieve more than 100% on occasion is a means to help achieve that.

Objective	Bus Value
1. Thermostat Over-the-Air Update	10
2. Next generation thermostat firmware (V300x only)	4
2. First pricing programs	10
3. Gateway Pointing Rearchitecture	6
4. Trade show demo by 3/15	10
5. Release v3.1 upgrade to channel	9
Stretch goals	
All thermostat versions	4
Pricing program 2	8

Figure 16–4 Objectives with stretch goals

---

4. We must be careful what we wish for. In my experience, teams that reliably meet 100% of their commitments without stretch goals are often not very high-performing teams in the aggregate. After all, they couldn't afford to take any risks, could they?

Summary

In the previous chapter, we described the motivation and mechanics of the Agile Release Train, which we use to drive strategic alignment and institutionalize product development flow. Integral to that is a series of rolling wave *release planning* events, which are used to communicate the Vision to the teams and gain commitments from the teams to a set of release objectives. In this chapter, we introduced the release planning event, a seminal event that is the pacemaker for every agile program. We provided a sample agenda and process for running this event, which have been used with good results in a wide variety of software enterprises.

The net result of the event is a set of release objectives for each *team*, which aggregates into a set of release objectives for the *program*. We described how to make these release objectives simultaneously ambitious and yet practical and manageable. Risks are actively recognized and addressed as well.

With these tools in hand, the enterprise can look forward to series of programs that stretch for the maximum feasible accomplishments and yet routinely address the variability inherent in software research and development. In this way, each program operates with a continuous flow of value delivery, predictable within acceptable limits. That's about as good as we know how to make it. This is software development after all.

Chapter 17

NONFUNCTIONAL REQUIREMENTS

WITH DON WIDRIG

The first 90% of the software takes 90% of the development time. The remaining 10% of the code takes up the other 90% of the time.

—Tom Cargill, Bell Labs

So far in this text, we have used *user stories* and *features* to describe the functional requirements of the system—those system behaviors whereby some combination of inputs (action) produces a meaningful output (result) for the user. We have invested many pages in exploring how to discover, organize, and manage, in an agile manner, the requirements that we must understand in order to build the system functionality our users need to go about their business or pleasure.

However, we haven't yet described how to discover, understand, or deliver the other class of requirements, the nonfunctional requirements (NFRs), that the users require of our system. These are the "ilities"—security, reliability, scalability, and so on—and other *system qualities* that affect the overall usefulness and, ultimately, the actual *viability* of the solution. Because if a system isn't reliable (crashes) or marketable (failure to meet some imposed regulatory standard) or scalable (doesn't support the number of users required), then, agile or not, we will fail just as badly as if we forgot some critical functional requirement.

Traditionally, one way to think about *all* the types of requirements that affect overall fitness for use has been the acronym FURPS, which stands for Functionality, Usability, Reliability, Performance, and Supportability [Grady 1992, Leffingwell and Widrig 2003].

The FURPS acronym reminds us that we must build and manage the behavior of the system from a number of different perspectives:

- *Functionality:* What the system does for the user
- *Usability:* How easy it is for a user to get the system to do it

- *Reliability:* How reliably the system does it
- *Performance:* How often, or how many of it, it can do
- *Supportability:* How easy it is for us to maintain and extend the system that does it

We've discussed functionality at length in the prior chapters. The "URPS" part of FURPS is a placeholder for organizing the NFRs, which serves as a reminder that we must also consider these other types of requirements in our system design, even when we approach implementation in a just-in-time agile manner.

In addition, in *Managing Software Requirements, Second Edition: A Use Case Approach* [Leffingwell and Widrig 2003], we found it useful to think about one additional requirements perspective, the perspective of *design constraints*. Each of these three types of requirements is defined in Table 17–1.

MODELING NONFUNCTIONAL REQUIREMENTS

In one perspective, all of these items can be considered to be *constraints* on new development, in that each eliminates some degree of design freedom on the part of those building the system. Here's an example:

> *"For compatibility with our partners, we have agreed to implement SAML-based Single Sign On (SSO is a functional requirement, basing it on SAML is a constraint) for all products in the suite."*

> *"Every product in the suite has to be internationalized (constraint), but only the Order Entry module must be localized to Korean (functional requirement) for this release."*

Table 17–1   Requirement Types and Descriptions

Requirement Type	Description	Examples
Functional requirements	Express how the system interacts with its users—its inputs, its outputs, and the functions and features it provides.	Display a pop-up on the TV when the utility sends a brownout warning.
Nonfunctional requirements	Criteria used to judge the operation or qualities of a system.	The system must be available to its users at least 99.99% of the time. The systems should support 100 concurrent users with no degradation in performance.
Design constraints	Restrictions on the design of a system, or the process by which a system is developed, but that must be fulfilled to meet technical, business, or contractual obligations.	Use Python for all client applications. Don't use any open source software that doesn't conform to the GNU General Public License.

So, in the information model, we have modeled NFRs as *backlog constraints*, as illustrated in Figure 17–1.

From the diagram, we see that a backlog item may be constrained by (zero, one, or more) nonfunctional requirements. An example from the case study appears in Figure 17–2.

Also, nonfunctional requirements apply to zero or more backlog items. For example, a nonfunctional requirement such as support 100 concurrent users might apply to zero, one, or many backlog items.

Once identified, relevant nonfunctional requirements must be captured and communicated to all teams who may be affected by the constraints. In agile, with its focus on the backlog, there is no obvious place to model them, so in the Big Picture, we just call them *backlog constraints* and represent them as shown in Figure 17–3.

Figure 17–1 Association between backlog items and nonfunctional requirements

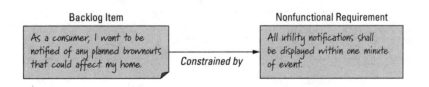

Figure 17–2 User story constrained by a nonfunctional requirement

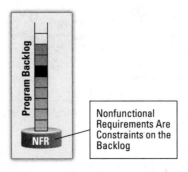

Figure 17–3 A backlog with backlog constraints in the Big Picture

Expressing Nonfunctional Requirements as User Stories

Given the predominance of user stories in agile and the more recent user voice form (as a <user role>, I can...), there may be value in expressing nonfunctional requirements in user voice story form. Often, it can clarify the source (<user role>) and the business benefit to the user or the solution provider. Sometimes it's worth this little extra effort to communicate a nonfunctional requirement more clearly, but sometimes it isn't. Figure 17–4 provides some examples.

Using the user voice form makes good sense for NFRs when it adds value, and it makes equally good sense not to when it doesn't.

EXPLORING NONFUNCTIONAL REQUIREMENTS

Understandably, there's a fairly long list of potential NFRs that may apply to a particular project context. Table 17–2 shows a superset of these considerations.

However, to think about them in a more organized way, we'll return to our URPS (usability, reliability, performance, and supportability) acronym. In the next sections, we'll use URPS (along with design constraints) as our categorization and provide some guidelines to help discover and record NFRs.

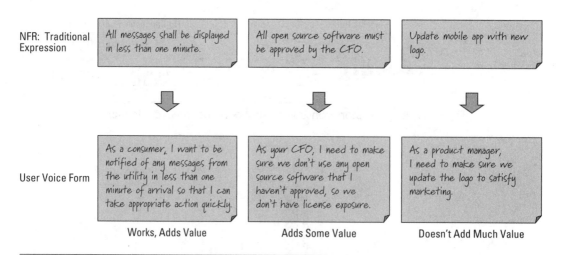

Figure 17–4 Expressing nonfunctional requirements in user voice form

Table 17-2 Examples of Nonfunctional Requirements

Accessibility	Extensibility	Quality
Audit and control	Failure management	Recovery
Availability	Legal and licensing issues	Reliability
Backup	Interoperability	Resilience
Capacity: current and forecast	Maintainability	Resource constraints
Certification	Modifiability	Response time
Compatibility compliance	Open Source	Robustness
Configuration management	Operability	Scalability
Dependency on other parties	Patent-infringement-avoidability	Security
Documentation	Performance/response time	Software, tools, standards
Disaster recovery	Platform compatibility	Stability
Efficiency	Price	Safety
Effectiveness	Privacy	Supportability
Escrow	Portability	Testability
		Usability

Source: Wikipedia

Usability

In today's software products, ease of use ranks as one of the top criteria for commercial success and/or successful user adoption. However, since usability tends to be in the eye of the beholder, specifying usability can present a challenge. There is no simple solution to this problem, but here are some things to think about.

- Specify the training time objective for a user to become minimally productive (able to accomplish simple tasks) and operationally productive (able to accomplish normal day-to-day tasks). This may need to be further described in terms of personas, such as novice users, who may have never used an application of this type before, and power users.
- Specify measurable task times for typical tasks or transactions that the end user will be carrying out. Although this could be affected by performance issues in the system (such as network speed, network capacity, memory, and so on), task performance times are also strongly affected by the usability of the system, and we should be able to specify that separately.
- Compare the user's experiences with other comparable systems that the user community knows and likes.
- Specify any required user assistance features such as online help, wizards, tool tips, context-sensitive help, user manuals, and other forms of documentation and assistance.

- Follow conventions and standards that have been developed for the human-to-machine interface. Having a system work "just like what I'm used to" can be accomplished by following consistent standards from application to application. For example, you can specify a requirement to conform to common usability standards, such as IBM's Common User Access (CUA) standards or the Windows applications standards published by Microsoft.

Reliability

Obviously, reliability is an absolute requirement for customer satisfaction. To achieve acceptable system behavior, we must give some thought to what requirements and performance measures we would ascribe to this aspect. Under the category of Reliability, we might want to consider the following issues.

- *Availability:* The system must be available for operational use during a specified percentage of the time. In the extreme case, the requirement(s) might specify "nonstop" availability, that is, 24 hours a day, 365 days a year. It's more common to see a stipulation of 99.9% availability or a stipulation of 99.99% availability between the hours of 8 a.m. and midnight.
- *Mean time between failures (MTBF):* This is usually specified in hours, but it also could be specified in days, months, or years.
- *Mean time to repair (MTTR):* How long is the system allowed to be out of operation after it has failed? A range of MTTR values may be appropriate; for example, the user might stipulate that 90% of all system failures must be repairable within five minutes and that 99.9% of all failures must be repairable within one hour.
- *Accuracy:* What accuracy is required in systems that produce numerical outputs? Must the results in a financial system, for example, be accurate to the nearest penny or to the nearest dollar?
- *Defects:* Defects may be categorized in terms of minor, significant, and critical. Eliminating all critical defects is always the goal, but large numbers of lower-priority defects can also substantially reduce the usability and users' satisfaction with the system. Total defects by type are a pretty good indicator of a user's likely experience with the system.
- *Security:* Application security is of paramount importance, and it is a critical business priority to design security into the system. Some security issues can be addressed in functional requirements (require strong passwords). However, security can also be specified with nonfunctional requirements such as detect denial-of-service attacks, as well as certain design and coding principles such as verify controls for buffer over-runs. Also, in mature markets, published security standards are likely to exist.

Performance

Performance is another broad category of NFRs that specify how responsive a system is to users or other systems and how a system is likely to degrade with increasing load. Types of NFRs in the performance category might include the following.

- *Response time:* Specify for transactions of a given type, average and worst case.
- *Throughput:* Specify in transactions per second, latency, overhead, data transmission rates, and so on.
- *Capacity:* Specify the number of customers, transactions, data, and so on, the system can accommodate.
- *Scalability:* Specify the ability of the system to be extended to accommodate more interactions and/or users.
- *Degradation modes:* Define an acceptable behavior for when the system has been degraded. For example, it may be permissible for a system to become slower with load, or even deny users access to certain services, as opposed to a system crash.
- *Resource utilization:* If the new system has to share hardware resources with other systems or applications, it may also be necessary to stipulate the degree to which the implementation will make "civilized" use of such resources as the CPU, memory, channels, disk storage, and bandwidth.

Supportability (Maintainability)

Supportability (maintainability) includes the ability of the software to be easily modified to accommodate enhancements and repairs. For some application domains, the likely nature and even timing of future enhancements can be anticipated (protocol changes, annual tax rule changes, standards compliance response timelines, availability of new data sources, and so on), and there may be a mandate for a team to be able to respond to these anticipated changes. Customers may also require service-level agreements for various types of defect fixes and system enhancements.

Design Constraints

As we mentioned earlier, design constraints are often treated as another class of nonfunctional requirements. Most typically, these are created to enhance supportability. Design constraints typically originate from one of three sources: some necessary restriction of design options, conditions imposed on the development process itself, and regulations and imposed standards.

Restriction of Design Options

Most stories allow for more than one design option. Whenever possible, we want to leave that choice to the developers or user experience experts rather than specifying it in the story, because they are in the best position to evaluate the technical and economic merits of each option. Whenever we do not allow a choice to be made (use Oracle DBMS), a degree of flexibility and development freedom has been lost. However, sometimes this is necessary to improve supportability. (Imagine the challenges that an internal support team or customer database administrator would face if each product in a multiple product suite chose a separate database to persist customer data.)

Conditions Imposed on the Development Process

Also, to assure systemic productivity in the agile teams, support the principle of collective ownership, and enhance the ability of team members to move from one project team to another (a key measure of business agility), teams will typically adopt common programming languages, unit testing tools, agile project management tooling, coding standards, configuration management, build environments, and so on. Examples include the following:

- *Application standards:* Use the class library from Developer's Library 09–724 on the corporate IT server
- *Corporate best practices and standards:* Compatibility with the legacy database must be maintained
- *Development standards:* Use our Java coding standards

With respect to coding standards, for example, agile teams take pride in their code. This is a prudent development practice that makes good economic sense. In addition to improving inherent code quality, coding standards improve the ability to refactor and maintain the code, improving the overall velocity of the team. To achieve this, good teams make the software as simple as possible, easy to read (more time is spent reading code than writing code), and easy to refactor. For guidance on this topic, we refer you to Bob Martin's *Clean Code: A Handbook of Agile Software Craftsmanship* [2009].

Regulations and Imposed Standards

Some industries, such as the medical device industry, have bodies of regulations and standards that govern development practices. Typically, these are too lengthy to incorporate directly and are therefore just included by reference (application must fail safely per the provisions of TüV Software Standard, Sections 3.1–3.4).

Incorporation by reference has its hazards, however. For example, a reference of the form The product must conform to ISO 601 effectively binds your product to *all* the standards in the entire document, so teams should be careful to incorporate specific and relevant references instead of more general references.

Managing Design Constraints

Design constraints are unique and may deserve a special treatment. You may want to include them in a special section of your backlog or perhaps even create a supplemental specification for that purpose. In addition, you may want to identify the source and rationale. This serves as a reminder of the derivation and motivation for the design constraint, so it can be appropriately applied in the individual team's context. That way, it can potentially be modified or eliminated if the business context changes.

PERSISTING NONFUNCTIONAL REQUIREMENTS

Another difference between user stories and nonfunctional requirements is that they typically need to persist differently in the development life cycle. We've described how user stories are lightweight and generally don't have to be maintained, which is one of the key benefits. We've also shown that the details of a user story are captured in the acceptance test, which persist inside the team's automated or manual regression test environment. That is why we can throw the user story away after implementation—because we have memorialized the important details in our test cases.

That can work for some NFRs, too, but it gets a bit riskier. For example, if a system must support 1000 concurrent users, we could develop an automated test that simulated that load and build it in the regression test suite. That would be an excellent practice because we could refactor the code at will, and if we accidentally created a performance bottleneck, it would be quickly discovered. In that case, we could forget about the NFR once we have seen it the first time, because the automated test remembers it for us.

There are other types of NFRs, however, that must be treated quite differently. Here are some examples:

- Maintain PCI compliance (credit card industry user security standards) in all applications
- Localize the application in all then-current, supported languages prior to release in any language
- No open source without a CFO license review

We surely can't forget these, and we can't write automated test cases for them, either. So, the teams must have an organized way to save them, find them, and review them when necessary. In practice, we've seen agile teams take a number of approaches to persisting NFRs.

- Create a separate backlog in the agile project management tool. Most enterprises will adopt agile project management tooling as a central repository for stories and tasks, as well as iteration and release objects that support scheduling, burndown, and feature status reporting. Teams can create a special project/product backlog to hold and maintain the NFRs within the tool. Access privileges must be granted to all team members who are working on the program.
- Store and manage them in a wiki. This method works well because it provides continuous visibility; is available to all team members; is persistent; fosters communication, comments, and interaction; and doesn't require any special tooling.
- Maintain a supplementary specification. This label/document was originally developed as an auxiliary document to RUP's use case models and use case specifications and served exactly this role (organizing nonfunctional requirements). Remember, as agilists, we "favor working software over comprehensive documentation," but that doesn't mean we can't create the documentation we need. Even more importantly, we like to do the simplest thing that can possibly work, and when we know something is important, it makes sense to write it down. Table 17–3 later in this chapter provides an example template for a supplemental specification.
- Build the NFRs into the definition of done, and point to the special backlog, wiki, or supplemental specification that contains the details. In this approach, a team can't be *done* until the NFRs are satisfied as well. Different definitions of done, requiring different amounts of regression testing, inspection, and so on, can be established for various iteration, potentially shippable increment, and release milestones.

No matter the approach, it is mandatory that the teams do *something* to maintain and manage these specifications, because they could make the difference between success and failure.

TESTING NONFUNCTIONAL REQUIREMENTS

The question arises as to whether these nonfunctional requirements are testable. The answer is assuredly *yes*, because most all of these constraints (*performance*, for example) can and should be objectively tested.

Recalling the agile testing matrix diagram in Chapter 10, we find ourselves in quadrant 4, the domain of system qualities testing, as shown in Figure 17–5.

Indeed, compliance to these requirements is just as critical as it is to meeting functional requirements, and we provide explicit support for this in the model, as illustrated in Figure 17–6.

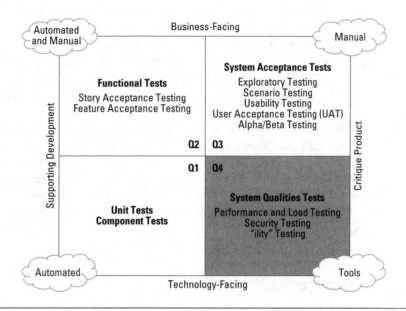

Figure 17–5 Quadrant 4, system qualities tests

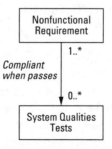

Figure 17–6 A system is compliant with its nonfunctional requirements when it passes its system qualities tests.

This is intended to better describe how this set of tests help assure that the system is in continuous compliance with its nonfunctional quality requirements. The multiplicity (1..* and 0..*) further indicates the following.

- Not every NFR has a qualities test (0..). For example, some design constraints (*program in Python*) simply aren't worth testing (other than perhaps by one-time inspection or acknowledgment).
- However, most NFRs (..*) should have at least one objective test associated with them. Moreover, some NFRs (for example, *runs on IE 8*) might require an entire *test suite* to assure conformance.
- Every system qualities test should be associated with some NFR (1..*) (otherwise there would be no way to tell whether it passes!), and some system qualities tests could assure compliance with more than one NFR.

Testing in quadrant 4 is quite different, because it doesn't tie directly to a functional implementation of a story or feature in a timebox. Some of the qualities tests (*no open source without approval*) will be more in the nature of a one-shot test at some appropriate milestone. Other tests will be recurring tests at critical release points (*PCI Credit Card Handling Compliance*). Regardless of the schedule, these tests are vital to the success of the product and must be factored into the team's thinking at iteration and release planning. Of course, the tests must respond to the type of NFR at issue. We'll provide some examples in the following sections.

Usability

Usability testing is a black-box testing technique, which tests how easy it is for users to achieve their objectives with the system. Typically, usability testing involves gathering a small number of users (three to five) together and then having them execute scripts that use the system in predetermined ways. During this process, those administering the tests typically focus on measuring four aspects of the user's interaction with the system.

- *Productivity:* How long does it take a user to perform a particular task?
- *Accuracy:* How many errors or missteps does the user experience along the way?
- *Recall:* How easily can a user recall how to use the system if they have been away from the system for a while?
- *Emotional response:* How does the user react to the experience of using the system—drudgery, acceptable, interesting, or fun?

Reliability

Reliability is somewhat easier to test because the objectives may be clearer, especially if the team has stated any service-level requirements such as availability, mean time between failures, and so on. In addition, there are many language-specific profiling tools that assist developers in performing low-level tests such as testing for memory leaks, potential race, and other code conditions that have shown to be typical root causes of reliability problems. However, there are still challenges.

- It may not be possible to test the product for the amount of time that would be required to collect such data. Instead, stress and load testing may be necessary to accelerate potential failure conditions.
- It can be difficult to simulate the user's real operating environment, because there could be many factors, such as other systems, environment, types of users, and so on, that affect the long-term results.

The team must develop a reasonable balance of reliability tests to operate the system under load, possibly with heightened environmental stress factors.

Security

Security is a special type of reliability testing, and it can be approached from two perspectives, white-box testing and black-box testing.

White-Box Testing

In white-box testing, the testing regime examines the actual code to look for potential coding practices and paths through the code that can allow security breaches. However, it is not generally practical to examine all possible pathways and combinations. Instead, the number of potential combinations must be pruned to a manageable set of tests, usually by deciding on the most likely and most important pathways through the code. The comprehensiveness of the testing is determined by the criticality of the product and its financial and legal impact. For example, a banking application for international wire transfers would require extreme rigor as compared to a web application for purchasing ring-back tones from a mobile operator.

Black-Box Testing

Black-box testing mimics the way in which real-life hackers try to defeat a system. Using scripts and tools, the test regime can inject various faulty inputs into the system and try to "break the system."

Story-level black-box testing can be performed in the course of the iteration because unit tests are comparatively easy to perform by the individual developer because of the limited scope of the required tests. For example, it is fairly easy to inject faulty data into a low-level routine at the time the code is written, observe its behavior, and correct any resultant security flaws in the design at that early stage.

Things get more complicated as the system evolves into higher levels of functionality. As the level of sophistication evolves, the unit tests, component tests, scripts, and tools will necessarily have to evolve too.

Performance

Performance testing is usually done with the assistance of specialized tools. At the scope of system-level testing, user and other system load simulators, measuring, and monitoring tools are available. These are used to simulate a heavy load on a server, network, system component, or other object to test its resilience and to analyze overall performance under different load types.

Open source and commercial tools offer differing capabilities, and the teams need to select an appropriate set. Custom, purpose-built tools may also be required for complex systems. To assure that each increment of the new system works as intended, this type of testing should be started in early iterations, and the tests need to be added to the daily build, iteration, or release-level regression testing criteria.

Supportability and Design Constraints

Supportability and design constraint testing involves testing adherence to any supportability requirements that may be imposed on the team by outside stakeholders or that teams have imposed on themselves. Typically, this may be done by inspection or retrospection, applying lessons learned from prior iterations to improve future outcomes.

In many cases, design constraints are one-shot tests that are performed by inspection early on. At a later stage, reconfirmation of the constraint might be in order, just to ensure that things haven't changed.

A more complex set of testing practices may be necessary if regulatory bodies are involved. For example, in the United States, developing a software-controlled medical device will likely be subject to a large body of process and product regulations from the U.S. Food & Drug Administration. If regulation is involved, it is critical to have these constraints made known at the beginning of the project, because many such regulations place demands on *how* certain things must be implemented, and redoing a process the team has already done could generate a significant amount of waste.

TEMPLATE FOR AN NFR SPECIFICATION

As we have described, there are many ways for a team to capture, organize, and communicate nonfunctional requirements. One such way is via a supplemental specification (document, database, or wiki), a template for which appears in Table 17–3.

Table 17–3 Template for a Supplemental (Nonfunctional Requirements) Specification

1. Introduction

  1.1. Purpose

     To record all nonfunctional requirements for the system.

  1.2. Scope

  1.3. Definitions, Acronyms, and Abbreviations

  1.4. References

2. Usability

  State any requirements that affect usability, and link them to specific domains of functionality where applicable.

3. Reliability

  State any requirements for reliability, quantitatively wherever possible.

4. Performance

  State any performance requirements of the system, expressed quantitatively where possible, and link to specific features or user stories where applicable.

6. Supportability

  State any requirements for system supportability or maintainability.

7. Design Constraints

  State any design or development constraints imposed on the system or development process.

8. Documentation Requirements

  State the requirements for user and/or administrator documentation.

9. Purchased Components

  List any purchased components used with the system, licensing or usage restrictions, and compatibility/interoperability requirements.

10. Interfaces

  Define any third-party interfaces that must be supported by the system.

  10.1. Software Interfaces and Communication Protocols

  10.2. Hardware Interfaces, Operating Platforms

11. Licensing and Security Requirements

  Describe the licensing and usage enforcement requirements or other restrictions for usage, security, and accessibility.

12. Legal, Copyright, and Other Notices

  State any required legal disclaimers, warranties, copyright notices, patent notices, trademarks, or logo compliance issues.

Continues

Table 17–3 Template for a Supplemental (Nonfunctional Requirements) Specification (Continued)

13. Applicable Standards

Reference any applicable standards and the specific sections of any such standards that apply.

14. Internationalization and Localization

State any requirements for support of internationalization, user languages, and dialects.

15. Physical Deliverables

Define any specific deliverable artifacts required by the user or customer.

16. Installation and Deployment

Describe any specific configuration or target system preparation required to support installation and deployment of the system.

17. Other Requirements

Describe any other issues and requirements not covered elsewhere.

SUMMARY

In this chapter, we introduced that important software system bugaboo of nonfunctional requirements. We described how to think about them, how to discover them, and how to organize them so that the teams can build systems that meet the requisite *functionality, usability, reliability, performance, and supportability* requirements. We do so in the hope that with this guidance, that last 10% of the code might take only the remaining 10% of the time. That way, teams can complete their work on time and meet the objectives they have established during release planning.

Chapter 18

REQUIREMENTS ANALYSIS TOOLKIT

There is no sense in being precise about something, when you don't even know what you are talking about.

—John Von Neumann

Smaller projects, such as those that can operate solely at the Team level, are usually so well contained that communication among the stakeholders is not a big issue. The team usually has easy access to each other, and it's easy to resolve ambiguities and confusion. Just lean over to the next workstation, and ask the product owner what they meant with a story!

However, as projects grow in scope and size, the communication pathways become more and more complex, and opportunities for misunderstandings arise. Indeed, as projects grow to the Program level, it's pretty much a given that different means of communication become necessary. In addition, there are cases in which the ambiguity of imperfect requirements communication is simply not tolerable, particularly when the stories deal with life-and-death issues or when the erroneous behavior of a system could have extreme financial or legal consequences.

Communication has always been an imperfect vehicle. Misunderstandings abound, and it's common to say or hear, "This story is perfectly clear. Why don't you understand it?" Indeed, it may be clear to the story writer, but others may not find it so obvious at all. For example, think back to the "estimating" exercise in Chapter 8 for an "obvious" statement of requirements, such as "count the pages in the workbook," and look at all the confusions that arise within the scope of that simple exercise. Now, consider your real world.

Even with user stories, so helpful in bridging the gap between developer and user communities, our pidgin language may be able to communicate fairly simple things in a simple way, sufficient to buy some beads or build a software widget, but sometimes far more precision is required (How exactly is that cardiac pacemaker algorithm supposed to work...?).

In other words, when we are building complex systems, there are clearly times when we need alternate and far more precise communication mechanisms.

> If the description of the story is too complex for natural language and if the business cannot afford to have the specification misunderstood, the team should augment the story with a more precise specification method.

In this chapter, we'll describe a number of *requirements analysis techniques,* more technical methods for specifying system behavior that the team can use to resolve ambiguity and build more assuredly safe and reliable systems. Such methods include the following:

- Activity diagrams (flowcharts)
- Sample reports
- Pseudocode
- Decision tables and decision trees
- Finite state machines
- Message sequence diagrams
- Entity-relationship diagrams
- Use cases

And there are many others.

We won't attempt to describe any of these techniques in detail since each is worthy of a chapter of its own. But we can provide a brief introduction to each so that you'll have a sense of what to use and when to use it.

Where possible, only one or two of these technical methods should be used to augment natural-language stories for a system. This simplifies the nontechnical reviewer's task of reading and understanding these special elements. If all the systems developed by an organization fall into one application domain, such as telephone switching systems, perhaps the same technical method can be used for all the systems. But in most organizations, it's unrealistic to mandate a single technique for all stories in all systems. Story writers and analysts need to select an approach that best suits the individual situation and help the users and reviewers understand how the technique expresses system behavior.

In this chapter, we'll describe each of these methods in summary form.

ACTIVITY DIAGRAMS

Flowcharts and their new and more precise incarnation, the UML activity diagram, have the advantage of reasonable familiarity. Even people with no computer-related training or background generally know what a flowchart is. Teams apply activity diagrams, such as the Tendril one in Figure 18–1, that specify the major steps and process steps necessary to provision a new release of a product. They could have written a long and involved text-based procedure, or they could simplify the steps into a single understandable flow diagram as in Figure 18–1. Although the same information could have been presented in a number of other forms, the UML notation provides a visual representation that is fairly easy to understand and relatively unambiguous.

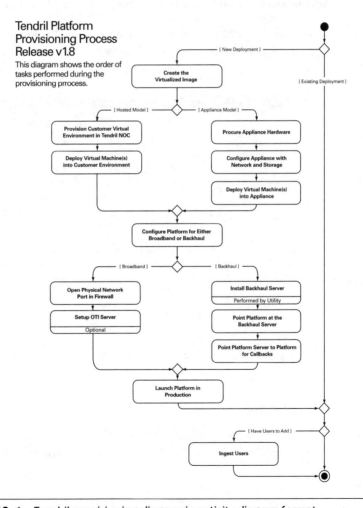

Figure 18–1 Tendril provisioning diagram in activity diagram format

SAMPLE REPORTS

Like the UI challenge we described in Chapter 7, users often don't know what they want to see in a report or other output until they see the report. Many times, teams churn code through a series of iterations, trying to get the right data presented in the right way, without simply stepping back and asking themselves, "What is it that they really want to see, and how do they want to see it?"

In these cases, a sample report format with mock data, generated by any number of desktop tools, might be all that is necessary to resolve most of the ambiguity. If the system is algorithmically intensive and the user cannot evaluate the report format without some real data and results, the team may need to invest some time in producing some real data. Figure 18–2 shows an example of a mock-up report.

Spikes are frequently invoked as research items to develop and validate sample reports with the product owner and users.

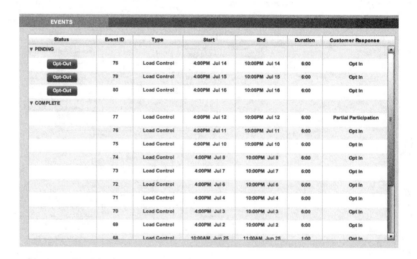

Figure 18–2   Sample event report format from case study

PSEUDOCODE

As the term implies, *pseudocode* is a "quasi" programming language, which combines the informality of natural language with the strict syntax and control structures of a

```
Set SUM(x)=0
FOR each customer X
        IF customer purchased paid support
               AND((Current month)>=(2 months after ship date))
               AND((Current month)<=(14 months after ship date))
               THEN Sum(X)=Sum(X)+(amount customer paid)/12
END
```

Figure 18–3   Example of pseudocode

programming language. In the extreme form, pseudocode consists of combinations of the following:

- Imperative sentences with a single verb and a single object
- A limited set, typically not more than 40 to 50, of "action-oriented" verbs from which the sentences must be constructed
- Decisions represented with a formal IF-ELSE-ENDIF structure
- Iterative activities represented with DO-WHILE or FOR-NEXT structures

Figure 18–3 shows an example of a pseudocode specification of an algorithm for calculating deferred-service revenue earned within a given month in a business application. The text of the pseudocode is indented in an outline-style format in order to show "blocks" of logic. The combination of the syntax restrictions and the format and layout of the text greatly reduces the ambiguity of what could otherwise be a very difficult and error-prone story. (It certainly was before we wrote this pseudocode.) At the same time, it should be possible for a nonprogramming person to read and understand the story's function in the form shown in Figure 18–3.

DECISION TABLES AND DECISION TREES

It's common to see a story that deals with a combination of inputs; different combinations of those inputs lead to different actions or outputs. Suppose, for example, that we have a system with three inputs—A, B, and C—and we see a story that starts with a pseudocode-like statement: "If A is true, then if B is also true, do action X, unless C is true, in which case the required action is Y." The combination of

IF-THEN-ELSE clauses quickly becomes tangled, especially if, as in this example, it involves nested IFs. Typically, nontechnical users are not sure that they understand any of it, and nobody is sure whether all the possible combinations and permutations of A, B, and C have been covered.

The solution in this case is to enumerate all the combinations of inputs and to describe each one explicitly in a decision table. In our example, if the only permissible values of the inputs are "true" and "false," we have 2^3, or eight, combinations. These can be represented in a table containing eight columns. We would then list the actions for each of those eight combinations. Figure 18–4 illustrates a real-life problem that many users encounter, a printer malfunction.

Alternatively, a decision tree can be drawn to portray decisions in a more graphical form. Figure 18–5 shows a decision tree used to describe a hypothetical emergency sequence.

		Rules							
Conditions	Printer does not print.	Y	Y	Y	Y	N	N	N	N
	A red light is flashing.	Y	Y	N	N	Y	Y	N	N
	Printer is unrecognized.	Y	N	Y	N	Y	N	Y	N
Actions	Check the power cable.			X					
	Check the printer-computer cable.	X		X					
	Ensure printer software is installed.	X		X		X		X	
	Check/replace ink.	X	X			X	X		
	Check for paper jam.		X		X				

Figure 18–4   Decision table for debugging a printer failure

Source: Wikipedia (en.wikipedia.org/wiki/Decision_table)

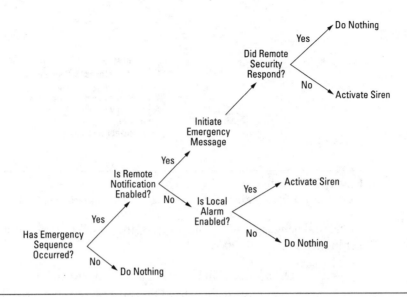

Figure 18–5 Example of a graphical decision tree

Source: *Managing Software Requirements: A Unified Approach* [Leffingwell and Widrig 2000]

FINITE STATE MACHINES

In some cases, it's convenient to model a complex system as a "hypothetical machine that can be in only one of a given number of 'states' at any specific time" [Davis 1993]. In response to an input, such as data entry from the user or an input from an external device, the machine changes its state and then generates an output or carries out an action. Both the output and the next state can be determined solely on the basis of understanding the current state and the event that caused the transition. In that way, a system's behavior can be said to be deterministic; we can mathematically determine every possible state and, therefore, the outputs of the system, based on any set of inputs provided.

Hardware designers have used finite state machines (FSMs) for decades, and a large body of literature describes the creation and analysis of such machines. Indeed, the mathematical nature of the FSM notation lends itself to formal and rigorous analysis so that the problems of consistency, completeness, and ambiguity can be largely mitigated using this technique.

Let's suppose that we have a light box with two lights (Even and Odd) and three buttons, On, Off, and Count, as shown in Figure 18–6.

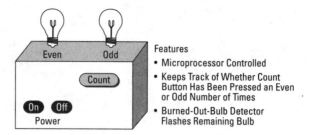

Figure 18–6 Light box

Source: *Managing Software Requirements: A Unified Approach* [Leffingwell and Widrig 2000]

In natural language, we could express the desired story thusly [Davis 1993, Leffingwell and Widrig 2000].

- After On is pushed but before Off is pushed, system is termed "powered on."
- After Off is pushed but before On is pushed, system is termed "powered off," and no lights shall be lit.
- Since the most recent On press, if Count has been pressed an odd number of times, Odd shall be lit.
- Since the most recent On press, if Count has been pressed an even number of times, Even shall be lit.
- If either light burns out, the other light shall flash every one second.

A popular notation for FSMs is the state transition diagram (Figure 18–7). In this notation, the boxes represent the state the device is in, and the arrows represent actions that transition the device to alternative states. We might note that the natural-language expression listed previously of "the other light shall flash every one second" is ambiguous. The state transition diagram in Figure 18–7 is not ambiguous

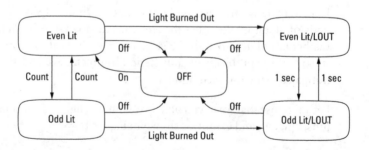

Figure 18–7 Example of a state transition diagram

and it illustrates exactly what the product owner desired. If a bulb burns out, the device alternates between attempting to light the Even light and attempting to light the Odd light, each for a period of one second.

An even more precise form of representing an FSM is the state transition matrix, which is represented as a table that shows every possible state the device can be in, the output of the system for each state, and the effect of every possible stimulus or event on every possible state. This ensures a higher degree of specificity, because every state and the effect of every possible event must be represented in the table. Figure 18–8 defines the behavior of our light box in the form of a state transition matrix.

With this technique, we can resolve additional ambiguities that may have been present in our attempt to understand the behavior of the device.

- What happens if the user presses the On switch and the device is already on? Answer: Nothing.
- What happens if both bulbs are burned out? Answer: The device powers itself off.

FSMs are popular for certain categories of systems programming applications, such as message-switching systems, operating systems, and process control systems. FSMs also provide a rigorous way to describe the interaction between an external human user and a system (consider, for example, the interaction between a bank customer and an automated teller machine when the customer wants to withdraw money). However, FSMs can become unwieldy, particularly if we need to represent the system's behavior as a function of several inputs. In such cases, the required system behavior is typically a function of all current conditions and stimuli rather than the current stimulus or a history of stimuli.

State	Event					Output
	On Press	**Off Press**	**Count Press**	**Bulb Burns Out**	**Every Second**	
Off	Even Lit	—	—	—	—	Both Off
Even Lit	—	Off	Odd Lit	LO/Even Lit	—	Even Lit
Odd Lit	—	Off	Even Lit	LO/Odd Lit	—	Odd Lit
Light Out/Even Lit	—	Off	—	Off	LO/Odd Lit	Even Lit
Light Out/Odd Lit	—	Off	—	Off	LO/Even Lit	Odd Lit

Figure 18–8 Example of a state transition matrix

MESSAGE SEQUENCE DIAGRAMS

A message sequence diagram is a kind of interaction diagram that shows how processes operate with one another and in what order. Message sequence diagrams (MSDs) are a convenient way to express a transactional relationship between two or more parties. Typically, MSDs are used to express relationships such as "A sends this message to B. B responds with this message to A." Figure 18–9 illustrates a typical MSD from the Tendril case study. MSDs identify the interested parties (subsystems in this case) across the top of the diagram, and the interactions proceed down the diagram as time evolves. In this case, the HAN initiates the action, and the messages flow from there.[1]

Limitations of MSDs[2]

Some systems have simple dynamic behavior that can be expressed in terms of specific sequences of messages between a small, fixed number of objects or processes. In such cases, MSDs can completely specify the system's behavior. Often, behavior

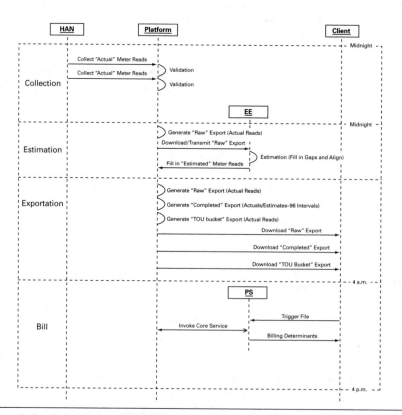

Figure 18–9   Case study example message sequence diagram

---

1. Thanks to Oliver Johnson of Tendril for this example.
2. See *en.wikipedia.org/wiki/Sequence_diagram* for further explanations.

is more complex, such as when the set of communicating objects is large or highly variable, when there are many branch points (for example, exceptions), when there are complex iterations, or when there are synchronization issues such as resource contention. In such cases, MSDs cannot easily describe the system's behavior, but they can specify typical use cases for the system, small details in its behavior, and simplified overviews of its behavior.

ENTITY-RELATIONSHIP DIAGRAMS

If the stories within a set involve a description of the structure and relationships among data within the system, it's often convenient to represent that information in an entity-relationship diagram (ERD). Figure 18–10 shows a typical ERD.

Note that the ERD provides a high-level "architectural" view of the data represented by customers, invoices, packing lists, and so on; it would be further augmented with appropriate details about the required information to describe a customer. The ERD does correctly focus on the external behaviors of the system and allows us to define such questions as "Can there be more than one billing address per invoice?" *Answer:* No.

Although an ERD is a capable modeling technique, it has the potential disadvantage of being difficult for a nontechnical reader to understand.

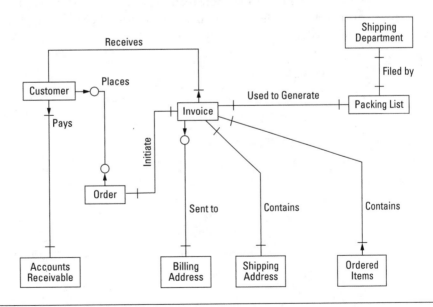

Figure 18–10   Example of an entity-relationship diagram

Source: *Managing Software Requirements: A Unified Approach* [Leffingwell and Widrig 2000]

USE-CASE MODELING

So far, our agile requirements story hasn't introduced use cases, which are a traditional way to express system behavior in complex systems. Use cases are the primary means to represent requirements with the UML. They are well described there as well as in a variety of texts on the subject. Use cases can be used for both specification and analysis. They are especially useful when the system of interest is in turn composed of other subsystems. But we won't ignore them any longer, because they are the entire subject of the next chapter.

SUMMARY

Agile development avoids big, up-front design (BUFD) and analysis wherever possible. However, your system still has to work and deliver the requisite reliability. When user stories and natural language aren't good enough, your team will need to apply more technical methods to reduce the risk of misunderstanding and to provide additional safety, security, and reliability for your system.

In this chapter, we introduced a number of specification techniques that can reduce ambiguity in specifying system behavior. In general, these technical methods should be used sparingly, and common sense should guide the decision as to which formal technique will be used in a project. If you're building a pacemaker or nuclear reactor control system, perhaps every aspect of the system is critical; in most systems, however, it's unlikely that more than 10 percent of the stories will require this degree of rigor. Choose the method that suits your team best, and apply it only where it is really needed.

Chapter 19

USE CASES

A user story is to a use case as a gazelle is to a gazebo.

—Alistair Cockburn

In Chapter 1, we provided a brief history of requirements methods and briefly mentioned the role of use cases as a form of requirements capture and expression. Popularized originally within the context of the Rational Unified Process (RUP), which was *use case–driven* and architecture-centric, for many, use cases have been the requirements analysis and communication expression of choice. Even outside RUP, they appeared in most contemporary works on software requirements and systems analysis. Use cases were also the container for functional requirements capture, analysis, and behavioral specification within the context of the Unified Modeling Language (UML). Those who used the UML most likely used use cases. If you have been doing iterative development, you are probably using use cases too.

In agile development, however, the picture changed as the user story (or even more simply, the backlog item in Scrum) became the predominant form. As we have described throughout this book, there can be no doubt of their value in lightening requirements expression, driving more and more incremental thinking, and generally increasing the agility of the teams that use them. User stories are good requirements tools. Use cases were largely banned from the agile tribes.[1]

As agile methods started to be applied to larger systems, however, something was missing: *context*. Simply put, although a nice itemized list of backlog items is easy to look at, tool, prioritize, and manage, it is inadequate to do the more complex analysis work that larger systems require. And even though we've called our backlog items user stories, they don't really tell much of a story after all, at least not one much beyond what any casual reader might understand.

---

1. One Certified Scrum Product Owner course stated, "Don't use use cases. They are too hard to write, and users don't understand them."

To this end, this chapter describes how to apply use cases in the development of complex software systems being developed in an agile manner. After all, who is building a simple software system with agile these days?

THE PROBLEMS WITH USER STORIES AND BACKLOG ITEMS

Alistair Cockburn is one agile thought leader with his foot in both of these camps. As both an authority on use cases [Cockburn 2001] and a respected agilist and signer of the Agile Manifesto, he bemoans the apparent loss of use cases from agile development. He notes that there are many problems with the user story and backlog forms of requirements expression:[2]

> User stories and backlog items don't give the designers a context to work from—when is the user doing this, what is the context of their operation, and what is their larger goal at this moment?
>
> User stories and backlog items don't give the project team any sense of scope or potential "completeness"—a development team estimates a project at (e.g.) 270 story points, and then as soon as they start working, that number keeps increasing, seemingly without bound. The developers and sponsors are equally depressed. How big is this project, really?
>
> User stories and backlog items don't provide a mechanism for looking ahead at upcoming work. Seeing a set of extension conditions (alternate flows) in a use case lets the analysts understand which ones will be easy and which will be difficult so they can stage the work accordingly. With user stories, the extension conditions are usually detected mid-sprint, when it is too late.

FIVE GOOD REASONS TO STILL USE USE CASES

Use Case

Use cases help explore the deeper interactions among *users*, the *systems*, and the *subsystems* of the solution. The use case also helps identify all the *alternate scenarios* that trip us up so often when it comes to system-level quality. This is especially the case when the team is building complex hardware and software systems, where system-spanning epics, features, and stories bob in and out of hardware and software like a surfacing porpoise. Cockburn notes "five good reasons to use use cases in agile development."

> ■ *The list of goal names provides executives with a short summary of what the system will contribute to the business and the users. It also provides a project planning skeleton, to be used to build initial priorities, estimates, team allocation, and timing. It is the first part of the completeness question.*

---

2. See *http://alistair.cockburn.us/A+user+story+is+to+a+use+case+as+a+gazelle+is+to+a+gazebo*. Portions reproduced here with permission. Minor edits by the author.

- *The main success scenario of the use case provides everyone with an agreement as to what the system will... and will not do. It provides the context for each requirement, a context that is hard to get any other way.*
- *The extension conditions of the use case provide a framework for investigating all the little, niggling things that somehow take up 80% of the development time and budget. It provides a look-ahead mechanism, so the customer/product owner/ business analyst can spot issues that are likely to take a long time to get answers for. The use case extension conditions are the second part of the completeness question.*
- *The use case extension scenarios provide answers to the many detailed, tricky business questions programmers ask: "What are we supposed to do in this case?" (normally answered by, "I don't know, I've never thought about that case"). It is a thinking/documentation framework that matches the if... then... else statement that helps programmers think through such issues.*
- *The full use case set (use case model) shows that the developers/analysts have thought through every user's needs, every goal they have with respect to the system, and every business variant involved. This is the final part of the completeness question.*

Since use cases can play such a beneficial role in agile development, this chapter will provide a basic grounding in use cases so an agile team or enterprise can understand how to apply them. For additional background and depth on use cases, we refer you to other texts on the subject.[3]

Use Case Basics

We'll start with a definition:

A use case describes a sequence of actions between an actor and a system that produces a result of value for that actor.

In other words, each use case describes a series of events in which a particular actor, such as Mark the *consumer*, interacts with a system, such as *the Tendril platform*, to achieve a result of value to Mark, such as shed some energy load in his area.

To further our understanding, let's look closer at this definition.

- *Sequence of actions:* The sequence of actions describes a set of interactions between the actor and the system. The sequence is invoked when the actor provides some input to the system. Each action is atomic; that is, it is performed either entirely or not at all.

---

3. There are dozens of books on the topic, including Cockburn's *Writing Effective Use Cases* [2001] and Leffingwell and Widrig's *Managing Software Requirements, Second Edition: A Use Case Approach* [2003].

- *System:* The system works for the actor. It executes some function, algorithmic procedure, or other activity. The system takes its orders from the actor as to when to do what.
- *A result of value:* Like a user story, the use case must deliver value to a user. Therefore, *the resident pushes the opt-in button* is not a good use case (the system didn't do anything obvious for the user). But *the resident pushes the "opt-in" button and the system starts to shed load* is a meaningful use case.
- *Actor:* The particular actor is the individual or device (Mark, the resident; a message from the utility) that initiates the action (*shed some load; create a message on the user's TV*).

Use Case Actors

Actor

An actor is someone or something that interacts with the system.

There are generally three types of actors to be considered.

- *Users:* Users act on the system; this is the type of actor most people think of when they think of a use case. For example, I am an actor on the word processing system I'm using to write this chapter.
- *Other systems or applications:* Most software interacts with other systems or other applications. This is another primary source of actors. Here's an example: The author's word processing application interacts with a Web service to access and insert clip art. The author's word processing application is an actor on the Web service.
- *A device:* Many applications interface to a variety of input and output devices. For example, the consumer's refrigerator is an actor on the Tendril platform.

Use Case Structure

The use case itself is a text-based structure of logical elements that work together to define the use case. Figure 19–1 provides a standard template.

A use case has four mandatory elements.

- *Name:* The name describes the goal, that is, what is achieved by the interaction with the actor. The name should be a few words in length, and it must be unique. Names such as *pop up an emergency warning message* and *shed refrigerator load* are good examples. They are short, are descriptive, and define the goal.

- *Brief description:* The purpose of the use case should be described in one or two sentences. Here's an example: this use case describes what happens when the Tendril system receives an event notification from the utility.
- *Actor(s):* A use case has no meaning outside the context of its use by an actor, so each actor who participates in the use case is listed with the use case.
- *Flow of events:* The main body of the use case is the event flow, usually a textual description of the interactions between the actor and the system. The flow of events can consist of both the *basic flow*, which is the main path through the use case, and *alternate flows*, which are executed only under certain circumstances.

It is the *alternate flows* (or *alternate scenarios*) that provide much of value to the agile system builder. It is here where they are forced to think through all the "what ifs" that might affect our user story. Here's an example: "what happens if the device does not respond to the message?" or "if I'm programming the system, and an event happens—what happens then?" Understanding all the alternate flows of a use case defines the various (usually less likely but equally important) scenarios that the system must handle with grace in order to assure reliability and quality.

```
                  Use Case Name
Description
Actor(s)
Flow of Events
       Basic Flow
             Event 1
             Event 2
             .........
       Alternate Flow
Preconditions

Exit Conditions
       Success Guarantee
       Minimum Guarantee
```

Figure 19–1 Use case template

In addition to the mandatory elements, a use case may have optional elements.

■ *Preconditions:* Preconditions are those conditions that must be present in order for a use case to start. They usually represent some system state that must be present before the use case can be used. For example, a precondition of the set thermostat to shed load use case is that the system must have opt-in for load shedding enabled.

■ *Exit conditions:* Exit conditions describe the state of the system after a use case has run its course. These can include both a *success guarantee*, which describes the state of the system after a successful execution, and a *minimum guarantee*, which describes the state of the system if the execution of the use case fails for some reason. For example, a *success guarantee* of the set thermostat to shed load use case is that the system remains in the load shedding state. A *minimum guarantee* might be that load shedding is not initiated but an error message is displayed.

■ *System or subsystem:* In a system of subsystems, it may be necessary to identify whether a use case is a system-level use case (one that causes multiple subsystems to interact) or a subsystem use case. In either case, the team needs to identify what system or subsystem a use case is identified with.

■ *Other stakeholders:* It may also be useful to identify other key stakeholders who may be affected by the use case. For example, a manager may use a report from the system, and yet the manager may not personally interact with the system and would therefore not appear as an actor.

■ *Special requirements:* The use case may also have special requirements that apply to that specific use case. Often these are nonfunctional requirements (support 10,000 homes without performance degradation) that apply to the specific use case.

A Step-by-Step Guide to Building the Use Case Model

An individual use case describes how a particular actor interacts with the system to achieve a result of value for that specific actor. The set of all use cases together describes the complete behavior of the system. The complete set of use cases, actors, and their interactions constitutes the *use case model* for the system.

Building the use case model for the system is an important analysis step, one that will become the basis for understanding, communicating, and refining the behavior of the system over the course of the project. We have found a simple five-step approach to be an effective way to build the use case model. However, these steps do not all happen at the same point in the project life cycle, and some steps will likely be revisited.

Step 1: Identify and Describe the Actors

First, identify all the actors that interact with the system. This is a matter of dividing the world into two classes of interesting things: the system we are building and those things (actors) that interact with the system.

The following questions will help identify actors.

- Who uses the system?
- Who gets information from this system?
- Who provides information to the system?
- Where is the system used?
- Who supports and maintains the system?
- What other systems or devices use this system?

Step 2: Identify the Use Cases

Once the actors are identified, the next step is to identify the various use cases that the actors need to accomplish their jobs. We can do this by determining the specific goals for each actor in turn.

- What will the actor use the system for?
- Will the actor create, store, change, remove, or read data in the system?
- Will the actor need to inform the system about external events or changes?
- Will the actor need to be informed about certain occurrences in the system?

We might discover use cases such as send consumers a notification of pending event as something that a power utility's network operations center (the actor) might want to do to the Tendril platform. Graphically, we could construct a simple diagram of use cases and actors as illustrated in Figure 19–2.

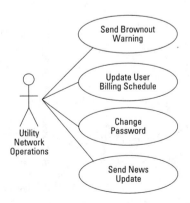

Figure 19–2   Use cases for the utility network operations center

Each use case has a *name* that represents the goal of the use case. The name is a few words or short phrase that starts with an action verb and communicates what the actor achieves. Names help communicate what the system does and create context.

Along with the name, there is a brief description that further describes the intent of the use case.

Step 3: Identify the Actor and Use Case Relationships

Although only one actor can initiate a use case, some use cases involve the participation of multiple actors. When the actors and use cases interact in concert, that's when the system becomes a system. In this step, each use case is analyzed to see what actors interact with it, and each actor's anticipated behavior is reviewed to verify that the actor participates in all the necessary use cases.

Step 4: Outline the Flow of the Use Cases

The next step is to outline the flow of each use case to start to gain an understanding of required system behavior at the next level of detail. Of particular interest at this time is the flow of events, including the basic and alternate flows, as Figure 19–3 illustrates.

Outline the basic flow first. This is the flow that represents the most common path (the "happy path") from start to finish through the use case.

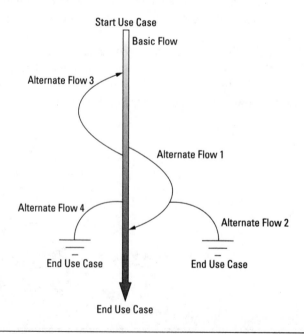

Figure 19–3   A use case has one main flow and some number of alternate flows.

In addition to the basic flow, the use case will have a number of alternate flows based on both regular circumstances and exceptional events. The following questions can help discover these paths.

- Basic flow
    - What actor's event starts the use case?
    - How does the use case end?
    - How does the use case repeat some behavior?
- Alternate flow
    - What else can the actor do?
    - How will the actor react to optional situations?
    - What variants might happen?
    - What exceptions to the usual behavior may occur?

Step 5: Refine the Use Cases

Later, the use case may be refined to another level of detail, or perhaps the team will move directly to the stories that implement the use case. There are a number of additional factors to be considered.

- *Consider all alternate flows, including unusual exception conditions:* It is usually straightforward to identify the primary alternate flows of a use case since these are driven by explicit actor choices. However, the "what ifs" are a primary source of concern, and these must be fully explored in alternate flows. "What if the resident is programming the system when an energy event occurs?" All these exceptions must be understood, coded, and tested, or the application may not behave as expected.
- *Preconditions:* The refinement process will identify state information that controls the behavior of the system. Preconditions describe the things that must be true before a use case starts. For example, a precondition to programming vacation settings might be that the user has set the time zone. If that has not been done, the use case cannot be successfully executed.
- *Exit conditions:* These describe the persistent states the use case leaves behind. They can include the success guarantee (state after successful execution) and the minimum guarantee (state after unsuccessful execution).

A Use Case Example

As an example, we'll describe a use case from the Tendril platform. One of the system features is the capability of the power utilities to notify their consumers of pending changes in power distribution. Suppose a utility is about to go into a "brownout." The utility would like to notify its consumers of the impending brownout event so they could plan accordingly. Figure 19–4 illustrates a use case for this.

Use Case Name: Issue brownout notification
Brief Description: Upon determining that a brownout condition is pending, the utility sends a message to all registered devices in the utility's Tendril domain. This will include notification to all the utility's registered on-premise displays, mobile devices, and portals.
Actors:
• Utility Network Operating Center operators (UNOC) (primary actor)
• Tendril customers
Basic Flow of Events:
1. A UNOC operator determines that a brownout event is pending.
2. The operator composes a broadcast message in TUP.
3. TUP sends the message to all affected customers, either over the utility backhaul or through an Internet (IP) connection, to all registered Tendril devices in the consumer's home, and logs that the message has been sent.
4. Each Tendril device in the home returns to TUP a confirmation of successful message receipt and presents the upcoming brownout message to the homeowner in its device-specific format.
5. TUP adds each confirmation to its record of confirmations received.
Alternate Flows:
• 4a. Home Tendril device fails to confirm (initially): At established intervals, TUP resends the brownout event notice to all Tendril devices that did not reply.
• 4b. Home Tendril device fails to confirm after the specified number of retries: TUP notifies the UNOC operator of the situation of the nonacknowledging Tendril home device.
Preconditions:
• Receipt of overload conditions pending on the utility grid.
• Determination of areas to be affected by brownout and matching areas to preset Tendril notification zones.
Success Guarantee:
• The brownout notice has been sent.
• Every home device has been accounted for, through either confirmation or total failure to confirm.
• The UNOC operator as been notified of all home devices that failed to confirm.
Minimal Guarantee:
• In the worst case, the TUP log has captured the state of all notification-confirmation pairs for every home device on the subscription list.

Figure 19–4   A sample use case

We can see from the example that a use case is not a trivial thing. Rather, it is an appropriate requirements artifact used to capture and define the behavior of non-trivial systems. One could imagine that a single use case like the one in Figure 19–4 could create dozens, or more, individual user stories. But the use case spawns these stories within a system usage context. That can be a tremendous aid to understanding for the customer, user, development team, and other key stakeholders alike.

APPLYING USE CASES

If your system is complex and is composed of subsystems (what complex system isn't?), use cases provide a mechanism to help developers think about all the possible paths through the system and subsystems that the users may encounter.

In turn, this helps the team understand where user stories are likely to be needed to implement the required functionality. Every time a new use case touches a subsystem, there are probably new stories that must be developed for that subsystem, as is shown in Figure 19–5.

Once identified, the use cases can then be used to drive incremental development, one story at a time, as Kroll and MacIsaac [2006] illustrate in Figure 19–6.

In this graphic, one can see how use case–spawned user stories can be implemented in iterations over time (story 1 in iteration 1, stories 2 and 3 in iteration 2, and so on). To the agile developer or product owner, this can be helpful in understanding the larger context that can be lost when the teams focus on understanding "just one user story at a time."

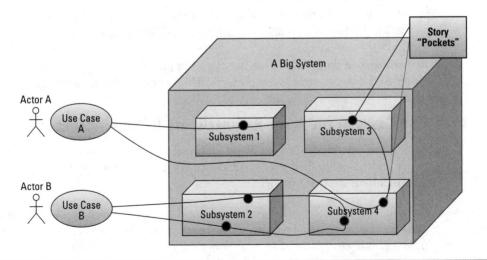

Figure 19–5   Use cases traversing a system identify where stories are needed.

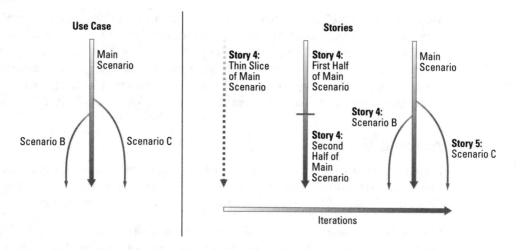

Figure 19–6   Sequencing user stories in iterations

Source: Kroll/MacIsaac, *Agility and Discipline Made Easy,* © 2006

Tips for Applying Use Cases in Agile

Finally, here are a few tips to keep in mind when you apply use cases in agile development.

- Keep them lightweight—no design details, GUI specs, and so on.
- Don't treat them like fixed requirements. Like user stories, they are merely statements of intended system behavior.
- Don't worry about maintaining them; they are primarily thinking tools.
- Model them informally—use whiteboards, lightweight tools, and so on.

Remember, you don't have to use use cases, but no one can tell you not to use them either. And if your system is complex, you'll likely be quite happy if you do.

Use Cases in the Agile Requirements Information Model

As we have described, use cases are an *optional* technique, which teams can use to better understand desired system behaviors. We haven't yet introduced them in the agile requirements meta-model.

Since functional system behaviors are captured as backlog items, we'll associate use cases there, as an optional requirements modeling and elaboration artifact. We illustrate this in Figure 19–7.

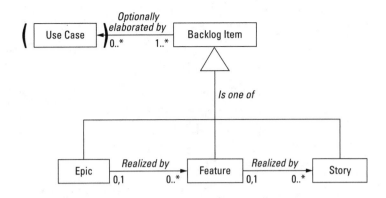

Figure 19–7   Use cases may be used to elaborate desired system behavior.

As the model indicates, you can apply use cases to describe more complex system behavior, most typically at the feature and epic levels, where they serve to better illustrate *what we mean by that big thing*.

SUMMARY

Throughout most of this book, we've used user stories, features, and epics to define the behavior of the systems we are building. They work well, and they have earned their place in the forefront of agilists' minds. As convenient as they are, however, they can do a poor job of helping teams define and understand the behavior of more complex systems, where we need to understand the user and the system *in context*, not to mention thinking through all the "what if" scenarios that happen with systems of any scale. For this we can apply use cases, which are a well-understood and proven tool that was invented for just this purpose.

Even though use cases aren't generally promoted in agile, as professionals we need to keep an open mind about these things. Ignoring techniques that have helped us manage complexity before is stupid. And being stupid isn't lean, agile, professional, or economically sound.

PART IV

AGILE REQUIREMENTS FOR THE PORTFOLIO

A system is a network of interdependent components that work together to try to accomplish the aim of the system. A system must have an aim. Without the aim, there is no system.

—W. Edwards Deming

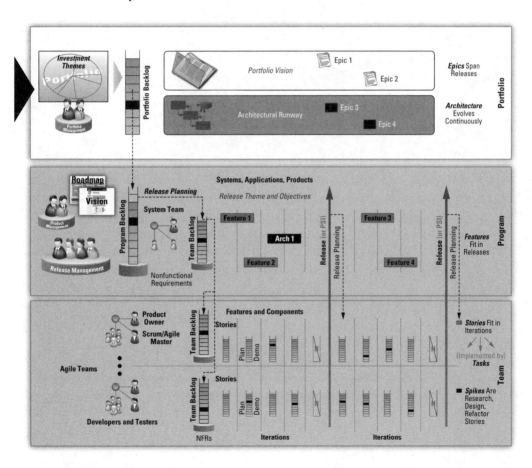

Chapter 20

AGILE ARCHITECTURE

Evolving big systems requires big thoughts.

INTRODUCTION TO THE PORTFOLIO LEVEL OF THE BIG PICTURE

As we reach the *Portfolio level* of the Big Picture (see Figure 20–1), the things we need to describe get bigger and more complex, so in order to keep our thinking crisp, we'll need to discuss them at a higher level of abstraction.

At this level, we'll need to understand the strategic *investment themes* that drive our decisions and resource allocations, the *portfolio backlog* (where new products, services, and systems arise), and the *epics* that we'll use to define, elaborate, and implement these bigger things.

In this chapter, we'll discuss the critical role that *system architecture* plays in helping us build robust, reliable, and scalable systems. We'll also describe how larger teams build and extend the *architectural runway* they use to host all those new features we need in order to keep our solutions competitive.

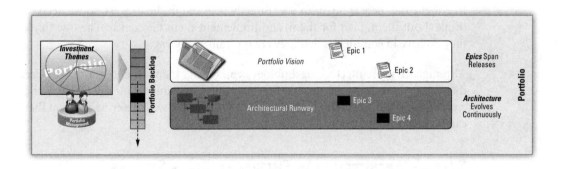

Figure 20–1 The Portfolio level of the Big Picture

We'll also elaborate on the concept of *architectural epics*. These are the larger-scale technology initiatives, or *infrastructure enablers*, that describe how we need to evolve our system so that it meets the needs we have identified today, as well as allows us to exploit new opportunities that present themselves in the future:

> Architectural epics are large, technology development initiatives that cut across one or more of three dimensions.
>
>> Time—affecting multiple releases of our products, systems, services, or solutions
>> Scope—affecting multiple products, systems, services, or solutions
>> Organization—affecting multiple teams, programs, business units

Examples of such epics include the following.

- Build a UI framework for porting all existing applications to mobile devices.
- Build a common installer and licensing mechanism for all products in a suite.
- Implement an industry security standard to lower our data purchasing costs.
- Refactor back-office transaction applications to run 64-bit servers.
- Support latest version of the customer's desktop OS, database, or platform.
- Implement the new UI standard with new corporate branding.
- Replace the search engine's underlying database with MySQL.

Of course, we wouldn't invest in these epics if they didn't deliver any value, but it isn't only *user value* that we must consider. There are other forms of value, including the *value to our business* in efficiency, operating, or transaction costs (…*lower our data purchasing costs, corporate branding*). More typically they drive user value, whether the value is obvious (*support latest desktop OS*) or not so obvious (*run on 64-bit servers*). In either case, there is often no user directly involved in the process, so we need to think about them, plan for them, and implement them differently. The one thing they do have in common is that they are typically really *big*.

Although these architecture (technology) epics aren't requirements per se, we'll see that they behave as if they are, and they play an equally important role. To keep the entire system lean and agile, in the chapter after this one, we'll describe a system that can be used to help *achieve architectural flow*.

SYSTEMS ARCHITECTURE IN ENTERPRISE-CLASS SYSTEMS

So far in this text, we've discussed requirements in a sort of "value-stream-only vacuum." That is, we've intentionally expressed requirements so as to focus solely on "what the system does" to deliver value to our users. In so doing, we consciously avoided overloading our users' thinking with "how the system goes about doing it."

This was reasonable and purposeful—trying to understand real value is hard enough—and the last thing we needed to do was to confuse the customer or ourselves with discussions of frameworks, technologies, and technical jargon about all the infrastructure we'll need to host those nifty new features.

However, in doing so, we must also be conscious of the fact that requirements and design (we'll just generalize that to *architecture* at this level) represent two sides of the same coin, the "what the system needs to do" as reflected in requirements expressions and the "how the system will be built to do it" as reflected in architectural constructs. And they are *not* independent.

In previous texts [Leffingwell and Widrig 2003], we've described the continuous give-and-take between design and requirements as follows:

> The requirements versus design activities must be iterative. Requirements discovery and definition and design decisions are circular. The process is a continuous give-and-take:

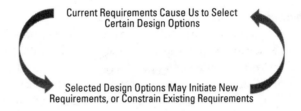

Current Requirements Cause Us to Select
Certain Design Options

Selected Design Options May Initiate New
Requirements, or Constrain Existing Requirements

So, the discriminator between "what a system is supposed to do" and "how it is supposed to do it" is really not so clear. In any case, as system developers, we need to understand *both*.

Does All Architecture Emerge in Agile?

At the level of the teams and programs, we didn't fuss about architecture and design decisions at all. After all, user stories and features were negotiable, so if we discovered that a story as stated was unnecessarily hard to implement, we negotiated one that delivered comparable value but was easier and more cost effective. That makes good economic sense. Indeed, that's a primary reason that *negotiable* lives in the INVEST model.

Some Does

We have also trusted in Agile Manifesto principle #11 (*The best architectures, requirements, and designs emerge from self-organizing teams*) as well as principle #5 (*... Trust them to get the job done*). Moreover, if we do worry a bit, as we probably should, we always have that *working software* (principles #1 and #3) to satisfy our curiosity about status. With the fast give-and-take between users, product owners, testers, and developers, we *trust them* to produce a system that is robust and reliable and meets current needs. They certainly don't need someone else to design it for them, and they *trust us* not to meddle in their business.

In addition, when it comes to evolving software, agile teams have their refactoring skills to rely on; they constantly improve the quality and performance of the system by continuously refactoring the design. This is an important skill, because with minimal "up-front" requirements and design, teams know they can't possibly get it right the first time. However, continuously refactoring and redesigning large-scale, emerging architectures becomes less economical as the size of the system grows. Even minor, system-level redesigns can cause substantial rework for large numbers of teams, some of whom would otherwise *not* have to refactor their module. It is one thing for one team to redesign their code based on lessons they have learned; it's quite another to require *ten* teams to do so based on *another* team's lessons learned.

But Some Doesn't

For developers, architects, and businesspeople who have experience building large-scale systems and portfolios consisting of systems, products, and services—with the extensibility and scalability a successful solution demands—a *solely emergent architecture* is counter to our experience. We know that some amount of architectural planning and governance is necessary to reliably produce and maintain such systems. Individual teams, products, and programs may not even have the visibility necessary to see how the larger, enterprise system needs to evolve. *It can't simply emerge. Something has to tie it all together.*

In addition, sometimes our architectural "evolution" is driven in spasms by unpredictable events. These can include the following.

- Mergers or acquisitions from which new product or system harmonization is needed.
- State changes in the business life cycle; for example, the need to compete with suites and solution offerings as opposed to point products.
- Maturity phases; moving from selling to innovators and early adopters to selling to the early and late majority requires more product maturity, and higher reliability, stability, and predictability. This, in turn, requires *stronger architectural governance.*

The Need for Intentional Architecture

But as we consider architecture at this level of the enterprise, we also are cognizant of the fact that it is the "lighter-weight" agile methods, specifically Scrum and XP, that are seeing the broadest adoption in the enterprise and that these methods provide virtually no guidance (at least as compared to FDD, DSDM, OpenUP, and others[1]) on the topic of architecture. They didn't have to—the methods weren't designed to be applied at the scale that we now apply them.

And that is one of our big challenges. The methods are based on the assumption that architecture emerges as a natural outcome of a rapid iteration cycle, implementation of prioritized value-driven user requests, and a continuous refactoring process. That works fine, up to a point. *This* is that point.

So, architecture can indeed emerge, but some of it needs to emerge intentionally. And because all software systems age and grow fragmented by competing demands over time, it will eventually be necessary to *rearchitect* major portions of the system. To do that, we'll also need a common architectural vision, strategy, and governance model.

So, our challenge is again to carry the desirable and qualitative agile benefits from individual teams to multiple teams and ever-larger systems but still do so in a lean and agile manner.

Business Drivers for Architectural Epics

It is the economics of the business itself that drive us to build the best possible software systems, because that is how we build our revenue and market share. Some of these business factors drive us to new technological solutions, which we objectify as architectural epics. These business drivers can include the following.

- *New product or service opportunities:* Many architectural initiatives are driven from the *portfolio backlog* (big things the company would like to do). They provide opportunity for growth of revenue, market share, or increased end user satisfaction, but they are not feasible in the context of the existing system's architecture.
- *Changes in technologies that affect multiple products and services:* Often the need is driven by evolving technologies—things that weren't feasible or even invented "back when" the initial system was built. Examples include new platforms and operating systems, mobile technologies, 64-bit chipsets, and so on.
- *Problems within the existing solution set:* Sometimes the change is driven by problems in the existing solution. For example, unanticipated market success can drive heavier user loads and highlight system-level bottlenecks.

---

1. For a deeper discussion on the methods themselves and their treatments of architecture more specifically, refer to Chapter 16 of *Scaling Software Agility: Best Practices for Large Enterprises* [Leffingwell 2007].

Examples include performance, size (runtime and download footprint), new security requirements, usability, upgradability, compatibility, and so on.

- *Architectural governance:* Some common, imposed constructs can ease usability, extensibility, performance, and maintenance. For example, something as simple as a common presentation design can result in higher end-user satisfaction. In addition, as stewards of many of the system-level nonfunctional requirements, architecture must also address needs such as internationalization, security, common platforms, and so on. This governance provides a balanced, focused long-term business and portfolio interest over near-term project and product interest.

- *Common infrastructure and avoidance of duplication of effort:* Sometimes the driver is simple software development economics, whereby it makes more sense to build a component only once and then have it be reused by many teams. Even if in agile "time to market trumps potential for reuse," some common, reusable components can provide substantial long-term user (usability, fitness for use) and business (economic) benefits.

- *Driving innovation:* Although agile development can certainly foster innovation by quickly driving solutions to meet real, rather than perceived, user needs, it can sometimes inhibit it, too. This can occur when the "tyranny of the urgent"—rapid iteration cycles and continuous commitment to value delivery—drives teams to avoid risky or innovative experiments. When everyone is committed and accountable to a near-term deliverable, who is scouting the next curve in the road?

- *Cost:* And finally, sometimes revising systems architecture can simply help lower the costs of the products and services the business provides. Examples include following security standards to lower data purchasing costs, supply chain investments, and so on. And operating cost affects business economics.

Role of the System Architect in the Agile Enterprise

Historically, within the larger enterprise, defining a system-level architecture was a primary function of some number of *system architects.* But here we have three small problems.

- The most common agile methods don't define (or even imply support for) such a role. This made some sense in the smaller context, because agile focuses on harnessing the power of the collective team, rather than any one individual. Clearly you can't have an omniscient system architect dictate technical direction to empowered agile teams.[2]

---

2. "Things are usually easier said than done, and software architects are notoriously good at coming up with things to say." —Timothy High

- Although these system architects have decades of experience, their expertise has likely grown outside of the agile process. They may not even be comfortable with agile in general because it seems less technically well-planned and more ad hoc. And they become even more uncomfortable when they no longer see a role for themselves!
- System architects may also be concerned about the potential architectural entropy of all the newly empowered and energized agile teams. They may also have strong opinions about the software development practices teams employ.

First: Relegitimize the Role

Clearly, if we fail to bring these key stakeholders on board to the agile paradigm, they could limit or kill the entire initiative. And most importantly, when building enterprise-class systems, we need them, their experience, and their expertise. Therefore, it is in the enterprise's best interest to include system architects in the agile enterprise process, where their input is highly valued. In any case, *we must relegitimize the role and avoid a battle between agile teams and system architects, because all will be losers in that fight.*

What System Architects Do

With that behind us, when you ask system architects what they do, they will typically respond with a number of common answers.

- Build enterprise architectural "blueprints" to help the team understand the broader enterprise picture.
- Fight unnecessary duplication at the system level.
- Define boundary conditions and constraints (including nonfunctional requirements) for the system. Help teams understand and work within those constraints.
- Define architectural governance rules and help teams apply them.
- Drive in-house use of industry standards and practices. Influence the industry and participate in development of emerging standards.
- Help teams find and implement common interfaces to increase system compatibility, flexibility, and separation of concerns.
- Define common vocabulary and terminology across multiple products, systems, and organizations. Help the team's interpretation and understanding.
- Collaborate with all stakeholders from business to technical. Serve as an interface (and translator) between the business owners and the development teams.

Given that these all appear to be sensible, high-value functions in the enterprise, let's see whether we can understand how that works in the context of agility.

EIGHT PRINCIPLES OF AGILE ARCHITECTURE[3]

As we extend and apply lean and agile requirements practices in the larger enterprise and incorporate systems architects in the process, we must constantly remind ourselves of our first principles, as driven primarily by the principles of the Agile Manifesto and product development flow.

However, although the spirit of these principles guides us, they are silent on the topics of enterprise-class systems and architecture in general. To help us reach the next level, we propose eight governing principles for the development and maintenance of intentional, enterprise-class architectures in the lean and agile enterprise.

These principles are as follows.

- *Principle #1:* The teams that code the system also design the system.
- *Principle #2:* Build the simplest architecture that can possibly work.
- *Principle #3:* When in doubt, code it or model it out.
- *Principle #4:* They build it, they test it.
- *Principle #5:* The bigger the system, the longer the runway.
- *Principle #6:* System architecture is a role collaboration.
- *Principle #7:* There is no monopoly on innovation.
- *Principle #8:* Implement architectural flow.

We'll describe each of these principles in the sections that follow.

Principle #1: The Teams That Code the System Design the System

This first principle is driven by the manifesto itself (*the best architectures, requirements, and designs emerge from self-organizing teams*), as well as the fact that agile teams are both empowered to deliver software *and* are accountable for the results.

For teams to be accountable, they must be allowed to make the decisions required to support that accountability. If not, they will be held accountable for decisions made by others, and that is an ineffective and demotivating model for team performance. Although this may now seem axiomatic, in our pre-agile world that was often the case, as Table 20–1 shows.

---

3. Thanks to Mauricio Zamora and Ryan Martens for contributing to an earlier white paper on this topic.

Table 20–1 Architecture Responsibility and Accountability in the Pre- and Agile World

	Pre-agile Practices	Agile Practices
Architect's Responsibility	Analyze and define requirements. Design the system. Interface to key business stakeholders and customers. Bid the work for teams. Only ones who understand how the whole system works.	Analyze architectural epics. Collaborate with business stakeholders and development teams. Get implementation feedback and development estimates from teams. Prevent the team from being "wagged" by changing business priorities. Filter potential changes through an analysis funnel (Chapter 21). Maintain system models and model future state based on new epics.
Team Responsibility	Inherits the plan and work estimates. Inherits the architecture. Left "holding the bag" and executes on a "best-efforts" basis.	Interface to business and customers via product owner role. Tech leads participate in virtual, extended system architecture team. Responsible for subsystem design. Estimates work for their area of concern. Commits on behalf of *themselves*. Accountable for the results.

Because they are closest to the implementation, local design and architectural decisions are most optimally made by the coders, tech leads, and team-based architects. Moving the primary responsibilities for design and architecture to the teams is a triple-win for the enterprise.

- A more optimum decision is likely to be made.
- Once a decision is made, the team will likely work very hard to make its decision work. If it doesn't work as planned, they will fix it.
- Regardless, the team is empowered, responsible, and accountable for its decisions.

Principle #2: Build the Simplest Architecture That Can Possibly Work

Agile is known for its focus on simplicity: Agile Manifesto principle #10 (*Simplicity—the art of maximizing the amount of work not done—is essential*). It's further characterized in the culture and lore:

What is the simplest thing that can possibly work?

—Attributed to Ward Cunningham

If simplicity is good, we'll leave the system with the simplest design that supports its current functionality.

—Kent Beck

YAGNI, You Ain't Gonna Need It.

—An XP mantra

Simplicity remains an essential attribute as complexity increases. For example, Amazon used agile and organically grew a system to handle 55 million customer accounts. Werner Vogels, Amazon's CTO, commented this:[4]

> The only way to manage a large distributed system is to keep things as simple as possible. Keep things simple by making sure there are no hidden requirements and hidden dependencies in the design. Cut technology to the minimum you need to solve the problem you have.

Simplicity wins. Even at scale.

Principle #3: When in Doubt, Code or Model It Out

Agile, with its highly iterative experience and code-based emphasis, allows developers to rely on their coding skills to move quickly through the decision-making process via fast feedback. This is helpful when selecting a design alternative or a high-impact infrastructure implementation choice. Even then, we may still occasionally find ourselves mired in technical debate, either within the team or between the team and the architects.

This third principle reminds us that when we have to make a tough choice, we can usually turn to a rapid evaluation in code. One- or two-week iterations give us fast feedback, and the demos at the end of the iteration provide objective evidence of results. The inherent visibility of the process through stories and demos allows all impacted stakeholders to see the reasoning and experimental results as they develop.

In addition, principle #2 reminds us that if a design alternative can't be coded and evaluated within a few iterations, it probably isn't the simplest choice. In practice, many decisions are usually fairly obvious after a few short technical spikes.

Here's another lesson learned from the Amazon Architecture:

> Use measurement and objective debate to separate the good from the bad...expose real customers to a choice and see which one works best...get

---

4. *http://highscalability.com/amazon-architecture*

rid of the influence of the HiPPos, the (Highest Paid People) in the room. If you have a question about what you should do, code it up, let people use it, and see which alternative gives you the results you want.

If It's Too Big to Code, Model It

But these are big, complex systems, and we are faced with big, complex problems. If the epic is really large and crosscutting, a few weeks in a coding exercise may be inadequate because the impact of the epic may touch many different systems in different ways. Fortunately, although we are agile, modeling is another tool in our toolkit, and agile (and nonagile) architects who use models to understand and reflect system behavior visually are valuable assets to the teams.

One set of consistent advice for modeling complex systems in iterative development comes from the Rational Unified Process and its companion modeling language, the Unified Modeling Language (UML). The views of architecture within the UML were derived in part from some of Kruchten's work on the "4+1 views of architecture" [2005].[5] Kruchten comments on the evolution of the importance of architecture for systems of scale:

> [Initially] many software systems weren't complex, the architecture could remain an implicit understanding among software developers. However, as systems evolve and grow to accommodate new requirements, things break in a strange fashion, and the systems do not scale up.... Moreover, designers lack the intellectual tools to reason about parts of the system. Not having an architecture, or using a poor architecture, is a major technical risk for software projects.

Architecture in UML is typically represented in a set of views, each view describing the system from the perspective of various stakeholders. There are two mandatory views.

- *Use-case (requirements) view:* The use-case view of the system illustrates the use cases and scenarios that encompass architecturally significant behavior, classes, or technical risks. More generally, this is the requirements "view" that is really not a view so much as it as an understanding of the imposed requirements. If the teams do apply use cases (Chapter 19), then it can be a graphical view, which summarizes the *use-case model.* Otherwise, in agile, this "view" is simply a pointer to the backlog.

---

5. Philippe Kruchten also gave me the best definition of software architecture I have seen: "Architecture is what you have left when you take away everything you don't need to explain how the system works."

■ *Logical view:* At the enterprise level, this view defines the relationship of the main entities in the system and their relationships. At the subsystem level, it illustrates packages and classes that encompass architecturally significant entities.

In addition, there are four additional, optional views that can be used depending on the importance of these aspects to the type of system being deployed.

■ *Process view:* This view is recommended when the system has more than one thread of control and the threads interact with one another. This view illustrates the process decomposition of the system, from mapping classes and subsystems to processes and threads.

■ *Deployment view:* This view is recommended when the run-time system is distributed across more than one node and when the distribution has architectural implications. The deployment view illustrates the distribution of processing across a set of nodes in the system, including the physical distribution of processes and threads.

■ *Implementation view:* This view is recommended when the implementation (source code, binaries, libraries, and so on) is not strictly driven from the design, that is, where there is a different distribution of responsibilities between corresponding packages in the design and implementation models. The implementation view is useful for assigning implementation work to individuals and teams. A proper implementation structure will support effective continuous integration, which is mandatory in agile.

■ *Data view:* This view is recommended when persistent data is a key aspect of the system, such as a system that contains schema, data definition, algorithms, and so on. At the enterprise level, this view illustrates the data relationships among the primary entities in the system.

The Model Documents the As-Built and Future State

Generally, the software teams themselves get to decide what documents to produce, so long as they follow any required standards or governance requirements. And of course, agile teams usually invest primarily in documents that provide only direct customer value. Modeling is informal, often sketched on whiteboards or on diagrams posted in the team's working area. The design is in the code.

However, at the enterprise level, modeling often takes on a more formal structure, because "the model is to the architects what the code is to the developer," that is, the way they think and reason about the system. So, system architects typically produce and maintain these model documents more formally and use them to communicate the as-built and future states to the teams, based on impending architectural epics.

Principle #4: They Build It, They Test It

Testing system architecture involves testing the system's ability to meet its larger-scale functional, operational, performance, and reliability requirements. To do this, teams must typically build a testing infrastructure that enables ongoing system-level testing. After all, if it can't be tested, it is assumed not to work.

Even when applying the simplicity principle, we are building systems that are ever more complex in nature. Who can possibly deal with testing systems that are so complex? Simply,

> It is the responsibility of the development teams themselves to develop, test, and maintain a system-testing framework that continually assesses the system's ability to meet its functional and nonfunctional requirements.

If the architecture is evolving, the testing framework must evolve with it. This responsibility cannot be given to any other testing resource or outsourced function. If they design and build it, they have to test it too. Anything else would be irresponsible.

Principle #5: The Bigger the System, the Longer the Runway

Value delivery focuses on delivering the features that customers need. The ability to deliver planned functionality predictably in a near-term (60 to 120 days) release is a hallmark of mature agile teams. That ability, in turn, allows agile enterprises to communicate near-term expectations to customers, whose businesses depend on this information.

Even experienced agile teams occasionally have trouble completing planned work. In general, that can be acceptable, because a team that reliably completes 100 percent of the commitment for each timebox may not be stretching enough to meet the demands of the marketplace. Furthermore, so long as the team is able to self-correct effectively, it also encourages a level of acceptable risk taking.

However, occasionally we see an iteration, or even a release, that is badly missed. In retrospectives, we usually find that some architectural work was at play, causing the team to underestimate the time it would take for a significant redesign or to lay in a new foundation. This leads us to the conclusion that an agile team's ability to meet value delivery commitments *is far more reliable when the foundation for the new features is already in place.*

Although we can't predict the future, we do stress the need for the continuous buildout of *architectural runway*—the system infrastructure that must be in place to deliver features on the nearer-term product Roadmap. Building this architectural runway is our primary mechanism for decreasing the risk of missed commitments.

Small Systems Don't Need Much Runway

For smaller teams, infrastructure sufficient to support a single iteration or release cycle may be all the runway that's needed. If it breaks, they'll fix it. Simply, it may be more efficient for those teams to be wrong initially and then quickly refactor the application than it is to invest more time up front trying to discover the undiscoverable.

Bigger Systems Need More

For larger teams of teams building larger systems, they will need substantially more runway so that they can "land" (successfully implement) larger features and epics in the course of the next PSI or so. Building this runway takes time, often far longer than a single short release cycle. Without such runway, the team won't be able to reliably "land" each release on schedule. This requires some additional foresight and investment and more careful planning. We'll discuss how to do that later in this chapter.

Principle #6: System Architecture Is a Role Collaboration

As we have described, system architects play an important role in the development of these large systems. After all, we are building systems of enormous complexity (even when we keep them as simple as possible), so it makes good economic and technical sense to leverage the skills of those who have the experience to match the challenges the teams face.

But how do we incorporate them into our team-centric agile model? As a metaphor, in object-oriented systems development, we learned to *design systems of collaborating objects, structured around well-defined interfaces, which work together to create an output that is greater than the sum of its parts.* We can apply this same approach to developing a system architecture, as we illustrate in Figure 20–2.

In a manner similar to how product managers and product owners collaborate to define the user value features and stories, system architects work with team-based tech leads and architects to define the design spikes they will use to collaboratively develop an agreed-to system architecture.

And *when in doubt, they code or model it out* (principle #3), using a series of technical spikes and architectural models to drive out risks.

In addition, leveraging the thoughts and strengths of development team members in this collaboration carries two strong messages for the teams: "the technical input of all development team members is respected" and "you do not have to be an architect to make a big contribution to design."

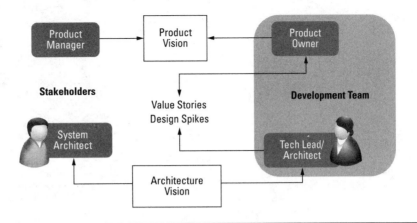

Figure 20–2   System architecture results from a role collaboration.

Principle #7: There Is No Monopoly on Innovation

We have seen how agile practices provide a disciplined, production-like ability to reliably meet commitments and rapidly evolve a system to meet customer requirements. But we've also described the "tyranny of the urgent," which may keep us overly focused on near-term deliverables. How do we stretch, identify, and take and manage risks, especially those that are longer term and extend beyond current project scope and team boundaries? Where does innovation come from in such a model?

Some of the innovation comes from empowering system architects as part of our advanced guard—exploring new technologies, patterns, and techniques that will help us innovate while we are building the existing solution.

But ours is a team-centric model, so we don't rely on architects as the sole source of such innovation. In fact, the team-centric model can foster innovation at an even greater pace than that generally seen in traditional software organizations. That's because innovators innovate at all stages of their career, and the team-centric model enables these people to flourish and contribute beyond what their level of experience may imply.

One way to foster innovation at the team level is by judicious backlog management that includes spikes for redesign and exploration of new ideas. This can work quite well, but given the tyranny of the urgent, even more purposeful and explicit models have been developed. For example, some teams have evolved an advanced development cadence, as illustrated in Figure 20–3.

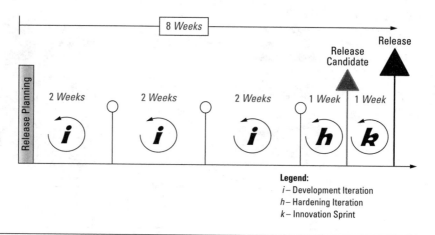

Figure 20–3   A cadence with one innovation "hackathon" per release

This figure illustrates a standard release cycle.

- "*i*" is a standard development iteration, providing new functionality for an upcoming release.
- "*h*" is a one-week *hardening* iteration to eliminate any remaining technical debt and assure quality meets the release-to-manufacturing criteria.
- "*k*" is an "innovation sprint." (Note: the "k" symbol comes from the informal, somewhat pejorative, and perhaps ill-advised use of the word *hackathon* for this purpose.[6])

The innovation sprint (hackathon) is the interesting part, because it is specifically designed to foster innovation at the team level. The rules of this special iteration are simple: Any team member can explore any technology in any way they want, so long as there is a correlation to the company's mission.

This gives the team some regular time to reflect, think, and experiment outside the everyday rigor and pressures of the iteration and release cycle. They are free to take risks, explore new technologies, and experiment in ways that are not conducive to the normal iteration value delivery cadence. Experience has shown that,

---

6. As we described earlier, management has a key role in driving lean and agile behavior at scale; we assuredly need their support for this key innovation mechanism. So, be careful what word you pick!

over time, many new product innovations will arise from this process.[7] And the teams love it too.

With a model like this, innovation is expected and programmatic, and there can be no ambiguity to the point of principle #7: *There is no monopoly on innovation.*

Principle #8: Implement Architectural Flow

The final principle on our list reminds us that even with agile principles at work, we must continually improve our process to achieve enterprise-level product development flow and thereby avoid the delays and overhead introduced by starting and stopping projects every time there is a new initiative. This means that we'll need to provide visibility and transparency, provide work-in-process limits, actively manage queue lengths, and do the other work necessary to build and control a continuous stream of architectural updates—just like we do with features and stories. Because the Agile Release Train is our synchronized and cadence-based implementation flow mechanism, the architects will need to interact with that mechanism in order to continuously extend the architectural runway.

This is such an important topic that is the subject of the next chapter, Rearchitecting with Flow.

IMPLEMENTING ARCHITECTURAL EPICS

Historically, implementing wholesale architectural changes to a large system was conceptually simple: Make a new branch, start the new development, and merge it to the baseline down the road somewhere. However, it was extremely difficult in practice: Make code changes in both branches, merge later, discover nasty errors in assumptions, rework, delay, continue maintaining two branches longer than anticipated, disappoint stakeholders.... It was an easy mental model but a really hard physical one.

In agile development, we don't do it that way. Instead, we commit to a continuous refactoring of the existing system, and we branch rarely, if at all, and even then only for very short periods. This creates a more complex conceptual model, and not a trivial physical one, but it dramatically reduces the risk of new development by providing fast feedback and leaving us with *a system that always runs.*

---

7. I once witnessed a product sales demo where the salesperson highlighted innovation after innovation that came from their use of the hackathon cadence.

Achieving this in the face of significant architectural changes is an art form—the art of the truly lean and agile software enterprise. In describing how to do this, we'll break the large-scale refactoring problem into three separate cases.

- *Case A:* The epic is big,[8] but there is an incremental approach to implementation. *The system always runs.*
- *Case B:* The epic is big, but it can't be implemented entirely incrementally. *The system will need to take an occasional break.*
- *Case C:* The epic is really big, and it cannot be implemented incrementally. *The system runs when needed; do no harm.*

Case A: Big, but Incremental; the System Always Runs

Building incrementally reduces risk, controls WIP, and avoids big-bang system integrations. Therefore, this is the best case by far for an agile program. The epic is split into architectural features at release planning boundaries (enablers, subepics, smaller chunks of stuff), and the full epic is realized over whatever course of time is necessary or feasible, as Figure 20–4 shows.

With this approach, the system always runs. Risk is mitigated, and each PSI is *really* potentially shippable. Moreover, each iteration has conceptual integrity as well, providing fast feedback and potential for deployment to alpha or beta customers. Value delivery (features) continues while the rearchitecting is done. This is the lowest-risk and lowest-cost approach and the most favorable model.

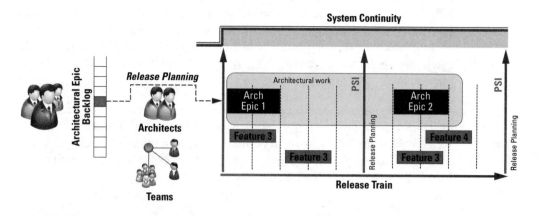

Figure 20–4   Case A: The system always runs.

---

8. Epics are big by definition. Smaller architectural changes can be done by the teams in the course of normal business, so long as they are prioritized in the backlog accordingly.

Case B: Big, but Not Entirely Incremental; the System Takes an Occasional Break

But what if you can't do it incrementally? First, if you find yourself in this case, *stop and rethink the problem*. In most of the cases, there is a way to retrench, redefine the epic if necessary, and return to case A, the optimum path. Typically, this requires some out-of-box thinking and perhaps a few seemingly unnatural software acts—extra stubs, temporary frameworks, and so on—but it is worth it because of the lower risk and faster feedback.

However, in other cases, I've been convinced by the teams, and by the apparent economics, that they can break the system down, do the refactoring work, and put it all back together before the next PSI boundary. If so, it's potentially more efficient than incremental refactoring. They don't have to do the extra work required to break it down further or any other unnatural acts—all hands on deck, one mission, one code line, no investment in stubs, and so on. In this case, the model looks like Figure 20–5.

Risk is increased during this time because there is no working system for a while. Plus, there may or may not be much additional value delivery in the PSI; given the risks the team has taken, it's better to lower expectations for value delivery during one PSI and be sure to complete it than it is to pass a PSI boundary with a nonfunctioning system.

Although this is not the preferred approach, we have seen it work in practice (example: wholesale replacement of an underlying database within a PSI), and the risk-versus-efficiency outcome was quite favorable.

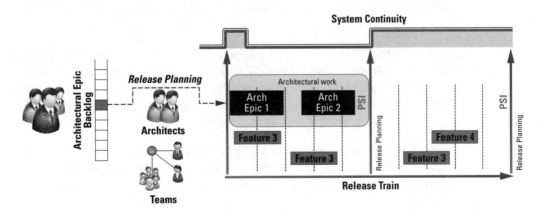

Figure 20–5   Case B: The system takes a break.

Of course, we've seen it fail too, causing missed PSIs. However, even that can still be acceptable, so long as it doesn't affect the external release commitments. Again, we must return to the economic basis for the decision. In this case, it's the trade-off between the potential cost of delay of a missed PSI versus a) the cost of longer and slower, incremental refactors, b) the risk of making a big system branch, or c) the additional investment required to use a set-based (multiple options) approach.

Case C: Really Big and Not Incremental; the System Runs When Needed; Do No Harm

There is a third and most challenging case, which occurs on occasion in the larger system context. In this case, the legacy system has reached some boundary where redesigning it incrementally, or even within a PSI, is impractical. A longer-term architectural initiative is required, and the product still has to be shippable in the meantime. This is the most complicated case and requires the most care and planning.

In this case, the teams can deploy a combination of case A and case B approaches, along with a third practice.

The team builds architectural epics in situ (in the main branch). But since a release cannot be missed and since some chunks of work cannot be completed in PSI boundaries, the new epics are built in and then isolated so as to *do no harm* to the running system. In other words, the architecture is redesigned and implemented in place, even though it is incomplete and not yet usable. It evolves slowly to the new technology paradigm.

At release time, much of the work may be hidden from the user via stubs and special scaffolding, until such time as all the pieces have come together and the new architecture can be safely exposed. This plan is represented in Figure 20–6.

This may appear to be a somewhat complex approach, one that requires teams to build and validate the extra scaffolding necessary to hide internal changes. That is true. However, it addresses a complex problem and helps manage the risk of really large rearchitecting projects. As such, it is still highly preferable to the *big branch – big bang – big crash*, waterfall approach of the past.

Feedback to the teams is still provided in fast iteration cycles; the system is always available at PSI dates; and the longer-term, large-scale refactoring objective is still accomplished, incrementally, as it should be, just so long as they *do no harm*.

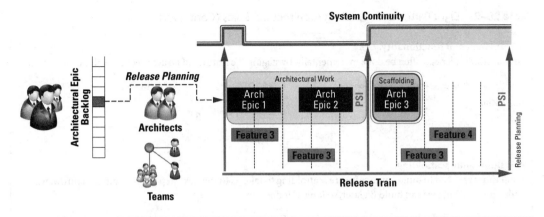

Figure 20–6 The system runs when needed: Do no harm.

Splitting Architecture Epics

No matter the approach, it is likely that it will be necessary to split architecture epics into smaller pieces, just as it is necessary to split user stories and features to fit in iterations and PSIs. Indeed, many of the patterns we applied for splitting user stories in Chapter 6 are equally applicable here. Plus, because of their technical nature, there are additional patterns for splitting architectural epics that we can leverage. Table 20–2 describes eight ways to split architectural epics into iteration, or PSI-sized, chunks.

Table 20–2 Eight Patterns for Splitting Architectural Epics

---

1. Partition by subsystem or product.

One opportunity, which is not so common when splitting user value stories, is the ability to split the epic into subepics or features that can be implemented one component of the system at a time.

All applications must run in native 64-bit mode.	…do one application each PSI.
	…do client side to support labeling claims to consumer first, defer server side for performance until later.

---

2. System qualities incrementally.

Technology epics are often used to address systemic performance, reliability, or security challenges, or sometimes just to make sure the system can handle the load brought about by market success. These can often be broken down in increments.

Support 10,000 homes per server deployment.	5,000 in PSI 1.
	10,000 in PSI 2.

Continues

Table 20–2   Eight Patterns for Splitting Architectural Epics (Continued)

3. Incremental functionality. Architectural epics can often be done incrementally, by staging the features of an architectural solution over time.	
Provide over-the-air software update for the thermostat.	*Enable OTA capability on device bootloader.* *Enable OTA capability on the radio.* *Integrate with server side.*
4. Build some scaffolding. Sometimes we need to build some software scaffolding to take us to the next step up. It might be a throwaway code, or something we can build on later, so long as it does no harm.	
Build an API to support a third-party integration.	*Build some resets into the system, and mock up the data, so our partners can test integrations.*
5. Major/minor effort. Sometimes an epic can be split into several parts where most of the effort will go toward implementing the first one.	
Major: Productize the APIs.	*First (major) epic: separate identified APIs from core service, use them internally.* *Then...* *(minor epics) Refactor to support standards and third-party use.*
6. Complex/simple. When the team is discussing an epic and complexity is constantly increasing, stop and ask, "Is this the simplest architecture we can envision?" Capture that simple version as its own epic, and worry about all the variations and complexities later.	
Complex: Productize the APIs.	*Simple: Build an adapter to expose only the meter API.*
7. Variations in data. As with user stories, data variations and data sources are another source of scope and complexity that can often be split by data type.	
Implement consumer home energy management devices through the new backhaul grid infrastructure.	*Implement on meter and backhaul vendor A protocol.* *Implement on meter and backhaul vendor B protocol.*
8. Break out a spike. Some architectural epics require a spike, or a series of spikes, to establish feasibility, estimate impact, and effort, or perhaps even determine how to split the epic!	
Support the new Zigbee radio chip.	*Get chips in house and run interoperability analysis.* *Test SE compliance.* *Validate feasibility and initial effort estimate.*

Each of these patterns is likely to find use in splitting architecture into incremental pieces. In point of fact, technology epics are often so large that they *typically require a significant combination of these patterns* to achieve our objective. That's fine. These are big systems. Rearchitecting them incrementally is not a trivial problem, so we'll need all the tools we can find at our disposal.

SUMMARY

In this chapter, we described how system architecture helps teams of teams build reliable, extensible, enterprise-class systems in an agile manner. To implement this practice, we empowered the role of the system architect as an integral part of "what makes an agile team of teams a team." To guide the process further, we've provided a set of guiding principles, Eight Principles of Agile Architecture, intended to be quintessentially agile and lean and yet provide guidance in an area where most agile practices have remained largely silent.

And since architectural epics are, by definition, *big*, we provided a set of patterns that teams can use to break down these large projects into manageable, incremental, PSI-sized pieces.

In the next chapter, we'll describe how to continuously prioritize and implement these pieces, by rearchitecting with flow.

Chapter 21

REARCHITECTING WITH FLOW

If you accept this fact—that the choices you make today will most certainly be wrong in the future—then it relieves you of the burden of trying to future-proof your architectures.

—Richard Monson-Haefel, author of
97 Things Every Software Architect Should Know

In the previous chapter, we introduced the role of system architects, as well as system architecture, in helping teams evolve reliable, robust, and scalable enterprise-class systems in an agile manner. We described a set of principles that enterprises can use to govern this activity, while keeping the teams agile and the enterprise lean. We also described the business need for some amount of architectural runway, which is system infrastructure that exists to host features on the near-term product map. Even then, however, it's economic folly to attempt to *future-proof* our solution, so occasionally, we run out of runway entirely, or our system becomes so unsuitable for the new market demands that we find ourselves needing to *rearchitect* the system.

Whether extending runway or rearchitecting the system, the eighth principle of agile architecture—*Implement architectural flow*—reminds us of the constant need to keep all of our practices lean and flowing. In doing so, we can achieve the maximum velocity of value delivery and avoid the negative economic impacts of long queues, project fits and starts, and thrashing across too many initiatives.

In this chapter, we'll describe a system that supports architectural flow and helps us match our wishes (new architectural initiatives) to our constraints (capacity of the development teams).

Before we do so, however, it's worth repeating here that agile teams and agile programs are fully empowered to handle those significant architectural refactors and redesigns that are under their local control.[1] We don't need this additional layer of architectural drivers and governance (or even this chapter) for that.

Therefore, the focus of this chapter is on large, crosscutting architectural epics (as we defined in the previous chapter) that are likely to affect some combination of multiple teams, multiple products, multiple components, multiple services, and, occasionally, even multiple product lines and business units. They imply a significant investment, and they will impact a significant number of teams. They are a pretty big deal.

ARCHITECTURAL EPIC KANBAN SYSTEM[2]

To rearchitect such systems and manage architectural epics that rise to this global impact level, we need a process for reasoning about scope and return on investment, for performing analysis and prioritization, and for analyzing capacity and assessing impact. We also need to keep all that activity visible to the stakeholders so they will know what we are working on, why, and when to expect results. We also need a systematic way to implement these large initiatives incrementally, in support of our basic agile and lean framework. To accomplish all this, we'll describe an *architectural epic kanban system*.

Objectives of the Kanban System

A lean, flow-based model for moving from architecture to implementation must accomplish four objectives.

- *Make architectural work in process (AWIP) visible:* Lean thinking drives us to make sure that *all work is visible.* As Reinertsen [2009] points out, invisible development work in process is WIP nonetheless.[3] Worse, since it can't be seen, it has "no natural predators," and therefore there is a natural tendency to overload those involved in such work. (Since we can't see it or quantify it and it seems like important stuff to do, why not do some more of it?)

  Our kanban system must make AWIP visible so that it can be owned and managed responsibly. Architectural backlogs, queues, and analysis work in

---

1. Agile Manifesto principle #11—*The best architectures, requirements, and designs emerge from self-organizing teams.*
2. Special thanks to the system architects and enterprise agilists at F-Secure Corporation for their substantial contributions to this chapter.
3. Principle of Product Development Flow Q1—*The principle of invisible inventory: Product development inventory is physically and financially invisible.*

process must all be visible, creating a shared understanding of current and future workload.

- *Establish AWIP limits to control queue sizes and help assure product development flow:* Limiting WIP helps us avoid the economic damage of large queue sizes, large delays, and the thrashing costs and inefficiencies of overloaded resources.

  First, we'll limit local AWIP to only that work that the architecture teams can actually do, thereby assuring that the architects are not thrashing across too broad a workload—starting many projects but finishing far fewer. That will increase the efficiency, productivity, and quality outputs of the architecture team.

  Second, in doing so, we will also be consciously limiting *global WIP.* This includes upstream, *portfolio WIP* (projects that drive new architectures), and downstream, *development WIP* (projects that build new architecture). In this manner, we'll match input objectives to implementation constraints, all across the enterprise.

- *Drive an effective collaboration with the development teams:* The tension between architecture and development is obvious. Eventually, architectural epics are going to be implemented by the development teams. It won't be helpful to surprise them with new stuff ("If we would only have known that sooner, we wouldn't have spent all this time...") or hold them accountable for implementing plans that they don't feel are actually workable. F-Secure's James Cooper notes the following:

  > Listen to developers—if they say there is a problem with the design, there probably is.

  If our model drives effective communication between these teams, things will naturally flow more smoothly.

- *Provide a quantitative basis for economic decision making:* Then we'll know that we are doing the right things in the right order.

OVERVIEW OF THE ARCHITECTURAL EPIC KANBAN SYSTEM

We'll need to implement a system that accomplishes these objectives with as much transparency and as little overhead as possible. Visually, such a system might appear as in Figure 21–1.

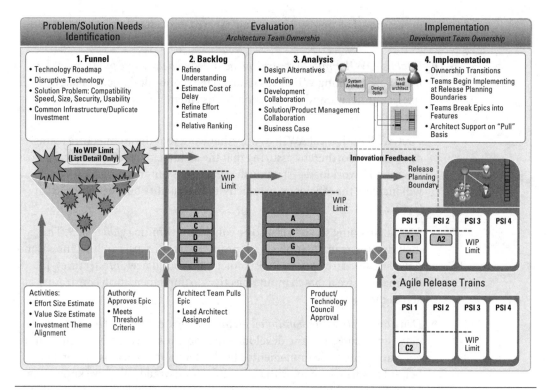

Figure 21–1 Graphic overview of the architectural epic kanban system

Queue Descriptions

The kanban system we'll describe processes epics through a series of four queues, each characterized by different activities on the part of the architecture and development teams, along with correspondingly increasing levels of investment. The queues are as follows.

1. The Funnel: Problem/Solution Needs Identification

The funnel queue is the "capture" queue. In this queue, all new "big ideas" are welcome. They can come from any source. They need no business case or estimates. Tooling is trivial—a document, spreadsheet, or simple list on the wall will suffice.

Since the investment of effort of items in this queue is minor, this queue is not WIP limited; all ideas are captured for consideration. Funnel epics are discussed on a periodic cadence established by the architecture team. Epics that meet the decision criteria are promoted to the backlog queue.

2. Backlog

Epics that reach the backlog queue warrant further investment of time. In this queue, epics are roughly sized, and some estimate of value is established. Time investment is controlled to discussion level and perhaps some very preliminary investigation. The epic may be elaborated to a paragraph or two.

Since the investment is increasing, this queue is WIP-limited to limit the number of active items in process. Backlog epics are discussed periodically. Epics are assigned a *cost of delay* (CoD). Epics that rise to the top of the queue are pulled into analysis as soon as space is available.

3. Analysis

Epics that make it to this queue deserve a more rigorous analysis and require further investment. An architect is typically assigned as the epic owner. An active collaboration with development is initiated. Design alternatives are explored. Options for internal development and/or outsourcing are considered. A lightweight business case, with a *go* or *no-go* recommendation, is developed.

Items in this queue use scarce resources, so it is WIP-limited based on the capacity of the architecture and development teams and the desired throughput rates for items in this queue. Promotion from analysis to implementation is an important economic decision for the enterprise that can be made only by the appropriate authority, based on the developed business case. Epics that meet the *go* criteria are promoted to implementation.

4. Implementation

In this queue, the primary responsibility for the epic is passed to the development teams. Architect resources remain available on a "pull" basis: The responsibility for implementation rests with the development teams, but the architect assists the teams and shares responsibility until the team has developed a sufficient understanding of the work required.

This queue is WIP-limited, in this case primarily by the capacity of the development teams and the amount of investment in architecture that is required.

Architecture Epic State Descriptions

Although the overview description provides a broad sense of how the system works, it does leave some questions. To better understand the system, we describe the various states that an epic goes through in Figure 21–2.

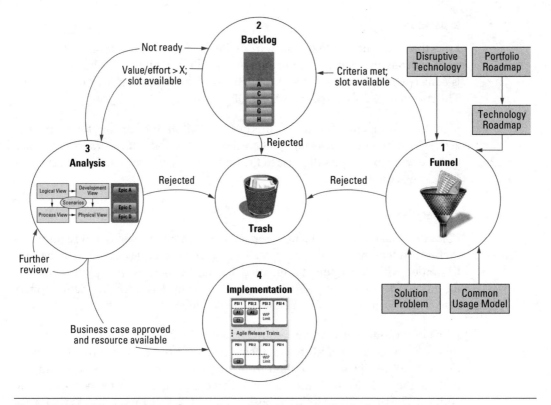

Figure 21–2   State transition diagram for architectural epics in the kanban system

The state diagram illustrates all the paths for an epic and the decision gates that drive the epics down these paths. Figure 21–3 summarizes the details of the activities for items in each queue, the decision criteria, and the decision authority.

Given this state model for the epics, we'll now describe each queue in additional detail.

1. The Funnel: Problem/Solution Needs Identification

The "funnel" is the simplest queue. In this queue, all ideas are welcome; anyone can contribute. As with all future queues, when an item enters this queue, it is date stamped so the teams will be able to tell how long it has been in the queue.

State	Activities to Transition	Transition Criteria	Next	Authority
Funnel	• Estimate Value • Estimate Effort • Test Against Investment Themes	1. Rank > Threshold 2. WHEN Slot Available 3. Fails Criteria	→ Backlog → Trash	Architectural Authority
Backlog	• Assign Cost of Delay • Effort Estimate Refined • Establish Relative Rank	Ranked Relative to Other Items Highest Ranked Item Pulled When Age of Item > Limit	→ Analysis → Escalate or Trash	Pull System Architectural Authority
Analysis	• Workshops, Modeling, Design Alternatives • Development Collaboration and Cost Estimates • Develop Design Spikes • Product/Solution Management Review • Implementation Options • Market Validation of Value • Business Case	Business Case with GO/NO GO Recommendation GO > Implementation NO GO 1 > More Elaboration Needed No GO 2 > Reject	→ Implementation → Stay in Queue → Trash	Product/ Technology Council

Figure 21–3   Architectural epic kanban activities and decisions

Sources of New Architectural Epics

Business drivers for new architectural epics come from a variety of sources both within and outside the enterprise. These include factors such as the following.

- *Technology Roadmap:* Driven by the portfolio Vision and Roadmap (Chapter 23), the system architects typically manage a technology roadmap that they use to monitor and implement key new technologies over time. Examples include converting back-office systems to service-oriented architectures, "webifying" current customer-facing applications, and so on.
- *Disruptive technology:* Some disruptive technologies may appear fairly suddenly and make their way to the roadmap in an expedited fashion. Examples include 64-bit chipsets, Single Sign On standards, Bluetooth, rapidly evolving wireless standards, and so on.
- *Common usage model and avoidance of duplicate investment:* In the larger enterprise, it is likely that a significant number of teams are developing code to solve the same problem for customers. This can be as simple as installation utilities, licensing mechanisms, access to common data sets, and so on.

If left to their own initiative, the teams will solve these problems in a way that suits the local team and their customers. However, that same customer is likely to be a user of a different product or service from the same company that will have implemented the same utility but in a different way. In this case, we have two significant economic problems:

- The enterprise is duplicating investment in common technologies and common code. Multiple teams are writing the same lines of code but in a different way. That doesn't always make economic sense.
- Worse, while simply trying to do the same function, customers are experiencing a wide range of user experiences. This causes confusion, higher training costs, lack of seamlessness for the user, and ultimately lower perception of quality and loss of customer confidence in the solution provider.

In these cases, architectural epics are used to drive common initiatives that decrease investment costs and improve product quality.

- *Problem with the existing solution:* Some architectural epics are driven by known problems with an existing solution. Examples include increasing performance and reliability, enhancing scalability to support market success, or even building workarounds for a patent challenge.

Activities: Ranking the Epic

The primary activity of the architect teams for epics in this queue is a periodic review and analysis of the item, establishing three relevant parameters.

- A preliminary estimate of the *size* (the relative "bigness") of the epic. The effort estimate is an aggregation of a number of factors that may include the following:
    - Estimate of the cost and time to implement
    - Number of teams, programs, products potentially affected
    - Technical risk
    - Complexity
- A preliminary estimate of the potential value of the epic, whether measured in customer retention, revenue, or market share value.
- A quick test to match the epic with the enterprise's current investment themes.

Once the teams have agreed on a set of metrics that work in their context, it's a fairly easy matter to create a calculation spreadsheet to rank a funnel epic relative to its peers. Table 21–1 provides one such example.

Table 21–1 Ranking Criteria for Epics in the Funnel State

Ranking Item	Scale
Effort size	1, 2, 3, 5, 8, 13, 20, 40†
Potential value	1, 2, 3, 5, 8, 13, 20, 40
Alignment to investment theme	0, .25, .5, .75, 1
Epic weight	= (Potential value/effort) * alignment

† We've used the modified Fibonacci series to indicate that uncertainty gets larger as the estimates get larger, but any appropriate scale can be used.

Once an item has been ranked and its value exceeds some threshold (or perhaps simply shows greater value than each of its ranked peers), it can be moved to the backlog queue, assuming space is available, because that queue is WIP-limited.

If the item fails some threshold test, it is deleted. Items can also be deleted from the funnel when they have been in the queue too long (perhaps six months). This indicates that the item was either too ambiguous for investment or perhaps simply didn't have high enough importance to warrant the attention of the team.

Work-in-Process Limits

Since this is the "capture" queue, there is no strict WIP limit associated with this queue, although periodic pruning may be necessary to keep the list to a workable size (perhaps 50 to 75 items).

Decision Authority

The funnel queue, and the final decision to move an item to the backlog, is managed by the appropriate architectural authority—often a chief architect or CTO.

2. BACKLOG

Epics in the backlog queue justify a little more time investment, so they are treated with additional rigor.

Activities: Cadence-Based Review, Discussion, and Peer Rating

The architecture team, working as a group, reviews and discusses all epics on the backlog on a regular cadence (typically every few weeks). During this review process, epics receive additional consideration and are further elaborated to advance understanding.

This includes the diligence required to further understand the epic, refine the estimates of effort and value, and measure alignment with the current strategic investment themes.

To rank the epic relative to its peers, epics may be placed into a quantitative evaluation matrix, based on whatever rating system the team establishes for items in this queue. Table 21–2 provides one such example of a template and rating system.

Table 21–2 Template and Rating System for Backlog Queue Epics

Name		Date entered backlog		
Version		Changes		
Description				
Stakeholder sponsors				
Prerequisites (if any)				
Teams, products, programs, markets affected				
Notes				

Ratings		Weight	Net	Comments
Effort size		1		(Scale 1, 3, 5, 8, 13, 20, 40)
Cost of delay				
Business value		1		(same scale)
Time value		1		(same scale)
Risk reduction value		1		(same scale)
Length of time in queue		.5		(see below)
Weighted rating†				= example: (BV+TV+RRV+(LT*.5)) / Size

† In the example, we've simply added these together, applied the weights, and then divided by size. Other schemes may also be used.

Prioritization and Rating System

In Chapter 13, Vision, Features, and Product Roadmap, we described a Weighted Shortest Job First (WSJF) scheduling system for rating features, which optimizes delivery value based on the economics of the CoD. In the template in Table 21–2, we've applied WSJF again with a few minor differences. The prioritization parameters include the following.

- *Estimated size:* See funnel queue size estimate.
- *Cost of delay:* An estimate for the cost of delay. As with features, the cost of delay includes three components.

    - Business value—an estimate of the size of the potential return for the business.

▶ **NOTE**   This parameter is stated as *business value*, rather than as *user value* (as we applied to features), because many system-level architectural refactors are driven by internal cost savings, maintenance concerns, performance and scalability, and new business opportunities, or otherwise have a more indirect relationship to near-term user value.

    - Time value—the way in which the value decays over time. A low rating indicates a stable situation; a high rating indicates a rapid potential decay on the business value.
    - Risk reduction/opportunity enablement value—the value associated with risk reduction and enablement of opportunities for new types of future features and services.

- *Length of time in the queue:* We've added this optional parameter to the list as a reflection on how long this epic has been in the system. This is intended to accelerate consideration and decision making on items that have been in the queue too long, because they continue to require review and investment and therefore drive overhead by some incremental amount.

    Example: 0–30 days = 2, 30–60 days = 5, 60–120 days = 8, over 120 = 13.

Weighted Rating and Decision Criteria

These attributes are combined into a single weighted rating, which can be used to prioritize the epics relative to each other based on the economics of a WSJF. Table 21–2 also applies an optional weighting system for the various attributes (we've weighted time in queue at 0.5).

Items with the highest rating rise to the top of the backlog for promotion to the next state.

Pull from Transition to Analysis

Since the next queue is WIP-limited, there may be no further decision criteria beyond the mature rating, and a pull system may be applied. In other words, so long as there is room in the analysis queue, any available architect can pull the highest-rated epic into the next queue.

Work-in-Process Limits

Since items in this backlog queue require additional investment, the queue is WIP-limited to some integer number of epics (perhaps 20 to 25). Like all WIP limits, the limit can be adjusted over time based on the capacity of the architecture team and the response time desired for items to move through the queue.

3. ANALYSIS

In the two queues we have described so far, work is limited to discussions and preliminary analysis only. Investment is minimal. The artifacts are lightweight. A fairly large number of epics are manageable.

In the analysis queue, however, material use of scarce resources (architects, team leads, product and solution managers, marketing/business analysts, development team members) is required.

Activities

When an item is pulled into this queue by the architect team, the epic is time stamped, and an architect is assigned to be the "epic owner." The epic owner is the "chief engineer" for the epic and is responsible for defining and spearheading the analysis work that follows. Work in this state may include some or all of the following:

- Consideration of design alternatives
- Requirements workshops and other discovery techniques (Chapter 12)
- Impact analysis: development, distribution, and deployment
- Evaluating internal resourcing versus outsourcing options
- Buy or build evaluation
- Architectural analysis and modeling[4]

---

4. Yes, architects still model in agile development, though lighter-weight approaches are often applied. More on this topic can be found at, for example, *www.agilemodeling.com*.

- Refined scoping of market potential
- Collaboration with development
- Collaboration with business analysts, solution managers, and/or product managers
- Market validation of value
- Business case (discussed later in this chapter)

Collaboration with Development

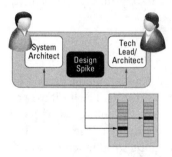

In the previous chapter, we described "intentionally emergent system architecture" as a result of a *role collaboration* between the system architects and the development team. That collaboration is initiated when an epic appears in this state. Typically, this involves engaging tech leads and architects associated with the agile teams in the analysis and design alternatives work. In addition, the *development teams themselves estimate the development cost* for each area impacted. This provides higher-fidelity estimates and a greater sense of buy-in from the teams.

In addition, some number of development teams will likely be involved in technical spikes designed to determine feasibility and reduce risk of the initiative. In a mature state, it is not unusual to see teams investing as much as 5% to 10% of their resources in technical spikes.[5] Of course, architects are also likely to be doing technical spikes and evaluating various design trade-offs in code. However, having the development teams perform the majority of the technical spikes has a number of benefits.

- There are far more resources in the development teams than in the architecture team.
- The development teams are closest to the current implementation; they have the best understanding of how to integrate the new architecture.
- The spikes give the teams time to explore the upcoming work and to socialize and integrate the new concepts into their backlogs, Vision, designs, and thinking.

---

5. Agile Architecture principle #3: *When in doubt, code it out.*

Collaboration with the Business: Solution Management, Product Management, Business Analysts

In a like manner, the impact on the marketplace and on the business must also be understood. Therefore, a second active collaboration is initiated with those in the business who can best assess these factors. In addition, the final value estimate should come from the solution manager, product manager, or business owner—whoever is in the best position to judge the potential value. More importantly, this engages these key stakeholders in helping manage the impact of the epic so as to best achieve that value. Without their active support and buy-in, the epic is likely doomed anyway and should be dropped from the queue.

Work-in-Process Limits

As we mentioned, epics in this queue consume scarce and valuable resources; therefore, this state is subject to rigorous work-in-process limits. The limit may be simply some number of epics (or the number and size of the analysis work) and may be adjusted over time. However, in our experience, the size of the epics is less material to this WIP limit; the number of epics undergoing simultaneous evaluation is a more controlling factor. Typically, some small number of epics (perhaps five to seven) would be manageable in this queue.

Architectural Epic Business Case Template

As we have described, the types of epics that have reached this queue are assumed to be large and crosscutting; in other words, they typically affect multiple teams, products, components, and services. They imply a significant investment, and they will impact a significant number of teams. Therefore, it is incumbent on the architects—in collaboration with the development teams and their product/solution manager-partners—to make a *go* or *no-go* recommendation to the business. In addition, the recommendation should be presented in such a way that the business owners have the background data they need to make a final decision.

To do so, we recommend that the primary artifact of an epic in this state is a *lightweight business case*, of one or two pages in length. As an example, an annotated template for such an artifact appears in Table 21–3.

When the architects think the analysis has been sufficiently thorough and that the business case is "ready enough," it is presented to the decision authority for action.

Table 21–3 Lightweight Business Case Template for Architectural Epics

Epic name:	Go or no-go recommendation:		Date entered backlog:	Architect epic owner:
Version		Changes		
Description				
Stakeholder sponsors	(Identifies key business sponsors who will be supporting the initiative.)			
Products, programs, services affected	(Identifies products, programs, services, teams, departments, and so on, that will be impacted by this epic.)			
Impact on sales, distribution, deployment	(Describes any impact on how the product is sold, distributed, or deployed.)			
Estimated investment	Story points:		Cost:	
Weighted rating	(WSJF rating from analysis)	**Type of return:**	(Nature and amount of potential return. Markets impacted, revenue, customer satisfaction, product line extension, customer retention, and so on.)	
In-house, outsource PR purchase	(Describes recommendations for where the epic is to be developed.)			
Estimated development timeline	**Start date:**		**Completion date:** (Estimated calendar date or number of PSIs.)	
Incremental implementation strategy	(Breaks initiative down into preliminary epics or subepics that fit the company's PSI cadence.)			
Reevaluation checkpoints	(If the epic is large, identifies potential milestones or checkpoints for reevaluation.)			
Analysis summary	(Brief summary of the analysis that has been formed to create the business case. Pointers to other data, architectural models, market analysis, and so on, that were used in the creation of the business case.)			
Other notes and comments				

Decision Authority

Because of the scope of the effort, the stakeholders who have the ultimate fiduciary responsibility for the product line, business unit, or enterprise must make the final decision about to whether to proceed with implementation. Typically, this responsibility rests with a portfolio management team (Chapter 22) or *product/technology council*, whether a formal or informal construct. Such councils typically include the chief executive for the domain, senior solution managers, line-of-business owners, sales and marketing representatives, the CTO, and senior development managers.

"No" Is an Acceptable Answer

However, even in the presence of a *go* recommendation case, the product council must take a broader view. For example, they must also consider the opportunity cost of the initiative (the opportunities lost to the business while this epic is being implemented) along with any other business cases at the same state of maturity. For example, if a product council is presented with 5, 10, or even 20 business cases with an estimated positive ROI (those with a negative ROI will not make it this far), that doesn't mean they could or should approve them all. After all, the *I* (investment) comes before the *R* (return), and the business must always work within its investment limits. In addition, the target is optimization of the overall portfolio, so individual epics must be considered in that light. So, *no* is an acceptable answer.

Indeed, one would hope that the business is managed in such a way that it is always presented with many opportunities for new investment, and picking the right ones means saying no to many others. That is one of the many reasons we keep the business cases lightweight, lest the personal time investment of those who developed the case may be prejudicial to the decision. The enterprise should consider only the marginal, forward-looking investment, ignoring any sunk costs and personal biases that may have occurred in analysis.[6]

Reasonable decisions include *not* initiating the project or, in the marginal case, perhaps asking for some additional analysis. In this case, the business must recognize that because of the WIP limits in the analysis queue, there is also an opportunity cost (other epics cannot enter analysis) in leaving the initiative in that queue.

"Yes" Is Too

However, many such initiatives will be approved or the organization will fail to innovate or keep the technology platform current for the longer view. When approved, the epic is moved to *implementation*.

---

6. Product Development Flow Principle E17—*The sunk cost principle. Do not consider money already spent.*

4. Implementation

Although the analysis work of the prior two queues uses scarce resources, the real cost begins once an architecture epic has been committed to implementation.

One major challenge in broaching this next state is an obvious one: "This new thing is big and no one is working on it now, so how, exactly, do we intend to actually do it?" That drives the enterprise to a serious consideration of resources and implementation paths as part of the business case in the last state. In practice, there are four implementation paths to be considered:

- Path A—internal development
- Path B—create a new team to build some runway
- Path C—outsourced development
- Path D—purchase a solution

Implementation Path A: Transition to Development

In this case, ownership of the epic moves to the development teams for implementation in the affected release trains, as Figure 21–4 illustrates.

The sponsoring architect remains on the team in a "pull " state, meaning that they provide whatever support the teams need to fully understand and implement the epic, but the responsibility now rests with the development teams.

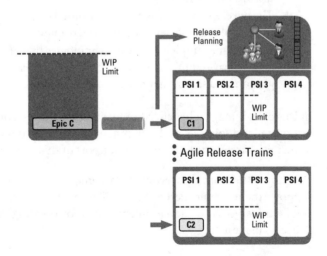

Figure 21–4   Epic C moves to development in two release trains.

Transitioning to development is the preferred case for a number of reasons.

- New development starts as soon as feasible within the context of the ongoing release trains for the affected products.
- Responsibility transitions immediately. Architects are freed up (except for the pull commitment) to work on other epics.
- Work remains in-house, the team's knowledge increases, and the company's core competence grows.

In this case, the new epics will be presented as part of the Vision and architecture overview at the next release planning session. There, epics are likely to be split, and the teams consume the smaller epics by subdividing them into the architectural features and stories they will use for implementation.

Thereafter, it is simply business as usual, and the architectural epic flow system is complete for that epic.

Implementation Path B: Create a New Team

Though the previous path is the preferred case, it is not always practical for a number of potential reasons.

- Sometimes the architectural epics represent a new technology or framework that must be built from scratch, or perhaps it still has significant risk associated or is otherwise too immature or uncertain to warrant immediate disruption of the teams.
- The development teams are so consumed by existing commitments that they cannot take on the new epic in a timely manner.
- The epic may implement new technologies that are unfamiliar to the teams and/or may require creation of some new infrastructure (continuous integration, and so on) that must be in place before development begins.

In this case, it may be beneficial to form a new team—consisting of the epic architect owner and some set of development resources—and charter that team to build some initial architectural runway in support of this epic, as Figure 21–5 illustrates.

Over time, the team may evolve to become a full-fledged development team that supports the new epic. Perhaps more likely is that the new framework will eventually be transitioned to development teams for ongoing development and maintenance, as in path A.

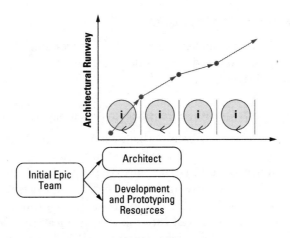

Figure 21–5 Building architectural runway for a new epic

Implementation Path C: Outsourced Development

There is a third path that must be considered as well. There are situations in which outsourcing can be the most effective path to implementation of new technology. This can occur when

- There is simply insufficient internal capacity to take on the epic
- There are outside sources who have more core competence in the new technology and can therefore more quickly build the needed runway

However, because the epic likely represents some new core intellectual property— one that the development teams themselves must eventually understand and master—internal development or architect resources should be assigned to the project so that knowledge transfer begins immediately.

Implementation Path D: Purchase a Solution

Purchasing a solution may also be a viable option under any of the following conditions.

- The product/service is needed to enable business, but it is not the company's core business.
- There is a solution available in the marketplace that is cheaper to buy than build.
- The enterprise can leverage the competence of the solution provider.
- Time to market is so critical that a more immediate solution must be delivered.

Work-in-Process Limits

The potential application of work-in-process limits for the implementation stage is not so obvious and is highly dependent on the path chosen. We'll look at each in the following sections.

WIP Limits for Path A: Transition to Development

In this path, WIP limits are highly subjective to the company's competitive and customer satisfaction context at the time of implementation. Rather than strict limits, it may be sufficient for the enterprise to know how much it is investing in new technology infrastructure for the near- to mid-term versus ongoing investment in feature delivery on the existing runway. That can usually be accomplished in the agile project management tooling, where features and stories driven by architectural epics can be categorized accordingly.

As a rule of thumb, we often see enterprises limiting new technology development to 10% to 15% of total investment. Yet there are times when we have seen a program devote as much as 60% of the effort, spread across multiple PSIs. This decision must be based solely on the company's context in the market at that time. It doesn't really matter how the company measures or limits it, so long as the WIP is visible.

WIP Limits for Path B: Create a New Team

WIP limits for this path are more obvious. Initiatives on this path consume scarce resources (architects, tech leads, senior developers) for substantial periods of time and, after that, *still* require a transition back to development for longer-term support.

Therefore, a typical business unit, product line, program, or smaller enterprise can typically support only *one or two* such initiatives at a time.

WIP Limits for Paths C and D: Outsourced Development and Purchased Solution

WIP limits on these parts are controlled by two factors: the availability of funding and the availability of architects or others to effectively manage the projects and to provide for information transfer.

Like path B, a limit of only *one or two* such concurrent projects may be suitable for the typical program.

Summary

In this chapter, we described an architectural epic kanban system as an example of a lean process that can be used to reason about, analyze, and make go/no-go recommendations for large-scale architectural initiatives.

This system is designed to make all architectural work in process visible, manage queue sizes of work awaiting implementation, and provide a quantitative way to evaluate epics relative to each other. The final output of this system is a lightweight business case for the architectural epics that can be used by the appropriate authorities to make a final decision on any individual epic. Those epics that make the cut will move to implementation, and the system architect's work is largely complete, subject to whatever support may be required based on the chosen implementation path.

These previous two chapters complete our discussion of agile system architecture. In the next two chapters, we'll move on to discussing agile approaches to managing the enterprise's full portfolio.

Chapter 22

MOVING TO AGILE PORTFOLIO MANAGEMENT

To succeed with agile, management's need for results must be greater than their need for control.

—Israel Gat, formerly of BMC Software

In the previous two chapters, we described the role that system architects and system architecture play in building robust and scalable enterprise-class systems. We did so because architecture is the "yin to our requirements yang"—the balancing force that keeps our systems evolving steadily and, ideally, ever-ready to meet customer's needs.

However, evolving architecture is not the only consideration at the Portfolio level, nor even the most important one. For here we find the executives and managers who are ultimately responsible for *portfolio management*, which is the function that ultimately makes the decisions as to *what we build and why*. They establish business and technical initiatives, priorities, and budgets. As fiduciaries, they are responsible for the ultimate success or failure of the business venture or business unit that they represent. These are serious folks with serious business challenges, and they too must evolve if our enterprise is to succeed with its lean and agile renovation.

PORTFOLIO MANAGEMENT

Mikko Parkolla describes portfolio management this way:[1]

> Portfolio management is a top-level authority that makes long-term investment decisions on strategic areas that affect the business performance of the company. In order to do this properly, deep knowledge of the market, environment, technology and financial landscape at a macro level are

---

1. Excerpt from Mikko Parkolla's master's thesis: *Product Management and Product Owner Role in Large Scale Agile Software Development*

429

needed. Implicitly, this responsibility requires high-level rank and rests with a vice president, executive team, or a business unit top management level decision making forum, depending on where these decisions are typically made within the company.

The main responsibility of portfolio management is to set the investment levels between business areas, product lines, different products, and strategic portfolio investment themes; these are a collection of related strategic initiatives. In an enterprise environment, these decisions can be also made at different levels as appropriate: for example, on an executive team level between business units, at a business unit level between product lines, for product lines between products. The investment level is the granted budget for the specific area, which cannot be moved, borrowed or used for another area. It is the fixed investment into this area for the defined amount of time, in terms of monetary budget, head count or allocation over the planned mid and long-term time interval.

Typically, the portfolio management function controls (or heavily influences) three sets of activities that are important to the financial and product development health of the business entity. These include the following.

- *Investment funding:* Determining the allocation of the company's scarce R&D resources to various products and services.
- *Change management:* Fact patterns change over time, and the business must react with new plans, budgets, and expectations.
- *Governance and oversight:* Assuring that the programs remain on track and that they follow the applicable corporate rules, guidelines, and relevant standards. As we will see shortly, this function is often under the auspices of the project management office (PMO).

So far in this book, we have spent most our time describing requirements practices and project-related issues that primarily affect the teams—and the teams of teams—that build the product, services, and solutions than we have discussing any issues at the Portfolio or governance level. That makes sense, because agile practices were designed by and for those in the trenches—those developers, architects, testers, product managers, and product owners who actually *define, build, and test* all the software assets the enterprise deploys to the market.

To achieve the next levels of agility in the enterprise, however, we must eventually come face-to-face with some of the existing, higher-level principles and practices that control projects, requirements, software development processes, and other aspects of the team's behavior. So, there comes a time when many of the "impediments" that arise from the lean-agile transformation rise to a ceiling that is beyond the control of the teams.

It could be a portfolio management function that creates fixed (and potentially impossible) requirements and delivery commitments. It could be a PMO that *manages the teams* with traditional project management practices and reports to executive management on that basis. It could be internal software process "police" that holds the teams accountable to waterfall-based software development mandates. Most of the time, it's some combination of these. Worse, the belief systems and practices they instantiate are so conflated and intertwined that it is exceedingly difficult for the teams to make changes on their own or even know how to go about influencing the key stakeholders that control them.

But change we must, or our enterprise will not achieve the full economic and motivational benefits of the lean/agile transformation. This chapter is dedicated to that challenge.

WHEN AGILE TEAMS MEET THE PMO: TWO SHIPS PASS IN THE NIGHT

Sometimes the ceiling is represented by the project management office (PMO), a place many agilists perceive to be "the mother ship of impediments." Indeed, if you mention the words *project office* or *PMO* among a group of agilists in the trenches, reactions will vary, but probably only from negative...to very negative.

I mention this not to stoke the fire but to simply acknowledge that for many enterprises these are "two ships that pass in the night." They may hear each other's foghorns and begrudgingly acknowledge each other's presence, but they hope to simply pass without damage and go on about their business. Doing so, however, will ultimately deny the enterprise its ultimate agile benefits—the ability to make a fast midcourse correction (even though it is a mighty big ship). It might be the ability to avoid a competitor's new obstacle or to find a slipstream to a major new opportunity—if only they could turn that ship, say 90 degrees to the right, and do so *right now*.

Ultimately, there comes a time when these two ships must meet and agree on a common course and direction. However, you don't want this time to come too soon. Rather, it should come at a time when the agile teams are standing on the credibility of their achievements, not promises, when some of the next impediments rest clearly at the door of the PMO, and when the PMO recognizes that becoming an agile enterprise is no longer business as usual. They too must recognize that the PMO must change, and change dramatically, to survive in an increasingly agile world.

LEGACY MIND-SETS INHIBIT ENTERPRISE AGILITY

Some time back, I was researching the industry trends in this area in order to help an enterprise adapt its portfolio planning and PMO to agile ways. While doing so, I ran across a case study from DTE Energy called *Establishing an Agile Portfolio to Align IT Investments with Business Needs* [Baker and Thomas 2008]. Here is the introductory "grabber" that piqued my interest:

> Those who implement agile software development and agile project management in a traditional corporate environment may encounter legacy corporate processes that reflect legacy mindsets and cultures. These remnant processes, mindsets, and cultures represent opportunities to improve the systemic value that agile approaches are capable of enabling.

As we described earlier, this is a reminder that *team agility* does not automatically engender *enterprise agility*, and, in most all cases, the team is just the beginning. The DTE case study is an example of how one such agile enterprise first *recognized* and then *began to address* the significant changes necessary to allow the emergence of true enterprise agility.

The white paper describes a number of legacy mind-sets that can inhibit achievement of the full benefits of the agile enterprise. These include pithy descriptions such as "widget engineering," "control through data," "order-taker mentality," and more. Recognizing these mind-sets is an important underpinning for the enterprise transformation, because one can't recognize solutions to a problem if one doesn't believe there is a problem to begin with.

The Problem Is Not "Theirs"; It Is "Ours"

Let's first admit that any enterprise that is fortunate enough to have lots of development teams, a portfolio management function, and probably a PMO is, almost by definition, a successful enterprise. Otherwise, how could they have grown to have all these teams and assets to manage—and all these project and program managers around to help manage them? It's hard to argue with success.

Let's also recognize that there are professionals on both of these teams—experienced project teams that have been willing to change and adopt agile methods and experienced portfolio and project managers with decades of experience in shepherding these programs to market. How, then, can these ships be at such risk of crashing in the fog?

We Taught Them Much of What They Know

In our earlier history of software development methods, we noted that the waterfall method was the most predominant for the last 20 to 30 years. "We"—developers, methodologists, thought leaders, executives, and managers—invented and applied that method. Naturally, governance evolved around that method as well. In addition, those with project management responsibility applied the traditional project management practices to manage software development. It should come as no surprise that our agile teams and programs are being held accountable to legacy waterfall practices for governance and traditional methods of project management. That was all there was. We have met the enemy that started all this, and he is us.

In the following sections, we'll take a critical look at those legacy mind-sets, but we do so with the humility that "we" are not smarter than "they." Indeed, *we* are *they*, so let's see what we can learn about our other selves.

LEGACY MIND-SETS IN PORTFOLIO MANAGEMENT

I once imagined that I would eventually expound on the legacy mind-sets described in the DTE white paper, but they are so well expressed and so symptomatic that I decided just to repeat them (with permission) here. However, the accompanying descriptions and paraphrasing are my own. These are based on my experience from two perspectives; *then*, as one of "them" (an executive, managing portfolios, and carrying some elements of these mind-sets) and *now*, as one of "us" (an agile executive attempting to change those mind-sets). The following mind-sets are often endemic, and they require immediate attention.

- *Widget engineering:* This mind-set is based on the belief that software development is a repetitive, readily controlled, and manufacturing-like business, rather than research *and* development with the incredible variability, risk, and opportunity that such implies. "Draw it up and build it like you drew it," goes the thinking.
- *Order-taker mentality:* Also known as "You build what we tell you to build." Founded on the belief that *they*—the customer (or portfolio or program or product manager or business owner; substitute your word here)—is always right, is all-knowing, and actually knows what the requirements for a never-as-yet-built-system really are. And, of course, they have already spent six months researching the requirements and writing them down. The development teams should "just build it."

- *Maximize utilization:* The belief that if all resources aren't fully utilized *on paper,* then they won't be fully utilized *in practice.* "Unless we keep them fully loaded, they'll just be idlers," goes the thinking. "Fully assign them to tasks well into the future or lose them in the next budget cycle," and "The more projects people work on, the higher the utilizations, the more efficient our enterprise becomes."

- *Control through milestones:* The belief that by asking for the right kind of data at project milestones—earned value metrics, design reviews, requirements, and test plans—we can tell where we are on the project. And then, "If we still can't tell where we are, we'll just ask for more detailed data." The belief that milestones are great program review markers, ignoring the fact that the later and slower the project is, the less frequent they are!

- *We can plan a full year of projects:* Conveniently disregarding our past 20 years or so of experience in *failing* to predict projects a year in advance, we assume it's a failure of *our planning,* not a failure of the basic *paradigm.* "If we only planned in more detail, we could really get it right this year." So, on we go to more and more detailed planning—tighter requirements, more analysis, and tighter commitments—the very problem that led to our predicament.

- *Just get it done:* The belief that our best case plans can be reality if the teams would only *try hard enough.* This is also known as "This is the plan we agreed to; now execute it," and "When the going gets tough, the tough get going." And lastly, the infamous "We know it's impossible; that's why we want you on this project."

In practice, the manifestation of these mind-sets creates huge problems for agile development teams, as Table 22–1 shows.

Table 22–1   The Problems Legacy Mind-Sets Create in Agile Development

Mind-Set	Manifestation	Problems Caused
"Widget engineering"	Fixed schedule, fixed requirements.	Detailed commitments made a year in advance.
	Big, up-front design (BUFD).	Analysis paralysis. Project is late when it's started.
	No allowance for innovation.	
	Unrealistic expectations.	Detailed specs and designs "handed off" to development.
"Order-taker mentality"	Do what you are told.	False agreements. No buy-in.
	We are the boss of you.	Misses innovation from development.
		Failure to meet expectations—mistrust.
		No empowerment, low motivation.

Mind-Set	Manifestation	Problems Caused
"Maximize utilization"	Resources committed long range.	No time to think or innovate.
	100% allocation before "what if."	Dedicate resources to tasks or lose them.
	Key resources assigned to multiple projects.	No resources for new, higher-priority projects.
		Thrashing. Low productivity. Burnout.
"Get it done"	Belief that best case plans must succeed.	Deferred recognition of plan versus actual.
		Late discovery and renegotiation.
		Loss of credibility, mistrust.
"Control through milestones"	Teams held to waterfall-based project milestones.	Start-wait-start-wait-start-wait projects.
	Unproductive artifacts.	Teams produce artifacts they don't need or want.
	Fine grain reporting and overhead.	Teams pretend not to work ahead of milestones.
		Slow value delivery.
"We can plan a full year of projects"	Detailed work breakdown structures, earned value metrics, Gantt charts.	Reporting overhead. Annoying the team.
		Metrics don't reflect actual progress.
		Plans are obsolete but not treated that way.

It's also obvious that these mind-sets are directly opposite to *so many* principles of product development flow, as Table 22–2 illustrates.

Table 22–2   Legacy Mind-Sets Are Contrary to Lean Principles

Mind-Set	Contra Lean Product Development Principles [Reinertsen 2009]
"Widget engineering"	V1: The Principle of Beneficial Variability—*Variability can create economic value.*
	V3: The Principle of Optimum Variability—*Variability should neither be minimized nor maximized.*
"Order-taker mentality"	D1: The Second Perishability Principle—*Decentralize control for problems and opportunities that age poorly.*
"Maximize utilization"	F1: The Principle of Congestion Collapse—*When loading becomes too high, we will see a sudden and catastrophic drop in output.*
	F6: The Cadence Capacity Margin Principle—*Provide sufficient capacity margin to enable cadence.*

Continues

Table 22–2   Legacy Mind-Sets Are Contrary to Lean Principles (Continued)

Mind-Set	Contra Lean Product Development Principles [Reinertsen 2009]
"Get it done"	W8: The Principle of Flexible Requirements—*Control WIP by shedding requirements.*
"Control through milestones"	D8: The Principle of Mission—*Specify the end state, its purpose, and the minimum possible constraints.*
	D3: The Principle of Layered Control—*Adapt the control approach to emerging information about the problem.*
"We can plan a full year of projects"	B7: The Psychology Principle of Batch Size—*Large batches inherently lower motivation and urgency.*
	V6: The Principle of Short-Term Forecasting—*Forecasting becomes exponentially easier at short time horizons.*
	D4: The Opportunistic Principle—*Adjust the plan for unplanned obstacles and variances.*

EIGHT RECOMMENDATIONS FOR MOVING TO AGILE PORTFOLIO MANAGEMENT

Well, enough carping about the current state; it's time to move on to some specific recommendations that can help a portfolio management team think, act, and be lean and agile. We'll divide these change recommendations into the three main activities we described earlier: investment funding, investment change management, and governance and oversight.

Rethinking Investment Funding

First, we'll provide some recommendations to assist in that critical up-front problem—determining what projects get funded and why.

#1: From "Too Many Projects" to Controlling Work In Process

In virtually every lean agile transformation I've been engaged in, many (or all) key resources are flitting like butterflies from project to project, rarely alighting long enough to make a meaningful contribution to anyone. Plus, every day they suffer the multiplexing tax, that 20% or so time penalty it takes to get "back in the flow" on *each new project they touch that day*. However, that's just the symptom. The root cause is "too many projects in flight at the same time."

When working with executives, one exercise that I use to help communicate this basic flaw in thinking is shown in Figure 22–1.

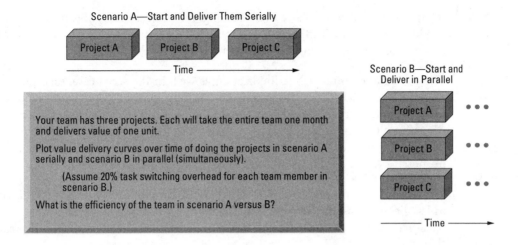

Figure 22-1   An exercise to show the negative economic effects of doing multiple projects in parallel

For the exercise, I have the executives plot the curve of value delivery for each approach, taking the projects on in parallel (which is their natural tendency; "We have to show progress, you know…") and then reconsidering the results if the projects were executed serially instead. Usually they ponder on it for a while, make a few scratches, and then the lightbulb goes on. The results are striking, as shown in Figure 22-2.

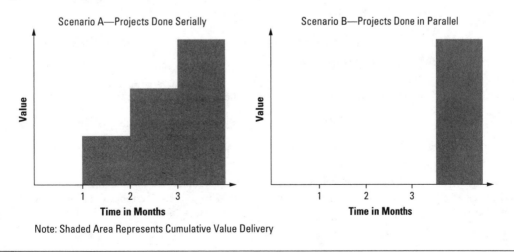

Figure 22-2   Value delivery results—serial versus parallel delivery

It can be seen from the figure that finishing one project before you start another produces economics (earlier value delivery) that are far superior. The advantages are obvious and compelling, as we further describe in Table 22–3.

There is another, more subtle implication as well. In the serial case, each project starts with a fresh set of requirements. For example, project C starts with requirements that are current at the start of the second month. In the parallel case, *all* projects suffer a three-month requirements decay, meaning that by the time of delivery, the requirements are stale, and the newly delivered project is less fit for the intended purpose.

When executives see the objective evidence of this simple exercise, they are inclined to learn about more actively managing work in process, keeping WIP visible, and releasing smaller blocks of content for implementation. We'll revisit that in the next chapter.

#2: From Detailed Business/Project Plans to Lightweight Business Cases

Funding for new programs has been traditionally justified by a business and project plan. These reflect the analysis that has been done, the potential return on investment, and, usually, a set of requirements for the program. The bigger the program, the bigger the document. This seemed sensible historically, but we note that it is a direct parallel to the software requirement specifications that we have largely abandoned in agile. The context is somewhat different, but the problem is the same: too-early commitment to requirements, a business case that has been developed by a business analysis team or individual who has become committed to the program (but who isn't going to actually do the work), and a detailed project plan with tasks forecast long into the future.

Instead, we want to evolve to a lighter-weight and more flexible model, as Figure 22–3 shows.

Table 22–3   Advantages of Serial Over Parallel Project Execution

Serial	Parallel
Value delivery begins after the first month, when the first project is completed.	Value delivery does not even *begin* until after three months.
Value accumulates rapidly as each project completes. The integration of value represents the potential profit over time.	The thrashing "tax" (caused when a team member switches projects) is estimated at from 20% to 60% and delays value delivery even further.
By the end of the third month, all projects are delivered.	*Nothing* is delivered at the end of three months.
Cost of delay is minimized.	*All* projects suffer a three-month+ cost of delay.

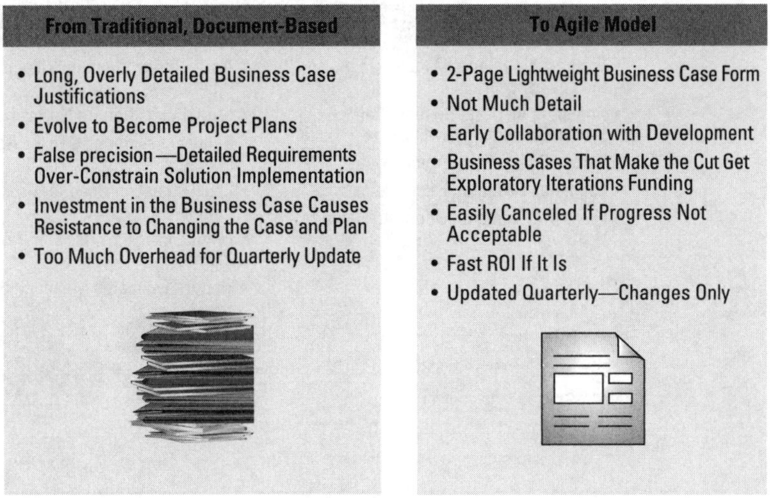

From Traditional, Document-Based	To Agile Model
• Long, Overly Detailed Business Case Justifications • Evolve to Become Project Plans • False precision—Detailed Requirements Over-Constrain Solution Implementation • Investment in the Business Case Causes Resistance to Changing the Case and Plan • Too Much Overhead for Quarterly Update	• 2-Page Lightweight Business Case Form • Not Much Detail • Early Collaboration with Development • Business Cases That Make the Cut Get Exploratory Iterations Funding • Easily Canceled If Progress Not Acceptable • Fast ROI If It Is • Updated Quarterly—Changes Only

Figure 22–3   Replace detailed business and project plans with a lightweight business case.

The resulting artifact is a lightweight business case template that can be updated quarterly. (An example template appears in the next chapter.)

Although some might worry that a lightweight document reflects lightweight thinking and therefore has the potential to inflict economic damage, there is little danger. As we will see, funding will be done incrementally, so there will be lots of opportunities to evaluate programs in process. At those standard intervals, funding (resources) can be moved to whatever projects, new or old, that are more deserving.

#3: From Work Breakdown Structure to Agile Estimating and Planning

To determine what projects get funded, there must be some means of determining the estimated cost of a project. Traditionally, this is done via a work breakdown structure, which decomposes the large initiative into a series of tasks in fine enough granularity so that they can be estimated with reasonably accuracy. The estimates for the task are summed up to provide the final cost estimate. This works reasonably well if you are trying to estimate the costs of building a bridge. However, it doesn't work very well at all for software. The results are often quite poor; estimates are typically off by 50% to 100%, with 200% to 300% not uncommon.

Instead, as we described in Chapter 13, agile brings new laws of software physics (maybe heuristics would be a better term), and we can apply those at the Portfolio level. Figure 22–4 summarizes the traditional versus agile estimating approaches.

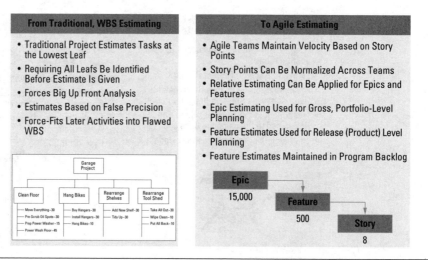

Figure 22–4   From WBS-based estimating to agile estimating

In addition, as the team's maturity increases, they will naturally start to keep current estimates for work remaining, or new features that are anticipated, in the backlog. This provides management with the forward look they need to understand estimated costs for completion.

Rethinking Change Management

In addition to rethinking investment funding, we must also reconsider the way in which we approach managing the inevitable twists and turns of a software endeavor. Again, the traditional approaches are not well suited to the objectives of the lean and agile software enterprise.

#4: From Annual to Incremental Funding

Another pernicious aspect of the legacy model is the tendency for "all-or-none" funding. This means that once funds are committed, they become virtually impossible to deallocate. Instead, they become inexorably bound to external commitments as well as dedicated, internal resources. Further, the commitments are included in the annual budget planning process, whereby every department needs to justify the continued use of resources throughout a fiscal year. To do that, managers often need to show how the individuals are dedicated to tasks well into the future. To do *that*, they need to create more detailed plans that justify the annual budget. This vicious cycle continues to result in *just the exact opposite of the behavior we are trying to achieve.*

Instead, funding should be done incrementally so bad paths can be truncated more quickly and resources can be moved to the best opportunities throughout the fiscal year.

When we base future, incremental funding on objective demonstrations of working software—instead of on milestones based on proxy documentation—then we have continuous opportunities to assess and adjust. And teams have real motivation to deliver immediate value.

5: From "Projects" to Continuous Content Delivery

We start with a dramatic suggestion: *eliminate the basic construct of the "project" itself.*[2] Here's why: Traditionally, based on a construction-like metaphor, a "project" gathered some resources together, a set of requirements, a mission, start and end dates, and a project manager. The project then binds these things to together in a package that tends to become fixed and immutable. Every project develops its own antibodies to change. No one wants to be part of a canceled project; jobs may be on the line, even if the result was a "successful early failure" of a new product or technology. How does one innovate in that environment?

Instead, we need to move to a mode of *project-free, continuous content delivery.* Figure 22–5 illustrates the many downsides of the traditional "project" approach and contrasts it to *continuous content delivery.*

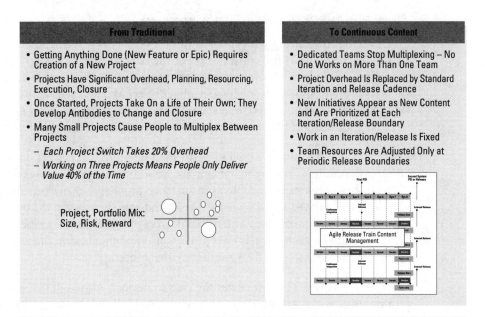

From Traditional

- Getting Anything Done (New Feature or Epic) Requires Creation of a New Project
- Projects Have Significant Overhead, Planning, Resourcing, Execution, Closure
- Once Started, Projects Take On a Life of Their Own; They Develop Antibodies to Change and Closure
- Many Small Projects Cause People to Multiplex Between Projects
  - *Each Project Switch Takes 20% Overhead*
  - *Working on Three Projects Means People Only Deliver Value 40% of the Time*

Project, Portfolio Mix: Size, Risk, Reward

To Continuous Content

- Dedicated Teams Stop Multiplexing – No One Works on More Than One Team
- Project Overhead Is Replaced by Standard Iteration and Release Cadence
- New Initiatives Appear as New Content and Are Prioritized at Each Iteration/Release Boundary
- Work in an Iteration/Release Is Fixed
- Team Resources Are Adjusted Only at Periodic Release Boundaries

Agile Release Train Content Management

Figure 22–5   From projects to continuous content management

2. Perhaps the project word is simply reused from the "construction world" and was meant for building and completing "one-off" things. But when you build a house, you don't have a release six of it that could be 100x bigger than the original. Software grows continuously, so the "project construct" doesn't imply the right things.

Moreover, in the project model, it was typically necessary to have individuals work on a number of projects at the same time (after all, we were doing them all in parallel and we had to show progress). This causes the thrashing (context switching) tax to be applied to most individuals on the project team, thereby significantly decreasing overall productivity.[3]

In the new model, new content is presented at fixed-cadence planning boundaries. Teams flex to the new content. Resources are adjusted at the same cadence. Multiplexing decreases. Portfolio management becomes "content management"—continuously prioritizing new content for the ongoing programs. No more "fits and starts" of building a new project every time we want to get something done.

Rethinking Governance and Oversight

No matter how empowered the teams and programs have become, the portfolio and project managers still have accountability to the business for understanding program progress, status of critical external deliverables and releases, and development cost accounting. We respect that. Governance and oversight is still important, even in the agile enterprise. But here again, the methods must evolve.

#6: From PMBOK to Agile Project Management

Of course, dispensing with the notion of a project is a cathartic event that must be considered in its full context. Part of the context is what to do with those who played the traditional role of project manager. If there are no projects, what happens to them? Indeed, if you look at what Project Management Body of Knowledge (PMBOK) trained project managers traditionally do, there is no obvious placeholder for many of their prior activities, as Figure 22–6 illustrates.

Most of the traditional activities performed by project managers on behalf of the teams, including "managing" them, are now gone. Instead, the teams themselves own these responsibilities. Because of these problems, many organizations have eliminated the project management role (and sometimes even the entire PMO) in their agile transformation, with mixed degrees of success. Moving the responsibility to the team to manage their own projects is one thing; having them actually know how to do that successfully is another matter entirely.

However, Figure 22–6 overstates the case somewhat. Although many of the recognizable activities are no longer necessary (WBS, PERT, Gantt, and so on), many traditional project management activities remain, and there are new, project-like activities to manage as well.

---

3. For example, during its transition to agile, one company diagnosed the "failures" of the first agile team's first few iterations. Their conclusion was that no one worked on the team long enough to accomplish anything!

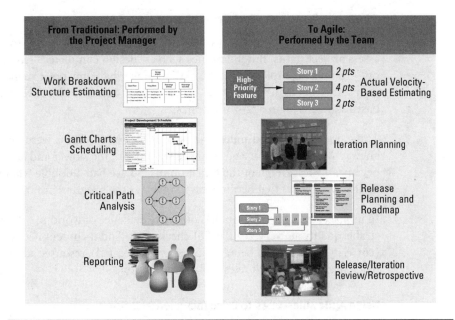

Figure 22–6 From traditional project management to self-management

We favor a model whereby project managers are retrained and repurposed as *agile project managers* and thereby fulfill a number of important responsibilities, some traditional and some new to the agile paradigm. These include the following:

- Organizing and facilitating release planning events, running release retrospectives
- Attending the Scrum of Scrums; working with the teams to resolve blocks and impediments
- Coordinating outside dependencies and suppliers; managing, packaging, and distributing team's deliverables
- Working in the existing accounting system to provide whatever adaptation is needed for existing cost accounting
- Facilitating Program-level demos and progress reviews
- Helping with backlog estimating and working with the portfolio management team to estimate and plan

All of these activities tend to fall somewhere outside the team's normal experience and competence (and sometimes interest). An able, agile project manager is a valued assistant to any agile program. For more on this topic, we refer you to *The Software Project Manager's Bridge to Agility* [Sliger and Broderick 2008].

7: From Milestone to Fact-Based Governance

Traditionally, we instituted various waterfall-legacy milestones to measure and assess project status. But milestones such as "design complete," "requirements sign-off," "test plan complete," and the like, no longer have any positive meaning to agile teams. Instead, agile governance is based upon routine, objective, fact, and code-based status, as Figure 22–7 illustrates.

These document-based milestone proxies for real progress were never very good anyway. Moreover, from a governance standpoint, the slower and later the program became, the less frequent the touch points. So, we had a double whammy—largely ineffective reviews that became less frequent as the program ran into more trouble!

In its place, the agile program has objective evidence of working code, with demonstrable quality at every, regular PSI checkpoint. And if content needs to be adjusted (correlated to a project being canceled or accelerated), resource adjustments can be made readily at the next release planning session.

Using Agile Milestones to Drive Incremental Delivery

However, for a number of reasons, the agile program is not necessarily milestone free. Indeed, a proper application of *agile* milestones can be used to drive incremental delivery in those parts of the organization that still tend to waterfall thinking. For example, an agile set of milestones might appear as in Figure 22–8.

From Traditional: Milestone-Based	To Agile: Fact-Based
• Teams Report Milestones with Document-Based Reviews • Subjective, Milestone Reports Do Not Correlate to Actual Project Status • Teams "Report to" Project Office (Leader as Conductor/Boss) • Teams *Cannot Proceed* Until and Unless They Pass Milestones (Start-Wait-Start-Wait Waste Cycle) • Scheduling Delays and Overhead • Process Changes Dictated by "Those Who Know Best"	• Primary Milestone: Working Code at Each PSI • Status and Quality Are Objective, Not Subjective • Project Office "Comes to Teams" (Enabling Leadership Model) • Teams *Default Model* Is to Proceed Unless Stopped by Business Case (No Process-Driven Delays/Waste) • No Scheduling Delays and Overhead • Process Changes Applied and Harvested from Team's Retrospectives

Figure 22–7   Moving from milestone-based to fact-based governance

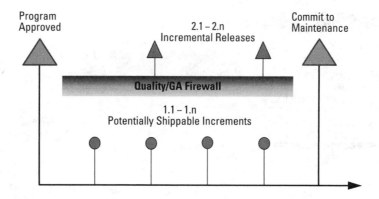

Figure 22–8 Agile milestones can drive incremental delivery.

In this figure, the presence of "1.1–1.n PSIs" communicates to the teams how assets are to be built incrementally, and the "2.1–2.n incremental release" milestones communicate the importance of early and continuous releases of value.

8: From Centralized Annual to Decentralized Rolling-Wave Planning

Traditionally, planning was often the province of the PMO or those project managers and project planners who would work with customers to understand requirements, estimate the work, and make the commitments for the teams. Although this was not necessarily without collaboration, the net result was that the project office and the project managers owned the plan and the team was left to try to achieve the commitments. In evolving our new planning model, the responsibility for planning is moved to the teams. At the Program level, this is accomplished primarily by the release planning function that we described in Chapter 16. In this model, planning is done on a standard cadence, independent of the status of the project and independent of release commitments. They *plan to replan*.

For many enterprises undergoing this transformation, this was a transition made in steps, as Figure 22–9 indicates.

Arriving at the third step, the *Agile Release Train* is no small feat for the enterprise. Indeed, in practice, this works best when the project office (surprise, surprise) takes an active role in driving the new planning process. It adds real value because

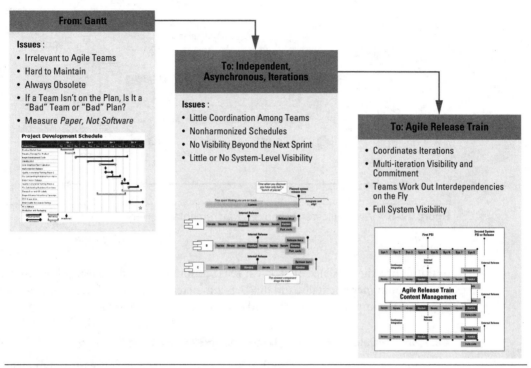

Figure 22–9   Typical stages of agile planning evolution

planning is hard. Also, there are a number of reasons why the teams can't actually plan at this level *entirely* by themselves.

- Logistically, it is difficult to even arrange such a planning function. It requires advanced scheduling, reservation of adequate facilities, commitments from product managers and key stakeholders to attend, and logistics on logistics.
- Release planning works best when it is facilitated. Neither of the two key stakeholders, product management or development, is in a neutral position to do this. Rather, a facilitator/planner from the PMO is often an excellent choice.
- While the teams are empowered to self-manage, they are not empowered to self-destruct or grow beyond previously agreed-upon boundaries. If a high-priority program in process needs additional resources; it should get them. And yet, what competent program would deprecate their own resources for a program they are committed to?

For these reasons, we suggest that an active governance role for the PMO is driving the release planning process. In addition to the benefits this provides the teams, there are many benefits to the PMO as well.

- Provides an integral, ongoing role in the agile enterprise, one that is directly supportive of the team's agile objectives.
- Provides the opportunity to attach to the programs. After all, the PMO always wants to know what the state of the program is, so how better than to help coordinate release planning activities?
- Provides a regularized opportunity to understand release status and capture release metrics, such as the release reliability metric, as well as to see when a program is in trouble.
- Provides additional value added by facilitating continuous improvement through release retrospectives and elimination of Program-level impediments.

SUMMARY: ON TO AGILE PORTFOLIO PLANNING

Although we've spent a fair amount of time in this chapter criticizing some mindsets and activities of the traditional portfolio and project management functions, we hope that we've added our own value by indicating ways that these functions can evolve to become staunch agile proponents and participants. By adopting these recommendations, these functions can evolve from being the "mother of all impediments" to "leaders of the lean and agile enterprise." In the next chapter, we'll put this new organization to work. Its first task: *agile portfolio planning*.

Chapter 23

INVESTMENT THEMES, EPICS, AND PORTFOLIO PLANNING

Greatness is not a function of circumstance. Greatness, it turns out, is largely a matter of conscious choice, and discipline.

—James Collins, author of *Good to Great*

In the previous chapter, we described ways in which the portfolio and project management functions can evolve to operate in a lean and agile manner, helping the full enterprise achieve the productivity and time-to-market benefits of agile development and the proven economic co-benefits of product development flow. In so doing, we left the requirements topic briefly in order to provide process guidance within which our agile requirements model can now be placed.

In this chapter, we return to the prime topic—agile requirements—but we do so at the Portfolio level, the highest level of the Big Picture and the enterprise, the place where all these requirements arise to begin with. We'll also further describe the last two requirements artifacts that we'll need to conclude our agile requirements story, *investment themes* and *business epics*, which are highlighted in Figure 23–1.

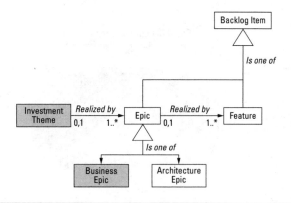

Figure 23–1 Strategic investment themes and epics in the requirements model

INVESTMENT THEMES

Investment themes represent the set of initiatives that drive the enterprise's portfolio by governing the investment in the various systems, products, and applications for which the teams are responsible.

▶ **NOTE**   Some product companies refer to these as *strategic product themes*. We'll use the more generic term of *strategic investment themes* (*themes* for short) here.

For example, the pie chart in Figure 23–2 illustrates the relative percentage budget allocations for the themes of a hypothetical "cloud computing device business unit."

The set of strategic investment themes drive the Vision for all products, systems, and services, and new *epics* are derived from this decision. As we described in the previous chapter, the responsibility for the investment decisions generally lies with the portfolio management team, which has fiduciary responsibilities to their stakeholders.

In most enterprises, these decisions happen at the business unit level based on annual or twice-annual budgeting process.

▶ **NOTE**   Although it's beyond our scope, the traditional budgeting process is not really up to the challenge of agile portfolio planning. Refer to Beyond Budgeting at *www.bbrt.org*. Member organizations follow the principles outlined in *Beyond Budgeting: How Managers Can Break Free from the Annual Performance Trap*, published by Harvard Business School Press.

The budgeting process determines the amount of funds available for each business unit or product set to invest in development.

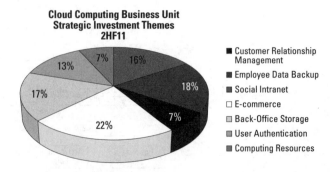

Figure 23–2   Budget allocations for a set of strategic investment themes

Within the business unit, the investment decisions are based on some combination of the following:

- Investment in existing product offerings—enhancements, support, and maintenance
- Investment in new products and services—products that will enhance revenue and/or gain new market share in the current or near-term budget period
- Investment in futures—product and service offerings that require investment today but will not contribute to revenue until outlying years

Balancing these investments is difficult, and we should appreciate the enormous pressures and conflicting priorities that are constantly present for those who make these decisions for our enterprise. But make them they must, or the enterprise will wander through time with an unfocused strategy. And we can all guess how that will work out.

The result of the decision process is a set of investment themes:

Investment themes are key product value propositions that provide marketplace differentiation and competitive advantage.

Themes have a much longer life span than epics. Indeed, even in the agile enterprise, a set of themes may be largely unchanged for up to a year or more.

Communicating Investment Themes

Although determining the investment mix is no small feat, communicating the decision via themes is fairly straightforward, because themes are very high level and are easily represented in bullet form. For example, one could imagine an enterprise business unit developing an online e-mail service deciding on the following themes for the upcoming year:

- Introduce voice and video chat
- Outlook integration
- Personalization
- Mail for Mobile devices 2.0
- Group chat from within mail

Why Investment Mix Rather Than Backlog Priority?

As opposed to epics, features, and stories, investment themes are not contained or represented in a backlog. The difference is subtle but important.

Backlog items are designed to be addressed in priority order. Investment themes are designed to be addressed on "a percentage of resources to be made available basis." For example, a lower-priority feature on a program backlog may not be addressed at all in the course of a release, and yet the release could well be a success (meet its stated objectives and be accepted by the product manager and the market). However, if the lowest-priority (smallest investment commitment) investment theme is not addressed over time, the enterprise *may ultimately fail in its mission, because it is not making its actual investments based on the priorities it has decided.*

From a lean perspective, allocating a percentage of investment to a theme is a form of *class of service*, each theme being given the resources (service level) required to achieve the appropriate level of investment.

Investment themes also do not share certain other backlog item behaviors. For example, as critical as they are, they are not really testable, because their instantiation occurs first through epics and then, finally, via actual implementation in features and stories, which have the specificity necessary to be testable.

If the enterprise is focused, only a few themes are active at any one time, so we shouldn't require a backlog management tool (spreadsheet or agile project management tool) to capture and maintain them. A simple list will suffice.

EPICS

Investment themes drive epics, which represent the highest-level expression of a customer or business need, as Figure 23–3 (a more obviously hierarchical representation) shows.

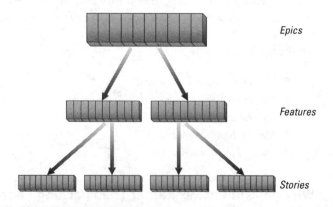

Figure 23–3   The hierarchical relationship between epics, features, and stories

Derived from strategic investment themes, business epics are development initiatives intended to deliver the value of the theme:

> Business epics are large, customer-facing initiatives intended to deliver new products, solutions, or services to the marketplace.

Business epics are identified, prioritized, estimated, and maintained in the *portfolio backlog*. They may be stand-alone (developed in a single program or business unit), or like architectural epics, they may cut across

- Time—affecting multiple releases of products, systems, services, or solutions
- Scope—affecting multiple products, systems, services, or solutions
- Organization—affecting multiple teams, programs, business units

Subepics

As a brief aside, we note that we've highlighted three levels of abstraction for expressing requirements—epics, features, and stories. However, we admit that these are arbitrary distinctions, essentially just labels to describe how to think about the system at various levels of abstraction. However, in admitting that they are arbitrary, we also admit that there is no perfect hierarchy. For example, prior to release planning, epics must be allocated to the appropriate programs, where they will eventually be decomposed into specific features. The features, in turn, drive release planning for the affected programs.

In such cases, a large epic, such as move CRM to the cloud will spawn a number of epics for individual programs, business units, and so on. To manage this allocation, some have found it convenient to split these epics into *subepics*, which create an additional level in the hierarchy. You don't have to add this level, but otherwise it may eventually become hard to understand what business epics drove these new program epics to exist. Although we won't add *subepics* to the requirements meta-model, the reader should know that others have found them convenient, and you can apply them whenever it makes sense to do so.

Expressing Epics

Epics may be expressed in bullet form, as a sentence or two, in video, as a prototype, in a short business case, or indeed in any form of expression suitable to express the intent of the product initiative.[1]

---

1. I was once at a meeting where an (otherwise) clever agilist, pushing back on what he considered to be delaying and excessive epic-level documentation requirements, told his PMO management, "You can even tell us in interpretive dance; we'll take it from there." Note, however, that this is not the recommended selling approach!

With epics, clearly, the objective is "the big vision," not specificity. In other words, the epic need only be described in detail sufficient to initiate a further discussion about who is impacted and what types of new features it implies.

Discriminating Epics, Features, and Stories

As we just described, epics, features, and stories are all forms of expressing user need and benefit but at different levels of abstraction. For example, earlier we hypothesized possible investment themes for a new, hosted e-mail service provider that include the following:

- Voice and video chat from within mail
- Outlook integration
- Personalization
- Support mobile devices
- Group chat

One can also imagine that personalization is a significant investment—one that the provider might hope would create a strategic differentiation from other providers and one that could evolve over years. In other words, personalization is a reasonable example of a well-stated strategic investment theme; you get the general idea, but you have no idea what exactly to do next!

To communicate better what to do next, prospective epics, such as emoticons and user background desktop themes, could have then been identified. Then, the teams responsible for user background desktop themes might well have brainstormed a multiple-stage implementation process, with the first releasable feature being apply a standard theme from mail theme catalog, followed by allow users to further customize a chosen standard theme.

In the first iteration, the teams might have decided to create an initial set of two stories, for example: implement a framework where selected themes could be cataloged, selected, and applied and also a user value story as an alpha tester, I can select and apply the first, prototype standard desktop theme so that I can provide early feedback on the concept.

In this hypothetical example, the requirements information model for this example would be as shown in Figure 23–4:

Still, we admit that there is no scientific way to determine whether a "thing you know you want to do" is an epic, feature, or story, but perhaps the discriminators of Table 23–1 will help.

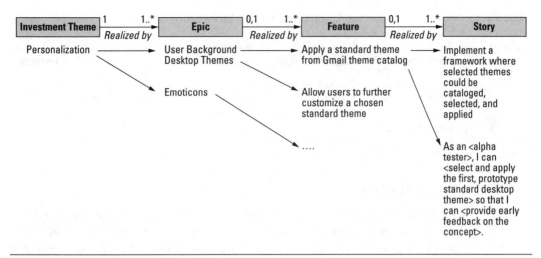

Figure 23–4   Example theme > epic > feature > story > hierarchy

Table 23–1   Discriminating Themes, Epics, Features, and Stories

Type of Information	Description	Responsibility	Time Frame and Sizing	Expression Format	Testable
Investment theme	*Big*, audacious, game changing, initiatives. Differentiating, and providing competitive advantage.	Business executives, Portfolio management.	Span strategic planning horizon, 12 to 18+ months. Not sized, controlled by percentage investment.	Any: text, prototype, PPT, video, conversation.	No
Epic	Bold, impactful, marketable differentiators.	Portfolio management. Business analysts, product and solution management, system architects.	6 to 12 months. Sized in points.	Most any, including prototype, mock-up, short phrase, or vision statement.	No
Feature	Short, descriptive, value delivery and benefit-oriented statement. Customer and marketing understandable.	Product manager and product owner.	Fits in an internal release (PSI), divide into incremental subfeatures as necessary. Sized in points.	Key phrase or user story voice form. May be elaborated with system use cases.	Yes

Continues

Table 23–1   Discriminating Themes, Epics, Features, and Stories (Continued)

Type of Information	Description	Responsibility	Time Frame and Sizing	Expression Format	Testable
Story	Small, atomic. Fit for team and detailed user understanding.	Product owner and team.	Fits in a single iteration. Sized in story points.	User story canonical form.	Yes

Types of Epics

We've already alluded to "types" of epics when we discussed architecture epics in the previous chapter. More generally, however, enterprises may want to classify epics into various types, which provide further clarity of the intended investment. For example, we have seen epics classified as follows:

- User/consumer experience epics
- Web services epics
- Distribution partner epics

This doesn't matter to the model; enterprises can create any type of epic that suits their needs. In the rest of this chapter, we'll just use the general term *business epics* to represent the types of epics that are managed in the agile portfolio planning process.

IDENTIFYING AND PRIORITIZING BUSINESS EPICS: A KANBAN SYSTEM FOR PORTFOLIO PLANNING

In Chapter 21, we described a kanban system for identifying and prioritizing architectural epics. This system included a kanban state model, a description of activities, and a prioritization model for moving epics from consideration to implementation. Although we introduced the model in the context of rearchitecting large-scale systems, in fact it is a general model that we can apply again here as well. To avoid repetition, we will not elaborate as much on the motivations or the descriptions of this model here. Instead, we'll just describe the highlights of the system as applied to prioritizing business epics.[2]

---

2. The architectural kanban system from the previous chapter and the business epic system in this chapter could be combined into one system. However, we've described them as separate systems, because in the larger enterprise, different teams are typically responsible for these different concerns.

The primary objectives of this system are as follows:

- Make the process of reasoning about future development work visible
- Establish WIP limits to control queue sizes and help assure product development flow
- Drive an effective collaboration with the development, solution management, sales/marketing, and executive teams
- Provide a quantitative basis for economic decision making

In summary, the system is designed to help those engaged in this most-critical decision-making process reason about their work. As their decisions go, so goes the fate of our enterprise.

Overview

Visually, such a system might appear as in Figure 23–5.

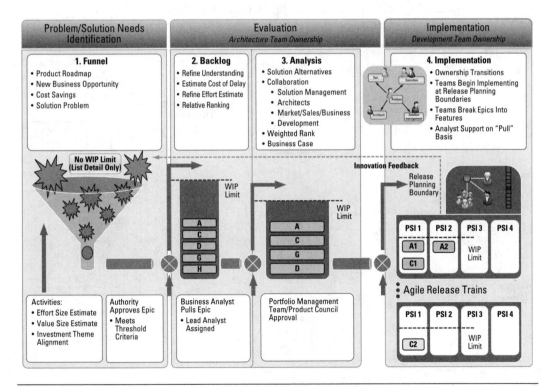

Figure 23–5 Graphic overview of the business epic kanban system

Just like before, epics that are eventually implemented go through a series of four queues, each characterized by different activities on the part of the business analysts and other stakeholders, along with correspondingly increasing levels of investment. The queues are as follows:

- Funnel (solution needs identification)
- Backlog
- Analysis
- Implementation

State Diagram View

As with the architecture kanban system, epics transition through a series of states, as we describe in Figure 23–6.

The state diagram illustrates all the paths for an epic and the decision gates that drive the epics down these paths. Figure 23–7 shows details of the activities in the queue, the decision criteria, and the decision authority.

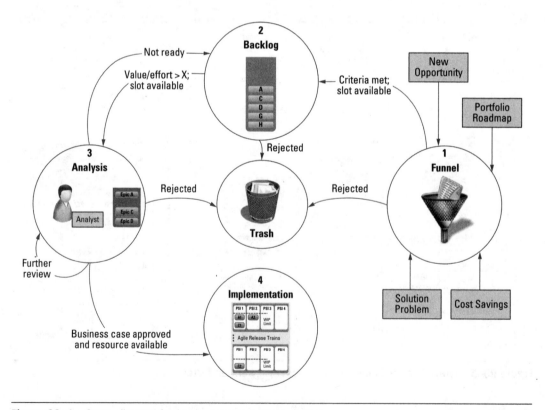

Figure 23–6 State diagram for business epic kanban system

State	Activities to Transition	Transition Criteria	Next	Authority
Funnel	• Estimate Value • Estimate Effort • Test Against Investment Themes	1. Rank > Threshold 2. WHEN Slot Available 3. Fails Criteria → Trash		Portfolio Authority
Backlog	• Assign Cost of Delay • Effort Estimate Refined • Establish Relative Rank	Ranked Relative to Other Items Highest Ranked Item Pulled When Age of Item > Limit	→ Escalate or Trash	Pull System Portfolio Authority
Analysis	• Solution Alternatives • Collaboration with Business, Architects, Development, Solutions Management • Cost Estimates • Implementation Options • Market Validation of Value • Business Case	Business Case with GO/NO GO Recommendation GO > Implementation NO GO 1 > More Elaboration Needed No GO 2 - Reject	→ Trash	

Figure 23–7   Business epic kanban activities and decisions

The Funnel: Problem/Solution Needs Identification

The funnel queue is the holding area for all business epics that have been identified. There is no formal filtering process; if a portfolio team member has an idea or gets an idea from another stakeholder, it goes right into the funnel and is date stamped at that time.

Sources of New Business Epics

Business drivers for new business epics come from a variety of sources, both inside and outside of the enterprise. Sources include the following.

- *Portfolio Vision:* Most of the new epics come from the portfolio Vision or Roadmap; they have been identified sometime in the past and are now reaching an appropriate implementation horizon.
- *New opportunities:* Some new epics originate from unanticipated changes in the marketplace, business acquisitions, entry of new competitors, and so on.
- *Cost savings:* Cost savings or other operational efficiencies drive many business epics. Examples include supply chain management, cloud-based hosting, and warehouse and inventory management.

- *Problem with the existing solution:* Some business epics are driven by known problems with an existing solution. Examples include increasing performance and reliability and enhancing scalability to support market success. (Generally, however, these would then be fed into the *architectural* kanban system, if such a system exists.)

Activities: Ranking the Epic

The primary activity for epics in this state is a periodic review and preliminary analysis of the item by the portfolio management team. A primary goal is to establish a relative ranking based on three parameters:

- A preliminary estimate of the *size* (the relative "bigness" of the item) to implement the effort. The effort estimate is an aggregation of a number of factors that may include the following:

  - Estimate of the cost and time to implement
  - Number of teams, programs, products, business lines potentially affected
  - Technical risk
  - Complexity

- A preliminary estimate of the value of the epics, whether measured in cost savings, customer retention, revenue, or market share
- Degree of alignment with the enterprise's current investment themes

Since the item is only in the funnel state, there's no reason to overinvest in estimating, so a simple spreadsheet as shown in Table 23–2 could be applied.

Once an item has been ranked and its value exceeds some threshold, it can be moved to the backlog as soon as space is available. If the item fails the threshold test, it is deleted. Items can also be either escalated (increase the cost of delay) or deleted from the funnel when they have been in the queue too long.

Table 23–2   Ranking Criteria for Business Epics in the Funnel State

Ranking Item	Scale
Effort size	1, 2, 3, 5, 8, 13, 20, 40
Potential value	1, 2, 3, 5, 8, 13, 20, 40
Alignment to investment theme	0, .25, .5, .75, 1
Epic weight	= (Value/effort) * alignment

Work-in-Process Limits

Since this is the "capture" queue, there is no strict work-in-process limit associated with this state, although periodic pruning may be necessary to keep the list to a workable size (perhaps 50 to 75 items).

Decision Authority

The funnel queue, and the final decision to move an item to the backlog, is managed by the appropriate authority, often a senior business analyst or solution manager.

Backlog

Items in the backlog queue deserve and require additional research.

Backlog Activities: Cadence-Based Review, Discussion, and Peer Rating

The analyst team, working as a group, reviews and discusses all epics on the backlog on a regular cadence (perhaps every two weeks or so). During this review process, epics receive additional consideration and are further elaborated to advance understanding.

This includes the diligence required to refine the estimates of effort and value. In addition, a cost of delay is assigned, which requires a more sophisticated understanding of the time element that drives the individual epic.

To rank the epic relative to its peers, epics may be placed into a quantitative evaluation matrix. Table 23–3 provides an example of a template for weighting an epic in the backlog queue.

Table 23–3 Template for Backlog Epics

Name		Date entered		
Version		Changes		
Description				
Potential stakeholder sponsors				
Prerequisites				
Teams, products, programs, markets affected				
Notes				
Ratings		Weight	Net	Comments
Size		1		1, 2, 3, 5, 8, 13, 20, 40, 100

Table 23–3   Template for Backlog Epics (Continued)

Cost of delay				
Business value		1		Same scale
Time value		1		Same scale
Risk reduction/ opportunity enablement		1		See below
Length of time in queue		.5		See below
Weighted rating (WSJF)				=(BV+TV+RRV+(LT*.5))/size

Prioritization and Rating System

Again, we use the Weighted Shortest Job First (WSJF) prioritization system for rating epics. The prioritization parameters in this case include the following:

- Estimated size (implementation effort).
- Estimated cost of delay for the epics. As was the case with features and architectural epics, the cost of delay includes three components.

  - *Business value:* Relative estimate of the size of the increase in revenue, market share, cost reduction, or customer satisfaction.
  - *Time value:* The way in which the value decays over time. A low rating indicates a stable (not time sensitive) situation; a high rating indicates a rapid potential decay.
  - Risk reduction/opportunity enablement. The way in which this epic reduces the risk of future epics, or enables other new business opportunities.

- Length of time in the queue.

  Example: 0–30 days = 2, 30–60 days = 5, 60–120 days = 7, over 120 = 10

Net Rating and Decision Criteria

These attributes are combined into a single weighted rating,[3] which can be used to prioritize the epics relative to each other, based on the economics of a WSJF. Items with the highest rating rise to the top of the backlog for promotion to the next state.

---

3. Add CoD and time in queue and divide by size.

Pull from Transition to Analysis

Since the next queue is WIP-limited, there may be no further decision criteria beyond the mature rating, and a pull system may be applied. Any available business analyst can pull an epic into the next queue.

Work-in-Process Limits

Items in this backlog queue require additional investment, so the state is WIP-limited. A reasonable WIP limit might allow an average of 25 or so items in this particular queue. The limit can be adjusted over time based on the capacity of the business analyst team.

Analysis

For the two queues we have described so far, the work on business epics is limited to discussions and preliminary analysis only. Investment is minimal. The artifacts are lightweight. A fairly large number of epics are manageable. In the analysis state, however, material use of scarce resources, including business analysts, architects, development team leads, product and solution managers, marketing/sales, executive team members, and so on, is both required and justified.

Analysis Activities

When an item is pulled into this state by the analyst team, the epic is time stamped, and a business analyst is assigned as the "epic owner." The epic owner is responsible for defining and spearheading the analysis work that follows. Work in this state may include the following:

- Requirements workshops and other discovery techniques
- Consideration of solution alternatives
- Competitive analysis
- Impact analysis—development, distribution, and deployment
- Buy-or-build evaluation
- Evaluation of internal resourcing versus outsourcing options
- Refined estimates for cost and impact
- Collaboration with development, solution managers, system architects, and executive sponsors
- Market validation of value; assignment of cost of delay
- Assigning an executive business sponsor

Collaborations

Much of the work in the analysis state is driving a set of collaborations with other key stakeholders to better understand and socialize the epic. Key collaborations include the following.

- *With development and architects:* To establish technical feasibility and impact on existing systems, the business analyst will involve development management, tech leads, and architects in the analysis and design alternatives work. The development teams themselves will estimate the development cost for each area impacted. In addition, some development teams and architects may be involved in technical spikes to determine feasibility.
- *With solution management/product management:* In a like manner, the impact on the marketplace and on the business must also be understood. Therefore, a second active collaboration is initiated with those elements of the business that can best assess these factors. In addition, the final value estimate should come from the solution manager, product manager, or business owner—whoever is in the best position to judge the potential value.
- *With executive stakeholders:* There are likely to be a few, key, executive-level stakeholders who have a keen interest in the opportunity or are likely to be impacted. The overall success of the new initiative will be dependent on them. Involving these stakeholders in the analysis phase serves to engage them early, actively solicits their input, helps assure buy-in, and serves as a check and balance on the potential cost and benefit estimates.

Work-in-Process Limits

The analysis queue is subject to work-in-process limits. The limit may be based on the number, or the number and size, of the epics and is adjusted over time based on the capacity of the business analysis team. Typically, some small number of epics (perhaps 5 to 10) would be manageable for this queue.

Epic Business Case Template

The types of epics that have reached this state are assumed to be quite significant, and they may affect multiple teams, products, components, and services. They imply a significant investment, and they will impact a significant number of teams. Therefore, it is incumbent on the analysts—in collaboration with the development teams and their product/solution manager-partners—to make a *go* or *no-go* recommendation to the business as an output of this state. In addition, the recommendation should be presented in such a way that the portfolio management team has the background data they need to make a final decision.

As is the case with architectural epics, we recommend development of a *lightweight business case*. Table 23–4 shows an annotated example template.

Table 23–4 Lightweight Business Case Template for Business Epics

Epic name	Go or no-go recommendation:		Date entered backlog:		Analyst epic owner:
Version		**Changes**			
Description of the epic					
Stakeholder sponsors	(Identifies key business sponsors who will be supporting the initiative.)				
Users and markets affected		(Describe the user community of the solution and any markets affected.)			
Products, programs, services affected		(Identifies products, programs, services, teams, departments, and so on, that will be impacted by this epic.)			
Impact on sales, distribution, deployment		(Describes any impact on how the product is sold, distributed, or deployed.)			
Estimated investment	**Story points:**		**Cost:**		
Weighted rating	(WSJF)	**Type of return**		(Nature of potential return. Revenue, market share, new markets served.)	
In-house or outsource development	(Describes recommendations for where the epic is to be developed.)				
Estimated development timeline	**Start date:**		**Completion date:** (Estimated calendar date or number of PSIs.)		
Incremental implementation strategy	(Breaks initiative down into preliminary epics or subepics that fit the company's PSI cadence.)				
Reevaluation checkpoints	(If the epic is large, identifies potential milestones or checkpoints for reevaluation.)				
Analysis summary	(Brief summary of the analysis that has been formed to create the business case. Pointers to other data, feasibility studies, models, market analysis, and so on, that was used in the creation of the business case.)				
Attachments	Project stakeholder needs assessment (see Chapter 7). System stakeholder needs assessment.				
Other notes and comments					

When the analysts think the analysis has been sufficiently thorough and that the business case is "ready enough," it is presented to the decision authority for action.

Decision Authority

Because of the scope of the effort, the portfolio management team (or some other set of stakeholders who have the ultimate fiduciary responsibility for the product line, business unit, or enterprise) makes the final decision as to whether to proceed with implementation. Such councils typically include the chief executive for the domain, senior solution managers, line-of-business owners, sales and marketing representatives, the CTO, and senior development managers.

"No" Is an Acceptable Answer

However, as is the case with architectural epics, even in the presence of a *go* recommendation case, the portfolio management team must take a broad view. They must also consider the opportunity cost of the initiative (the opportunities lost to the business while this epic is being implemented) along with any other business cases at the same state of maturity.

Indeed, as was the case with architecture epics, one would hope that the business is managed in such a way that it is always presented with many opportunities for new investment, and picking the right ones means saying no to many others. That is one of the many reasons we keep the business cases lightweight, lest the personal time investment of those who developed the case may be prejudicial to the decision. The enterprise should consider only the marginal, forward-looking investment, ignoring any sunk costs and personal biases that may have occurred in analysis.[4]

Reasonable decisions include *not* initiating the project or, in the marginal case, perhaps asking for some additional analysis. In this case, the business must recognize that because of the WIP limits in the analysis state, there is also an opportunity cost (other epics cannot enter analysis) in leaving the initiative in that state.

"Yes" Is Too

However, many such initiatives will be approved or the organization will fail to innovate and maintain a competitive advantage. When approved, the epic is moved to the next and final state, *implementation*.

---

4. Product Development Flow Principle E17—*The sunk cost principle. Do not consider money already spent.*

Implementation

Although the analysis work of the prior two states uses scarce resources, the real investment in mass and cost begins once a business epic has been committed to implementation.

As was the case with architectural epics, the enterprise must consider resources and implementation paths as part of the business case in the last state. There are four implementation paths to be considered:

- Path A—transition to development
- Path B—create a new team to explore feasibility and build some architectural runway
- Path C—outsourcing
- Path D—purchase a solution

Because we've explored each of these paths in the prior chapter on implementation options for architectural epics, we won't repeat them here.

SUMMARY

In this chapter, we introduced *investment themes*, which are the set of initiatives and relative budgets that drive new development in the agile enterprise. We also introduced the construct of the *business epic*, which is the requirements object we use as a container to define new initiatives and estimate and prioritize larger-scale business value items. In addition, since decision making at this level is so critical to the economic success of the business, we introduced a kanban system for portfolio planning that makes work in process visible, drives collaboration with the key stakeholders, builds the business case for each epic, and provides a framework for decision making based on the economics of each new business opportunity.

Our hope is that this chapter, and the business epic kanban system we described, will help your enterprise implement an agile approach to deciding *what* to develop and *when*. Surely, this will drive the best possible economic outcomes for your agile enterprise, because that is the ultimate goal of this entire book.

In the next and final chapter, we'll summarize what we've discussed into a more complete framework for reasoning about enterprise-wide *agile software requirements*.

Chapter 24

CONCLUSION

We started this book by noting that software development is one of the world's most important technologies. Simply, our modern world runs on software, and where it doesn't now, it likely will soon.

In support of this criticality, the move to lighter-weight, more flexible, more adaptable, and more user-centric software development methods—generally couched under the label of agile and lean software development—is an inexorable force. This is not just a whim of some thought leaders or a simple pushback from management oversight by a few thousand grumpy software developers. Rather, the trend is driven by the business benefits these models can deliver—rapid increases in development productivity and delivered quality as well as improved morale of those doing this important work. The net benefit is better software development economics, and those economics are driving enterprises, small and large, to adopt and further improve these new methods.

But as powerful as they are, they are only now advancing to the point of providing broad, practical, and standardized guidance for that odd combination of art, science, and engineering that is the software development process. Central to this process are the software requirements, those abstractions we use to drive a conversation with our customers, as well as to communicate among ourselves, what the new software solution is supposed to do for them and what benefits it is designed to deliver.

In this book, we have attempted to address this central part of the larger puzzle by providing principles, practices, and techniques that development teams, architects, product managers, and businesspeople can use to define, communicate, implement, and test the requisite behaviors of these complex new systems. In so doing, we've built on the governing principles of agile—as primarily expressed by the Agile Manifesto, as well as lean development as primarily expressed by Reinertsen's Principles of Product Development Flow—to help assure that the recommendations are as lean and agile as we can possibly make them.

In Part I, we provided an overview context—an organization, process, and artifact model—that teams could use to reason about software requirements, starting with the Team level, moving to the Program level, and finally, moving to the full enterprise portfolio management challenge.

In Part II, we described the most basic—though certainly far from trivial—practices that software teams can employ to do their local work. We introduced user stories, stakeholders, user personas, agile estimating and velocity, iterating, backlog, throughput and kanban, the role of the product owner, acceptance testing, and a set of requirements discovery techniques that teams can use to both identify the appropriate sources and describe intended system behavior.

In Part III, we elevated the discussion to those practices and techniques that teams of teams could use to manage requirements at the Program level, where they build larger systems, applications, and product suites. We introduced additional roles and artifacts, including Vision, features, Roadmap, the role of the product manager, the Agile Release Train, release planning, nonfunctional requirements, use cases, and, finally, a requirements analysis toolkit that teams can use when the enterprise cannot afford to have the intended behavior misunderstood.

In Part IV, we took the discussion to the managers and executive suites and discussed approaches to identifying and prioritizing those business and technology epics that we used to describe new solution and technology initiatives. We described a set of guiding principles for providing the necessary architectural oversight and governance. We introduced a kanban system for defining, prioritizing, and implementing large-scale, crosscutting technology initiatives that help teams rearchitect their system to meet ever-increasing user demands. We described how to change some of the legacy mind-sets of portfolio management to more agile ways of thinking. Finally, we introduced investment themes, business epics, and a kanban system for agile portfolio planning.

Of course, describing all this is the easy part (well, perhaps not that easy at times), but the real work is left up to you, the reader. It is our sincere hope that this book will provide a thinking aid with the practical guidance you need to be able to successfully implement a lean/agile—and yet fully scalable—requirements process in your organization so that you can reap the benefits. After all, that's the only real value delivery opportunity we have.

The rest is actual software, and that's up to you.

Good luck.

FURTHER INFORMATION

For further information, and for discussions and extensions to the ideas expressed in this work, visit *www.agilesoftwarerequirements.com* or e-mail the author at *deanleffingwell@gmail.com*.

Appendix A

CONTEXT-FREE INTERVIEW

In Chapter 12, Requirements Discovery Toolkit, one of the tools we introduced was the context-free interview that teams or product owners can use to better understand prospective user requirements. Refer to that chapter for descriptions of the application and how to use the interview template that follows.

Part I: Establishing the Customer or User Profile

Name:

Company:

Industry:

Job title:

(The above information can typically be entered in advance.)

What are your key responsibilities?

What outputs do you produce?

For whom?

How is success measured?

Which problems interfere with your success?

What, if any, trends make your job easier or more difficult?

Part II: Assessing the Problem

For which [application type] problems do you lack good solutions?

What are they? (Hint: Keep asking, "Anything else?")

For each problem, ask the following questions.

- Why does this problem exist?
- How do you solve it now?
- How would you like to solve it?

Part III: Understanding the User Environment

Who are the users?

What is their educational background?

What is their computer background?

Are users experienced with this type of application?

Which platforms are in use?

What are your plans for future platforms?

Are additional applications in use that are relevant to this application? If so, let's talk about them a bit.

What are your expectations for usability of the product?

What are your expectations for training time?

What kinds of user help (for example, hard copy and online documentation) do you need?

Part IV: Recapping for Understanding

You have told me:

(List customer-described problems in your own words.)

■

■

■

Does this adequately represent the problems you are having with your existing solution?

What, if any, other problems are you experiencing?

Part V: Analyzing the Customer's Problem

(Validate or invalidate assumptions.)

(If not yet addressed.) Which, if any, problems are associated with the following? (List any needs or additional problems you think should concern the customer or user.)

■

■

■

For each suggested problem, ask the following questions.

- Is this a real problem?
- What are the reasons for this problem?
- How do you currently solve the problem?
- How would you like to solve the problem?
- How would you rank solving these problems in comparison to others you've mentioned?

Part VI: Assessing Your Solution (If Applicable)

(Summarize the key capabilities of your proposed solution.)

What if you could:

-
-
-

How would you rank the importance of these?

Part VII: Assessing the Opportunity

Who in your organization needs this application?

How many of these types of users would use the application?

How would you value a successful solution?

Part VIII: Assessing the Reliability, Performance, and Support Needs

What are your expectations for reliability?

What are your expectations for performance?

Will you support the product, or will others support it?

Do you have special needs for support?

What about maintenance and service access?

What are the security requirements?

What are the installation and configuration requirements?

Are there special licensing requirements?

How will the software be distributed?

Are there labeling and packaging requirements?

Part IX: Addressing Other Requirements

Are there any legal, regulatory, or environmental requirements or other standards that must be supported?

Can you think of any other requirements we should know about?

Part X: Wrapping Up

Are there any other questions I should be asking you?

If I need to ask follow-up questions, may I give you a call? Would you be willing to participate in a requirements review?

Part XI: Summarizing

After the interview and while the data is still fresh in your mind, summarize the three highest-priority needs or problems identified by this user/customer.

1.

2.

3.

VISION DOCUMENT TEMPLATE

In Chapter 13, Vision, Features, and Roadmap, we introduced the Vision document as one mechanism for defining and communicating a Vision for the solution. A template for such a document is provided in the pages that follow.

VISION DOCUMENT TEMPLATE

Company Name

Vision Document for [Program Name]

© 20XX [Company Name]

Revision History

Date	Revision	Description	Author
mm/dd/yy	1.0	Initial version	Author name

Table of Contents

1   Introduction

This section provides an overview of the Vision document.

1.1 Purpose

This document defines the strategic intent of the program. It defines high-level user needs, any applicable user personas, key stakeholders, and the general system capabilities needed by the users.

1.2 Solution Overview

State the general purpose of the product, system, application or service, and any version identification.

- Identify the product or application to be created or enhanced.

- Describe the application of the product, including its benefits, goals, and objectives.

- Provide a general description of what the solution will and, where appropriate, will not do.

1.3 References

List other documents referenced, and specify the sources from which the references can be obtained. If a business case (Chapter 23) was developed to drive the program, refer to it or attach it.

2   User Description

To provide products and services that meet users' needs, it is helpful to understand the challenges they confront when performing their jobs. This section should profile the intended users of the application and the key problems that limit the user's productivity. This section should not be used to state specific requirements; just provide the background for why the features specified in Section 5 are needed.

2.1 User/Market Demographics

Summarize the key market demographics that motivate your solution decisions. Describe target-market segments. Estimate the market's size and growth by the number of potential users or the amount of money your customers spend, trying to meet needs that your product/enhancement would fulfill. Review major industry trends and technologies. Refer to a market analysis, where available.

2.2 User Personas

Describe the primary and secondary user personas (see Chapter 7). A thorough analysis might cover the following topics for each persona:

- Technical background and degree of sophistication
- Key responsibilities
- Deliverables the user produces and for whom
- Trends that make the user's job easier or more difficult
- The user's definition of success and how the user is rewarded
- Problems that interfere with success

2.3 User Environment

Describe the working environment of the target user. Here are some suggestions.

- How many people are involved in completing the task? Is this changing?

- How long is a task cycle? How much time is spent in each activity? Is this changing?

- Are there any unique environmental constraints: controlled environment, mobile, outdoors, and so on?

- Which system platforms are in use today? Future platforms?

- What other applications are in use? Does your application need to integrate with them?

2.4 Key User Needs

List the key problems or needs as perceived by the user. Clarify the following issues for each problem.

- What are the reasons for this problem?

- How is it solved now?

- What solutions does the user envision?

Ranking and cumulative-voting techniques for these needs indicate problems that *must* be solved versus issues the user would *like* to be solved.

2.5 Alternatives and Competition

Identify any alternatives available to the user. These can include buying a competitor's product, building a homegrown solution, or simply maintaining the status quo. List any known competitive choices that exist. Include the major strengths and weaknesses of each competitor as perceived by the end user.

2.5.1 Competitor 1

2.5.2 Competitor 2

3 Stakeholders

Identify the program stakeholders, their needs, and their degree of involvement with the system. A table such as the following can be effective:

Project Stakeholder	Degree of Involvement	Product Needs	Program Needs
Stakeholder 1			
Stakeholder 2			

4 Product Overview

This section provides a high-level view of the solution capabilities, interfaces to other applications, and systems configurations. This section usually consists of five subsections, as follows.

4.1 Product Perspective

This subsection should put the product in perspective to other related products and the user's environment. If the product is independent and totally self-contained, state so. If the product is a component of a larger system, this subsection should relate how these systems interact and should identify the relevant interfaces among the systems. One easy way to display the major components of the larger system, interconnections, and external interfaces is via a system context block diagram.

4.2 Product Position Statement

Provide an overall statement summarizing, at the highest level, the unique position the product intends to fill in the marketplace. Moore [1991] calls this the product position statement and recommends the following format.

For	(target customer)
Who	(statement of the need or opportunity)
The (product name)	is a (product category)
That	(statement of key benefit, that is, compelling reason to buy)
Unlike	(primary competitive alternative)
Our product	(statement of primary differentiation)

A product position statement communicates the intent of the application and the importance of the program to all stakeholders.

4.3 Summary of Capabilities

Summarize the major benefits and features the product will provide. Organize the features so that the list is understandable to any stakeholder. A simple table listing the key benefits and their supporting features, as shown below, might suffice.

Solution Features	Customer Benefit
Feature 1	Benefit 1
Feature 2	Benefit 2

4.4 Assumptions and Dependencies

List any assumptions that, if changed, will alter the vision for the product.

4.5 Cost and Pricing

Describe any relevant cost and pricing constraints, because these can directly impact the solution definition and implementation.

5 Product Features

This section describes the intended product features. Features provide the system capabilities that are necessary to deliver benefits to the users. Feature descriptions should be short and pithy, a key phrase, perhaps followed by one or two sentences of explanation.

Use a level of abstraction high enough to be able to describe the system with a maximum of 25 to 50 features. Each feature should be perceivable by users, operators, or other external systems.

5.1 Feature 1

5.2 Feature 2

6   Exemplary Use Cases

[Optional] You may want to describe a few exemplary use cases, perhaps those that are architecturally significant or those that will most readily help the reader understand how the system is intended to be used.

7   Nonfunctional Requirements

This section records other system requirements including nonfunctional requirements (constraints) imposed on the system (see Chapter 17).

7.1   Usability

7.2   Reliability

7.3   Performance

7.4   Supportability

7.5   Other Requirements

7.5.1 Applicable Standards

List all standards the product must comply with, such as legal and regulatory, communications standards, platform compliance standards, and quality and safety standards.

7.5.2 System Requirements

Define any system requirements necessary to support the application. These may include the host operating systems and network platforms, configurations, communication, peripherals, and companion software.

7.5.3 Licensing, Security, and Installation

Licensing, security, and installation issues can also directly impact the development effort. Installation requirements may affect coding or create the need for separate installation software.

8 Documentation Requirements

This section describes the documentation that must be developed to support successful deployment and use.

8.1 User Manual

Describe the intent of the user manual. Discuss desired length, level of detail, need for index and glossary, tutorial versus reference manual strategy, and so on. Formatting, electronic distribution, and printing constraints should also be identified.

8.2 Online Help

The nature of these systems is unique to application development since they combine aspects of programming and hosting, such as hyperlinks and web services, with aspects of technical writing, such as organization, style, and presentation.

8.3 Installation Guides, Configuration, "Read Me" File

A document that includes installation instructions and configuration guidelines is typically necessary. Also, a "read me" file is often included as a standard component. The "read me" file may include a "What's New with This Release" section and a discussion of compatibility issues with earlier releases. Most users also appreciate publication of any known defects and workarounds.

8.4 Labeling and Packaging

Defines the requirements for labeling to be incorporated into the code. Examples include copyright and patent notices, corporate logos, standardized icons, and other graphic elements.

9 Glossary

The glossary defines terms that are unique to the program. Include any acronyms or abbreviations that need to be understood by users or other readers.

Appendix C

RELEASE PLANNING READINESS CHECKLIST

In Chapter 16, Release Planning, we described the release planning activity as a key component of the Agile Release Train. We noted that a simple checklist is a useful way to assure preparedness for this important event. An example is provided here.

No.	Item	Description	Yes/No
Part I: Organizational Readiness			
1.1	**Planning scope and context**	Is the scope (product, system, technology domains) of the planning process understood? Do we know what teams need to plan together?	
1.2	**Planning time frame, iteration, and release cadence**	What are the release planning dates? Is the iteration (sprint) and release (PSI) cadence defined? Do we know what release period we are planning for?	
1.3	**Agile teams**	Does each feature/component team have an identified Scrum/Agile Master and product owner?	
1.4	**Agile team attendance**	Are all team members present in person, or are arrangements made to involve them remotely?	
1.5	**Team agile estimating ability**	Do the teams have a known velocity and the ability to do story estimating?	
1.6	**If no to the above**	If not, will training be provided prior to that time? Or will adequate coaching be present during the session?	
1.7	**Executives, business owners, participation**	Do we know who will set the business context and present the product/solution Vision?	
1.8	**Business alignment**	Is there reasonable agreement on priorities among the business owners and product management?	
1.9	**Other attendees**	Do we know what other key stakeholders (documentation, support, IT, infrastructure, and so on) should attend?	
1.10	**Development infrastructure**	Do we understand the impact and/or plans on SCM continuous integration and build environments?	

Continues

Part I: Organizational Readiness (Continued)			
No.	**Item**	**Description**	**Yes/No**
1.11	Agile project management tooling	Do we know how and where features, iterations, releases, stories, tasks, status, burndown, and so on, will be maintained?	
1.12	Continuing agile education	Is there to be any continuing education provided? If so, by whom, and does it fit the planning schedule?	
1.13	Agile technical practices	Is there a strategy for unit testing and test automation? Any other practice guidelines?	

Part II: Release Planning Event Content Preparation			
No.	**Item**	**Description**	**Responsible**
2.1	Scope, context, and organizational readiness established	Review items from Part I.	All
2.2	Final agenda	Final agenda with start and stop times, timeboxes, speaker callouts, and so on.	All
2.3	Facilitator preparation	Facilitator understands context, mechanics of event, and facilitator guidelines.	Facilitator
2.4	Introductory briefing	Establishes schedule, objectives, context, requirements for session.	Facilitator
2.5	Executive briefing	Defines current business context and investment themes.	Executive identified
2.6	Product Vision briefing(s)	Briefings prepared by product managers. Handouts/backlogs prepared with supporting detail (features, priorities, market reports, use cases, UX guidelines, and so on).	Product managers and business owners
2.7	Architectural Vision briefing	Communicate any new architectural epics and system qualities (nonfunctional) requirements	CTO/architects, security directors, and so on
2.8	Development context briefing (optional)	Agile development process known; infrastructure and process initiatives understood. Guidelines for agile technical practices.	Senior development management
2.9	Meeting notice	Finalize agenda and send meeting notice to attendees with venue, access requirements, and so on.	Facilitator or project manager

No.	Item	Description	Responsible
		Part III: Facilities Checklist	
3.1	Facilities	Roomy enough for all attendees with separate breakout rooms (if necessary, depending on size of group). Note: Ideally, some teams can remain in the plenary session room.	
3.2	Room accessibility/security	Is facility available before and after hours (in case teams stay to continue planning)? Can teams access the breakout rooms?	
3.3	Refreshments and lunch arrangements	As appropriate based on venue, time, culture.	
3.4	Internet connectivity	Needed to access backlogs and other planning resources.	
3.5	Projection equipment	Projector available, working (spare bulb).	
3.6	Audio	If there are more than 30 to 40 attendees, a working audio system is required. Ideally, one lapel mic for the speaker and one handheld mic for reviewers.	
3.7	Room arrangement	Workshop setting. Tables seating entire teams (7±2) preferred.	
3.8	Remote communications arrangement	Arrange connectivity, phone, Skype, webcam, WebEx, or whatever to engage team members who will participate remotely.	
3.9	Release planning bill of materials	For *each* team: • Two Super Sticky Ultra Notes, 4x6, five colors, three 90-Sheet pads/pack • Two 3M Post-it® Super Sticky Meeting Flip Chart White Pk 2 • Set of markers • Name table tents, if useful	

		Scrum/Agile		# On-site	# Off-site	Breakout
(1)	Team Name	Master	Product Owner	Attendees	Attendees	Room (2,3)
1						
2						
3						
4						
5						
6						
7						
8						
9						
10						
11						
12						

Part IV: Program Planning Roster

Notes:

1. Suggest limit: 100 people, 12 teams maximum. More typically, 50 to 75 people in 7 to 10 teams.
2. Breakout rooms may require teleconference equipment for remote team members.
3. Can typically keep four to five teams in the plenary session (auditorium) unless they have remote attendees that require video and audio.

AGILE REQUIREMENTS ENTERPRISE BACKLOG META-MODEL

In this book, we've introduced an extensive, agile requirements artifact meta-model (note: "enterprise backlog model" might be a better label)—a model that defines the requirements artifacts used by agile teams, as well as the relationships among these artifacts. As an aid to understanding, we introduced it incrementally, in the context of the discussions of each section.

Figure D–1 shows the fully elaborated model, from Team through Program through Portfolio, including the application of use cases for optionally elaborating system behavior. If the full model appears complex, that's because contemporary software development at scale is complex, even with agile methods. Besides, if you don't need it all, don't use it all.

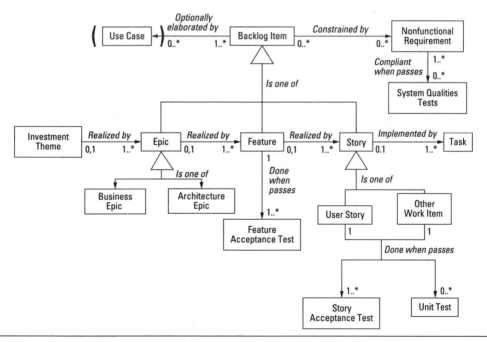

Figure D–1   Requirements meta-model

BIBLIOGRAPHY

Anderson, David J. *Kanban.* Sequim, WA: Blue Hole Press, 2010.

Baker, Steven, and Joseph Thomas. "Establishing an Agile Portfolio to Align IT Investments with Business Needs." Proceedings of the Agile 2008 Conference, IEEE Computer Society, pp. 252–258, 2008.

Beck, Kent. *Extreme Programming Explained: Embrace Change.* Boston, MA: Addison-Wesley, 2000.

———. *Test-Driven Development.* Boston, MA: Addison-Wesley, 2003.

Beck, Kent, with Cynthia Andres. *Extreme Programming Explained: Embrace Change.* Second Edition. Boston, MA: Addison-Wesley, 2005.

Beck, Kent, with Martin Fowler. *Planning Extreme Programming.* Boston, MA: Addison-Wesley, 2005.

BMC Software Inc. and Rally Software Development Corp. "How BMC Is Scaling Agile Development." 2006.

Boehm, Barry. "A Spiral Model of Software Development and Enhancement." *Computer* vol. 21 no. 5 (May 1988): 61–72.

Cockburn, Alistair. *Writing Effective Use Cases.* Boston, MA: Addison-Wesley, 2001.

Cohn, Mike. *Agile Estimating and Planning.* Upper Saddle River, NJ: Prentice-Hall, 2006.

———. *Succeeding with Agile: Software Development Using Scrum.* Upper Saddle River, NJ: Addison-Wesley, 2010.

———. *User Stories Applied: For Agile Software Development.* Boston, MA: Addison-Wesley, 2004.

Cooper, Alan. *The Inmates Are Running the Asylum: Why High Tech Products Drive Us Crazy and How to Restore the Sanity.* U.S.: Sams, 1999.

Crispin, Lisa, and Janet Gregory. *Agile Testing: A Practical Guide for Testers and Agile Teams*. Upper Saddle River, NJ: Addison-Wesley, 2009.

Davis, Alan M. *Software Requirements: Objects, Functions, and States*. Englewood Cliffs, NJ: Prentice-Hall, 1993.

Denne, Mark, and Jane Cleland-Huang. *Software by Numbers: Low-Risk, High-Return Development*. Upper Saddle River, NJ: Prentice Hall, 2004.

Gause, Donald, and Gerald Weinberg. *Exploring Requirements: Quality Before Design*. New York, NY: Dorset House Publishing, 1989.

Grady, Robert B. *Practical Software Metrics for Project Management and Process Improvement*. Upper Saddle River, NJ: Prentice-Hall, 1992.

Highsmith, Jim. *Agile Project Management: Creating Innovative Products*. Boston, MA: Addison-Wesley, 2004.

Jeffries, Ron. "Essential XP: Card, Conversation, and Confirmation." *XP Magazine* (August 2001).

Kniberg, Henrik, and Mattias Skarin. *Kanban and Scrum: Making the Most of Both*. Raleigh, NC: Lulu.com, 2010.

Kroll, Per, and Bruce MacIsaac. *Agility and Discipline Made Easy: Practices from OpenUP and RUP*. New York, NY: Addison-Wesley, 2006.

Kruchten, Philippe. "The 4+1 View of Architecture." *IEEE Software* vol. 12, no. 6 (2005): pp. 45–50.

Ladas, Corey. *Scrumban: Essays on Kanban Systems for Lean Software Development*. Seattle, WA: Modus Cooperandi Press, 2008.

Larman, Craig. *Agile and Iterative Development: A Manager's Guide*. Boston, MA: Addison-Wesley, 2004.

Larman, Craig, and Bas Vodde. *Scaling Lean and Agile Development*. Upper Saddle River, NJ: Addison-Wesley, 2009.

Leffingwell, Dean. *Scaling Software Agility: Best Practices for Large Enterprises*. Boston, MA: Addison-Wesley, 2007.

Leffingwell, Dean, and Don Widrig. *Managing Software Requirements: A Unified Approach*. Boston, MA: Addison-Wesley, 2000.

————. *Managing Software Requirements, Second Edition: A Use Case Approach.* Boston, MA: Addison-Wesley, 2003.

Liker, Jeffrey. *The Toyota Way.* New York, NY: McGraw-Hill, 2004.

Martin, Robert. *Clean Code: A Handbook of Agile Software Craftsmanship.* Upper Saddle River, NJ: Prentice-Hall, 2009.

Middleton, Peter, and James Sutton. *Lean Software Strategies: Proven Techniques for Managers and Developers.* New York, NY: Productivity Press, 2005.

Moore, Geoffrey. *Crossing the Chasm.* New York, NY: HarperBusiness, 1991.

————. *Dealing with Darwin: How Great Companies Innovate at Every Phase of Their Evolution.* New York, NY: Portfolio Press, 2008.

Mugridge, Rick, and Ward Cunningham. *Fit for Developing Software.* Upper Saddle River, NJ: Prentice-Hall, 2005.

Pichler, Roman. *Agile Product Management with Scrum.* Boston, MA: Addison-Wesley, 2010.

Poppendieck, Mary, and Tom Poppendieck. *Implementing Lean Software Development: From Concept to Cash.* Upper Saddle River, NJ: Addison-Wesley, 2007.

————. *Lean Software Development: An Agile Toolkit for Software Development Managers.* Boston, MA: Addison-Wesley, 2003.

QSM Case Study. "Cutter & SLIM Tools Highlight Unprecedented Agile Gains at BMC Software." http://www.qsma.com/re_news.html, 2007.

Reinertsen, Donald G. *Managing the Design Factory: A Product Developer's Toolkit.* New York, NY: Free Press, 1997.

————. *The Principles of Product Development Flow: Second Generation Lean Product Development.* Redondo Beach, CA: Celeritas Publishing, 2009.

Royce, Winston W. "Managing the Development of Large Software Systems: Concepts and Techniques." WESCON Technical Papers, vol. 14 (1970). Los Angeles: WESCON. Reprinted in Proceedings of the Ninth International Conference on Software Engineering (1987): pp. 328–338.

Schwaber, Ken. *Agile Project Management with Scrum.* Redmond, WA: Microsoft Press, 2004.

———. *The Enterprise and Scrum*. Redmond, WA: Microsoft Press, 2007.

Schwaber, Ken, and Mike Beedle. *Agile Software Development with Scrum*. Upper Saddle River, NJ: Prentice Hall, 2002.

Shalloway, Alan et.al. *Lean-Agile Software Development: Achieving Enterprise Agility*. Upper Saddle River, NJ: Addison-Wesley, 2010.

Sliger, Michele, and Stacia Broderick. *The Software Project Manager's Bridge to Agility*. Upper Saddle River, NJ: Addison-Wesley, 2008.

Standish Group. "Charting the Seas of Information Technology—Chaos." West Yarmouth, MA: The Standish Group International, 1994.

Thomas, M. "IT Projects Sink or Swim." *British Computer Society Review* (2001).

Wake, William. "Invest in Good Stories and SMART Tasks." www.xp123.com, 2003.

Wiegers, Karl E. *Software Requirements*. Redmond, WA: Microsoft Press, 1999.

Index

The Agile Software Development Series

9780321502759

978032148965

9780201721843

9780201699692

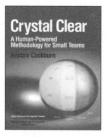

9780201699470

9780201498349

9780201702255

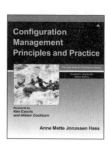

9780321117663

9780201760439

9780321219770

9780131111554

9780321458193

9780201758207

9780321150783

9780321268778

9780321286086

Addison
Wesley

REGISTER

THIS PRODUCT

informit.com/register

Register the Addison-Wesley, Exam Cram, Prentice Hall, Que, and Sams products you own to unlock great benefits.

To begin the registration process, simply go to **informit.com/register** to sign in or create an account. You will then be prompted to enter the 10- or 13-digit ISBN that appears on the back cover of your product.

Registering your products can unlock the following benefits:

- Access to supplemental content, including bonus chapters, source code, or project files.
- A coupon to be used on your next purchase.

Registration benefits vary by product. Benefits will be listed on your Account page under Registered Products.

About InformIT — **THE TRUSTED TECHNOLOGY LEARNING SOURCE**

INFORMIT IS HOME TO THE LEADING TECHNOLOGY PUBLISHING IMPRINTS Addison-Wesley Professional, Cisco Press, Exam Cram, IBM Press, Prentice Hall Professional, Que, and Sams. Here you will gain access to quality and trusted content and resources from the authors, creators, innovators, and leaders of technology. Whether you're looking for a book on a new technology, a helpful article, timely newsletters, or access to the Safari Books Online digital library, InformIT has a solution for you.

THE TRUSTED TECHNOLOGY LEARNING SOURCE

Addison-Wesley | Cisco Press | Exam Cram
IBM Press | Que | Prentice Hall | Sams

SAFARI BOOKS ONLINE

informIT.com
THE TRUSTED TECHNOLOGY LEARNING SOURCE

InformIT is a brand of Pearson and the online presence for the world's leading technology publishers. It's your source for reliable and qualified content and knowledge, providing access to the top brands, authors, and contributors from the tech community.

Addison-Wesley   **Cisco Press**   EXAM/**CRAM**   **IBM** Press.   **QUE**   **PRENTICE HALL**   **SAMS** | Safari Books Online

---

LearnIT at InformIT

Looking for a book, eBook, or training video on a new technology? Seeking timely and relevant information and tutorials? Looking for expert opinions, advice, and tips? **InformIT has the solution.**

- Learn about new releases and special promotions by subscribing to a wide variety of newsletters.
  Visit **informit.com/newsletters**.

- Access FREE podcasts from experts at **informit.com/podcasts**.

- Read the latest author articles and sample chapters at **informit.com/articles**.

- Access thousands of books and videos in the Safari Books Online digital library at **safari.informit.com**.

- Get tips from expert blogs at **informit.com/blogs**.

Visit **informit.com/learn** to discover all the ways you can access the hottest technology content.

Are You Part of the **IT** Crowd?

Connect with Pearson authors and editors via RSS feeds, Facebook, Twitter, YouTube, and more! Visit **informit.com/socialconnect**.

---

informIT.com THE TRUSTED TECHNOLOGY LEARNING SOURCE   PEARSON

Addison-Wesley   **Cisco Press**   EXAM/**CRAM**   **IBM** Press.   **QUE**   **PRENTICE HALL**   **SAMS** | Safari Books Online

Try Safari Books Online FREE

Get online access to 5,000+ Books and Videos

FREE TRIAL—GET STARTED TODAY!
www.informit.com/safaritrial

Find trusted answers, fast
Only Safari lets you search across thousands of best-selling books from the top technology publishers, including Addison-Wesley Professional, Cisco Press, O'Reilly, Prentice Hall, Que, and Sams.

Master the latest tools and techniques
In addition to gaining access to an incredible inventory of technical books, Safari's extensive collection of video tutorials lets you learn from the leading video training experts.

WAIT, THERE'S MORE!

Keep your competitive edge
With Rough Cuts, get access to the developing manuscript and be among the first to learn the newest technologies.

Stay current with emerging technologies
Short Cuts and Quick Reference Sheets are short, concise, focused content created to get you up-to-speed quickly on new and cutting-edge technologies.

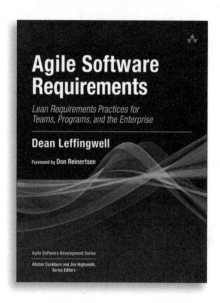

FREE Online Edition

Your purchase of **Agile Software Requirements** includes access to a free online edition for 45 days through the Safari Books Online subscription service. Nearly every Addison-Wesley Professional book is available online through Safari Books Online, along with more than 5,000 other technical books and videos from publishers such as, Cisco Press, Exam Cram, IBM Press, O'Reilly, Prentice Hall, Que, and Sams.

SAFARI BOOKS ONLINE allows you to search for a specific answer, cut and paste code, download chapters, and stay current with emerging technologies.

Activate your FREE Online Edition at
www.informit.com/safarifree

> **STEP 1:** Enter the coupon code: BULOZBI.

> **STEP 2:** New Safari users, complete the brief registration form.
> Safari subscribers, just log in.

If you have difficulty registering on Safari or accessing the online edition, please e-mail customer-service@safaribooksonline.com